T0246122

JIMMY

JIMMY

THE SECRET LIFE OF JAMES DEAN

JASON COLAVITO

APPLAUSE
THEATRE & CINEMA BOOKS

APPLAUSE
THEATRE & CINEMA BOOKS

Bloomsbury Group, Inc.
4501 Forbes Blvd., Ste. 200
Lanham, MD 20706
www.rowman.com

Distributed by NATIONAL BOOK NETWORK

Library of Congress Cataloging-in-Publication Data
Names: Colavito, Jason, author.
Title: Jimmy : the secret life of James Dean / Jason Colavito.
Description: Essex, Connecticut : Applause Press, 2024. | Includes
   bibliographical references and index.
Identifiers: LCCN 2024019893 (print) | LCCN 2024019894 (ebook) | ISBN
   9781493085651 (cloth) | ISBN 9781493085668 (ebook)
Subjects: LCSH: Dean, James, 1931-1955. | Motion picture actors and
   actresses--United States--Biography. | Gay actors--United States--Biography. |
   Gay men--United States--Biography.
Classification: LCC PN2287.D33 C66 2024 (print) | LCC PN2287.D33 (ebook)
   | DDC 791.4302/8092 [B]--dc23/eng/20240528
LC record available at https://lccn.loc.gov/2024019893
LC ebook record available at https://lccn.loc.gov/2024019894

♾™ The paper used in this publication meets the minimum requirements of American National Standard for Information Sciences—Permanence of Paper for Printed Library Materials, ANSI/NISO Z39.48-1992.

Being an actor is the loneliest thing in the world. . . . You are all alone with your concentration and imagination, and that's all you have. . . . Being a good actor isn't easy. Being a man is even harder. I want to be both . . . and I will before I'm done.

—James Dean[1]

Contents

Note on Terminology

The words used to describe sexuality are constantly in flux. Rather than attempt to impose modern labels on people from the past who never used them and may not have recognized what they represent, in this book I have employed the historical terms *homosexual* and *gay* and, to a lesser extent, *queer*, which were in use in the 1940s and 1950s. These terms are true to how people of the era, including those with same-sex or bisexual attractions, talked about and thought of themselves, even if today they may seem more limiting or less precise than more recent terminology.

INTRODUCTION

On Wednesday, October 10, 1956, the glittering gala premiere of famed director George Stevens's new epic drama *Giant* sparkled with the light of dozens of stars. Hollywood had come to New York's Roxy Theatre, a six-thousand-seat movie palace, the second-largest in the world, to celebrate what promised to be the biggest movie of 1956, both in length—it was three and a half hours long—and in box office. The flashbulbs went off one by one, capturing images of movie royalty, including *Giant* stars Elizabeth Taylor, Rock Hudson, and Mercedes McCambridge, as they smiled and waved their way through cheering crowds into the Spanish-style "cathedral of the motion picture" and to their seats rising above the wide, shallow stage, where the theater's ice-skating dance troupe, the Icy Roxyettes, twirled in perfect synchronization to the sound of the Roxy Theatre Orchestra's *Fall Fantasy* musical revue. Police struggled to hold back what a reporter described as the thousand-strong "seething, screaming, seemingly somewhat insane sea of starstruck humanity" who had crowded around rope barricades strung across the corner of West Fiftieth Street and Seventh Avenue to see the arriving celebrities and to cheer for one who wasn't there. Inside, executives, socialites, and stars filled the seats, at as much as $15 a ticket, the money going to a charity to fight muscular dystrophy.[1] The event, the papers noted that week, was bigger than the World Series, which had ended across town that afternoon with the Yankees beating the Dodgers.

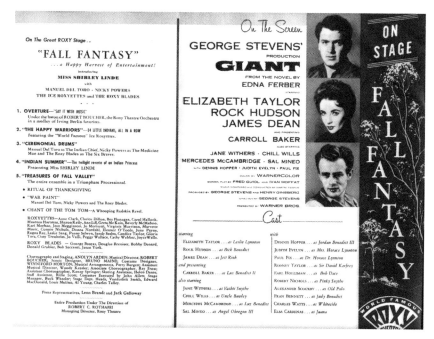

The program for the world premiere of *Giant* at the Roxy Theatre in New York City listed an ice show and a concert before the screening of the film. *Author's collection.*

As more celebrities, like actress Natalie Wood and comedian Henny Youngman entered, a massive phalanx of sixty or more reporters from twenty-seven cities vied to ask questions. Singer and actress Jayne Meadows and actor Chill Wills hosted live television coverage in front of the doors to the theater's cavernous lobby, fully packed shoulder to shoulder with attendees, and fashion models served as ushers. The movie's cast stopped one by one to speak with WRCA-FM's popular hosts Tex McCrary and Jinx Falkenburg, who were recording a special show devoted to *Giant* to air the next night. Despite the star power on display, Tex and Jinx, as the pair were known, were most interested in an absent actor, his name staring down silently from the movie palace's massive, illuminated marquee: James Dean. Rumors swirled that the young *Giant* actor, who had died in a car accident at the age of twenty-four almost exactly a year prior, would soon receive an unprecedented second posthumous Academy Award nomination. Although he had starred in only three films, by most measures he was the most famous man in the world. He had fan clubs from L.A. to Paris to Jakarta. Tex and

Jinx wanted to know how each star remembered their fallen colleague. Taylor praised Dean lavishly and told the pair that had he lived, he would have become one of the era's finest actors. McCambridge spoke of Dean's kindness to her. Hudson, in gruff dissent, informed the radio hosts that he did not really know Dean, whom he found aloof.[2]

And yet inside the theater and on the street outside, hundreds, even thousands who came out that night did feel as though they knew James Dean, just like millions of his fans across America and around the world. Had they not seen the handsome young man bare his soul on celluloid and felt his pain and known they had glimpsed the real boy behind the flickering image? A thousand of Dean's biggest fans packed the Roxy's highest balcony and stomped their feet loudly when his name appeared in the opening credits and shouted uncontrollably when their idol's face graced the screen for the first time. The special guests and reporters down below heard unearthly wailing from the throng above. Some of them must have looked twice at Larry Chandler, a Los Angeles photoengraver who used his vacation time to come to New York for the premiere. He told a reporter who noticed his unmistakable resemblance to Dean that he was also a huge Dean fan, and like an uncountable number of other fans, he read every scrap of information he could find about Dean. Hundreds of magazine articles obsessively chronicled the dead star's life for millions of readers, who demanded still more, and now in the bookstores dotted around Manhattan, like the Doubleday Book Shop, where Dean once shopped, and across the country, notices advertised a new biography of the star written by his best friend, on sale in mere weeks. Promotional photos of the book's black cover showed Dean's face emerging from a shadow like a ghost.

For the stars looking out from the Roxy's lobby at the teeming throng, Dean's phantom must have seemed to be everywhere. His face peered out from magazine covers on every newsstand, from the popular *Look* magazine to the tawdriest tabloid. Cardboard cutouts of him promoted *Giant* wherever it played—except the Roxy, where the cardboard idol was removed because it had become covered head to toe in patrons' lipstick kisses. Gazing at the people gathered to cheer James Dean, it was all too easy to see his face reflected in theirs. Young men and teenage boys combed their hair high to look like his, dressed in blue jeans to look like photos of him, and scowled and slouched and mumbled to imitate his gruff manner. James Dean ranked at the top of national polls of young men's favorite movie stars.³ The novelist John Dos Passos looked at the boys and young men dressing like James Dean, with their "resentful hair" and "scorn on the lip," and called them hypocrites, soft children of privilege pretending to be real men.⁴ He named them "sinister adolescents," but the scorn did nothing to stop boys from clipping Dean's picture from magazines, studying his three films, and learning from a dead man's celluloid shadow how to be men.

Even now, generations of men wear Dean's influence every day—quite literally—in their casual clothes and tussled hair and in the way they talk and walk. So ingrained has his style become that it is simply an American idiom, the language of modern masculinity, almost as invisible as the air. It's hard to imagine that in the 1950s someone needed to invent it. But still today, seven decades after James Dean, his name continues to stand for a particular type of young manliness. We see it most often in the young men proclaimed to be the "next James Dean" or who named Dean as a role model, men like Dennis Hopper, Bob Dylan, Elvis Presley, Martin Sheen, Brad Pitt, Johnny Depp, Luke Perry, River Phoenix, Nicolas Cage, Leonardo DiCaprio, Heath Ledger, Austin Butler, Jacob Elordi, and countless more. But his echo can be found everywhere.

There was a tremendous unspoken irony in young men celebrating James Dean as the ideal man. Dean died in the heart of the 1950s, a time when homophobia ran rampant. In Congress, legislators thundered against homosexual "sex perverts" and forced hundreds of gay men from government. President Eisenhower had banned gay people from federal jobs, and employers across the country followed suit. Newspapers and magazines screamed with lurid headlines about the "Homosexual Menace," warning that "Geniuses Are Potential Queers" and that TV, movies, and universities had become "Home Sweet Homo." A columnist darkly complained that homosexuals, as gay and bisexual people were then called, had infested American culture: "It is time for the American public to face the facts of homo-sexuality like it has faced the facts of cancer, tuberculosis, epilepsy," she wrote. Movie stars, Broadway actors, and athletes pretending to be straight were, the columnist declared, the "most dangerous type of male homo-sexual." These "perverts," she thundered, "perform on our motion picture screens and stages. They write our books, paint our pictures, sometimes compete in our best athletic events."⁵ They had to be stopped. Such sentiments were far from atypical.

Thousands of articles warning against the dangers homosexuals posed to America filled the media. They were so common in the 1950s that no literate American could miss them.

The young men who dressed like James Dean took such warnings to heart, vigorously enforcing unwritten codes of masculinity against any boy who seemed too much of a "sissy," and across the country, teenage boys had made a game of "fag hunting," patrolling parks and roadsides by night to lure men with promises of sex in order to rob and beat them. And yet, the man they looked up to and wanted to be was not straight.

I became interested in untangling James Dean's dual legacy, both as exemplar of (straight) manliness and as a queer icon, when I watched his most famous movie, *Rebel without a Cause* (1955), for the first time during the pandemic lockdowns of 2020. For most of my career, I had researched science fiction and horror, genres where aliens and monsters symbolize social forces that we can't quite express. Therefore, as a gay man attuned to subtext, I immediately saw in *Rebel* a very clear love story about two boys, only very lightly veiled for 1950s propriety. *Rebel without a Cause* became, in Dean's hands, a summation of the new world being born, an encapsulation of the emerging, raw, and more emotional manliness that critics of the time mistook for androgyny, and through his electrifying acting, it also became the screen's first positive depiction of young queer love and the only one onscreen during the two crucial decades when modern sexual identities formed. In the film, Dean's teenage character, Jim, forms a deep and intense relationship with Plato, a fellow teenage boy, played by Sal Mineo, one that overshadows Jim's pairing with Judy, played by Natalie Wood. Dean purposely made the movie into a reflection of his own experiences, directing Mineo to play the role as a lovestruck puppy, which he reciprocated in kind. Mineo recalled that his character was, "in a way, the first gay teenager in films. You watch it now, you *know* he had the hots for James Dean. You watch it now, and everyone knows about Jimmy, so it's like he had the hots for Natalie and me. Ergo, I had to be bumped off, out of the way."[6] The torrent of grief that poured from Dean at Plato's death became a cathartic explosion.

But straight critics then, as now, just didn't see it. *Variety*'s Robert J. Landry thought the movie was really about costar Natalie Wood's "bosoms, lipstick and sex feelings," while the *Hollywood Reporter*'s Jack Moffitt wrote

about an ending to the movie that *never happened* to avoid remembering Dean's character breaking down in tears to mourn the boy he loved.[7]
Although straight critics were blind to it, gay boys then and now recognized,
understood, and for a moment saw themselves and their lives raised to dignity and art. In trying to answer the question of why my perception differed
so much from that of straight critics, I discovered that everything I saw in
the film applied equally and more to its star, James Dean. This resulted in me
writing an article for *Esquire* magazine in 2021 examining Dean's legacy as
queer icon—and correcting a piece *Esquire* ran attacking Dean in 1956—and
this book was born.[8]

In death, James Dean had come to embody the reckless, impetuous, red-
blooded, heterosexual all-American male, a role ill-suited to his slight, delicate frame; artistic interests; and emerging queer sexuality. It was this tension
between the real person and the image he projected that gave him a power
that his rivals could not match, a magnetism that fascinated all who saw
him. In his life and through his death, he transcended the limits America's
political and cultural leaders placed on sexuality and masculinity and forged
a new idea of manhood that forever changed what it means to be a man, and
he inaugurated a revolution in America's attitudes toward masculinity and
sexuality that is not yet complete.

This book is not a traditional biography. It does not dwell on elementary
school art projects or the financial details of movie contracts. It does not discuss every person Dean ever met nor detail every conversation that he had.
Others have done that work. Val Holley explored the minutiae of Dean's daily
life exhaustively in 1995's *James Dean: The Biography*.[9] While Holley's book
is somewhat outdated, it is not my intention for this book to simply repeat
prior biographies. This book is instead an effort to explore how midcentury
society's conflicts over sexuality and masculinity shaped the life and the cultural impact of the man who came to define both his era and the very image
of young American manhood. It tells one story about James Dean's life, not
every story.

In writing about these issues, the problem of history becomes inescapable. This book is told in narrative form, but to tell a story that flows with
a sense of immediacy and drama, I made hard choices while faced with
decidedly imperfect sources. When writing about queer history, the sources

are especially imperfect because so much of that history has been forgotten and the sources, intentionally obscured, fragmentary, or never written due to decades of oppression and suppression. Much has been destroyed. The Federal Bureau of Investigation, for example, surreptitiously collected more than 300,000 pages of material on the sex lives of queer Americans, including many celebrities, in the mid-twentieth century, and in 1973, they destroyed it all. Many of the men whose lives we should know about left little written record of their thoughts and feelings, either because they self-censored or because friends and relatives destroyed what was left behind. Many lives can only be reconstructed from scattered scraps, occasional newspaper stories, and memories recalled long after the fact.

These problems plague any discussion of the life of James Dean. Because Dean died so young, he left behind very little by way of written records and only a handful of interviews, and many of his papers were purposely destroyed after his death. Despite his massive fame, primary sources are surprisingly rare. Every biography of James Dean relies on three original, detailed, and well-researched 1956 accounts of his life: William Bast's book-length biographical memoir *James Dean*, Joe Hyams's *Redbook* biographical study "James Dean," and George Scullin's *Look* magazine biographical article "James Dean: The Legend and the Facts."[10] These three life stories established the basic framework of facts guiding all future accounts, and all three contained fabrications and distortions, both intentional and accidental. As writers of their time, they relied heavily on Freudian ideas to assign motivation to Dean, seeking to attribute his behavior to the trauma of losing his mother or the disappointment of an absent father. All three also drew heavily on Warner Bros.' official studio biography of Dean, produced under the supervision of Walter Ross, their head of publicity, who went on to write a poisonous novel about the "immoral" Dean.[11] Its ultimate source was Dean himself, with studio "improvements."

Most of the rest of what passes for the story of Dean's life comes from the recollections of those who knew him, mostly remembered long after the fact and often colored with significant bias and the fuzzy shadow of memory. In attempting to bring Dean back to a semblance of life, I had to select among competing memories to create a coherent narrative from an impossible bundle of contradictions, self-serving narratives, and fabrications. Aside from a few basic names and dates, virtually no fact about James Dean's life has passed undisputed. It is therefore extremely fortunate that as I prepared this book, a large cache of nearly four hundred of James Dean's legal, business, and personal documents held by his agent, Jane Deacy, covering the years from 1952 to 1955, were made public for the first time. This unprecedented window into Dean's life in his own hand and through the eyes of his closest colleagues provided several unexpected revelations and the only independent archival confirmation of many of the claims known otherwise from disputed secondhand stories. The documents included letters written by Dean; letters received by Dean; financial documents; business records; and, most surprisingly, legal documents related to an ex-boyfriend's previously unknown efforts to sue Dean for the return of money spent supporting him during their relationship.[12]

In telling Dean's story, I have dispensed with the old, widely repeated, but outdated Freudian framework parroted uncritically since the 1950s. With little direct evidence, past authors have sought to reduce Dean's life to a wild, failed effort to reunite with his dead mother or reconcile with his absent father. Instead, I began with documented primary sources and the indisputable facts and then selected the most plausible recollections and testimony to layer atop those facts without contradicting the historical record. Significant divergences in sources are discussed in the notes, but this method necessarily involves rejecting claims, rumors, and legends that are chronologically impossible or that gainsay establish facts. The result, I hope, is a coherent and cohesive account of a life too often presented as inexplicable and irrational, revealing a rational but troubled soul beneath the wildly rebellious façade. In 1957, *Real*, a men's magazine, labeled James Dean "our weirdest national hero." The year before, *Look* magazine, *Life*'s great rival, called him the "strangest legend since Valentino."[13] Comparing Dean to other men of similar background and ambition who shared the experience of growing up queer in an intolerant America, James Dean's "weird" behavior becomes recognizable and familiar, part of a spectrum of responses queer men adopted as armor against a hostile and dangerous world.

Therefore, no account of James Dean's life can pass without dealing with the question of his sexuality, a subject of rumor and controversy since he was alive. Dean had sexual relationships with both women and men, but his family, friends, and colleagues all came to different conclusions about what, if anything, these relationships meant to him; thus, previous authors who have told his story all depicted him differently, as well. One biographer noted that Dean's friends and lovers have called him gay, straight, bisexual, and asexual, as have his biographers.[14] Dean himself is no help, once telling the U.S. government that he was a homosexual and the women he dated that he was not. There is no way for us to peer inside a dead man's heart, and debating whether he would today have labeled himself gay, bisexual, heteroflexible, homoflexible, demisexual, queer, or something else is both irrelevant and ahistorical—a misunderstanding of how men of his time understood sexuality.

In the 1940s and 1950s, a young man who had a sexual interest of any kind in other men, however slight, would have conceived of that attraction in one way, as "homosexual." Although terms like *bisexual* were used in academic literature, popular media rarely used them. Most Americans did not believe bisexuality truly existed, no matter what Alfred Kinsey claimed in his famous sexual scale; and in popular understanding, a man who experienced attraction for another man was a homosexual, regardless of whether he also engaged in sexual intimacy with women. Indeed, as Edmund Bergler, a famed psychoanalyst who claimed to "cure" gay people, wrote in 1959, "'Bisexuality' counts as homosexuality, popularly as well as scientifically." *Confidential* magazine, a popular tabloid read at its height by more than 10 percent of all Americans, went so far as to label bisexuality a myth in 1957.[15] Indeed, many bisexual men were branded "latent homosexuals" under the theory that only social opprobrium prevented a man from abandoning women for the seductive pleasure of sodomy. Thus, in the twentieth century's middle decades, *homosexual* did not simply mean *gay*, as we conceive the term today, but was something closer to the wider range of identities encompassed by the modern use of *queer*. To that extent, however you choose to interpret James Dean's words and actions, he was a homosexual by the standards of his day.

And he hated that—because he had been taught to hate himself.

"The past," William Faulkner once wrote, "is never dead. It's not even past." The postwar world echoes our own, and the struggles and pain of those who lived and died in the shadow of imaginary virtue and toxic conformity remind us of the dangers when society seeks to harm its most vulnerable in the name of a vindictive moral purity. The interlocking panic over masculinity and sexuality that centered on teenagers and young adults finds its match in our contemporary struggles with the same issues playing out from statehouses to sitcoms to social media. The story of James Dean is also the story of our times, and there is still much to learn from one who blazed a trail forward, attempting, however imperfectly, to live a twenty-first-century life in the twentieth century's stifling embrace.

1
THE EVIL WITHIN

"Are gentlemen sissies?" In January 1947, a few weeks before James Byron Dean's sixteenth birthday, etiquette doyenne Emily Post weighed in on the masculinity question in her widely read national newspaper column. In big cities and small towns, from the coasts to the heartland, many young men had come to believe that good manners were outdated relics of the prewar world, a sign of weakness, effeminacy, or even homosexuality. A real man, the argument went, practiced aggression and spoke with his fists. "Unfortunately, I notice many young men today who seem to think they are expected to put their strong-headedness first," Post wrote with disapproval. "They frown on good manners, become purposely careless." But she cautioned that masculinity and manners were not mutually exclusive, and well-mannered males were more likely to become leaders in the "world of men."[1] Nevertheless, on the Indiana farm where James Dean had cultivated strong-headedness and carelessness as a kind of masculine armor to protect him from the world, Post's "gentleman" would have seemed like a creature from another world.

Classmates and teachers remembered the teenage Dean as headstrong and gifted, prone to strong passions and long periods of wanting to be left alone. When he enrolled in Fairmount High School in the fall of '45, one of his first teachers was amazed at his wide reading and knowledge of almost every subject. In the manner of curious boys who spend a great deal of time by themselves, he had read broadly but not deeply of whatever was at hand, be it the classics or instruction manuals, and he had the conversational gift to use what he knew to make a person think he knew more than he did. Despite his curiosity and evident intelligence—he claimed to have done the work of a high school senior in junior high—he never made the effort to do well in high school, saying he preferred "to live."[2] His grades were poor in all but a handful of subjects, notably psychology and the arts. The budding actor's great project, and great failure, was understanding himself.

In many ways, James Dean in 1947 was a typical teenage boy of the postwar years. Adolescence had hardened his features over the past months, turning the formerly cherubic and round-faced boy of freshman year into a striking sophomore with close-cropped hair, whose sharp jawline and piercing eyes leapt out from the surrounding photos in the 1947 Fairmount High School yearbook. Handsome and athletic, if a little self-conscious about his five-foot-eight height and the nearsightedness that hid him behind large, round glasses, he played basketball and baseball and would

James Dean as a teenager (center front) in uniform for the Fairmount High School baseball team. *Photofest.*

even try pole vaulting. He succeeded through sheer force of will, often over the objections of exasperated coaches who wished he would listen to them. He called sports the "heart beat of every American boy" in an essay he wrote about himself for his high school principal. He loved going fast, whether on the motorcycle he had purchased a few months earlier or the next year, when he had learned to drive, in the borrowed cars of friends. Dean had never crashed his bike and couldn't imagine he ever would. The boys Dean called friends in high school remembered him speeding dangerously in and around town, doing stunts and tricks on his bike, and winning drag races behind the wheels of their cars. Some of it was true, and some of it was high school legend.

Dean's other boyish interests were less shrouded in awe and myth. He loved hamburgers and was mad for ice cream—a combination of raspberry and coffee especially. He liked banging on bongo drums and reading Western stories, and he idolized Billy the Kid, the orphaned outlaw whose crime spree ended in his death at the age of twenty-one. In the coming months, he would develop a fascination with bullfighting, an exotic sport that spoke of a world beyond the farm and beyond America, an exciting dance of death between man and beast. Dean hated dressing up in grown-up clothes and preferred T-shirts and jeans. "Unless I absolutely have to dress up off-screen," he later said, "I would rather jump into old dungarees and a T-shirt."[3] He liked to be called Jimmy. All the young men Dean would ever know would grow and change and leave behind boyish things, but not Dean. The bullfighting and bongos, the ice cream and the blue jeans, would stay with him forever.

When he was younger, Dean had read through the books shelved by the staircase downstairs in the white fourteen-room farmhouse, built in 1904, that he shared with his aunt and uncle: Bibles, moralizing biblical stories for young readers, and recently reprinted volumes of the Rover Boys adventure novels. The last were decades-old stories of fun-loving teenage boys who challenged authority, played pranks, and wooed women while traveling abroad and experiencing all the worldly wonders a farm boy might aspire to. Brothers Tom, Dick, and Sam Rover must have appealed to Dean because they moved through their lives with a haughty disregard for others and treated the world as their plaything, and their jokes had a recklessly cruel edge that straddled the line between audacious and criminal. Yet they always came out ahead and received the adoration of women and admiration of men. Had he seen it when he was eleven, he might even have found the Warner Bros.' *Merrie Melodies* parody cartoon "The Dover Boys" hilarious.

He had a taste, though, for morbid stories (the more dramatic and gruesome, the better), particularly for acting out dramatically. The Women's Christian Temperance Union sponsored a dramatic reading competition, and as a small child, he reveled in dramatizing the violent, hysterical "crimes" of those besotted with alcohol, even as he lamented that the "gory odes" were too moralizing and didactic. The previous school year, as part of the drama club, he had acted in *The Monkey's Paw*, a gruesome little supernatural tale based on the classic short story, in which he played a young man killed in a work accident after his parents ran afoul of the cursed title object, whose power could rewrite reality to grant wishes, though in the most ironic way.

"Why, we're all going to be rich and famous and happy," Dean dramatically proclaimed as Herbert to the kids playing his character's parents, doing his utmost to make the audience believe that a wish could unmake reality and make dreams come true. He might even have believed it himself. It didn't work out for Herbert, but Dean hoped that the right story and the right wish might make it true for him. In his second play that school year, *Mooncalf Mugford*, he had the starring role as a senile old man who fantasizes a world of dreams and convinces his wife to join in his delusions. Long after, audiences remembered how his performance of the final scene haunted them with his wistful longing for an imaginary better world. Adeline Brookshire, his high school drama teacher, recalled, too, that in his enthusiasm and consumed by the freedom afforded by performance, he paid too little mind to the others on stage and had nearly throttled the girl playing his wife.

The summer after sophomore year marked seven years since Dean and his grandmother had shared a long train ride from his parents' home in Los Angeles back to his family's seat in Fairmount, accompanying the body of his beloved mother, Mildred, to her final rest after losing her battle to cancer, an event that forever haunted him. From his birth in Marion, Indiana, on February 8, 1931, until his mother died on July 14, 1940, Dean had basked in maternal love, a closeness rooted in a shared passion for the arts that his father had found suspect and unmasculine. Winton had never really wanted a child, and with Mildred gone, he had taken the opportunity to place his son in the care of stolid relatives Ortense and Marcus Winslow, who treated the

Young Jimmy Dean lies on the ground of the Winslow family farm near Fairmount, Indiana. *Photofest.*

moody, taciturn youth with kindly indulgence, even giving him their own bedroom and its maple furniture because he liked it better.[4] The Winslows showered Dean with attention and love, but they noticed that he rarely shared his inner world with them. He could effortlessly make them feel his joy or his sadness with a glance, but the reasons for those moods were often opaque.[5] During high school, they felt him pull away from the family. "He became hard to handle, and we didn't know what was the matter," Marcus Winslow recalled to the gossip journalist Joe Hyams. "He didn't take any more stock in us."[6] In truth, Dean was starting to think of himself as an outsider, an alien, a creature from some other world.

The exotic lands and faraway planets he read about in his favorite pulp adventure magazines, with their lurid covers of square-jawed heroes and half-naked women, must have seemed a welcome escape from Fairmount, a sleepy farming town of just 2,600 people. Its main street, made up of mostly nineteenth-century buildings, stretched a whopping two blocks. It proudly sported fifteen churches, but its newspaper was published only once a week. Newspapers from the bigger cities, Indianapolis and far-off Chicago, and the radio kept the town connected tenuously to the world, but the endless stretches of farmland extending in every direction could make the town seem to be lost in space and time. It certainly seemed that way to Dean, who would stare at the vast nothing surrounding the farm where he lived with his aunt and uncle and the vaster infinity of the stars in the pitch-black sky and dream of worlds beyond the dull little town and its small-minded denizens. "My town thrives on dangerous bigotry," he would later write in a poem. Fairmount was like every other small midwestern town, mostly White, deeply religious, wary of outsiders. It sat in the heart of what had been Ku Klux Klan country not all that many years before, and conversation among the town Quakers often enough slid into racism and barbed asides about Catholics and Jews. Like most places in America, the townsfolk looked askance at soft, effeminate men and held "homos" and "fags" in contempt.

The young Dean had always felt he was different from the other boys, however, and the adults' hateful comments about "sissies," "queers," and "homos" silently stung.[7] He loved art and drew and painted and made little clay sculptures with important names, indulgences that the practical men and boys of Fairmount found suspect. He loved theater and performing but was sensitive to criticism and terrified of being humiliated. He dreamed of becoming an actor, though the menfolk tended to think of the theater with suspicion, as the province of queers. The Winslows tried to open the artistic youth to a more conventional life, but Marcus's efforts to introduce him to farming failed, as did Ortense's attempt to fix him up with a friend's daughter of his age. Their meeting was awkward, and the date ended badly. Marcus said Dean responded to the potential love match by quickly producing a water-color painting of wine spilled on a tablecloth, which he said was an artistic representation of the waste of his time. The story might have been true, or maybe not, but everyone who heard the story said it sounded like something he'd do. Dean didn't want to farm or mine or work forever in the cannery where he briefly held a job or live in a town he could survey from end to end just by turning around.

But he knew he was different from the other boys in another way, too. Sometimes, he thought about boys the way one was only supposed to think about girls, and it frightened him. So much ink has been spilled in the decades since trying to parse exactly what went on in the young man's heart, but he may never have truly known himself. "Well, I'm certainly not going through life with one hand tied behind my back," he was supposed to have once said of his sexuality.[8] He could and did take his pleasure with women and men, and he could play the great lover with girlfriends, though rarely for very long. His most lasting and intimate relationships were with men, but they were not exactly romances; the most loving of them slid between brotherly affection and sex and back again. In every case, man or woman, he always had some reason that the natural progression of love had to stop short. In later years, William Bast, with whom Dean had his longest-lasting and deepest friendship, thought that in a better world, the two of them would have been happy together for the rest of their lives. Liz Sheridan, the only girlfriend to share a home with Dean, thought the same thing about herself and Dean at the same time.

Whatever he truly felt, his behavior would forever remain much like every boy who agonized over feelings for other boys. "You learned that you should have played sports in high school in order not to have been chastised as a sissy," the novelist and critic Jack Ricardo, who grew up gay in a similar small town a few years after Dean, recalled. "You learned to go steady with a girl in order to defend your masculinity and keep faith with your so-called friends. You learned not to talk about homosexuality because just by mentioning the word you were criticized and categorized."[9] Dean would learn these sad lessons far too well.

But here, now, in the summer of 1947, the teenage Jimmy Dean only knew that he sometimes felt things he shouldn't feel, things he wouldn't or couldn't talk about. What was there to say? He knew well enough what the dour Quakers at his church and his pious family thought about sexual immorality, and any boy reasonably curious about the world couldn't help but notice the newspapers and magazines he consumed voraciously painted these feelings as monstrous. *Life* magazine recently had told thousands of boys like Dean that "neurotic" homosexuals were among the leading groups treated by psychoanalysts, while *Cosmopolitan* wrote that June that only psychoanalysis could cure homosexuality and lead the afflicted to a "happy marriage."[10] The June edition of the science fiction magazine *Amazing Stories*, so popular with teenage boys (nine in ten of whom read pulp fiction publications), devoted an article to a legend of God's vengeance on ancient homosexual giants, speaking with disgust of the "ugly acts committed by them for the purpose of self-gratification."[11] On June 9, *Newsweek* ran an article about "Homosexuals in Uniform" and screamed about the "abnormality" of the "inverts" who had penetrated the U.S. military, labeling them "neuropsychiatric cases" and insisting they were "undesirable."[12] No single word might have been better chosen to hurt Jimmy Dean.

According to the magazine, the military deployed psychiatrists to hunt down homosexuals in their ranks, looking for them "(1) by their effeminate looks or behavior and (2) by repeating certain words from the homosexual vocabulary and watching for signs of recognition." The most likely homosexuals, they determined ominously, were intelligent White men from broken homes with overbearing mothers. They also claimed that testing a man's urine could find homosexuals through the presence of excess estrogen. Suspected homosexuals were evacuated to hospitals, where psychiatrists would evaluate whether they could be "cured." Only half, they said, could change. To combat the menace of homosexual soldiers, the Army imposed a new policy, effective July 1, that would automatically eject any man found to have engaged in homosexual activity with a dishonorable discharge, thus marking him as undesirable for life.[13]

Jimmy Dean wouldn't have known that this would become one of the first tremors in a massive nationwide panic over the supposedly evil influence of homosexuals in America that would see the United States expel thousands of gay and bisexual men from government service over his lifetime and enact new laws and policies to persecute them, but he certainly understood how society thought of men who were different, and it marked him. Such thoughts echoed angrily against his deep fear from childhood that God had punished him by taking away his mother and his father. His secret feelings would have been yet another punishment. He began to read about life after death and the occult mysteries of the world, and he would forever after be interested in the question of what happens to the soul after the body passes.

His high school art teacher, Gurney Maddingly, remembered having conversations about the occult, space aliens, and ancient mysteries with the curious teen, no doubt inspired by science fiction stories and purportedly true articles from pulp magazines like *Amazing Stories* that called out to teenage boys with their lurid and exciting full-color covers filled with monsters, alien vistas, and manly he-men. One such conversation was prompted by a painting Dean made of bodies rising from the grave: "We talked about mediums who contacted the dead, particularly Harry Houdini, and we discussed whether the pyramids were built by the Egyptians or people from outer space. He said, 'When we finally die we'll know all those things but we'll have to wait until then.'"[14] Most who heard Dean talk that way assumed that he hoped to be reunited with the spirit of his mother. But he also worried for his own soul. As an adult, his favorite book was a 1943 children's story, *The Little Prince*, about a boy from outer space who learns about the evils of the world and the truth of love. The boy begs his only friend on Earth not to be sad when he kills himself and leaves his dead body behind so he can return home to the stars.

When sixteen-year-old James Dean raced his motorcycle at fifty miles per hour down the main drag of Fairmount, around the S-shaped curve near the cemetery, and on the long stretch of road from town to the Winslow farm, the engine roared so loudly that townsfolk could hear him coming a mile away. Speeding under endless sky in the summer sun, his head filled with the mysteries of this world and the next, it must have seemed that if he could only go fast enough, he might finally break free and escape to another, better world just beyond the horizon.

When Fairmount High School let out for the summer in May 1947, the long months ahead promised plenty of unstructured time for Dean to indulge his interests in art and literature, now that class was over and sports had ended for the year. Again, the next year, he earned generally poor marks. Dean always feared letting the other boys know that he was smart, worried that it would lead them to think he was effeminate, not masculine enough, homosexual. "I'd rather not get good grades than be called a sissy," he told Ortense by way of explanation.[15] His logic was not entirely unsound. That summer, psychiatrists in New York City issued a report complaining that there were too few mental hygiene clinics to treat adolescents and young adults with homosexual tendencies.[16] Such feelings were pathological—a sickness. To be a sissy was tantamount to admitting to be sick, diseased, evil.

Dean was already suspect, a loner who had trouble making friends and spent his after-school hours practicing theatrical monologues with his drama teacher, Adeline Brookshire, and rehearsing for plays. With no girlfriend or even dates, he was doubly suspect. Girls took a shine to him, but classmates recalled that he never seemed interested in them. According to the newspapers that year, athletics could serve as a "means of keeping our boys normal males, even if occasionally some homosexual athlete gets found out." Thus, "ladylike or effeminate boys should be encouraged to engage in the rough and tumble of play life with normal boys."[17] To earn the respect, if not the acceptance, of the other boys and to provide cover for his dramatic inclinations, during the school year, he threw himself into baseball, basketball, and track, competing so fiercely to show his manly worth that over his school career, he broke fifteen pairs of glasses. "I had to prove myself back there," he said.[18] In class, he would play the part of the contemptuous rule breaker, once offering a shocked Brookshire a cigarette in the middle of class.

It was a performance of masculinity and bravado, creating a new story about Jimmy Dean, star athlete and daredevil he-man, straight out of one of his favorite boys' adventure novels. It was only partly effective. When the boys would arrive for practice or for games, they came in boisterous, friendly

James Dean's high school basketball coach recalled that Dean would often arrive to and leave practice alone. *Courtesy David Loehr / The James Dean Gallery.*

groups, but Dean almost always arrived and left alone. He never seemed to be able to relax and be comfortable around teammates or classmates, his basketball coach Paul Weaver recalled. "He was a little different from most boys," Weaver added without ever quite understanding why.[19] At night, Dean often awoke crying from a recurring dream of being locked in a glass box, unable to break free, forced to watch other people laughing and playing around him without being able to connect with them.[20] Even his racing friends were more the type to sit side by side, working on their bikes, than to share secrets. They would recall that he would entertain them by imagining them in fictional races, with him as a radio announcer offering the play-by-play, an observer from afar. His was a world of imagination and pretend.

The summer months were usually quieter, however. Over the course of the summer, when he wasn't baling hay, working part-time at the local cannery for 10¢ an hour, or racing his motorcycle, he would spend hours consuming whatever reading material he could. He even took a stack of old books and almanacs he had come across to his bedroom and mined them for intriguing anecdotes and stories while lying beneath a rosette award for raising a grand champion Guernsey cow. He received that decoration from the 4H Club one summer, not for raising a cow, but for a grand exhibit he had made from soil samples he collected while a gas well was being drilled on the Winslow farm. The county agent didn't have an award for soil science, so Dean proudly hung up this bullish honor in substitute. It made for a good story.

Farm work tended to fall by the wayside when something more interesting came along or even when it didn't. "Now, this was a real farm I was on and I worked like crazy—as long as someone was watching me," Dean recalled in an interview years later. "The forty acres of oats was a huge stage and when the audience left I took a nap and things didn't get plowed or harrowed."[21] His uncle tended to let it slide. After seven years, he had about given up getting Dean to do anything he didn't want to do. He had watched as Dean developed one enthusiasm after another, like the time he had to know every mechanical facet of Marcus's newest piece of farm equipment. He worked tirelessly to master the subject and then dropped it forever as soon as he decided he had learned everything worth knowing about it. "Why did God put all these things here for us to be interested in?" Dean recalled asking.[22] The stories, however, seemed to be a constant. He was always reading stories, acting out stories, and listening to them, wrapping himself in other lives and other worlds, an armor against the world and against himself.

In the summer of 1947, had he been in New York or Los Angeles, the two cities where he hoped to one day live, it would have been impossible for James Dean not to see himself reflected in the stories important people were talking about—stories of boys not a world apart from him and stories that, unbeknownst to him, would one day define his life and legacy. A novel, a failed movie script, a Broadway play—the connections tying together seemingly disparate events in 1947 would shape Jimmy Dean's future in ways Dean could not have anticipated at sixteen.

A sensational new novel would soon set fire to the best-seller lists and enflame the passions of parents, who condemned its nearly pornographic depictions of juvenile delinquents and the darkness hiding in the hearts of teenage boys. Irving Shulman's 273-page *The Amboy Dukes*, published by Doubleday, told of violent, psychopathic, but seductively cool Jewish teenagers who prowled the streets of Brooklyn, battling one another with knives and guns and raping and murdering with wild abandon.

Shulman believed there was a sickness in American society, born of a rotting social structure, a cruelty fostered by capitalism, and failure in the nation's schools. He argued that young men were naturally drawn to deviance in the absence of leadership, but society, in its mindless quest to dominate and exploit, led teenage boys to their destruction.

When Avon Books released a paperback version two years later—with all references to Jewishness strangely excised—it started to sell and sold more than three million copies by 1955. The prose left educators and parents, and eventually Congress, concerned about and for high school boys, whom they worried were both budding criminals and susceptible to seduction toward delinquency. For now, though, few read the heavy hardcover. Its publication, however, did not go unnoticed at Warner Bros. Pictures in Hollywood, where Shulman was soon hired as a contract writer, in part to forestall competition because a very similar story was already in production for a planned late 1947 release, provided they could find the right star.

In January, Warner Bros. producer Jerry Wald told the *New York Times* that he intended to produce a film called *Rebel without a Cause* as a "consideration of juvenile delinquency and its causes." However, on the day the *Times* talked with Wald, the *Mildred Pierce* producer was much more enthusiastic about his current project, an adaptation of Charles Jackson's recent novel *The Fall of Valor*, the first American best-seller to bluntly discuss homosexuality. In that book, the protagonist's failing marriage collapses completely when he falls in love with a handsome Marine. Wald loved the story, except for one little detail. The homosexual material, he told the *Times*, had been "quietly dropped on the floor."[23] Instead, the film version would be a "clinical" dissection of a dead but decidedly heterosexual marriage. In so doing, Wald followed the path being taken by *Crossfire*, a 1947 murder mystery based on a 1945 novel, *The Brick Foxhole*. In the book, the murder victim was gay, but the film industry's prohibition on depictions of "sexual perversion" led RKO Radio Pictures to make him Jewish instead.

In February of the previous year, for $5,000 Warner Bros. had secured the film rights to the book *Rebel without a Cause: The Hypnoanalysis of a Criminal Psychopath*, a nonfiction study of a teenage criminal psychopath by the thirty-year-old psychoanalyst Robert M. Lindner. When released in 1944, the book caused a sensation by reporting on the secret world of a teenage delinquent and the psychological factors that supposedly drew him to a criminal lifestyle. Lindner's methods were suspect: He gained his insights through hypnosis, using leading questions and undue pressure to force his subject's life to conform to the ideas of Sigmund Freud. He claimed, preposterously, that the teenage boy he hypnotized had grown to loathe society because he hated his father after watching his parents copulate when he was one year old and mistaking the sex act for an attack. Parental hatred transferred to social hatred. But Lindner's key findings resonated with the upcoming generation. He spoke disapprovingly of disaffected young men who dissented from the social contract governing American life and rebelled against society, authority, and morality but with no clear ideas about what should replace them. Each was a "rebel without a cause, an agitator without a slogan, a revolutionary without a program."[24]

While the rebel may have had no cause to champion, he was himself the product of a specific cause. Lindner blamed the closing of the American frontier and the resulting calcification of a society with no more boundaries to push, no more new lands to explore: "Concentration in cities coincident with the disappearance of frontiers—both physical and psychological—is the responsible social factor in the genesis of the psychopathic pattern.

Behaviorally regarded, the psychopath's performance is of the frontier type."
For Lindner, the wild freedom from rules, morals, and laws typical of the
Old West of myth was also the freedom sought by young men who lacked
economic possibility, felt caged by "repetitious occupational activity," and
were plagued, "in a word, by social disinheritance."[25] These boys, often isolated and seeking solitude, had within them the spark of evil. Had he met
young James Dean, he might have noted grimly the lonely boy's idolization
of frontier outlaw Billy the Kid and predicted that Dean would rebel against a
stifling society, even at the expense of his own happiness. Lindner, however,
saw in angry young men the seeds of fascism and demanded a solution. History itself, he said, had assigned America the task of "cleansing civilization of
the predatory creature," the teen boy rebel, in order to "make of him a good
citizen in a new world."[26] His was a dream of conformity.

Wald had read of the critical acclaim afforded to *Rebel* and was intrigued
by the suggestion of a new social issue that could be turned into a didactic
film warning of another moral panic. These "issues" movies were peren-
nially popular, if moralistic and preachy, and the arrival of a new social
issue—juvenile delinquency—could provide a dramatic reinvention of the
studio's previous run of less-realistic films about the hardscrabble lives of
disaffected youths starring the Dead End Kids in such popular fare as *Angels
with Dirty Faces*.

Jerry Wald had a twenty-eight-page treatment for *Rebel* developed in mid-
1946, telling the story of a mentally ill boy driven to murder by his memories
of a traumatic childhood. Studio boss Jack Warner was on board. A partial
script by Peter Viertel was completed in April 1947, and in June, Theodor
Geisel, later known as Dr. Seuss, took a turn revising the script. Wald wasn't
happy with the scripts and asked Irving Shulman to give it a go, to no avail.
Warner talent executive William Orr considered the film a potential star-
making vehicle for the up-and-coming twenty-three-year-old actor Marlon
Brando, a brash young disciple of the emotionally driven Stanislavski system
of acting, with its total commitment to character and realism, which Brando
had learned under Stella Adler and Elia Kazan, the latter a onetime member
of the Communist Party in the 1930s. This was of no concern to the studios
that employed the Greek-born Kazan, but soon enough the U.S. government
would take notice.

The young Marlon Brando made an indelible impression on stage in *A Streetcar Named Desire*. He would soon become James Dean's acting idol. *Library of Congress, Prints and Photographs Division, Carl Van Vechten Collection, LC-USZ62-128582.*

This spring, however, Orr was hearing great things about Brando while scouting talent in New York. Brando brought a raw naturalism to acting that polarized audiences but might make him a dynamic lead for a movie about a mercurial killer. That same May, in New York, Orr invited the five-foot-ten, 170-pound Brando to test for *Rebel without a Cause*, playing a character named Harold from Viertel's unfinished script. In the test shot, depicting Harold returning home to his girlfriend, Brando is dressed casually in a striped T-shirt but looking more like a mature adult man than a teenager. He shouts to the actress playing his girlfriend, "I hate your stupid face!" as he rages and cries about his parents and plots a robbery and an escape to South America.

Brando, though, turned down the proffered role to stay on the stage, and when by August none of the Warner Bros. directors would agree to take on a script that even Orr admitted was terrible, the studio abandoned the project.[27] Juvenile delinquency wasn't yet the major panic it would become in the succeeding years. Brando returned to the stage, where late that summer Elia Kazan cast him in a Broadway production of Tennessee Williams's *A Streetcar Named Desire* and changed Brando's life forever. His electric performance in the role of Stanley Kowalski wowed critics and proved Brando had made the right call turning Warner Bros. down.

By the end of summer, the people and the projects that would, in due time, come together to make James Dean an immortal star had already entered each other's orbit, and had Dean known how his own gravitational pull would link him to the names he read in the newspapers, he would have called it fate, for he had made an important decision about his future.

One day, while drying dishes in the Winslows' neat little kitchen as Ortense washed, Jimmy Dean told her that he wanted to leave town after high school and become an actor. She told him that those kinds of dreams weren't for people like them, from places like this, as the silent trees, vacant yard, and empty fields spread endlessly beyond the big window over the sink.[28] But his drama teacher thought otherwise, and the new school year brought with it new opportunities to act in plays, perform dramatic oratory, and debate for the forensics team. His first play of the year would be in October. Varsity basketball also promised more chances for attention, adulation, and success. The wooden gym floor and the wooden auditorium stage boards blended into one platform fit for a star. All of the attention, however, didn't quite make up for the secrets he kept inside, the ones he couldn't quite bring himself to express, until finally he found someone he could tell some of those secrets to.

A while back, Fairmount had seen the arrival of a Wesleyan Methodist minister, the Reverend James DeWeerd, a dynamic former Army chaplain of eccentric personal style and an intensely emotional manner of preaching. He spent his time extolling fundamentalist views on sin and the devil in a traveling revival show and collecting donations from the faithful, but he made his home in Fairmount.[29] The bachelor clergyman had returned to town after years away at school and war. He lived with his mother in a grand house full of antiques and curiosities, surrounded by sumptuous beds of flowers. The jovial DeWeerd was, by Fairmount standards, exceptionally cultured and worldly. He had studied in England, knew Winston Churchill, and could speak of art, literature, and music. But he also had war wounds and a reputation for bravery from his service days. He was especially fond of teenage boys and made a special effort to befriend the boys of Fairmount High in the hope of providing spiritual guidance. For these past few summers, he had surrounded himself with boys, taking them on trips to the YMCA and museums and sparking gossip because the "prissy" fellow some of the townsfolk jokingly called "Dr. Weird" asked the boys to swim nude with him. No boy ever accused the pastor of any wrongdoing, but decades later, some townsfolk looked back and wondered.

In the summer of 1947, in unintentional echo, Lieutenant William T. Murphy of the Juvenile Bureau of Washington's Metropolitan Police pleaded in the newspapers for stronger laws to combat sexual perversion, to protect boys from the predations of homosexuals. "In practice," he warned, "an adult will strike up an acquaintance with a young person whom he happens to meet casually on the street. A show will be taken in, a little money will be spent." The youth would see in the older man the "appearance of a social success" and would soon "accept as morally and socially right whatever the pervert says and does." If not stopped, the "child's character and personality will be damaged beyond repair," and the boy will become a homosexual himself.[30]

Dean found himself drawn to DeWeerd, the most worldly and sophisticated man he had ever met and someone he felt understood him better than most. He could offer Dean something that stolid Marcus Winslow couldn't:

a glimpse of the world beyond Fairmount. DeWeerd was happy to oblige, seeing in Dean the only boy in town who could genuinely appreciate the higher parts of culture. They soon developed a friendly relationship, and DeWeerd invited Dean to spend his free time in his home. They would dine together and speak of philosophy and poetry. DeWeerd showed him amateur 8 mm movies of his adventures with bullfighting, and the exotic wonder of the violent spectacle captured Dean's imagination. His house became, for Dean, something of a second home, a respite from the world. "Jimmy was usually happiest stretched out on my library floor, reading Shakespeare or other books of his choosing," DeWeerd recalled a few years later. "He loved good music playing softly in the background. Tchaikovsky was his favorite."[31] DeWeerd told Dean that he would excel as a romantic lead in a Shakespeare play.

But DeWeerd wasn't simply an avatar of the arts for Dean. He was also a spiritual man who offered a sympathetic ear and imparted moral teachings alongside his lessons in literature and philosophy. Although he was a Wesleyan by trade, he had a penchant for the mystical side of faith. He taught Dean that knowledge and experience were twin paths to enlightenment and that conformity was cowardice. Truth to oneself was a paramount virtue, an authenticity that marked the elect from the common. Most people, DeWeerd insisted, were small, closed, almost unreal—the "square root of zero," he called them. This reinforced Dean's own decision years before to reject the rigid morality of small-town Christian hypocrites. In turn, Dean shared with DeWeerd some of the pain lurking within his heart and "poured out" his feelings of sadness, self-loathing, and despair. One day he showed DeWeerd a slumped, faceless clay figure he had sculpted. "It's me," he said. "I call it 'Self.'"[32] He told DeWeerd he worried that he was evil, that God had punished him for his evil by taking his mother and driving away his father, and that if anyone knew how evil he must be inside, then no one would ever love him.

DeWeerd offered his faith's unsparing response, which confirmed Dean's worst fears: "I taught Jim that he was depraved and vile, that he had to seek salvation."[33] The nature of Dean's evil remained between him and DeWeerd, but those who knew Dean felt DeWeerd's words alluded to sex.[34] All was not lost, for salvation could come to all who believed in Christ, and DeWeerd could guide him on the path of faith. But could Dean believe? DeWeerd told

Dean that the mental world was far more powerful than the corrupt and fallen world of matter. "I taught Jimmy to believe in personal immortality," DeWeerd said. "He had no fear of death because he believed as I do that death is merely control of mind over matter."[35] The physical world was but a temporary illusion, a gauntlet of trial and pain that would one day fall away, replaced by an immaterial forever, at least for those who were saved. "Why are we compelled to live in one world, to wonder about the other world?" Dean wrote in a high school homework assignment.[36] A friend recalled often seeing the sleepless boy racing his motorcycle down a blue road beneath the midnight stars out to the small graveyard on the old Dean farm where his ancestors lay to pray and plead with God or the gods or the spirits for guidance and support and courage.[37] Somewhere beyond, there would be another, better world.

Over the course of Dean's last two years of high school, he grew increasingly close to DeWeerd, who named the youth in his diary as one of his "closest friends," and long decades later, stories spread in the press that their relationship had taken a sexual turn.[38] It had started, or so the story went, with some touching during drives in DeWeerd's convertible, and these touches progressed to more sexual intimacies. Dean alluded to this only once, years later, when, in a rare unguarded moment late one night, he confessed that his minister had molested him.[39]

Whatever had transpired, the two had grown emotionally intimate in ways that both recognized had to remain private. Neither man spoke publicly about their relationship during Dean's lifetime. DeWeerd would soon rise to national fame as an evangelist and radio and television preacher, and he had no desire to invite unwelcome questions. "Jimmy never mentioned our relationship nor did I," gossip writer Joe Hyams said DeWeerd once told him. "It would not have helped either of us."[40] Indeed, requests for DeWeerd to lead evangelistic meetings had all but ceased by the late 1950s, when rumors may have first quietly circulated—seeming proof of DeWeerd's fears. Soon after, DeWeerd left the Wesleyan Methodist Church for another denomination.[41] But the secretive friendship did teach Dean lessons about the walls that would forever keep the many parts of his life and his soul separate and in conflict.

2
PROLOGUE TO GLORY

Separating himself worked, and for a time it became possible for Jimmy Dean to imagine he could live two parallel lives: the sensitive artist and the aggressive jock. Over the course of his junior and senior years of high school, Dean had come to believe that if he could keep these halves balanced, his dreams would not only come true but also that destiny itself had decreed his success. In his final year of high school, he had moved from one triumph to the next.

As an artist, his roles in school plays found him expanding his range into comedy and accent work and demonstrating such talent for acting that he became convinced his future lay in that field. He had even become a junior Lon Chaney, mastering the art of stage makeup. He made one of his characters so distinct that his classmates couldn't recognize him and ended a Halloween 1948 show with a grotesque take on Universal Pictures' definitive Frankenstein's Monster that repulsed his teachers and classmates.

And his other self, the jock, found equal success. His athletic talent made him famous around town. The *Fairmount News* had declared him an "outstanding threat" on the basketball court, and important people like the school superintendent chatted him up in the school halls. The younger boys looked up to him and copied his distinctive slouch. Even his whims succeeded. Told that his small stature precluded him becoming a pole vaulter, he took up the sport, broke the county pole-vaulting record, and

Teenage James Dean in a basketball team photo at the height of his high school athletic career. *Courtesy David Loehr / The James Dean Gallery.*

dropped it after he had secured his triumph. He signed his photo in innumerable yearbooks his junior year—everyone wanted his signature—with his nickname, "Rack," appropriated from his tennis-loving uncle, but he never let anyone see exactly how much work went in to making success seem effortless.[1]

In the fall of 1948, the start of his senior year, Fairmount High's new principal, Roland Dubois, asked his students to submit autobiographies so he could get to know his new charges. Dean took to the task with a blunt assessment of himself as a goal-driven man of destiny, calling his life story his "case study." He told the plain facts of his life and explained that his mother's death "still preys on my mind." He judged with perspicacity, if not humility, the path he was destined to take:

> I think my life will be devoted to art and dramatics. And there are so many different fields of art it would be hard to foul up, and if I did there are so many different things to do—farm, sports, science, geology, coaching, teaching, music. I got it and I know if I better myself then there will be no match. A fellow must have confidence. . . . As one strives to make a goal in a game there should be a goal in this crazy world for each of us. I hope I know what mine is—anyway, I'm after it.

Dean confessed to Dubois, however, that his own life was the "hardest subject to write about considering the information one knows of himself, I ever attempted."[2]

In short order, though, Dean's inkling that he had a goal in life and that self-improvement would take him toward success flowed easily into the mystical lessons about immortality and the divide between mind and matter that the Reverend DeWeerd had taught him. Privately, he started to believe that he was destined for greatness. He would visit his mother's grave and say as much to her spirit: "I'm gonna show you! I'm gonna be great!" he said. To a college friend two years later, he explained that "there's only one true form of greatness for man. If a man can bridge the gap between life and death, I mean, if he can live on after he's died, then maybe he was a great man. To me, the only success, the only greatness, is immortality."[3] His life's work, whatever that was to be, would live on after him for decades, centuries, forever. To achieve this artistic immortality, there could be only ceaseless striving toward a better tomorrow in a better world. "There is no top," he said.

He felt—no, knew—that some power beyond him was pushing and guiding him upward. "Have you ever had the feeling it's not in your hands?" he asked his friend before explaining for the first time the core of his personal myth, the story he told himself about his life and destiny. The powers above had showed him just enough to see the outlines of the story but not enough to know what he worked toward. "Do you ever just know that you've got something to do and you have no control over it? See, all I know is, I've got to do something. I don't know exactly what it is yet, but when the time comes, I'll know. I've got to keep trying until I hit the right button."[4] That great work, he said, was not acting or even directing. "There's got to be more to it than just that," he said. But that transcendent purpose, that great work of immortality—the powers above kept it hidden, a destiny he could feel in his bones but not fully know.

Dean may have felt his future touched by the divine, but the world around him remained a disappointment, something heartless and cruel and not entirely real, a realm of base matter awaiting a superior mind to transcend it. Somewhere, beyond the striving and struggle, something more solid awaited. It had to, or else the sadness and the alienation and the bottomless loneliness had no purpose. "I want to grow away from all this crap," he said.

> You know, the pathetic little world we exist in. I want to leave it all behind, all the petty thoughts about the unimportant little things that'll be forgotten a hundred years from now anyway. There's a level somewhere where everything is solid and important. I'm going to try to reach up there and find a place I know is pretty close to perfect, a place where this whole messy world should be, could be, if it'd just take the time to learn.[5]

A collegiate future was increasingly on Dean's mind during his senior year of high school, a looming uncertainty full of promise and peril. In his fantasies, he imagined it a stepping stone, vaulting him to Hollywood as rapt audiences bowed in awe to his natural talent. But the messy, crazy, imperfect world stubbornly refused to fully flatter Dean's Promethean vision of seizing fire from the gods or to let Dean forget that he, too, was mortal.

In Fairmount, Dean had grown into a minor god of sorts, his talent and drive setting him above his peers, but his confidence started to outrun reality. DeWeerd had taken him to the Indianapolis 500, and Dean developed a new passion for cars and auto racing. He started to borrow friends' cars to speed through town, imagining himself a future racer. His homeroom teacher, Bette McPherson, nearing thirty and newly separated from her invalid husband, developed a crush on Dean, showered him with attention, and imagined he was in love with her. He thought an affair a good way to bury his sexual traumas and doubts and to make his time with DeWeerd seem less suspicious.

When DeWeerd invited McPherson and Dean to dinner, Dean became embarrassed by DeWeerd's effeminate manners and made crude jokes about him behind his back to prove *himself* all man. McPherson, caught up in her own excitement and oblivious decades later to the possible impact that an adult (a trusted teacher, no less) sleeping with a teen might have, later implied that she had bedded the teenager. Boys like sex, right? Dean, however, insisted he was still a virgin well into his college years. Over the summer, when both were in Los Angeles, Dean impetuously offered an ill-considered marriage proposal, which McPherson declined, before he eventually forgot about McPherson entirely.[6]

Dean spent his last months of high school in the beginning of 1949 working with Adeline Brookshire to perfect a piece of dramatic oratory to present at the National Forensic League state finals. He chose a Gothic, macabre monologue from Charles Dickens's *The Pickwick Papers*, in which a madman confesses to driving his wife insane and trying to murder her brother. As would occur so often in his career, he found himself reflected in his chosen role, imbuing his character's words with his own inner pain:

> I knew I was mad, but they did not even suspect it. How I used to hug myself with delight, when I thought of the fine trick I was playing them after their old pointing and leering, when I was not mad, but only dreading that I might one day become so! And how I used to laugh for joy, when I was alone, and thought how well I kept my secret, and how quickly my kind friends would have fallen from me, if they had known the truth.[7]

He delivered a near quarter-hour of dramatic monologue with an astonishing range of tone, emotion, and action, delirium curdling into rage, leaping, crouching, and embodying madness.

However, the fine trick that kept Dean's two lives separate did not always hold, and when he could not fully wall off artist from jock, sensitive from aggressive, the unspoken desires from the public performance, he exploded in unexpected fits of shocking, confusing rage.

That spring he had become accustomed to his audience of classmates and teachers sitting in rapt attention and astonishment, mesmerized. But a younger boy, David Fox, who found the spectacle overwrought, turned to his classmates and smirked, snorted, and laughed through Dean's final rehearsal. "What're you trying to do, Dean?" he asked. "We know you're a great talent, a regular John Barrymore." Dean snapped, chased Fox down a stairwell, and beat him with such fury that only intervention by two teachers and the principal could break up the pummeling.[8] Principal DuBois demanded to know who started the fight and, receiving no response, expelled both boys until Dean fell on his sword and confessed to throwing the first punch.

During Dean's expulsion, he painted a series of watercolors in which he appeared to exorcise his frustrations through art. The series depicts an oversized stylized version of Dean standing on the Earth, atop Indiana, while an extraterrestrial monstrosity approaches from space. The Lovecraftian horror is a mass of wriggling eyeballs on stalks or tentacles emerging from a mysterious monolith sitting atop a floating platform. The monster abducts Dean into space and crushes him beneath the monolith as its bloodshot eyes watch curiously.

Two days out of school taught Dean no lesson, and he continued to resist any affront to the integrity of his performance. Brookshire reminded him that the Forensics League had a strict time limit that was two minutes less than his speech, but he refused to cut any of Dickens's words, taking the rules as implicit criticism of his artistic vision. Similarly, he refused to honor the league's unwritten dress code of blazer and tie as an imposition on his freedom to depict his character's madness. "How the heck can I go crazy in a shirt and tie?" he asked a fellow debater who proffered the same critique. Dean's stubborn conviction won out, and his dramatic declamation took first place in the regional competition and then again at the Indiana state finals in Peru, Indiana, in early April —but with a warning from the judges about running over time.

The win came as a surprise to Marcus and Ortense because Dean had neglected to tell them about the competition. They read about it in the local newspaper, which carried a headline about Dean's win on its front page, complete with a large photograph of Dean pulled from the school yearbook. On April 27, Dean and Brookshire took a train to Longmont, Colorado, for the National Forensic League's national competition. He stayed with a host family, and Brookshire was shocked to find that the night before his big speech at the local high school, he had charmed his hosts into letting him borrow their car to go driving around town. The next day, April 30, during the first round of dramatic declaration against a field of a hundred students from twenty-four states, he delivered his big monologue his own way, dressed in blue jeans, speaking unabridged despite the length, and opening with a primal scream, sure his talent and his destiny would carry him to victory. He made it from the first to the second round, with a warning from the judge to stick to the time limit. He ignored the admonishment, insisting on the integrity of his art. Another participant warned him he'd never win in blue jeans. "Then I won't win, that's all," he replied. "I don't need to win."[9] He didn't believe it, but he said it.

For the first time, the guiding hand of fate failed him in his artistic ambitions. Five finalists moved on to the last round, and Dean placed sixth. The boy who had been a god in the town of Fairmount and a king in the state of Indiana failed to take the throne on the national stage. His self-image as the man of destiny, guided toward supernatural success, had crashed into the reality of an all-too-human world that shared none of his faith. He disappeared, slinking into the school gymnasium, climbing to the top of the bleachers, and sitting in utter silence hour after hour, stunned, brooding, devastated. Eventually Brookshire found him and tried to get him to speak. When he finally did, there was no warmth in his voice. He blamed *her* for his loss, complaining that she had failed to intercede with the judges, had offered damaging criticism that threw him off, had somehow caused the disaster.

She must have flashed back to a similar incident from Dean's freshman year, when his first dramatic monologue ended in failure after the judges took away the chair he and Brookshire had planned for him to use as a prop. Refusing to perform, he unleashed a raging torrent of misplaced invective against her that she would still remember with horror half a century afterward. Now, at the end, it was as at the beginning. When the shock and the anger eventually wore off, Dean would amend his destiny with a grim coda reflecting his dim view of others, one he repeated to a gossip columnist years later: "But let me say this: no one helps you. You do it yourself."[10] He would never again take his art lightly. Even fate required effort and sacrifice.

The forensics loss stung Dean harder than anything since the death of his mother, and it irked him for the rest of his life, no matter how he tried to massage it into destiny's plan. In the coming years, he would complain about it to his college roommate, and as an adult, he would even tell the story of his state championship to gossip columnists and newspaper reporters, emphasizing his artistry and physicality and strategically omitting his national loss.[11] In the immediate aftermath, however, he needed to restore his sense of manhood and pride before high school ended in two weeks.

He returned home just in time for the senior class at Fairmount High to take a final field trip to Washington, D.C., on May 7 and 8 to tour the monuments, the National Mall, and the Smithsonian, crossing the same parks by day where each evening Metropolitan Police and groups of vigilante boys Dean's own age patrolled for homosexuals in hopes of "knocking off a queer," as one teenage thug put it.[12] Dean quietly sneaked away from the group to visit Ford's Theater, where Lincoln had been killed. As the stifling heat of Saturday began to turn miraculously toward the springtime cool of Sunday, Dean imagined himself once more a god among boys by securing a case of beer and secreting it back to the Roosevelt Apartments, where the class was staying. The tipsy boys tied bedsheets together to climb down to the floor below, where the girls resided. The chaperones mostly looked the other way. Back home, with school ending, prom came, and Dean banged a drum alongside the other boys, providing music in the gym, all the better to distract from his lack of a prom date—and lack of interest in one.

On the way home from Washington, the senior class of 1949 had elected him to give the benediction at their May 16 graduation, and in the yearbook, Dean joked that he would bequeath his temper to David Fox. A fortuitous letter from his long-absent but now-remarried father, Winton, opened a new opportunity. Winton Dean invited his son to come live with him in Los Angeles—the home of Hollywood—and he would give Dean room and board during his college education. Winton thought his son would make a fine sports coach, and Jimmy thought it was a great chance to explore acting in entertainment's capital.

Dean graduated twentieth in his class of forty-seven, receiving awards for both athletics and art. His friends and family, with the Reverend DeWeerd notably absent, threw him a going-away party on June 13, the night before he left, serenading him with verses from "California, Here I Come," and the *Fairmount News* dutifully reported the happening: "James Dean Was Honored at Farewell Party Monday Night," read the headline. The article said Dean was headed to UCLA, but that was an optimistic boast. Dean didn't know where he'd go to school once he got to L.A.

The next morning, he left Indiana for the destiny he knew awaited him, and he only rarely thought about the people he left behind, many of whom would never leave Fairmount. Dean had grown used to being the center of the world, for good or for ill, and he had come to believe it was his rightful place. Everybody else—well, they were still the square root of zero.

Dean arrived in California still very much a boy, all gangly legs and too-short hair, with glasses and clothes that seemed at once a size too big and too small, matched by a Hoosier accent a little too thick.[13] If he had any thoughts over the four days he spent on the bus about leaving behind bigoted Fairmount and the strange and complicated relationship he shared with the Reverend DeWeerd, he kept them to himself. Friends and family remembered only his excitement on the morning of his departure, how anxious he was to leave as he made his final goodbyes in the stifling summer heat and checked one last time on his motorcycle in storage.

No one observed anything amiss, but deep inside, putting distance between himself and DeWeerd's insistence that he was evil, that the feelings he could barely admit to himself condemned him before God, might have offered at least some relief. He may well have hoped California would give him a fresh start—perhaps in his silent fantasies, he even shared a secret thrill about visiting cities big enough to have a "Queer Street," "Queens Boulevard," "Fairyland," "Fag Alley," or "Birdcharmer Square," the colloquial names for neighborhoods where queer people gathered—but wherever he turned during the preceding year, it became increasingly inescapable that the world around him sought only to ratify DeWeerd's verdict.[14]

Magazines, movies, every outlet that once gave him escape insisted he was depraved and vile. *Cosmopolitan* ran a story that May on the "unmentionable minority," homosexuals, saying all "right-minded" people viewed their "illness of defect" with "disgust." *Newsweek* reminded its readers in the fall that homosexuals were all potential monsters, equivalent to sadists and pedophiles, their unnatural desires too easily sliding into violence and murder: "The sex pervert, whether a homosexual, an exhibitionist, or even a dangerous sadist, is too often regarded merely as a 'queer' person who never hurts anyone but himself. Then the mangled form of some victim focuses public attention on the degenerate's work."[15] Under the euphemistic name of "morals charges" and using language indirect enough to pass unnoticed, newspapers of the late 1940s carried countless stories of men arrested for engaging in relations with other males and choosing to end their lives rather than face life as an outcast.

The association of homosexuality with destruction extended to the artistic world Dean longed to join, where homosexual attraction almost inevitably led to shame, villainy, suicide, or murder—when it was depicted at all. Several novels published in the late 1940s and reviewed in the papers and magazines Dean read pushed boundaries by dealing with gay characters, but with rare exceptions, like *The Fall of Valor*, the moral expectations of the reading public required those characters to meet their doom. Even a sympathetic portrayal of a gay man and the underground world of homosexuals, like Gore Vidal's *The City and the Pillar* (1948), makes its protagonist a violent murderer when his sexual advances are frustrated.[16]

In 1949, the future novelist James Baldwin, then twenty-five years old, a friend of Marlon Brando, and desperately in love with a seventeen-year-old high school boy, decried the new trend of novels that took pleasure in depicting violence against gay people. He argued, with some justification, that the growing number of books introducing gay characters, primarily to murder them, had less to do with homosexuality than with the degraded American relationship between men and women and an effort to reinforce the proper definition of masculinity by exorcising those males who, by breaking boundaries, threatened traditional ideas of manliness and enacted a pantomime of femininity to trap real men. After all, if men could find pleasure among themselves, then what purpose did the burden of wife, home, and child serve? For Baldwin, the homosexual and the woman both suffered figurative and literal violence under the toxic rule of American masculinity because heterosexual men saw them both as inferior by virtue of failing, by gender or by sex role, to be men's equals. Enforcing masculinity's most rigid form, he said, had become for America's novelists a "panic close to madness."[17] His insightful essay went largely unnoticed, published in the small journal *Zero* and read by nearly no one.

In the movies of the 1940s that Dean came of age watching, homosexuality was rarely mentioned explicitly, but characters meant to be gay appeared as effeminate "sissies" or as predatory villains, in both cases stereotyped as weak, sensitive, intellectual, and often wearing glasses—the opposite of gruff American cowboy manhood. Many of these were also traits Dean willed himself to overcome or at least to suppress. Clifton Webb, a gay actor, specialized in such clandestinely homosexual characters, including "sissy" roles in *Laura* in 1944 and *The Razor's Edge* two years later. Frank Faylen made his gay nurse in 1947's *The Lost Weekend* notably disquieting. Such characters never bore the name *homosexual* of course, not since the motion picture industry voluntarily adopted a Production Code in 1934 to forestall calls for government censorship of violent and sexualized films. Although the code's moralizing clauses did not explicitly mention homosexuality, its prohibition on "sexual perversion" was understood to encompass all forms of deviant sexuality.

Morals clauses in actors' contracts forbade sexual immorality—an actor must "conduct himself with due regard to social conventions and public morals and decency," as the lawyers put it—and led actors and directors into double lives and conspiracies of silence.[18] In creating a movie of his life in 1946, composer Cole Porter erased his own homosexuality. The celebrity magazines, society columns, and gossip reports of the era made little or no mention of bisexual and gay actors' real love lives, subsisting instead on a steady diet of tempestuous but false relationships stage-managed by the studios for publicity.

Paramount Pictures promoted the moody Montgomery Clift, then twenty-nine, as the hot new star for 1949 on the strength of his 1948 screen debut in the clandestinely homoerotic *Red River*, in which he shares a charged flirtation with another cowboy, and his second picture, *The Search*. Deeply involved in every aspect of his performance and his image, Clift had secretly rewritten the Oscar-winning script for the latter. The studio marketed him as a sex symbol to a nation of women who soon swooned over his performance opposite Olivia de Havilland in *The Heiress*. None of the women writing letters to de Havilland to complain that her character treated Clift's poorly (or James Dean, watching with rapt attention) had any idea that behind the scenes, Clift had relationships with both men and women and agonized over keeping up the right public face. His close friend Elizabeth Taylor considered him gay, and Clark Gable contemptuously called him "that fag." The consequences of not conforming were obvious to all. James Whale, the director of *Frankenstein*, refused to pretend he wasn't gay, and the studios refused to employ him.

As a result of media censorship and a culture of silence, millions of Americans in the late 1940s were unaware homosexuality even existed or at least that it was anything other than a rare and dangerous disorder. The young Rock Hudson, like Dean a midwestern farm boy with big dreams, once thought himself the only homosexual in the world. Katharine Hepburn professed not to know what a homosexual was until Spencer Tracy took her aside and spent an evening explaining it to her. In 1938, she had starred alongside the bisexual Cary Grant in *Bringing Up Baby*, in which Grant's character, by comic circumstance wearing Hepburn's negligée, jumps up and down and shouts, "I just went *gay* all of a sudden!" What did she think he meant? That unscripted moment, ad-libbed by Grant, remained the only Hollywood use of the word *gay* to mean *homosexual* until the liberalization of the Production Code two decades later. Jimmy Stewart didn't realize in 1948 that the two men his character investigated for murder in Alfred Hitchcock's *Rope* were meant to be gay, but the Production Code censors did, complaining of "homosexual dialogue" in the film. Clift and Grant both turned down roles in the film, fearing its gay subtext. But what did James Dean see when he watched these films?

In this climate of repression and oppression, the scientific report *Sexual Behavior in the Human Male* published in 1948 by Alfred Kinsey, a zoologist at Indiana University, landed with the thunderous snap of a storm breaking on a summer's day. Within three months, Gallup found one in five Americans had read the book or read about it in the hundreds of articles covering its claims, and it would have been impossible for Jimmy Dean not to have heard something about it over the course of the year before he left for college, even if secondhand.

Kinsey's volume stated in blunt, seemingly scientific language what the movies could only hint obliquely: Millions of American men were leading double lives outside the boundaries of acceptable morality. After interviewing more than five thousand men over a fifteen-year period, Kinsey concluded that nearly half had experienced attraction to someone of the same sex in their adult lives, that more than a third of all men had acted on such attractions, and that one in ten had been or would be "exclusively homosexual" for at least three years in their adult lives.

Kinsey further shocked the public by declaring sexuality a spectrum ranging from exclusive heterosexuality to bisexuality to exclusive homosexuality, which he rated on a seven-point scale. "Males do not represent two discrete populations, heterosexual and homosexual," he wrote.[19] But rather than recognizing a continuum of experience varying by life stage and circumstance, by the time Dean struck out for California, many journalists and even politicians saw only evidence that anyone might be clandestinely homosexual and a secret subversive. No one wanted shades of gray. They wanted a firm duality between good and evil, heterosexual and homosexual.

Indeed, psychiatrists and sociologists condemned Kinsey's research, upset that he concluded that such "abnormal" sexual behavior as homosexuality was "natural" and not the result of extreme emotional disturbances. The then-current model of homosexuality, derived from the ideas of Freud, held that human males progressed from childhood asexuality to a homosocial stage in early adolescence that culminated in the arrival of full heterosexuality in late adolescence, provided that parents and teachers properly taught the correct beliefs and behaviors. Homosexuals, they believed, suffered from the emotional disturbance of bad parenting, and thus their homosocial stage never ended, perverted into a mania for one's own sex. Kinsey, however, challenged this belief by undermining the neat dichotomy between homosexual and heterosexual.

Kinsey's ideas seemed to find unexpected support in the unexpurgated text of Oscar Wilde's *De Profundis*, which reached bookstores in 1949, half a century after publishers had stripped Wilde's meditation on the connection between artistic genius, romantic individualism, and homosexuality of the wounded, angry love letter to his longtime lover, Lord Alfred Douglas, that enclosed it. The married Wilde wrote the letter while in prison, convicted of gross indecency in an infamous British trial focusing on Wilde's homosexual activity. "Reason does not help me," Wilde lamented. "It tells me that the laws under which I am convicted are wrong and unjust laws, and the system under which I have suffered a wrong and unjust system. But, somehow, I have got to make both of these things just and right to me."

James Dean would soon own a copy of the book and kept it with him for life, often reading parts of it aloud to friends and looking in it for answers to questions he never spoke aloud. "Most people are other people," Wilde wrote in words that must have resonated with Dean. "Their thoughts are some one else's opinions, their lives a mimicry, their passions a quotation." The artist, Wilde said, is the only true individual, expressing his soul as the essence of life: "To the artist, expression is the only mode under which he can conceive life at all. To him what is dumb is dead."[20] The past called out to the present with prophecy and warning.

Jimmy Dean found self-expression unexpectedly challenging when he started his first day of classes at Santa Monica City College in August 1949 and began to struggle to turn the churning stew of dualities within him into a coherent idea of what he would be as a man. He stood before the growing college's temporary campus on Pico Boulevard, the man of destiny who feared an inner evil, the passionate young man who found himself hobbled by insecurity, the athletic star who dreamed of the arts, the would-be cosmopolitan who spoke with a thick rural accent, the physically maturing man who loved boyish things, the handsome youth who knew he should date girls but who secretly had unwanted thoughts about boys.

He had disembarked the Greyhound and arrived at his father's two-bedroom home in Santa Monica, near where he had lived for four years as a child before his mother's death. He had a growing sense of isolation and dislocation. He had never felt at one with the family back in Fairmount who raised him, nor did he feel a part of this family, close neither to his distant father or to the stepmother he barely knew and who seemed anxious around him. Now he had two families, but neither was satisfactory. The Winslows thought he should get a job and start a responsible life. Winton's only fatherly words for his son were to become a lawyer for the money or a basketball coach for the satisfaction. Dean, who would only call Winton "Father," never "Dad," became eager to start school, both to get out of his father's house during the day and in the hope of finding friendship and companions in this strange new city that had once been home.

He met a professor at UCLA who used to live in Fairmount and who introduced Dean to the theater department. To his family in Fairmount, he excitedly wrote that he would be taking classes at UCLA and had joined a local theater troupe, where he had no acting role, but "my knowledge of the stage and the ability to design and paint sets won me the place of head stage manager for the next production."[21] His grandparents Charles and Emma Dean sent the letter to the local paper to be printed for the whole town to read. But Dean's high school grades were too poor to matriculate at UCLA, so he registered for classes at Santa Monica's junior college to earn credits that could transfer toward a bachelor's degree at the four-year school. In later years, rewriting his past, he elided his community college year, hiding it under his sophomore success in entering a more prestigious school.[22]

At college, Dean tried to pull the same trick that had carried him through high school, carefully bifurcating his education and his extracurriculars so that a façade of masculine responsibility would provide cover for his less-respectable artistic interests. Such a feat seemed oddly appropriate because his new school, then constructing a new campus, had its temporary classrooms in Santa Monica High School alongside secondary students, as though Dean weren't really growing up.

He registered as a prelaw student and divided his class schedule in two. One half looked toward an academic future, with courses in English and American history, and the other indulged his passion with courses in theater arts and acting. Similarly, he bifurcated his extracurricular life by throwing himself into the basketball team with the same zeal as the jazz club and minor jobs in student theatrical productions. He also tried to reinvent himself, playing around with his appearance and even his name. He avoided wearing his glasses as much as possible, even on the basketball court, because he thought he looked better without them. He experimented with going by his middle name, Byron, which he insisted was a prophetic link to the great Romantic poet Lord Byron, the notoriously bisexual model for the rebellious, passionate, self-destructive heroes of literature and cinema. Byron had died tragically young.

But Dean soon found that it was easier to make a mark as one of only a couple hundred high schoolers in a town of a few thousand than one of sixteen hundred Santa Monica City College students among the nearly two million residents of Los Angeles County. His classmates remembered him as a walking contradiction, ambitious and driven and yet painfully awkward and shy, an opportunist who looked down at his peers but craved their approval, an alien confused by a world he wished to master.[23] To his shame, his drama teacher, Gene Owen, and his classmates complained about the former Indiana state forensics champion's poor diction and their inability to understand him. They blamed it on his rural accent, and he insisted it was the effect of a daredevil childhood accident that had left him with two false teeth. So Owen worked with him for a semester on his speech by having him reading *Hamlet* aloud, and his teacher soon found herself in awe of the artistry Dean brought to the title role, granting the pained, foredoomed young prince a vulnerability that "touched my heart," she said.[24] She was only the latest person not to notice that Dean's acting success seemed to correlate directly to his ability to discover his own sadness, his own fear, and his own life reflected in the characters he played. When they aligned, he spoke with the voice of the gods, but when they did not, he was all too often merely human.

Dean's father was much less touched by his subterfuge and bifurcation and demanded Dean drop his theatrical ambitions. When he refused, father and son mutually disengaged. Dean spent more and more time away from his new home but to no avail. He indifferently took girls from school out on dates when classmates tried to involve him in their outings, but the girls found his attentions lacking. One remarked that he was more interested in watching the waves crash onto the Santa Monica shore than in talking to her on the beach. He made no close male friends either, though Richard Shannon, a much older classmate, took a paternal interest in him and spent time before and after class answering the curious youth's many questions, sometimes about acting and more often about life.[25]

Soon enough, lonely and bored, Dean had tired of college, which he found simultaneously pretentious and unchallenging. "I couldn't take the . . . tea-sipping, moss-walled academicians, that academic bull," he recalled five years later.[26] He found more satisfaction in underlining the many sexually explicit passages—and likely noting the occasional frank but sympathetic discussions of homosexuality—in a copy he somehow obtained of *My Life and Loves*, a 1922 memoir by Frank Harris, a journalist and friend of Oscar Wilde, banned as obscene in the United States. These and the memoir's many photographs of nude women he shared with members of the basketball and football teams to try to bond with them.

However, despite his academic displeasure and middling grades, he was named to the Opheleos Men's Honor Service Organization, representing the college's twenty-one most outstanding male students each year, "outstanding" being a somewhat elastic term. After receiving a Selective Service eligibility survey by mail in April 1950, as the Korean War draft ramped up, he must have felt some pressure to maintain his student deferment. He desperately wanted to avoid military service.[27] With his father's grudging assent, he made plans in June 1950 to give college another try and to transfer to UCLA for his sophomore year. He spent the summer working as a camp counselor to earn money for the transfer, and he finished the season with a two-week return visit to Indiana. Marcus Winslow found it odd that Dean never told his high school friends he had come home but less odd that Dean spoke barely a word during the trip.

It was during this August homecoming that Dean took his motorcycle, alone, to Marion, where he had been born, to see a movie called *The Men*, a recent tearjerker about wounded war veterans. Watching the drama of traumatized young men struggling to rebuild a sense of manhood and purpose moved Dean with an emotional intensity he had never before experienced and never forgot. He was immediately overwhelmed by the earthshaking performance of the film's star, Marlon Brando, making his screen debut. Dean had seen nothing like it and had never known acting could mean so much. There, by himself in the cool of a darkened theater on a hot summer's day, while outside the first battles of the Korean War stirred talk of expanding the draft in America, random chance shaded imperceptibly into the hand of fate. Jimmy Dean saw his future and emerged from the theater reborn. For a moment the gods spoke through light dancing on a silver screen. And who dared question the gods?

3
KEEP OUR HONOR BRIGHT

From his first days on the UCLA campus, Jimmy Dean's classmates noticed something a bit off about him. Sullen, quiet, and often alone, Dean rarely spoke to other students, made no real friends, and seemed possessed by a single-minded desire for success. He stalked the campus with his ever-present rolled-up newspapers stuffed into his back pocket; two entertainment industry trade papers, *Daily Variety* and the *Hollywood Reporter*, were his favorites. When the theater kids, most of whom had known each other since freshman year, ate their lunches together on the lawn behind the Romanesque red-brick Royce Hall, they would see Dean in the distance, sitting by himself beneath a tree, recognizable even from afar thanks to his striking good looks.

On occasion, Dean would hesitantly try to relate something about himself, though typically to classmates he did not know very well, who often were unsure exactly what he was trying to tell them. One night, Dean accompanied an older student, John Holden, a war veteran, back to his car and asked him what he knew about gay bars—"those bars" Dean called them, apparently struggling even to say the word *gay*—and if he had ever been to one. "I could detect that he was seeking information about gay life in a very oblique way," Holden remembered decades later. Taken aback and unwilling to discuss homosexuality with Dean, Holden quickly changed the subject and rebuffed Dean's inquiries.[1]

As a student, James Dean could often be found stalking around the UCLA campus, including near the Powell Library, alone with his newspapers. *Library of Congress Prints and Photographs Division, Historic American Buildings Survey, HABS CA-2678-A.*

Dean's fellow students met his halting efforts to share a fraction of his inner life with some combination of indifference, disapproval, and contempt. But even these small steps were likely difficult for someone so used to keeping so much to himself, made harder by the news stories he read every day in the papers he carried with him. The newspapers and the magazines he read religiously were becoming increasingly insistent that the Reverend DeWeerd was right about inner evil.

While Dean certainly never saw Minneapolis *Spokesman* columnist Nell Dodson Russell's April 1950 jeremiad comparing homosexuals to cancer and tuberculosis and expressing anger that they had infested the arts, particularly the theater, the sentiment could be found in almost every newspaper and magazine. Homosexuality, she said, is the "haven of the unwanted, the frustrated, the bored and the least loved. It collects some of our most brilliant people and our most vicious people. . . . It must be a sign of the times that the frustration, the dissatisfaction has made physical and emotional perverts of so many people."[2] A similar column in Dean's local paper, the *Los Angeles Times*, decried the "earthy language" used to condemn "perverts" but nevertheless informed Dean and other readers that homosexual feelings were a "personal tragedy" that required government effort to "clean up an unpleasant subject."[3]

Dean would likely have seen the frequent and insistent ads in the *Los Angeles Times* for an upcoming *Coronet* magazine exposé on the "moral menace" of homosexuality that September, scaled down to teenagers but linking perversion and pedophilia on Main Street U.S.A. specifically to the homosexual hazard that politicians like Senator Joe McCarthy said was threatening Washington, D.C. Under a colorful cartoon cover of a model nuclear family done up in cowboy duds, Ralph H. Major Jr. wrote that homosexuals were hidden in plain sight, ever ready to "seduce" teenage boys, and a source of criminal activity. Major related stories of pedophilia, sexual abuse, and teenage prostitution, suggesting that these were the fruits of degeneracy. He blamed the pederasty he conflated with homosexuality on the stress of city life and the difficulties of making a living, which led men to lust for the innocence of boyhood. Major advised parents to fight back against the "doomed" life of the homosexual by teaching their children heterosexual sex practices from an early age and to monitor their friends, teachers, and coaches for signs of homosexuality. After disputing Alfred Kinsey's liberal sexual attitudes, Major quoted California's attorney general in warning that the homosexual was an "inveterate seducer" who sought to convert teenagers to homosexuality to create "degenerate companions" for himself. "Through knowledge of the facts," Major concluded, "plus a concerted attack, the sinister shadow of sexual perversion can be removed from the pathway of America's youth."[4]

Though James Dean seemed ready to make a few halting steps toward exploring homosexuality in these months, public attitudes about homosexuality were quickly hardening. Two years earlier, one could find newspapers praising Gore Vidal's gay-themed *City and the Pillar* as an "artistic achievement," in the words of the Washington *Evening Star*'s Carter Brooke Jones. But Jones's review of Vidal's new novel *Dark Green, Bright Red* in the *Evening Star* for October 8, 1950, lauded Vidal's turn away from the "abnormal" and offered this high praise: "There are no homosexuals or other psychically sick persons in [it]."[5]

Something was changing, and fast. Dean must have understood how dangerous even his hesitant efforts to learn about homosexuality could be. That year, Philadelphia police were arresting two hundred men per month on charges of indecency and disorderly conduct, most stemming from homosexual encounters, and other cities offered similar numbers.[6] In 1950, Washington boasted of one thousand annual homosexual arrests. By 1950, Los Angeles, where James Dean uneasily wondered about life as a homosexual, had seen its arrests for "sex perversion"—homosexuality—rise by nearly 90 percent in just three years, approaching three thousand annually.[7]

One of those three thousand L.A. arrests in 1950 would eventually prove fateful and have an unintended impact on James Dean's life five years later. But for Dean's difficulty socializing and the random caprice of fate, it easily might have been him. On the afternoon of October 14, 1950, an undercover deputy detective in the Los Angeles vice squad, whose name was withheld from later press coverage, made his way into one of the city's gay bars intending to gather intelligence on illicit gay activity in the city as part of a program designed to infiltrate homosexual gatherings and arrest participants.

The officer ordered a Scotch and water and struck up a conversation with two men who seemed rather excited. They told him that they were planning to attend a party for a certain kind of person that evening at 2501 Hope Street in the L.A. suburb of Walnut Park. The detective bought the men a few more rounds of drinks, loosening their tongues until they offered the handsome officer an invitation to the party. There was one catch—it was a pajama party, and he'd need to bring some sleepwear. He agreed but secretly called for reinforcements before rejoining his companions and heading out for the party.

The three men arrived at the unassuming Spanish-style bungalow around 10:30 p.m., and one of the guests was already in pajamas. The detective counted twenty-four men milling about the house and two deep-voiced women in men's clothing that he assumed to be lesbians. They were a cross-section of young L.A. life—students, salesmen, actors with bit parts on their résumés. One strapping boy stood out from the crowd. Arthur Andrew Gelien was nineteen, just like Dean, blond and well-muscled, nothing like the delicate, feminine types the detective had presumed most men at parties like this to be. Like Dean, he divided his life between traditionally masculine pursuits (as a teen, he had lied about his age to serve in the Coast Guard) and less manly ones, having once been a teenage figure skater. Similarly, he had been a loner in youth, had a poor relationship with his father, and was quick to respond with anger if anyone suspected his homosexual inclinations. His former Coast Guard buddies nicknamed him "Hollywood" because he preferred watching movies to chasing women and going to bars.

For half an hour, the detective watched as the two dozen men socialized and courted one another and occasionally danced together, until he could slip away to the window and subtly give a signal to the team officers waiting outside. Within seconds, vice cops raided the house and hauled all twenty-six partygoers to the Firestone Park sheriff's station, where they were booked and sent to the Los Angeles County Jail. Gelien, who had come to the party at a friend's invitation for the free food, was in the kitchen making a peanut butter sandwich when the cops grabbed him.

When the booking sergeant called Gelien up for processing, he asked his name, which Gelien gave. He asked for his Social Security number, which he also gave. He told the sergeant his place of birth, New York City, and his age. But when the sergeant asked for his occupation, Gelien lied. "None," he said. He didn't want the cops or any of the other men from the party to know that he was an actor or that his agent, Henry Willson, had assigned him a new name, Tab Hunter. He had recently appeared in a movie, *The Lawless*, but now the sergeant booked him in violation of California Penal Code section 647.5, restricting "idle, lewd or dissolute persons, or associates of thieves." Homosexuals were, in California's eyes, "lewd," even within the walls of private houses.

Four months later, the district attorney knocked the charge down to disturbing the peace, and Gelien got off with a $50 fine, a thirty-day suspended sentence, and a year's probation.[8] The incident was quickly forgotten, and soon enough the Warner Bros. publicity machine began promoting Hunter as an all-American boy next door—athletic, handsome, and robustly heterosexual. Indeed, Hunter would later falsely claim his very attendance at the party was a mistake and that he had no idea *homosexuals* would be present.[9] The illusion held for five years, by which time Hunter and Dean would find themselves rivals living parallel lives.

When Dean settled in on campus in the fall of 1950, just before Tab Hunter's arrest, a UCLA committee was in the midst of a years-long study on the "sexually deviate student." In summarizing their results in 1955, UCLA's

Although James Dean (right) would not meet Tab Hunter (left) until 1955, Hunter's growing career and sexual secrets quietly shaped and influenced Dean's rise. *RGR Collection / Alamy Stock Photo.*

dean of students noted that "society does not understand nor tolerate sexually deviate behavior, nor should it," but cautioned his fellow administrators that "in our lack of toleration, we are much more likely to adopt punitive than remedial measures" and these could be counterproductive. He and his coauthor approved of the trend that had begun in the early 1950s of campus psychiatrists treating student homosexuality as a mental disease. As far as administrators were concerned, this had the fortunate side effect of hiding the true number of "deviates" on campus from public knowledge, just as students like Dean disguised themselves, and therefore gave less reason for meddling state and federal politicians to demand stricter control over colleges.[10]

As was his wont, Dean had started the academic year in September with the intention of bifurcating his life into two equal halves: a public-facing side with a respectable major pointing toward law school, papering over his real passion, his minor in theater. "Just for the hell of it," he recalled somewhat facetiously, he had "signed up for a pre-law course at U.C.L.A." But he didn't enjoy the sophistry, even if there was an ironic connection to acting. "That did call for a certain knowledge of histrionics," he later quipped.[11] His course in anthropology was more interesting, covering the world and its people, but he remained indifferent to the actual course work. He absorbed enough to unsuccessfully attempt to help a classmate pass the final exam during a cigarette break, but the student who had managed to stay engaged enough to pass all his courses the previous year had gradually stopped caring over the course of the fall term as he poured his energy into acting. "I guess the university life was much too slow for him," one of his professors recalled. "I wasn't happy in law," Dean stated frankly.[12]

Although he wanted more than anything to act, he remained concerned about what others would think of him. When Dean needed a place to live while he attended school, he chose to pledge the UCLA chapter of the socially prominent Sigma Nu fraternity to secure a room in its house at 601 Gayley Avenue in Westwood. It cost less than the university dormitory, and a part-time job could cover the reduced expenses. Despite the initial excitement he expressed for Greek life in letters written that fall, in later years, he tended to quickly gloss over his time in the frat: "I even joined a fraternity on campus," he said, "but I busted a couple of guys in the nose and got myself kicked out."[13] That flippant summary wasn't quite the whole story.

Sigma Nu, a prestigious all-White fraternity that officially forbade "Negroes" and "Orientals" in its "unamendable" statutes and bylaws, was popular with jocks, especially members of the football team.[14] It offered a credibly masculine facade for Dean. Smaller—"runty," as he put it—than the others and no longer a jock, being far too short for the UCLA basketball team, he stood out from his frat brothers.[15] The other boys considered him a bit odd. He spent too much time alone in his room, they thought, drawing his strange pictures of surrealist landscapes dotted with disembodied eyeballs. But his warm laugh was endearing, especially when some remark struck him as funny and left him rolling on the floor. His boyishly mischievous habit of playing with his food and sticking bits of it up his nose to amuse or repulse his companions was always entertaining. One on one, he could be friendly and fun. But in a group, he tended to withdraw, and more often than not, his brothers enjoyed making fun of the strange little fellow, whom they nicknamed "Plowboy" after his rural roots. When they went swimming, they mocked, too, his two-tone body: tan on top but with blinding-white legs because he wore blue jeans even at the beach. Dean desperately wanted to be accepted, to be one of them—to find in the boisterous, playful group something that he had sought his whole life: brothers, equals.

But the frat boys weren't quite so keen on Dean. Their ribbing developed a cruel edge, and soon enough he was no longer so keen on them, either. They had started to suspect that he was perhaps a little too theatrical, a little less masculine than they'd like, maybe even homosexual.[16] Behind his back, they would gossip about him from time to time, whispering about the weirdness of having a *theater* person in their frat. The president of the fraternity had made plain that theater majors weren't welcome, and even Dean's minor might be suspect. Sure, there was one theater major in the house, but he was a *football* player, which made him an acceptably masculine member. It didn't help matters that in the first weeks of October, Dean auditioned for and won a fairly large role in the upcoming December student production of *Macbeth*, undercutting the front he put up for the brothers. Nevertheless, landing a role for the first time since high school excited him. He wrote to the Winslows to share the news: "After the auditioning of 367 actors and actresses, I came up with a wonderful lead in *Macbeth* the character being Malcolm (huge part)."[17] But "false face must hide what false heart doth know"—the line, though it was not one he spoke, hung over Dean. To help save face with his brothers, however, he started dating Jeanetta Lewis, a friend of the girl playing Lady Macduff. Although Lewis was smitten, the new relationship didn't go anywhere in particular over its first weeks.

While the other pledges went through the typical embarrassments and humiliations of a frat hazing, the brothers reserved for Dean extra degradations and a special test of manhood to prove himself worthy of initiation. They told him to lay at the bottom of a swimming pool, atop the drainage vent, which they would turn on. If he could swim out of the suction, he'd be in. People who knew Dean told two versions of what happened next. The more dramatic had Dean nearly drown as his indifferent fraternity brothers made only minimal efforts to prevent a tragedy. The more plausible found Dean refusing to participate in the planned hazing, rejecting with justifiable moral outrage the dangers and disgraces they demanded of him.[18]

Soon enough, things came to a head. Over the long course of the fall semester, Dean had made no friends on campus or in his frat, except maybe for one, James Bellah, and he wasn't even sure about him. In private, Bellah called Dean nice but "fucked-up."[19] Dean was lonely and sad, and he had started to become disagreeable and to lash out at his brothers. The strain was beginning to show. The $45 he owed in back dues didn't help, money the fraternity would never see.

Keeping up appearances was harder work when living with one's audience all day and all night, without a break, instead of performing only a few hours each day, as he had in high school and junior college. During rehearsals for *Macbeth*, however, Lewis introduced Dean to her friend's boyfriend, William Bast, while Dean was in the dressing room in costume amusing himself by bouncing his kilt's leather sporran off his crotch. Bast was taken aback by the sight. Over the next week, the four went on a series of double dates, and it gradually dawned on both Dean and Bast that they were growing to like one another. They had a lot in common, both being transplants from the Midwest, both studying theater, both looking for a Hollywood career, both largely indifferent to their academic studies, and both very lonely on a large campus where few wanted to be their friends. Bast also happened to be gay, hiding behind a sexless relationship with the girlfriend he was deceiving even as he guiltily accepted the occasional favors of strange older men who propositioned him in quietly coded language on the streets of Beverly Hills and Hollywood.

Bast told himself then that he wasn't attracted to Dean, though from their first meeting and for more than six decades after, he couldn't stop himself from describing Dean as golden and "chiseled," likening him to a statue of a Greek god freed from confining marble. And like a marble statue, Dean was initially cold and silent, until, little by little, Bast's Pygmalion brought the stone to life. After a few double dates, Dean had developed an infatuation, as he would many times in life, finding a new plaything he had to explore in all

James Dean (right) in costume as Malcolm in the UCLA production of *Macbeth*. *Photofest*.

its details. Bast seemed to be exactly what Dean had wished for, an equal who was just like him, with broad interests and artistic tastes, someone who might finally *get* him. Lonely, Bast liked the attention, to a point. "At times," Bast said, "he was so attentive that he made me feel uncomfortable."[20]

Shortly after, *Macbeth* ended in a humiliating failure that Dean struggled to revise into a success to match the myth he had made of his life. His thick accent left the audience struggling to understand him, and the campus newspaper singled out his performance as particularly awful. Even Dean admitted that his acting hadn't met the mark. But a few days later, still hungover from a night of heavy drinking, he joined his fraternity brother James Bellah to make a quick $10 as an extra in a Pepsi-Cola commercial, a job arranged by Bellah's agent, Isabelle Draesemer. He spent a day in Griffith Park in the shadow of the gleaming temple-like Observatory, a building four years younger than him, shooting the ad on a carousel with a pack of other college kids.

To Bellah's annoyance, Dean alone got called back for a second day of shooting and an additional $55—not based on his acting talent but on his looks. Draesemer quickly signed him as a client, figuring he was handsome enough to make some cash from, regardless of his talent. Dean didn't want to admit that his face had achieved what his skill could not. So when he got back to campus, he lied and told Bast and others that Draesemer had attended *Macbeth* and showed up backstage to sign him on the spot. Bast believed him and was amazed.[21]

A little after, the two boys and their girlfriends took a road trip down to Ensenada in Baja, Mexico. Late at night—boys in one room, girls in the other, for propriety—Dean and Bast confessed to each other that they were virgins, though Bast strategically omitted his frequent fellatio with strangers and used some verbal gymnastics to talk around the acts he refused to speak aloud. Back on campus for the spring term that January, Dean had a capital idea that left Bast uneasy. He asked Bast to come join Sigma Nu. In his mind, it would solve everything: He would have a friend, a brother, and an ally in the frat house.

Bast remained wary of the masculine cruelty of fraternities but agreed to a lunch with Dean and the other brothers to please his new friend. A last-minute conflict kept Dean away, and the slight, bookish Bast found himself alone at a long table in the Sigma Nu house, intimidated by a dozen muscled jocks who took little time in concluding Bast was gay. They didn't say it to his face, of course, but the way they disparaged theater made it plain. Even Bellah privately complained that Bast was too effeminate. Bast left lunch shaken and upset and told Dean he wouldn't be joining, to Dean's disappointment.

At the frat's next alcohol-soaked party, the brothers began to harass Dean about the theater boy he had brought into their house and what it implied about Dean. He got the message. "So they started on me for being in the theater arts and all," he told Bast afterward. "Like there's something a little, well, peculiar about a guy who'd go in for that kind of stuff." Underneath the indirect allusions, Bast could see the truth: They had called Bast gay, and one of the brothers made a crack about Dean being effeminate to his face because no normal boy would knowingly involve himself with a *queer*.[22]

Dean had weathered the jokes and the pranks and the cruelty to be one of the guys, but this was the one accusation he could not absorb, the only one that could impel the quiet, artsy boy to violence. He punched his supposed brother in the nose, and the next day the fraternity forced him out of the house for good. "I guess I just can't take a riding," he told Bast on a bus ride back from Hollywood, where they both had been hunting for work.[23] In retrospect, it seemed obvious to Bast that Dean had tried to say without using the words that if Bast were gay, then it was all right with him. But that day the message didn't quite come through.

That fraternity fight might have seemed to be just another small squabble among young men prone to immature shows of bravado, but Dean's punch landed with the weight of history colliding with irony. Sure, Bast was gay, and Dean felt things for other boys, as well, but neither knew that the cocky jocks enforcing masculine purity were not themselves precisely pure. Four miles down Sunset Boulevard from campus, on Cordell Drive, the famed director George Cukor held Sunday night "all-boy" pool parties at his Mediterranean-style villa and paid beautiful boys—college jocks were a favorite once the postwar influx of former soldiers abated—to skinny dip and entertain his high-powered guests with their athletic beauty and hard bodies.[24]

Nor was he the only one to make such offers or to have them accepted. College boys were always welcome at the bars lining West Hollywood, and the well-known ex-Marine-turned-gigolo Scotty Bowers, who counted Cukor as both friend and regular client, would happily help clean-cut young men from the local colleges find a paying companion for a quick trick. Indeed, he sent more than a few Cukor's way to be on the receiving end of the emotionally detached director's coldly mechanical fellatio.[25] The friends and teammates of the Sigma Nu brothers might well be among those selling their bodies for cash, and for all anyone knew, so might some of the fraternity boys themselves. Dean lashed out at a truth that could not be spoken and hit a lie that pretended to speak for virtue.

An illusory avenue had closed, but on that long bus ride back to Westwood, past the side streets where wealthy power brokers held raucous parties and paid college boys for sex, Dean latched onto the only real friend he had made in years. Secrecy and misdirection had failed him with his fake brothers, but now, perhaps for the first time, he let down some of his guard. "You know, you and I would make a good team," he told Bast. "We sort of complement each other. I mean, you know a lot of stuff I should know. And there's a lot I could help you with, I guess. Maybe, if we stuck together—you know, combined forces—it might make for easier going." Bast hemmed and hawed, unsure. "I was thinking maybe we could get a place together," Dean continued. Bast thought Dean was laying it on thick, but his attraction to Dean won out, and he agreed to be a team and to live together.

They sealed their agreement with a handshake, and Dean was all smiles, like an excited kid. Suddenly, words started to pour out of him, words he hadn't said aloud before for fear of seeming crazy. "I think I can trust you," he said, momentarily vulnerable and uncharacteristically honest. He told Bast about his philosophy of life, about the hand of destiny he felt pushing him toward some unknown end and his towering ambition to achieve greatness and change the world, about bridging the gap between life and death and his desire to transcend the mundane and ascend toward a perfect world beyond, and about immortality, personal and professional. And when he finished, he offered a sheepish smile and closed with the nonsense phrase he always used to fill the gaps in conversation. "Well, then, there, now," he said. "Guess I shot my wad. Anyway, now you know what a nut I am."[26]

Bast didn't know what to make of any of it, weird and strange and far beyond his more conventional ideas, but he understood that he had gotten a glimpse behind the façade, and what had emerged was more exciting and more terrifying than any false face. Both young men got off the bus with the strange feeling that in those few minutes of unexpected honesty, they had each discovered a true friend and their lives had forever changed.

4
NO ROOM

James Dean packed up his room in the Sigma Nu frat house on a Friday afternoon in January 1951 and moved back to Santa Monica, where just that morning he and Bill Bast had rented a $300-per-month furnished place on Tenth Avenue grandly advertised as a penthouse.[1] Although it cost more than the boys could afford, having almost no money between them, Dean loved the rich Aztec Revival and Mexican interior design theme and thought it fate that his first real place should look like he imagined a bullfighter's home to be. He planned to pay for it with hypothetical acting jobs and Bast's new ushering position at CBS. That weekend, they lived by candlelight because the power company wouldn't turn on the electricity until Monday.

During the long winter nights those first weeks in the new apartment, the young men got to know one another, sharing their life stories and their imagined futures as they practiced their diction reading plays and poems to one another. Dean talked, perhaps for the first time in years, about the traumas of his childhood. Bast shared his experiences, too, including a first-place finish in a regional forensics contest. Dean beamed with pride in describing his own forensics experiences, recast here as one triumph after the next, because even a sixth-place national finish had him outranking Bast.

Bast later realized that he had barely noticed as they talked that Dean subtly but consistently boosted himself just a little bit above whatever Bast had accomplished, not so much from grandiosity, but insecurity, to even out what

Dean considered a disparity between his spotty education and Bast's more secure intellectual footing. Bast mentioned that he was a decent fencer. Dean had learned fencing from James Bellah at Sigma Nu and had boasted falsely in a letter home to the Winslows that he was on the UCLA fencing team. He proved himself the superior swordsman, defeated Bast in a match, and, so far as anyone could recall, never fenced again.[2]

Dean even insisted on measuring their heights repeatedly, as though he might one day prove himself taller. But in compensation, he spent hours questioning Bast on all manner of historical, literary, and cultural topics, his boundless curiosity exhausting Bast with a breadth that exceeded Bast's admittedly indifferent intellectualism. It was an honor to be taken for a sage, he thought, at least until Dean's growing store of facts finally outstripped Bast's.

Still, Dean also tried to play the wise man for Bast, and for years he would spout half-baked proverbs that the Reverend DeWeerd had included for memorization in the letters he had obsessively sent to Dean almost daily for the past two years. "You're running so fast, it's all passing you by," Dean would intone sagely, quoting from a letter. "You've got to bounce the ball," he randomly repeated on another day with seeming profundity. Bast began to dread the onslaught of confusing ersatz aphorisms. "I would struggle through a few days, trying desperately to divine what he meant," Bast said. Yet he repeatedly found himself drawn back to Dean for more supposed wisdom, until he developed a "nervous reaction to the thoughts he was trying to put into my head."[3]

Bast wished so intently to see in his roommate a dynamic leader and master of fate that he began to imagine darkly designed psychological manipulation in even the most innocent efforts at human connection. He hadn't realized that these early days in their shared apartment, a few weeks shy of Dean's twentieth birthday, were Dean's first honest try at forging something akin to a true friendship, so he bristled at Dean's painfully awkward, uncertain, sometimes overeager attempts to bond with him. Like too many in Dean's life, he mistook for manipulative design the grasping efforts of a man emotionally much younger than his age.

Bast also had difficulty understanding Dean's diffuse interests and unconventional behavior, exaggerated now that Dean was living free from those who might judge him. He noticed right away that Dean was at his most boyishly friendly and warm when he had a project to work toward, typically an acting job or even a piece of art, anything that directed him toward the future. When he had nothing planned, he became sullen, withdrawn, unpleasant, as though all his energy had turned inward, consuming him with doubt until the next new thing restored him. Sometimes these changes of mood came so suddenly that Bast found himself unable to relax, not knowing which Dean would tear through the door next. He also disliked Dean's indifference to personal grooming and general lack of interest in the everyday necessities of running a household. In a clean-shaven era, Dean often sported stubble.

Similarly, Bast was frequently baffled by Dean's art, annoyed that Dean wasted so much time on drawings, paintings, sculptures, and mobiles, as well as reams of poetry, that he produced with an almost supernaturally single-minded focus, talking quietly to himself as he worked. Bast balked at the surrealist subject matter. Bast barely understood it, and he had no interest in contemplating it. Dean titled an oil rendering of an emaciated green figure emerging from a tunnel of verdant ooze *Man in Woman's Womb*. A pencil drawing of an anthropomorphic male ashtray depicted a cigar passing through a mouthlike hole in its head. Such works recontextualized the symbolism of life—birth imagery, sexual penetration—as annihilation and death.

Similarly, a series of drawings depicting bullfighters in their dance of death with their dangerously horned opponents performed the reverse. The matadors, whose clothes he rendered in careful detail, revealed massive erections beneath their tight *trajes de luces*. Here, he used the nearness of death as an affirmation of life, the defiant, proud tumescence in the presence of inevitable mortality, the ultimate fulfillment of the masculine principle. Bast and the boys' girlfriends just saw dirty cartoons. Well, they *were* that, too. Double meanings and hidden layers were his specialty.

Freed from the conventional limits of his family and the stricter scrutiny of the fraternity, Dean's sexual and social interests had awakened from dormancy, but their long slumber had left him years behind his peers and often a little off. Dean took a special glee in spending a whole night sculpting a vagina from green clay, into which he placed a tall burning candle whose white wax dribbled down over the sculpture. He replaced Bast's alarm clock with the creation, leaving Bast utterly confused when he awoke to Dean laughing uproariously.[4] Bast spent half a century unsuccessfully trying to tease out what Dean really meant by the prank rather than simply asking him.

Dean was also quite excited to obtain from a sympathetic Sigma Nu brother a clandestine French copy of Henry Miller's *Sextus*, a semiautobiographical 1949 account of life and love, banned as obscene in the United States due to its sexually explicit passages. The lure of forbidden knowledge was too much for Dean, and he eagerly read aloud the most licentious paragraphs to Bast and the girls. "I ran my hand up her wet cunt," he dramatically proclaimed. "I felt the hot juice trickling through my fingers."[5] The prudish young women begged him to stop, but when the girls thought the boys weren't looking, they giddily kept reading. Propriety and offense were performances Dean had never mastered.

Dean might have reveled in the contraband titillation, but if he had only wished to shock, any back-alley pornography would have sufficed and been easier to obtain. *Women's Home Companion* ran an alarmist article that year complaining that an extensive "smut-racket" had made Los Angeles the center of the obscene book and magazine trade, and teenagers, its fastest-growing market.[6] But Miller's book wasn't smut; this was illicit *literature*, forbidden art. The book's themes of death and rebirth through sexual awakening and artistic fulfillment resonated with Dean's own interior philosophy. "The world would only begin to get something of value from me the moment I stopped being a serious member of society and became—*myself*," Miller wrote in *Sextus*. "From the little reading I had done I had observed that the men who were most *in* life, who were molding life, who were life itself, ate little, slept little, owned little or nothing. . . . They were interested in truth and in truth alone. They recognized only one kind of activity—*creation*."[7] They might just as well have been Dean's words. Double lives, insecure striving, unfulfilled longing—these were the outlines of Dean's world, hidden depths masked beneath a shocking audacity that might blind all but the most perceptive to secret truths. As in Miller's work, a certain seriousness always undergirded Dean's performance of outrageousness.

At least literature acknowledged the complexities of sex and sexuality, an honesty Dean would have appreciated, at least when he had money for books and time to read. A lack of both meant Dean missed out on the year's most important and controversial novel, J. D. Salinger's best-selling *Catcher in the Rye*, the finished version of material Salinger had been publishing piecemeal since 1945. This may have been a good thing, given how closely Dean would have seen himself sketched in the book's teenage protagonist—and how readily he would soon be compared to the book's narrator, Holden Caul-field. Beneath the fiery red cover image of a carousel horse just like the one Dean rode in his Pepsi ad debut, he would have found an almost unbeliev-ably uncanny funhouse-mirror version of his own life—past, present, and future—shuffled and twisted into something strange and sad.

In *Catcher*, Salinger's lonely adolescent protagonist involuntarily exits his all-male prep school after failing every subject, save English, the only course that embodies his passion to write and to write more honestly than his brother, who sold his pen to Hollywood to scribble sad stories devoid of meaning. Holden's classmates neither understand nor appreciate his sensi-tivity or his yearning for authenticity, and their bafflement ends in a fight in the dorms and a punch to the nose, ostensibly over a girl but with hints of homoerotic desire.

Departing for New York, he spends a long Christmas odyssey behaving obnoxiously amid a corrupt and fallen world of "phonies," seemingly unable to care for or about anyone but himself. He frightens his occasional girlfriend, pays a prostitute just to talk, and harasses an intellectual former classmate whom he suspects of being gay, or a "flit." He recalls years past when his class-mate would entertain the boys with stories about which manly movie stars were homosexuals: "He said half the married guys in the world were flits and didn't even know it. He said you could turn into one practically overnight, if you had all the traits and all. He used to scare the hell out of us. I kept waiting to turn into a flit or something."[8] Such dishonor was a fate worse than death.

Yet Holden seeks out the company of potentially homosexual men and shuns intercourse with women. He tries to find solace in the home and the advice of his trusted former English teacher Mr. Antolini, only to fall asleep and awaken to what he believes to be a homosexual advance. This sends Holden into a panic over "perverts" and their attraction to him. Flit perverts came on to him twenty times in his life by his count, and he reacted each time with terror, fear, and sweat. "I can't stand it," he says. By the novel's end, Holden is in a mental institution, being psychoanalyzed, unsure if he can resume a conventional American life of school and girls and a hollow future. With pained nostalgia, he misses the men who belittled and beat him in his failed effort to release his emotions and angst.[9]

Even though Dean almost certainly did not read *Catcher* and therefore did not need to wonder how so much of his life ended up in print or how he was less unique than he believed, he most likely saw at least one of the reviews that ran in the major newspapers he consumed with dedication. He may well have noticed reviewers' allusive language and furtive, disapproving references to the "queer" teacher and the "pitiful," "raw," and "absurd" Holden. "There is nothing wrong with him that a little understanding and affection, preferably from his parents, couldn't have set right," the *New York Times* declared.[10] Dean might have nodded in agreement.

By contrast, the Hollywood movies Dean devoted so much time (and so much of his money) to seeing that year, much more influential than novels, pursued the path of denial. In 1951, Production Code censors asked producers of *Everybody's Girl* to cut a gay joke: "Did you ever have a fairy godfather?" one character asks. "No. But I have an uncle in Chicago we're not too sure about."[11] *A Streetcar Named Desire*, Elia Kazan's powerful 1951 adaptation of his own production of Tennessee Williams's 1947 stage play, was a huge draw, after some judicious editing of the source material. Marlon Brando reprised his stage role in a star-making performance—James Dean was left stunned and speechless after sitting through two screenings of the film in Santa Monica that fall—even as Kazan worked with Warner Bros.' censors to tone down or excise the play's references to homosexuality. Alfred Hitchcock's *Strangers on a Train* had homoerotic undertones between the two male leads looking to escape the women in their lives, though with the director's trademark implication of psychological sickness. In movies like *My Son John*, which started filming in the summer of 1951, Hollywood adopted politicians' equation of homosexuality with communism, depicting parents' horrified discovery of a haughty, cold, and intellectual young man's communism exactly as the magazines depicted parents' distraught terror upon learning of a son's homosexuality.

Just as the films James Dean watched could not fully hide what they tried to cut away, Dean tried and failed to keep hidden parts of himself that Bill Bast was gradually starting to uncover. As Dean's finances faltered and the rent came inevitably due, moments of professional advancement helped to create hope that disaster was not inevitable. The boys economized, and Dean experimented with combining nonperishable staples. He developed an inexpensive favorite meal of dried oatmeal mixed with mayonnaise and jam, which he would eat by the bowlful. It tasted something like a poor man's Waldorf salad, even if the gritty, viscous texture wasn't quite as satisfying.[12]

He had lost interest in his classes and considered a degree little more than an empty expedient, and his sporadic attendance at UCLA gradually faded, maintained mostly for a chance to act in the spring play. He didn't get a part and stopped attending classes two weeks before final exams. He never returned. But the director of his Pepsi commercial had cast him in an Easter TV production as the Apostle John, which aired on *Father Peyton's Television Theater* on March 21. Dean had a cold, and he geared his performance a bit too grandly for the production, as though he were in a Technicolor epic instead of a local TV play. But he looked handsome and radiant on-screen, and a local Catholic high school started a short-lived fan club for Dean, who lapped up the younger girls' attention at a party in his honor.

Over the course of that spring, Bast introduced Dean to Oscar-nominated actor James Whitmore, a student of Kazan, whom Bast had met when Whitmore came to CBS's studios. At Dean's insistence, Bast convinced Whitmore to lead a regular acting study group for them and their friends. Dean held back in early sessions, afraid to make a mistake that might inspire criticism. But Whitmore showed Dean how to center his acting in his character's motivation rather than the script, and having internalized the lesson, Dean improvised a scene with Bast that left him so overexcited that the two began to aggressively wrestle on the floor. (His thief character was trying to steal another man's watch.) Their pretend fight turned personal, Dean calling Bast "pompous" and Bast needling Dean about his poor eyesight. As they grappled, the boys experienced an uncomfortably sexual arousal that left them shaken and silent.[13] Dean appreciated the advice Whitmore had given him. "I guess you can say he saved me when I got all mixed up," he later told a reporter. "He told me I didn't know the difference between acting as a soft job and acting as a difficult art. I needed to learn these differences."[14]

The spring of 1951 found Dean struggling to rebalance the scales after his acting plans had stalled and after his efforts to channel his "mixed-up" feelings into friendship and art had faltered. Behind the back of his girlfriend, Bast had started seeing a new girl, Beverly Wills, a seventeen-year-old radio actress on *Junior Miss* and wealthy daughter of TV star Joan Davis, and brought her around to the penthouse to meet Dean. Wills quickly took notice of the knife's edge that now separated Dean's boyish excitement for new success from abject despair when he failed. "When he was happy," she said, "there was no one more lovable, but when he was depressed, he wanted to die. These low moods became so violent that he began to tell me that he was having strange nightmares in which he dreamed he was dying."[15]

In his darkening mood and woefully inexperienced in the emotion and propriety of both friendship and love, he sabotaged his relationships in a reckless gamble to grasp professional success. Life, Dean believed, was like a basketball game—a competition to be won at all costs.[16] In rapid succession, he had ingratiated himself with Wills behind Bast's back and made a play for her affections in the hope of parlaying a potential relationship into an invitation to her world of wealth and power. He secretly strung Jeanetta Lewis along while dating Wills, whom he escorted to her senior prom in a rented tuxedo and soon offered to marry. They planned to elope once the high schooler turned eighteen. The pair told Bast they were dating, and Dean cruelly let slip to Bast's other girlfriend that Bast had been unfaithful.

Dean had considered his girlfriends to be mere accessories to his incipient greatness, and he had disregarded Bast's feelings altogether. His haughtiness, his self-centering, somehow only made him more attractive to both his girlfriends and especially to Bast, like a cat everyone wanted to pet precisely because it refused the proffered hand. All three wanted to be with him, even when he angered them, and only physical separation ever worked to cool their passions. Bast, who valued Dean's love above his sham romance with Wills, forgave Dean after making a halfhearted attempt to feign outrage at the clandestine relationship. He received a sad confession from Dean that he had behaved badly. "I'm a serious-minded and intense little devil," as Dean would later say, "terrible gauche, and so tense that I don't see how people stay in the same room with me. I wouldn't tolerate myself."[17]

But Bast continued to more than tolerate Dean, even as the two circled each other, coming ever closer to saying the unspoken truth neither dared admit. Bast continued to seek fellatio with strange men on his way home from work, and one evening he met a young Marine he called Craig outside CBS and shared an unexpectedly intimate emotional connection that led to Bast's first romantic kiss with another man. Craig was about to be deployed to Korea and was certain he would die at war, and over the course of a single night, Bast bonded with the handsome Craig and felt his heart break at the thought of the Marine's death. When Craig missed the last bus of the night tarrying with Bast, Dean volunteered to drive the pair to Camp Pendleton to drop Craig off. On the late-night drive, Bast could see Dean's curious eyes in the rearview mirror studying the two in the back seat. When they returned home, Bast was an emotional wreck, and unbidden, Dean lay down beside Bast and held Bast as he slept without speaking a word. Nor did they ever again mention the unexpected intimacy, leaving Bast confused about Dean's feelings and how much Dean understood of Bast's romantic inclinations.[18]

Despite such moments of grace, their clashing personalities and Dean's need for silent time alone to think, rest, and restore—and his hostility when those contemplations were interrupted—upset Bast. Bast thought Dean was depressed and bitterly resented the hours Dean refused to speak or when he left to take nighttime walks around town alone, wandering silently through the patchwork of light and shadow or listening to the rush of the black waves crashing against the darkened beach, communing with the gods and spirits until dawn. "I had never known such lack of communication," Bast complained when recalling this period.[19] What he meant, though, was that he wished Dean had shared his inner world and more with him. He was hurt that Dean did not, though he was himself hiding, none too well, his own evening assignations and furtive longings.

One spring night, to glimpse that secret world, Bast secretly followed Dean on one of his nocturnal walks. He found Dean stretched provocatively on a bus-stop bench beneath a streetlight, smoking and lazing until a car pulled up and the man inside lowered the window. Any of the men who drove down these silent streets in search of male companionship would have recognized the scene; it was a standard method young men used to advertise their availability to passing motorists, either for pleasure, for pay, or for both. Dean stood, leaned into the car, listened, and then pulled out a borrowed jackknife, waving it at the driver. The rubber tires squealed as the driver tore away in panic. Dean was testing himself and the world, walking up to the edge of something frightening he could only express furtively in a mixed-up, destructive flash of sex and violence, a reckoning with buried feelings he could not contain but did not yet accept. Nor could he cut them away. Bast was shaken and confused. Roadside fellatio he would have understood, but this was something else. He worried that Dean might become violent with him in the same way.[20] And once again neither young man spoke a word to the other about what had occurred.

By the end of June, Bast accepted that Dean no longer saw him as his other half, his equal, and he didn't want to continue living with someone he both loved and feared. After Bast accidentally revealed Dean's two-timing and betrayals to a humiliated and enraged Jeanetta Lewis, she convinced Bast to salvage his pride and move out. When the two told Dean that Bast was leaving, the confrontation turned violent, with Dean angry and afraid, slapping Lewis with the back of his hand when she inserted herself between him and a numb Bast. She knowingly goaded Dean, taunting him that she had torn his life apart in revenge, daring him to hit her, wanting him to suffer. "Honey, I'm enjoyin' this!" she told Bast after Dean collapsed in shame at his unexpected violence. Dean apologized and cried, devastated by his own emotions, only some of which he understood. "I trusted you," he kept repeating to Bast through his anger and tears as Bast left him, alone and broke and broken, the mirror image of their bonding bus ride half a year before.[21] The loss of Lewis, by contrast, meant nothing to him.

Unable to afford rent on his own, even with a $45 payday from a bit part in a *Bigelow Theatre* drama, Dean wasted no time taking up an offer of a job from Ted Avery, a friend he had met during a brief, failed attempt to work as an usher at CBS. Avery got Dean work as a parking valet next door to the CBS studios, where industry big shots tended to tip attractive young men very well, letting Dean pay the rent, with a little help from Wills. Not for the last time, his face would reward him with the success that his talent and temperament had failed to provide.

One Saturday that July, Dean parked the car of wealthy advertising executive Rogers Brackett of Foote, Cone & Belding, the firm that produced the weekly CBS afternoon radio drama *Alias Jane Doe*, about an undercover magazine reporter, now halfway through its six-month run.[22] The tall, handsome Brackett, his head full of curly hair, had come in for a half-day's work overseeing the recording of that week's episode, but he was struck by the golden beauty of the youth who took his keys, a boy fifteen years his junior but looking smart in his uniform. Brackett thought it might be pleasant to strike up a conversation with the attractive boy—he preferred the company of very young men—and the advertiser bragged a bit about his radio work to impress him. Dean grew excited and blurted out that he was an actor. Brackett found his enthusiasm charming and offered to pay for coffee. They talked and smiled and laughed and exchanged telephone numbers. Brackett promised to keep Dean in mind for acting roles, and as he drove back to his Sunset Plaza Drive sublet in West Hollywood, he couldn't stop thinking about the boy he had just befriended.[23]

Rogers Brackett, seen here in a 1946 CBS headshot, was known in the media industry for his charm and humor. In the gay community, he was known for his interest in much younger men. *Photo by CBS via Getty Images.*

Brackett was smitten, so he called Dean and offered him a small part on *Alias Jane Doe* that July, and Dean eagerly accepted. He appeared in at least four episodes, which Dean triumphantly but falsely referred to as "lead" roles.[24] Brackett got Dean a few other bit parts and a radio commercial for his client and *Alias*'s sponsor, Toni Home Permanent. Amid weekends with Brackett exploring the high life, Dean found himself developing feelings for the older man, known in the radio industry as a droll and charming, if somewhat effete, character whose cosmopolitanism, intelligence, and success might be the equal to his own ambition, talent, and drive.[25] Although these feelings scared Dean—the Reverend DeWeerd's aphorisms about morality and evil and sin still arrived regularly by post—Brackett unlocked something Dean had kept so closely guarded that it had threatened to break him.

In short order, Dean blew up his relationship with Wills. Not long after Wills's belated eighteenth birthday party in Beverly Hills in early August, Dean spent a weekend in Paradise Cove, an oceanside resort community near Malibu, where Wills's father lived. At an evening dance at the Paradise Pavilion, Wills seemed to be flirting with another young man from a group of well-off teenagers she had known for years. She frequently danced with other boys in front of Dean without incident and indeed enjoyed riling him up, but this time something was different. "Go on! Dance your fool head off!" a livid Dean, red with rage, shouted. He accosted the young man, with whom he already had bad blood. The boy's group of male friends considered Dean a social inferior in shabby clothes and had only reluctantly invited him to join an earlier surfside football game at Wills's insistence. Dean's unnecessarily aggressive play, perhaps to prove himself to them or perhaps to seek revenge, caused the young man and his friends to cast Dean out. Afterward, the group refused to speak to Dean.

Now, an embarrassed Wills fled, and Dean stormed off onto the beach after her, kicking the sand as he marched. An intense argument between Dean and Wills ended their relationship. Wills later wrote that she believed Dean had cared in that moment more about the young man rejecting him than he did about his relationship with her. "I should have realized that this was his way of paying back a member of the crowd who had hurt him," Wills recalled. Dean's agent, Isabelle Draesemer, however, cynically wondered if Dean had staged the breakup because Wills had failed to help his career, speculating that he might try to land a gay director next.[26]

Dean returned to Los Angeles, where in late July he had traded his expensive Santa Monica penthouse for a money-saving stay on Ted Avery's Hollywood couch while Avery's wife was out of town. Dean told Brackett that Avery's wife was about to return home and he would be homeless. Brackett took a gamble and suggested that Dean move in with him, and they could share a bed and perhaps a life. The boy who only a few months earlier had reacted violently to the suggestion of homosexuality now allowed himself to feel what he had tried so hard to repress, made easier by the glorious career he saw Brackett making possible. For the first time in his life, Dean felt something like love, and the youth, who began the year claiming to be a virgin and ignorant of sex and love, ended the summer knowing a little of both.[27]

When Dean moved in with Brackett, he gave Draesemer his new address and phone number and told her he was Brackett's boarder. She didn't buy it. "I wasn't so easily fooled," Draesemer recalled. "He said we could have twin beds," Dean lied. Dean failed to dupe her, but she accepted the lie anyway. No matter how phony Dean might have felt telling the lie, or Draesemer for accepting it, you couldn't have people thinking a future star was a pervert.[28]

5
SOMETHING FOR AN EMPTY BRIEFCASE

August and September 1951 had been a whirlwind of activity for Jimmy Dean, a fever dream. Brackett had opened doors for Dean, helping him get bit parts in a few films and introducing him to directors and other powerful Hollywood movers and shakers. For a few weeks, Dean felt like he was finally starting to get somewhere. But not all of these efforts ended well. Dean's contempt for small talk and undeserved hierarchy, for casual hypocrisies and indirect discussion, kept showing through. A meeting with screenwriter Leonard Spigelgass, then a story editor at MGM, left the studio official fuming at Dean's poor manners. "He flicked ashes on the rug and behaved like an animal," Spigelgass said. "The boy was absolute poison."[1] He told Brackett that Dean would destroy his sterling reputation.

The wealthy and powerful at the parties the pair attended together felt the same, but at least the beautiful people, and Brackett's acquaintance, the notorious gay talent agent Henry Willson, infamous for extracting sex from his male clients, understood why they might enjoy each other's company. After all, more than a few of them had their own pet boys, and those who didn't made use of the rented pleasures of Scotty Bowers's stable of young men, some younger than Dean, in the regular round of late-night orgies. More than one employed a "chauffer" or "valet" who served as a third in their marriages.[2] The writer of short fiction George Bradshaw was left aghast when Dean accidentally set fire to his favorite armchair during a party, but Brackett kept bringing Dean to soirees and to dinners. "Jimmy was like a child," Brackett recalled. "He behaved badly just to get attention"—or perhaps to stave off the unwanted attentions of wealthy men who preferred their boys obedient and well-behaved. "He was a kid I loved," Brackett said, "sometimes parentally, sometimes not parentally."[3]

Dean picked up on Brackett's mix of romantic and parental feelings— *incestuous* was the word Brackett used—and he found it easy to slip into the role of roguish son, playing up his boyishness. At La Rue, one of L.A.'s best restaurants, he always ordered the vichyssoise and cheekily pronounced it "swishy-swashy." When Brackett praised a mobile Dean had made from chicken bones, he innocently pretended not to know the word *mobile*.[4] He lazed restlessly about the Sunset Plaza pool and took up photography. He acted like an overexcited kid when Brackett took him to Mexicali for a weekend trip so film director Budd Boetticher could give him the chance to fight a real-life, albeit tame, bull. He begged to borrow Boetticher's red-felt bullfighting cape—"I've never held a real fighting cape before. Can I take it home tonight?" he asked—and absconded with it. He bragged to Bill Bast after they tentatively patched up their friendship that the cape had been a gift to mark his exceptional bullfighting prowess, and the gullible Bast again believed him.[5]

Dean eagerly consumed the many books Brackett gave him, everything from Guy de Maupassant's horror stories to Albert Camus's novels of alienation to Dean's immediate favorite, *The Little Prince* of Antoine de Saint-Exupéry, the rights to which Brackett had recently attempted to buy for a "dramatized musical album" he was producing.[6] Brackett's taste ran toward the grandiose, the existential, and the outré. Such interests befitted a former "walking delegate and member extraordinaire" of the Fortean Society, a group of eccentrics and nonconformists, including some celebrities, devoted to paranormal and pseudoscientific mysteries.[7] Dean amazed Brackett by finishing the books left for him while Brackett was at work and then asking for more. "I like books that are on the serious side," Dean would later say. "I read everything from books on culture, expressionist literature, and philosophical books."[8] The pair performed scenes from *Hamlet* on the Sunset Plaza's sweeping main stairs, and Dean patiently absorbed Brackett's lessons on literature, modern art, philosophy, and classical music, an echo of his tutelage by the Reverend DeWeerd. But it wasn't quite enough.

From his reading of Oscar Wilde's *De Profundis* and other writers, like Frank Harris, and perhaps from Brackett's many gay friends who emulated Wilde, Dean would have learned that there were other ways of thinking about love between men besides the shame and evil he had known. Unlike the newspapers and magazines that screamed of a homosexual menace—J. Edgar Hoover had recently announced a new system to identify and fire homosexuals in government—and the psychiatrists who warned of the pathological insanity of sexual deviance, Wilde had rhapsodized about the love of an older man for a younger man as the noblest form of human affection. "The 'love' that dare not speak its name in this century is ... a deep spiritual affection that is as pure as it is perfect," he had said at his sodomy trial in 1895. "It is intellectual, and it repeatedly exists between an elder and younger man, when the elder man has intellect, and the younger man has all the joy, hope and glamour of life. That it should be so the world does not understand."[9]

Older writers and scholars of a certain persuasion, like John Addington Symonds in the late 1800s and Hans Licht in the 1930s, had analyzed ancient Greek models from Homer to Plato, describing the idealized form of "heroic" male love between equals, like Achilles and Patroclus, as a passion intense, pure, and noble—the highest love two humans could achieve. They spoke, too, of an earthier embodiment in classical Athens, the *paiderastia*, or "boy-love," between a young adult man and an adolescent boy, a mixed relationship where the man played second father, brother, and lover to the boy.[10]

Dean had thought he had found in Brackett a heroic equal, but the more Brackett treated him like an unruly son, the harder it became to sustain the illusion. The old doubts and insecurities returned. How could he love or trust anyone but a perfect equal? He feared opening himself to anyone strong enough to hurt him. One evening, Brackett returned home and found Dean crying in their bedroom. He asked Dean what was wrong. "I can't love and I can't be loved," he wailed.[11] But he meant that he couldn't let himself love or be loved.

Dean took solace in his beloved copy of historian and occultist Gerald Heard's influential 1939 book *Pain, Sex, and Time*, in which the openly gay but voluntarily celibate author wrote of the imperative for humankind to deliberately evolve its consciousness through the release of pain and sexual energy to overcome the limits of time and the material world and enter a higher realm beyond, and he hinted that homosexuals could lay equal claim to an honorable, mystical experience of reality.[12] Like Wilde, Heard saw art as a cathartic release of spiritual and psychic forces that could harness and transform sexual energy, a message Dean took to heart. But, Heard had warned, the transformation to greatness would come only by suppressing one's sexual desires and redirecting them toward the spiritual and the eternal. For Dean, the arts alone were eternal and thus became his path to transcendence.

Though the crisis seemed to abate for a time, Dean wavered between a desire to embrace his new life and a deep discomfort with being seen as gay. Dean took Brackett on an awkward trip to meet his father, and Brackett brought Dean to meet his mother, almost as a courting couple might. But around boys his own age, Dean put distance between himself and Brackett. James Bellah visited him and Brackett while they were living together, and Bellah was aghast at Brackett's unmanly, arch cosmopolitanism. He took Dean aside and said in warning, "This guy's a fairy." Dean nodded, "Yeah, I know." Bellah left convinced that Dean was still "fucked up," and Dean chafed at the notion that Bellah might think of him as a fairy, too.[13]

Dean soon became restless, wanting more than Brackett could provide, and faster. "They'll never really give me a chance out here," he said to another actor after shooting a brief film appearance in *Fixed Bayonets* on August 11. In fact, the whole Hollywood scene disappointed him. Casting directors complained he was either not good looking enough or, in one humiliating instance, too good looking. "My, isn't *she* pretty?" one had asked, likening his face to a woman's. Brackett's seemingly brilliant friends slowly revealed themselves to be small, shallow, unserious, more concerned with sex and gossip than art. Dean made a bet with Brackett that his friends would mention La Rue's restaurant more than fifteen times in an hour: "We kept count and I won," he told Bast. This was not the transcendent experience of universal truth he imagined avatars of the arts would provide. It was, he said, a "pile of crap." He started to tell Bast over lunches that he regretted "dancing" for them—apparently his oblique way of expressing his regret at rushing into a sexual relationship—and that he would rather go out in a blaze of glory, maintaining his dignity and integrity, than continue like this.[14]

In *Fixed Bayonets*, directed by a friend of Brackett's, Dean played a newly drafted Korean War soldier sent to the front. But Dean saw his one line cut from the final print.[15] One of the other actors, Neyle Morrow, noticed while shooting that Dean stood off by himself and wasn't eating lunch. He realized

Dean lacked money for a hamburger. Despite Brackett's wealth, Dean wasn't going to be a kept boy. If he hadn't earned money, then he had no money. Instead, he charmed his way into Morrow providing him a free meal. He was his friendliest, trading warm conversation and unexpected truth for a hamburger.

Echoing career advice James Whitmore had given him, he told Morrow he was working to earn money to go to New York and meet Elia Kazan. Here, away from Brackett, he slipped into his old pattern, confessing indirectly to someone who wouldn't understand a truth he couldn't otherwise speak, testing out the idea of leaving Brackett for a new life in New York. His relationship with Brackett had moved from flirtation to something like marriage in just weeks. It was too much, too fast for a youth of twenty, and it frightened him. Dean fantasized about putting space between them, and he expressed that desire through vaunting career ambitions. He made a great show of writing down Morrow's name on a matchbook and promising to look him up when he returned from New York. "I knew of course he'd never keep it," Morrow recalled, and sure enough Dean forgot about him the moment he was out of sight.[16]

Yet Dean learned far too quickly not to push Brackett too far away. Before Dean could plan his new life in New York, a letter arrived from the United States Selective Service System out of Marion, Indiana, drafting Dean into military service and ordering him to report for an October 9, 1951, induction physical, the same day he was scheduled to shoot a bit part in a film then called *Oh Money, Money*. He became despondent, convinced that his dreams would die on a foreign battlefield, with only *Fixed Bayonets* left behind to ironically tell the tale. Dean and Bast strategized how to respond to the draft board, and every path led to only one answer. He could try claiming conscientious objector status as a Quaker, but to ensure he remained a civilian, he would have to declare himself a homosexual to use the government's prejudices against them. He agonized about whether doing so would destroy his career as thoroughly as death in Korea.

He needed advice, so he asked Rogers Brackett for help. The prospect of Dean leaving for war terrified Brackett, who saw with adult eyes the empty places of the men, friends included, who never returned from the last war. "With his quasi-jock predilections," Brackett recalled thinking, "he'd have never made it back."[17] Under Brackett's advice, and with Bast's editorial

James Dean's selective service registration. Confusion over his 1951 claim to be exempt from service due to homosexuality led to a false rumor that he had registered as a homosexual when he turned 18 in 1949. *The National Archives.*

assistance, Dean wrote a letter explaining that he was a homosexual and therefore ineligible for service. Brackett used his power and wealth to keep Dean safe. He sent him to a compliant psychiatrist for a series of sham sessions to prove his homosexuality, but this tore at Dean's fragile masculinity. "What is it about me that attracts them?" he asked a friend about homosexual men after a later therapy session. "I'm a man, but if they don't let up soon, I'm going to begin to doubt myself." Brackett quietly made it known to the doctor and the draft board that Dean had been sharing a home with him, a known homosexual. The doctor's concurrence persuaded the government that under the antihomosexual policies of 1947, Dean was undesirable. "As Jimmy was 'living' with me," Brackett recalled, "there was no question that his unsuitability for military service was valid, or so they were led to believe." Dean would receive a 4-F designation exempting him from military service on November 14, but he worried for the rest of his life that someone would find proof written in his own hand that he was gay.[18]

A few hours after Dean reported for his induction physical and presented the military doctors with his declaration and proof of homosexuality, he found himself facing down irony on the set of *Oh Money, Money*—soon to be renamed *Has Anybody Seen My Gal?*—as the subject of unwanted attentions from one of the movie's male stars. That fall, Rock Hudson was an up-and-coming star, pegged as the next big thing. *Gal*, a period comedy set in the 1920s, offered a large role for Hudson, who would soon headline his own films. James Dean had a bit part, playing a teenager ordering an ice cream sundae from the soda fountain where Hudson's character works. But Hudson's reputation preceded him. On-screen and in the press, he was a tall, muscular, and masculine man who played every woman's dream lover. But every man in Hollywood, Dean included, knew that Hudson was gay and preferred good-looking younger, athletic men, especially those with sandy hair.

Hudson frequently solicited the attentions of attractive young stuntmen and extras in his movies. On the set of *Gal*, Hudson spent part of the day hitting on the handsome Dean, and Dean rebuffed him, developing an instant if ironic antipathy for Hudson's sharp divide between public and private behavior. Dean told Bast over lunch the next day that he was less offended about Hudson hitting on him than he was about Hudson daring to present himself as a masculine, heterosexual male while secretly being gay—an outrage Bast silently found almost shockingly hypocritical coming from Dean.[19]

Indeed, had Hudson tried to get to know his younger colleague rather than simply seek sex, each might have learned how much Hudson had in common with Dean. Hudson was six years older and a war veteran but, like Dean, a midwestern farm boy who grew up wanting to act and felt pressure to project a front of manliness. "I knew I wanted to be an actor when I was a little boy," he recalled decades later. "But living in a small town in the Middle West, I didn't say so, because that's just sissy stuff."[20] Like Dean, Hudson struggled to make friends in the big city and to adapt his rough country manners to high society. He had his first sexual experience with a much older man, dated women publicly, and met men in secret. He went further than Dean, though, to keep his secret from the press, maintaining a second phone line to make late-night plans with male lovers. Moviegoers might be fooled, but when he went out to places like the Mocambo Club in West Hollywood, the girls warned one another, "Hands off—he doesn't like women. . . . He likes boys."[21]

But it was their differences that stood out for Dean. Dean hoped to be a great actor, but Hudson, equally ambitious, hoped to be a great movie star,

Secretly queer, Rock Hudson kept a second phone line strictly to make sexual plans with other men. Perhaps because they had so much in common, James Dean took an instant dislike to Hudson, who would eventually return the favor. *Photofest.*

prioritizing commerce over art. While Dean prided himself on embracing masculinity in public and in private despite his slight, boyish frame, Hudson wore his masculinity only as a performance, building an athlete's body and taking lessons in manliness at his agent Henry Willson's insistence to butch up for the cameras. He had even changed his name from Roy Fitzgerald to Rock Hudson to sound manlier. He and Dean would share many of the same friends and acquaintances, but where Dean held himself apart from homosexual men, Hudson fully embraced life in Los Angeles's underground gay community.[22] Dean was depressed, but Hudson was, more or less, happy. Faced with someone so much like himself but everything he was not and more successful to boot, it was perhaps inevitable that Dean would bristle.

Rock Hudson might have represented everything Dean hated about Hollywood, but Dean had already turned his attention elsewhere. On September 22, the canceled *Alias Jane Doe* had aired its last episode. Now, in mid-October, Brackett was preparing to leave L.A. because his bosses had called him back to Chicago to work on a local children's radio show. Suddenly, Dean had a decision to make, and he wasn't willing to give up his career to follow Brackett to Illinois. It smacked too much of a public declaration of love, too much of a wife following a husband. He had a career and an image to consider, and he needed space.

Whitmore had advised going to New York. Brackett now agreed—albeit with a cynical motive—that it was the right move for Dean's career, promising that he would follow on to New York in the coming months to be with him. Even if Brackett never mentioned it, Dean must have known from the local L.A. newspapers he read that Brackett already had plans to go to New York that winter to open a musical revue on Broadway with his close friend, the composer Alec Wilder.[23]

Dean hoped that the more sober world of New York theater would provide him with the transcendent artistic experience superficial L.A. couldn't. He knew his skill came through investing his characters with himself and his limits, and he swore he would never be Rock Hudson. "I'm not the bobby-sox type, and I'm not the romantic leading-man type either," he said to a fellow actor around this time. "Can you imagine me making love to Lana Turner?"[24] He believed his great work, whatever it was to be, had to happen before he turned thirty and lost his boyish looks.[25]

Once he made his decision, that was final. He didn't bother with goodbyes. A day or two after Dean finished his day shooting *Has Anybody Seen My Gal?* Bill Bast came home to find a note from his landlady: "Mr. Dean called. Gone to New York."[26]

When Dean's train, the *Twentieth Century*, arrived in New York in late October 1951, his excitement mixed with fear.[27] He had come east to shore up his self-respect, but it had been a tiring week. Brackett had driven him from Los Angeles to Chicago, where Dean scandalized the Gold Coast by marching through the paneled lobby of the Ambassador East Hotel in a T-shirt and blue jeans with his matador's cape slung over his shoulder. After a few restless days in the hotel, Brackett sent him on by train to visit the Winslows in Fairmount and the Reverend DeWeerd at his new home in Indianapolis, where DeWeerd gave him $200. DeWeerd accompanied Dean back to Chicago, but Dean apparently said nothing to him about Brackett, instead sharing a hotel room with DeWeerd until the latter left town.

Dean then saw Brackett briefly and went on alone to Manhattan and a room at the Iroquois Hotel at 49 West Forty-Fourth Street near the Broadway theaters. He felt small, disoriented, and alone among the city's teeming throngs, relentless motion, and constant noise. "New York overwhelmed me," he recalled. "For the first few weeks I was so confused that I strayed only a couple of blocks from my hotel off Times Square. I saw three movies a day in an attempt to escape from my loneliness and depression—spent $150 of my limited funds on movies alone."[28] He watched Marlon Brando in *A Streetcar Named Desire* and Montgomery Clift in *A Place in the Sun* countless times, and on one occasion a few months later, he disturbed his friends by suddenly rending his shirt in the middle of a bar and shouting "Stella!" in an impromptu imitation of Brando's famous line.

It would have been difficult not to notice, though, the signs displayed in bars in Greenwich Village and Times Square where he ventured with the friends Brackett had arranged to meet him those first weeks: "If you're gay, please stay away," or "It is against the law to serve homosexuals." The irony was rich—Brackett's friends were mostly gay or bisexual, and one who likely wasn't, Alec Wilder, immediately sized Dean up as "masculine . . . but . . . homosexual," as though his manliness must be an act.[29]

Despite being forewarned Dean was "wild," Brackett's friends couldn't quite make sense of him. Theirs was a different world, one of city life, where, behind closed doors, men acted as they chose, companions in vice, open in their desires. But Dean always seemed to be performing some unseen role. He was, photographer Roy Schatt, who met him later, said, a "loner—he was a loner in every possible way." In his loneliness, he wandered the city at night, walking for hours alone, waiting for destiny to call.[30]

He fixated on Brando and Clift in hope of touching the sublime. For months, he inserted discussion of one or the other into conversation with whomever would listen. He watched their movies repeatedly, imitated their lines, and plotted ways to meet them. He phoned the actors' answering services regularly, hoping in vain one would call back. He never quite said what he hoped to get from meeting Brando and Clift, but it was obvious he considered them personal heroes, men whose equal he expected to be and who might pave the way for him. He would later say to a fellow actor that he saw himself as an ideal combination of the two, surly and wild like Brando and vulnerable and pleading like Clift. "And somewhere in between is James Dean!"[31] Like Oscar Wilde, he knew that art opened the way toward a transcendent, immaterial truth, and he persisted in believing that great artists must therefore be wise and deep and masters of this reality and the one beyond.

He never abandoned that belief, despite perpetual disappointment when reality fell short of his imagination. Although Brackett's friend, the bisexual director James Sheldon, had found him an agent, Jane Deacy, to smooth his entry into the New York television world and manage his finances, it wasn't enough for Dean.[32] He auditioned for roles and interviewed for jobs and fumed with rage when they didn't pan out. Directors complained that he treated the roles on offer, like his bit part as a student in an episode of the ABC sitcom *Trouble with Father* that December, as beneath him. When he did appear on television or radio, he inevitably alienated the production crews during rehearsals by folding into an irritable porcupine while working out characterizations in his head that they considered irrelevant. They didn't need him to stand silently and think; they needed him to recite his lines on cue.

He confounded them by claiming not to care about his pay. In the new year, his athleticism won him a position testing stunts (including taking seltzer and cream pies to the face) for the CBS television game show *Beat the Clock*. He baffled the crew by spending countless unpaid hours mastering every stunt just to show himself no challenge remained insurmountable.[33] He lost the job because he was better at the stunts than any contestant. "This crazy world seems to be a continuous chase around the table," Dean wrote to DeWeerd shortly after. "Nature has patterned it so I must run in the opposite direction to complete the game. Boy! I'm running? It's a tiring game, but I'm younger. Horrible!!"[34]

As fall turned to winter, Dean became desperate for companionship of any kind. He haunted used bookstores and spent hours with whatever artist or actor he happened to meet. He even took to calling his new agent, with half-joking affection, "Mom" because she volunteered to handle his chaotic finances, loaned him money against future earnings, and nagged him to show up to auditions on time. He professed a filial love for her as her "little monster."[35] He also loitered in the lobby of the Rehearsal Club, a boardinghouse for young women in the arts. The girls doted on him, moved by his worn-out clothes and air of sadness. He liked the attention and the free meals the girls gave him. He had been living off of milkshakes, rarely eating.

At Christmas, Brackett visited New York. In his absence, Dean had grown to miss him, particularly in his cramped but cheap new quarters at the YMCA by Central Park, and at their reunion, Brackett took Dean Upstate to Garrison, across the Hudson from West Point, for a romantic "old fashioned country Christmas" in a picturesque bed and breakfast.[36] It briefly lifted his mood, and around this time, in his room at the YMCA, he wrote cheerfully to DeWeerd that he now loved New York—"as fascinating as it is big"—and especially skating in the Rockefeller Center ice rink.[37]

Dean accepted Brackett's offers of financial help, though likely with great reluctance. Over the coming year, Brackett would spend more than $1,000 supporting Dean, paying $450 of Dean's hotel bills and more than $700 in gifts and loans. But when Brackett left for Chicago and Dean returned to New York, Dean tried to put more than miles between them. He spun fantasies for his acquaintances, like those he later told about running with the bulls in Pamplona or spending a night in jail—anything to be seen as more of a real, independent man. Beverly Wills passed through New York, and over dinner she showed off her engagement ring. When she told Dean that she would soon marry Bill Bast, Dean grew jealous. He made infrequent but insistent calls to Bast urging him to come to New York.

On a rainy January night at the Rehearsal Club, Dean asked to borrow an umbrella from a young dancer named Elizabeth "Dizzy" Sheridan as they read amusing lines from magazines to one another.[38] Intrigued that they both enjoyed bullfighting—she noticed he wore an unusual lapel pin, a matador's sword, of which he was inordinately proud, on his tattered blue jacket—they quickly fell into conversation, and Dean, as he had done a year before with Bast, developed one of his infatuations.[39] He saw in her a mirror of himself and imagined that she might be the even match he had so longed for. She was everything he thought himself to be—broad and deep, curious, consumed by theater and the arts, an aspiring matador (or so she let him believe). She thought he needed a friend. Together, they wandered the city in the night and read poetry and plays to one another until even Sheridan marveled that Dean could maintain such intensity for so long. They often ate dinner at Jerry's, an Italian restaurant on Fifty-Fourth Street—an almost deliberate contrast to Brackett's preferred gourmet French fare—and when Dean had no money, a sympathetic waiter named Louie de Liso sneaked him his new favorite meal, spaghetti.

It seemed a lot like love, but Sheridan, more emotionally perceptive than Dean, realized that a certain desperation marked their relationship, a sense that they were clinging to one another. For Dean, friendship and love, brotherhood and intimacy, intellectual engagement and sex were impossibly mixed up, and he perpetually sought to find as many of them together as he could while failing time and again to have them all. He believed in the Platonic ideal, where what he called "true unions of mind, spirit, and body" formed bonds of heroic love between equals, as he told an uncomprehending Bast a few months later.[40] He hoped this time he could gather enough to sustain him.

As he had done with Bast, Dean had a capital, if irregular, idea. He asked Sheridan to move in with him after two weeks, somewhat scandalous and unseemly for an unmarried couple. With little money between them, they took an uncomfortably small room with peeling wallpaper in the Hargrave Hotel on West Seventy-Second Street. They hung Dean's drawings on the walls and ate shredded wheat by candlelight and "real crazy dishes" he concocted for them from scraps.[41] They used his stolen matador's cape as a blanket, though she hated the unwashed, bloody cloth's smell. He read her *The Little Prince* and confessed that he saw himself in the book's hero, a space alien hovering uncomfortably above a world not his own. He identified with the author's "escapist attitude, his refusal to adjust to anything earthbound," he once said. "I hate all earthlings," he would joke, imagining himself floating above the Earth.[42]

She remembered being charmed when she awoke to find he had left for some audition and had cooked her breakfast, a hardboiled egg, on which he drew a cartoon face. They convinced each other that they both wanted to avoid the temptation of friends and live only with and for themselves in their room. She noticed that he lacked a certain enthusiasm for sex. "Jimmy never seemed to me a sexually driven or sexually obsessed young man," she recalled, and to a young woman in 1952, that seemed swell.[43] She told him she loved him. He replied, "Oh, wow."[44]

And Dean wanted to believe that he had finally found his equal, his match. But it wasn't enough. They had an intellectual connection and an emotional one, but as the weeks passed and Dean's initial infatuation faded, he found it hard to ignore the missing pieces in their union. Sheridan was, if anything, too much like Dean. He needed and wanted a teammate, someone who complemented him as much as reflected him, a source of mutual support on a climb ever upward, and Sheridan offered nothing he didn't already have.

"He did not want to be gay," Sheridan recalled decades later, but all things being equal, she was a woman, and that was less than satisfying in the quest for the ideal form of heroic love, no matter how much he tried to deny it. He loved her, it was true, but it was not the passion of *eros* but the steady affection of *philia*, and their connection faded little by little from fiery intensity to a comfortable sibling warmth. Unconsciously, Sheridan felt it, too. In later years, she chose an odd but telling simile, pregnant with unspoken layers, to describe their time together: "We felt separate from the rest of the world, like the brother and sister who live in the attic in *Les Enfants Terribles*."[45]

Like the dangerously destructive siblings in Jean Cocteau's novel, Dean started to tell her lies, small and large. He lied pointlessly about meeting the author of *The Little Prince*, and when she believed him, soon enough he lied about Rogers Brackett, who had returned to New York in February. He told her Brackett was stalking him, that he had followed Dean from Los Angeles after he had shamefully succumbed to Brackett's advances out of desperation for career help, and that he hated himself for it. The self-loathing may well have been true. Sheridan willed herself to believe him.

Yet Dean could push things only so far. One spring night, he took Sheridan to Brackett's apartment and introduced her to him as his girlfriend, as though together they might somehow free Dean from his discomforting hypocrisy by forcing his dualities to collapse into one. She spent the meeting icy and rude, treating Brackett like a romantic rival and dryly noting that the impeccably stylish Brackett wore tailored clothes the exact shade of beige as his apartment's tasteful wallpaper—and his hair. Brackett was polite, if a bit patronizing, to Sheridan and sipped a snifter of brandy until she excused herself. Dean found it amusing and perhaps familiar, but he couldn't bring himself to end things with Brackett.[46] "We live here in every world," Dean wrote in a poem he inscribed in one of his paperback books around that time. "Secret loft in azure habitat."[47] No one could say which secluded apartment he had in mind.

After less than two months, he and Sheridan ran out of money, and Sheridan moved in with a friend, while Dean said he had taken a room at the Iroquois, though he spent most nights with Brackett.[48] He had gotten Dean a job presenting the end credits for the *Hallmark Hall of Fame*, which Brackett's advertising firm oversaw, and took him to glamorous parties, where Winston Churchill's daughter lectured him about his boyishly mischievous behavior. Sheridan was no fool and knew both what was going on and where she stood.[49] But she compromised, with herself and with him, seeing how much happier Dean was with her when he also had him. She did not see that Dean had fallen into his most comfortable retreat, a bifurcated life that divided his dualities and desires. It hurt her, and when later that year Dean impulsively proposed marriage, she said no. When they fought, she called him "queer." He called her a "cunt."[50]

Around the time that James Dean read in the papers that the director he ached to work with, Elia Kazan, had departed Manhattan on a trip to Washington to name suspected entertainment industry communists to the House Un-American Activities Committee, Dean was all too happy to learn Bill Bast, lovelorn and lonely, planned to follow Dean to New York City that spring. Perhaps he need not choose only one true self after all. He had recently turned twenty-one and had but one year's understanding of real friendship and half a year's knowledge of love and less of professional acting. The world demanded of him the unnoticed hypocrisies and numbing compromises of a maturity beyond his experience. And when he failed to close the gap between the dreamy adolescence he could not outgrow and the cold conventions of a misunderstood manhood, he pasted a comforting passage from *The Little Prince* into the portfolio he carried to auditions, humorously marked "Matters of Great Consequence," and imagined himself a space alien, outcast from two worlds, in this world but not of it, the hero of some cosmic drama whose outlines he might glimpse but whose outcome he would only know once he lived among the immortal stars.

6
RUN LIKE A THIEF

Jimmy Dean's world seemed a little less hostile when Bill Bast knocked on the door of Rogers Brackett's spacious, air-conditioned fifth-floor studio apartment early one morning in May 1952. Dean had missed his first real friend and had agitated intermittently for months for Bast to join him in New York. When he opened the door, clad in only boxer shorts and glasses, and invited Bast in to gawk at Brackett's pricey furniture and original works of modern art, it seemed as though something broken had started to heal.

In high spirits, he treated Bast to a daylong comedy of manners in the style of Oscar Wilde, where both spoke archly and elegantly past one another without ever quite saying what they meant. It was all glossy surfaces and smiles, but a paper-thin veneer covering unacknowledged truths. They acted more like unrequited lovers than reunited friends, and they both knew it. Bast complimented the decor and asked if everything in the apartment was Brackett's. "Not quite," Dean replied after pulling on his clothes, and they both pretended Dean wasn't referring to himself.

Over breakfast at a diner, Dean tried boyishly to amuse Bast by popping out his false teeth so they could watch the other patrons gawk in horror. He spoke expansively about his life in New York, especially his TV roles. He said cryptically that if you "let things happen," good things follow, and he mentioned by example how the director Richard Levy had helped him make connections. Bast couldn't discern whether Dean had been speaking philosophically of opening himself to destiny or literally about offering his toes to Levy's notorious foot fetish. At least this time, he seemed to mean the former, because a few months later, he discussed destiny with a reporter in the same way: "I have a hunch there are some things in life we just can't avoid. They'll happen to us, probably because we're built that way—we simply attract our own fate . . . make our own destiny."[1] His high-minded philosophy covered over, however, the lustful glances and indecent offers Brackett's powerful friends had started to make, the pressure Dean felt to give in, and his distress that Brackett's libertinism (sex for him and his friends was recreational and transactional, rarely emotional) made him less Dean's protector than his pimp.

Bast was amazed that Dean already knew and didn't care that Bast had made and broken an engagement with their mutual ex, Beverly Wills. Dean reminded him that Wills was famous, and their engagement had been in all the papers, and also that she had told him herself. Bast didn't say that while with her, he had emulated Dean and conducted his own affair with a powerful older man, a CBS art director. They both pretended Bast hadn't thrown away his L.A. life mostly to join Dean. Bast made light of receiving a draft notice and escaping service at the last minute only due to a convenient digestive problem, and Dean joked about "pretending" to be gay to avoid service. Bast didn't share with Dean the terror he felt when the draft notice came or that when actually faced with the choice between shipping off to his death and admitting to being gay, death "seemed the better bet."[2] He laughed along instead.

Dean pulled Bast through a rapid tour of his Manhattan, bringing him to meet Dizzy Sheridan so the three of them could run wild through Central Park like kids, making faces at the zoo monkeys and the tourists. He lied shamelessly, telling Bast that Sheridan was nobody serious and offered none of the "challenges" of other "females," which Bast, wishfully perhaps, took to mean not wanting sex. He noticed that Dean and Sheridan never kissed or held hands. Sheridan suggested innocently that the boys find a place together, and Dean considered it a great idea. It would also, conveniently for her, separate Dean from Brackett.[3]

The boys tore through Manhattan's best residence hotels at lunchtime, knowing they couldn't afford any of them, until Dean's acquaintance Roddy McDowall, a gay friend of Brackett's and an intimate of Montgomery Clift living at the expensive Algonquin Hotel, told them to try the neighboring Iroquois.[4] Dean made a bad joke of their departure from the Algonquin, saying only Indians must live there because the desk clerk asked if he had a reservation. They took a gray-green room at the Iroquois for $90 per month, and Dean pretended never to have seen the place before, despite twice being a resident. He packed up his matador's cape, his shelf of books, and his clothes that afternoon and moved into their new quarters without telling Brackett. Dean had again begun to resent being treated as a dependent rather than an equal, and the distance helped even the scales. First thing, Dean hung his bull's horns over his bed. He kept seeing Brackett all that summer, even as he drew strange cartoons of Brackett as an ugly lizard monster, an atavistic revenant he didn't know how to escape. But Brackett clung to Dean with unhealthy tenacity.

To win him back, Brackett brought him into a circle of brilliant, mostly gay artists and entertainers who met at the Blue Bar in the Algonquin Hotel like Dorothy Parker's Round Table of old. They cast with sparkling words the illusion of genius, professed to take *The Little Prince* for a revelation and a sacred text—a sort of *Dianetics* for the rich and artsy—and amused themselves by feting Dean as the Little Prince incarnate. The songwriter Marshall Barer developed a crush on Dean, as did Bradley Saunders, an Air Force pilot in their circle with a penchant for adolescent boys.[5] Bast witnessed one of their number going into a rapture when Dean played the role of prince for him, as though touched by the divine. Here, the great men of art playacted an epiphany with James Dean as their pretend messiah, a wild boy to be "tamed" as the book's characters had tamed each other into love. Although the group's practice of theatrical effeminacy offended Dean's masculine sensibility, he received their feigned adulation, and for a time, he reveled in the attention, however false.

But their ethereal playacting had an earthier edge. When Dean spoke with some of the men on the phone, they would launch into sexual stories and tell him, "I really want to cock you."[6] Dean persisted in thinking that the great men of letters and the arts thought great thoughts and might take an interest in his ideas, his talents, his dreams. His head swirled with visions of the union of heroic equals, but it was not their minds that tingled when they made him offers of help. "I know one guy in particular who I introduced him to who gave Jimmy a couple of jobs," James Sheldon, then an ad executive, recalled.

"I know that they had sex." Sheldon added glibly that while *he* never had sex
with Dean, Bob Stevens, more than a decade Dean's senior, "had just gotten his director's job at CBS and they had a little thing before Jimmy really
took off."[7] Dean himself recalled one such "little thing." After an unnamed
television performance, the show's much older director invited Dean to his
apartment for a drink and pressured Dean to let him perform oral sex on him.
While his boss fellated him, Dean retreated from his own body, focusing on
a fly walking across the ceiling until the blow job ended. "It's no big deal," he
told himself, but beneath his show of bravado, it made him feel like a whore.[8]

These experiences—and there had been more than one, he sometimes
hinted—taught Dean that a sex act meant nothing to him unless he felt an
emotional connection to the other person. He wanted a friend, brother, and
lover together, but none of the men—not even the increasingly desperate,
manipulative Brackett, really—cared to look beyond his body. His mechanical responses to their advances never reached the ethereal heights of his imaginary idea of love. So he turned to the one person who had tried to engage his
mind and tried to understand his emotions in the only way he knew: through
stories. He poured out his conflicted feelings in a comedy of manners that
Bill Bast did not realize he had fallen into. On an early summer night, Dean
staged an elaborate, theatrical seduction scene, ridiculous and sweet in equal
measure, but stopped short of letting it reach its obvious end.

In their room at the Iroquois, Dean sat down beside Bast and put an arm
around him. He kissed him gently and tried, in his goofily awkward way, to
find out how experienced Bast was with men, if he had ever performed the act
before, and confessing his own gay experiences. Bast, whose roadside encounters had possessed him of an encyclopedia of carnal knowledge, lied and professed innocence. A giddy Dean told him to do exactly what he was bidden.
He handed him an address and shoved him out the door with instructions to
open himself to experience and call Dean if he ran into trouble.

Bast found himself at the Astor Bar near Times Square, an ancient gay
bar one street over from where women sold their bodies openly on the corner. A middle-aged man came on to him aggressively and maneuvered the
conversation to encourage Bast to call Dean, even giving him a nickel for the
phone. Bast called Dean, who asked Bast if he wanted to go home with the
other man. Bast demurred, and Dean said, "You're right. It ought to be with
someone you've tamed first." He told Bast softly that he didn't belong in that

James Dean sent Bill Bast to the gay bar in the Hotel Astor (center) in Times Square in a confusing attempt to sort through the two men's homosexual feelings. *Photo by Angelo Rizzuto / Library of Congress Prints and Photographs Division, Anthony Angel Collection, LC-DIG-ppmsca-69784.*

place and should come home. Bast rushed back, anticipating consummation, only to find the room empty and *The Little Prince* on Bast's bed with a note in Dean's hand: "For a gift, one is always beholden." It was a line heralding the protagonist's disappearance at the end of the second act of *The Moon Is Blue*, a then-current Broadway play written by F. Hugh Herbert that Bast had never seen. Alternately heartbroken and hopeful, he treasured the gift but longed for the absent man it represented.[9]

Dean had seemingly choreographed the whole night as a gay mirror of Herbert's play, in which a virgin woman meets a playboy atop the Empire State Building and returns to his apartment, where she encounters his rakish neighbor. She wants to talk of intellectual things, and the men lust to deflower her. She slips out with her virtue intact but finds the lovelorn playboy at the Empire State Building the next day, having nearly gone out of his mind with anger, sadness, and fear at her disappearance.

In Dean's production, the "virgin" Bast escaped a lusty man with virtue intact and awaited the playboy Dean's return, but Bast assumed Dean meant the evening as a push to help Bast accept himself as gay. When Dean returned deep in the night from wherever he had hidden, he might have expected to find Bast confused, demanding an explanation, or worried by his absence and in his anger speaking the truth about what he felt but refused to say. Any of those reactions would have told Dean that Bast loved him, mind, body, and soul, as the virgin learned from the playboy's pain. Instead, he found Bast asleep, clutching Dean's *Little Prince* to his chest. He was no heroic equal. This was a different type of love—devotion—but would it suffice? When dawn broke, the boys, as they had so often, acted as though nothing had happened.[10]

Throughout 1952, James Dean could not escape the notion that every boon came wrapped in pain, every success painted in trauma. He had irregular television work but had to write to Marcus and Ortense Winslow for $10 to keep himself afloat. A wealthy businessman, Louis Fabrikant, took a shine to him and treated him to elaborate dinners, but too often Dean went hungry.[11] All that year and even into the first months of the next, despite their fading relationship, Dean was still accepting work that Rogers Brackett occasionally threw his way.[12] He placed his hopes in joining the Actors Studio and following the path Marlon Brando had blazed.

After months of preparation, more than a little panic, and some beer, he passed his audition to join the Actors Studio, beating out 150 competitors. "*We . . . all of us . . . are alone*," he dramatically intoned at the end of his audition scene set on a desert island.[13] Finally, he could study the Method under Lee Strasberg and Elia Kazan. But his hopes of finding a temple of the arts crumbled before Strasberg's insistence that the techniques of psychological torture would cut away every emotion until only a pure actor remained. Dean chafed against Strasberg's efforts to unmask Dean's hidden core, that part of him he wouldn't admit even to himself. He worked hard to create a dramatic matador scene for the class, only to have Strasberg slice and dice both it and him to shreds. Dean stormed out, protested Strasberg's attempt to "cut off my balls," and vowed not to return.[14]

His anger extended beyond just Strasberg or even New York to encompass the whole world. All that long summer, he would rant and rave about Senator Joe McCarthy and his witch hunts against anyone McCarthy considered a "Communist or a cocksucker," becoming so angry that Dean could barely form the words to express his hatred for attacks on Hollywood and homosexuals he knew might someday come for him.[15] He found his relief wandering the streets of Manhattan, striking up conversation with interesting people, the winos and hobos and street musicians, hoping to learn from their lives something of how people thought and why their thoughts were so different from his.

In August, Brackett had paved the way for a desperately poor and out-of-work Dean to ingratiate himself with Lemuel Ayers, a married gay Broadway set designer sixteen years Dean's senior who was planning to produce that fall *See the Jaguar*, the story of a naive and sheltered teenage boy who makes a doomed foray into the hostile world beyond his home. Brackett knew Ayers through their mutual friend, Alec Wilder, and all three had worked together in 1950 on a failed production of Wilder's opera *The Impossible Forest*.[16]

After some weekend forays at the Ayers estate, at Ayers's invitation, Dean took a job as a deckhand aboard his yacht, the *Typhoon*, for Ayers's annual ten-day Cape Cod cruise, hoping to prove himself right for a role and charm his way into a part. In previous weekends at the Ayers' Hudson Valley home with Brackett, he had noticed Ayers looking at him a bit too long, but this was supposed to be a safe trip. He would be one among a full crew, and Ayers's wife would be right there, too.

It was a strange trip from the start. When telling the story to a fellow actor while drunk one night a few months later, Dean giggled uncomfortably when he recalled how Ayers had dressed him as the sea god Neptune. Ayers had sat him on a throne in costume, an old ritual once used to haze sailors crossing the equator for the first time, now employed improperly to mark Dean's first yacht trip. Dean had never sailed before, and the dark skies and brilliant stars revealed the infinite heavens that the bright lights of the city had so often kept hidden from him. In the sparkling darkness, Ayers came to him while his wife pretended not to see. Ayers held Dean's future in his hand, a demand for sex separating Dean from the glory he knew to be his destiny. Whatever happened on the wine-dark sea, the wanderer returned from his odyssey a different man.[17]

When Dean returned home to move into cheaper new quarters with Bill Bast and Dizzy Sheridan as roommates and playacted his bullfights with them through the living room, Bast pressed him for details. Dean tried to avoid admitting what happened and would only mumble that he had "put out" before clamming up again and changing the subject to something more amusing. It should have been obvious that the unwanted sex had left him feeling shame and guilt, but Bast considered giving and receiving oral sex simply a part of the "game" and wondered why Dean wouldn't provide him with the gossipy details of Ayers's orgasms and went back to complaining that Dean was late with the rent.

At some point, Dean began to recognize that for all the affection he had for his two closest friends, Sheridan and Bast, he had no one who truly understood him or his pain, no one who saw into his soul, not least because he trusted no one with all his secrets. When he had mumbled some words about how those older men had violated him, Sheridan had called him a "queer" and now refused to discuss the subject again, and his best friend made plain his opinion that Dean should be a more wanton whore to get more from the men. He started to badmouth them behind their backs as "the flake and the chick."[18] When he retreated into adolescent fantasy and played matador to escape the world, his friends grew bored and tired and annoyed. When he spoke of the heavy books he read—five or six at the same time, he claimed—and the deep thoughts about history, art, and eternity that swirled in his head, friends and colleagues stared at him in their uncomprehending blankness, by turns incurious and dismissive.[19] But they were all amused when he acted like a jackass, so that would be the role he played. "I am lonely," he would write in the coming months. "Forgive me. I am lonely."[20]

Sometime that summer or fall, Dean started reading a book about Aztec civilization and found within confirmation of his own sense of predestination, for the Aztecs had believed that ancient myths foretold the coming end of all things. His macabre taste reveled in the grotesquery of the Aztecs' unceasing human sacrifices—tens of thousands killed each year, some with their hearts ripped out and their skins turned to priestly coats—blood offerings intended to delay the inevitable end of the world age.

One story of sacrifice may have resonated. The Aztec priests chose a young man Dean's own age to play the role of Tezcatlipoca, the capricious, omniscient god of night and destiny. The youth served a year in the role, walking the streets of the capital playing a flute—more of a recorder, really—with four beautiful companions. After the year ended, he ritually broke his flute, and the priests sacrificed him. Dean had learned to play the recorder a few months back, practicing incessantly; sitting in the window of his room clad only in boxer shorts; pushing out sad, quiet melodies, the music of the spheres.[21]

He took special interest in the clockwork fulfillment of ancient prophecy. "They had a legend that their god Quetzalcoatl had predicted they would be conquered by strange visitors from another land," he explained, echoing the comic book language of Superman, another "strange visitor from another planet," recently making his syndicated television debut. "They had such a weird sense of doom that when the warlike Spaniards arrived in Mexico, a lot of the Aztecs just gave up, fatalistically, to an event they believed couldn't be avoided," Dean told a reporter that fall. As he read the book, he came to see himself in the Aztecs, in their submission to the power of fate. "With their sense of doom, they tried to get the most out of life while life was good; and I go along with them on that philosophy." There were, he thought, inevitabilities preordained, outcomes set in motion long before he was born. But around the edges, room remained for finding moments of grace, for experiencing the "good in life while it is good."[22]

The good, however, wasn't always easy to find. The compromises he had made had begun to wear, and his dark moods lasted longer. Rarely one to drink heavily, in the coming months he started to get drunk more often and smoked his first joint, and without really knowing why, he decided to accept an invitation from his father to escape the city and go back to his childhood home in Indiana for a while, to spend time with the family he loved and hoped to one day provide for. "I just upped and took off back home for Indiana," he shrugged in telling the story a few years later.[23] Sometime that fall, he bought and read a used 1947 expurgated biography of the gay playwright Federico García Lorca. After he, Sheridan, and Bast hitchhiked out to the Winslow farm in Fairmount and back—hitching a ride through the Ohio and Indiana rye fields with an actual catcher, Clyde McCullough of the Pittsburgh Pirates—he began reflecting on how life in New York had changed him from the boy he had been in high school. "My town is not what I am," he wrote in a poem he inscribed in the book. "I am here."[24]

During the trip, Ayers called for him. At first, Ayers had had no intention of casting Dean once he had gotten what he wanted from him, and Ayers had chosen another actor for the role. But Rogers Brackett and Alec Wilder had put pressure on him to give Dean an audition, and Brackett had even brought Dean to test readings of the play meant for potential financial backers, placing

Dean front and center in the audience, none too subtly reminding Ayers that he owed Dean. When Ayers's original choice fell through, he relented and gave Dean a chance. His first reading went poorly, which he blamed on cracked glasses, and Ayers rejected him. But the play's director, Michael Gordon, thought he looked right for the role and gave him another chance, and he aced it. *See the Jaguar* in short order would not just include James Dean but also star him.

He knew something had changed, that the stars had aligned and the future he had always felt to be his had started to come to pass. He would defy Strasberg's harsh judgment and perform on Broadway, but he could never forgive himself that his body and not his talent had been the handmaid of destiny. That could never happen again. He bought a large switchblade knife with money meant to replace his broken glasses and started carrying it everywhere.

Just before his Broadway debut, Dean gave a radio interview to Jack Shafer to promote *See the Jaguar*, and he dumbfounded the reporter. Shafer noticed Dean was carrying a book about the Aztecs, and at Shafer's politely mild interest, Dean built into a long monologue about doom and destiny and human sacrifice, becoming animated and excited at the chance to show off his thoughts on history and fate. He couldn't stop himself, and he nearly forgot to talk about the play.

See the Jaguar opened at the Cort Theatre on West Forty-Eighth Street on December 3, 1952, and garnered terrible reviews for its contrived script and heavy-handed symbolism. But critics agreed that James Dean acted far above the material. The *Herald Tribune*'s Walter Kerr praised his "extraordinary performance in an almost impossible role," bringing to convincing life a confused youth experiencing the cruelty of the world for the first time.

Bast and Sheridan sat in the opening-night audience in awe of Dean, immediately aware that the trajectories of their lives had begun to diverge. Although the play flopped and closed three days later, it had given Dean an incalculable boon. Suddenly, he was a star. Television offers poured in, and in the new year, he could be seen on the small screen almost weekly, usually depicting a rebellious, sensitive, or delinquent youth. The roles kept getting bigger as the year progressed. The best of these was the violent, sensitive young man he played in "A Long Time till Dawn" on *Kraft Television Theatre* late in 1953, a character whose father describes him with evident confusion as a boy who could be sweet and gentle one moment and a thug the next. "I

James Dean (right) made himself appear younger and more vulnerable to depict an innocent teenager in *See the Jaguar. Photofest.*

can't imagine anyone playing that particular role better," the show's writer, Rod Serling, recalled, not fully aware that he had, through some preternatural magic, polished his plodding script about an impulsive youth consumed with deadly nostalgia for boyish innocence into a twisted mirror of Dean himself. "I think this was his first big role in television and his behavior was very restrained and uncomfortable, but even then there was an excitement and intensity about him that he transmitted viscerally to the television audience."[25] Dean agonized over how to play the role until an hour before broadcast, only deciding at the last minute to take a friend's advice and give his character a distinctive and symbolic Freudian tic, drawn from his own unconscious habit of sucking his shirt collar for comfort, like a baby at his mother's breast.

With producers competing for him, there would be no more unwanted fellatio from sweaty older men. Indeed, he had decided he would no longer think of himself as a victim—his word—or give in to the "vampires," as he now called the predatory men who pressured him for sex. "I refuse to be sucked in to things of that nature," he wrote in a letter, adding in parentheses, "pun, ha ha."[26] Around the same time, he typed a letter to the Reverend DeWeerd, whom he addressed as the "King of the Wood" from *The Golden Bough*—the aging priest who must die so a handsome young man might achieve his destiny—lamenting that after playing so many roles, he was no closer to understanding his true self.[27]

Before 1953 dawned, Dean had moved out of his friends' shared apartment and to his own room in the Iroquois, where he began reading smatterings of Greek philosophy and Roman history and quickly forgot about Sheridan, a discarded infatuation who soon faded from his life. He retained a distant affection for her, but it was the ghostly afterglow of an extinguished flame, blown out along with other former obsessions, like pole vaulting and farm equipment. He had already replaced her with a new girl, Barbara Glenn, who found him looking sad and alone before the premiere of *See the Jaguar*. She soon became his new obsession.

Bast had developed his own social life with a group of young gay men, a group he kept separate from Dean, worried that they would find him the wrong kind of queer, not open and libertine and unabashedly free like them. Sexual researchers of the time had proposed a spectrum of homosexuality running from "exhibitionist fairies," who could not hide the effeminacy they flaunted, to the overly masculine "hoodlums," who feared any challenge to their manhood.[28] Bast had gravitated closer to the fairies, and Dean, to the hoodlums. Dean encouraged Bast to take a separate room at the Iroquois, their windows facing each other close enough to talk easily across the lightwell. Dean kept him as something of a devoted pet, someone to visit when he felt lonely, to talk with into the night until they fell chastely asleep beside each other on Bast's bed, Dean on his side with knees pulled halfway to his chest, hands tucked warmly between his thighs, his face twitching with motion, lips miming the silent words of an active mind restless even in sleep.[29]

And soon enough, Bast was gone, too, off to Los Angeles in the spring of 1953 to write for television. They parted with a long, warm hug in front of NBC's Radio City studios, and Dean gave Bast a hardcover copy of a recent English translation of André Maurois's collected stories. He wrote in it, "May flights of harpies escort your wingéd trip of vengeance," an encouraging go-get-'em allusion to Maurois's "Harpies on the Shore," a story Dean told Bast to read and from which Bast realized Dean sometimes pulled themes and ideas. The story told of the two wives of Antoine Vence, a writer so consumed with finding a perfect match of mind, body, and soul that he neglected the flesh-and-blood love right in front of him, until his first wife exposed the weakness beneath his façade of greatness, the flaws in his artistic pretentions, the teenage boy cowering in the man. Although he professed hatred for her in their divorce, until his death he could never escape the only person who made him truly human. To be a great man, to rise from poverty to riches, he had to wear a false face and, in his striving, failed to see how he hurt those who loved him. The story ends with Vence's first and last wives selling his life story to the movies and watching Hollywood transform the fragile, flawed man into a demigod and hero, his complicated sex life reduced to cinematic pablum. Dean's first message of affection was obvious and sad and completely lost on Bast. But Dean made his second meaning plain when he signed his note to Bast not with his usual "Jimmy" or affectionate "Deaner" but with "James Dean." Now, without the person who made him human, he would become someone else: a great man.[30]

7
THE FOGGY, FOGGY DEW

Of course, there was professional trouble for James Dean on the path to greatness. Many days in the lonely, dull months after *See the Jaguar* closed followed much the same pattern. When he had roused himself from bed, he headed to Midtown for the usual round of morning casting calls, stopped by his agent's office on the off chance that something big had arrived in the night, got coffee at Cromwell's, and spent the afternoon in contemplation, as often as not at the Museum of Modern Art. When bored, he telephoned Montgomery Clift or Marlon Brando, though he rarely planned anything to say. Brando listened in but never responded to the messages left with his answering service.[1] Clift recalled the barrage of phone calls that came to his East Side apartment. Clift said little as the quiet voice on the other end stumbled through an attempt at greeting: "Uh—hello, man—uh—this is Jimmy Dean—uh—how are you?" It was all too much. "What the fuck was I supposed to say?" an exasperated Clift wondered. "'Hello, man—uh—how are you' back?"[2]

Clift asked Elia Kazan, then preparing a new gay-themed drama for the stage, if he knew anything about the strange boy calling him. Kazan passed on a bit of gossip about Dean's sexuality swirling among the Broadway community: "They say he likes racing cars and bikes, waitresses—and waiters. They say you're his idol." Wary that Dean might want a sexual relationship with him, Clift would only remark, "Dean is *weird*," even as he avidly followed the gossip about Dean's activities. Particularly juicy was word from the

New York television scene that the young star never paid any attention to the bevy of young actresses who hovered around him on set. He seemed indifferent to female attention.[3]

With Bast gone, Dean began to spend more time with David Diamond, a much older gay composer and friend of Alec Wilder and Rogers Brackett who had the room next door to Dean's at the Iroquois. Diamond composed the themes to CBS's *Hear It Now* radio show and *See It Now* TV series but felt his career had stalled because of his open homosexuality. Over evenings spent in lessons and discussions about music, Dean developed an intense emotional intimacy with Diamond, who presented as less effeminately flamboyant than Wilder or Brackett, something Dean appreciated, especially because, like Dean, even Diamond found the Algonquin group occasionally too theatrically queer. Diamond was disappointed that the beautiful youth—whose very scent he found enchanting—saw him as a father figure, not as an object of desire, even if Diamond later claimed defensively that Dean was not his type.

Dean soaked up Diamond's affection, sought his praise and approval, and once charmed the composer by resting his head on Diamond's chest when Diamond hugged him, as though signaling a hard-earned trust. For a moment perhaps, Dean felt safe—safe enough to lounge or bathe nude in his room in Diamond's presence. And yet Diamond, like so many other men in Dean's life, soured on their bond when Dean pushed for a deeper emotional connection than Diamond was willing to give. In his diary Diamond would write that Dean had become a problem. Dean was quietly upset that Diamond had developed an unrequited crush on another boy, the twenty-two-year-old Martin Russ, who happened to be heterosexual and recently returned from service in Korea with plans to write a book about his time there.

When Dean learned that Diamond was returning to Italy and to his young Italian lover of more than a year, Ciro Cuomo, who was to be his long-term companion, Dean felt betrayed. Diamond called it jealousy and questioned in his diary why it was not enough merely to be Dean's friend, as if to ask whether Dean really expected emotional intimacy or fidelity, like a woman. Diamond crudely believed that any man with homosexual inclinations would inevitably ask for sex if alone long enough with another man. And yet Dean did not. Uninterested in serving as a father, brother, or soulmate, Diamond preferred to sneak glimpses of Dean's erections and pubic hair in the bathtub, fantasize about Dean's inviting sensuality and muscular pecs and thighs, and gossip with Alec Wilder about why Dean didn't ask him for sex.[4] Once again, vulgar reality disabused Dean of his ethereal hope for the union of heroic equals, and he soon broke away from Diamond.

Gradually, though, the unpleasant days grew fewer in number as TV roles began to come faster in the first half of 1953, accompanied by welcome contracts for $200; $300; or, by year's end, as much as $1,000 per appearance.[5] Dean played roles in sixteen television productions in 1953, most in the early months, from a laboratory assistant in a science fiction story on *Tales of Tomorrow* to a series of disaffected teenage hoodlums in tepid, ramshackle scripts Dean imbued with more life than they were worth. His ability to convey big emotions with the smallest movement—a catch in his voice, a pause for breath—put him in a class beyond the stiff, wooden standard of TV acting. His lively delivery and lithe movements, as in "Something for an Empty Briefcase" when playing a reforming thief on a self-improvement kick, could be delightfully charming, even when his acting was uneven, and the scripts, uninspired.

Soon enough, many days became an exercise in preparation, digging into the meat of the new role each week's broadcast offered. For a cowboy part, he took to biting his fingers to make the tips more sensitive so he could feel the gun more readily and draw it faster. But Dean could never understand why others found him difficult to work with. Directors complained about the switchblade he brandished at auditions, seemingly to signal he was dangerous. His castmates complained when he spoke quietly for the camera rather than loudly for them, and when he tried to break the tension by being funny—once turning his glasses to the side of his head, contorting his features, and yelling that he was a Picasso; another time placing a prop bottle in the crotch of his pants and miming an erection—they hated his jokes.

He expected the cast and crew to uphold the highest standards of art, to build toward the ideal, just as he worked tirelessly to do, and he struggled to mask his disappointment when workaday concerns compromised the imaginary perfection dancing across his mind's eye. In a typical incident, with just twenty-two minutes to air on a live production, Dean changed the blocking of a scene on a whim, confusing the cast and crew. "I was trying something new," Dean told his costar Hume Cronyn. "I wanted to confuse you—you should be confused." When Cronyn fumed in rage, Dean apologized—temporarily. A few weeks later, chancing upon him on the street, Dean cheekily told Cronyn he forgave him. "You were nervous," he said. Cronyn was speechless with astonishment.[6]

Similarly, Dean found the public's response to his television appearances both heartening proof of his greatness and another reminder that however ethereal his view of art, the world continued to see him in baser terms. "A comparative newcomer, James Dean, stole the spotlight," *Variety* wrote in a September 2, 1953, review of "Death Is My Neighbor," an episode of the CBS crime anthology *Danger,* singling out his "magnetic performance that brought a routine meller [*Variety*'s slang for *melodrama*] alive. . . . Dean's performance was in many ways reminiscent of Marlon Brando's in *Streetcar,* but he gave his role the individuality and nuances of its own which it required. He's got quite a future ahead of him."[7]

Dean clipped the review and proudly sent it to Barbara Glenn. He didn't tell her that women were proposing marriage over the phone, to his astonishment. He found both amusing and embarrassing letters from much older women instructing him to wear tighter pants. He discovered that a club of women aged fifty to seventy-five watched TV to lust after young men. "They sit there checking the cats out," he said, slipping into his growing collection of bohemian slang, "then write these dirty letters. It's really hard to believe."[8]

But the newspapers also contained disturbing rumbles. *Los Angeles Mirror* columnist Edith Glynn scowled at TV's new crop of sensitive young men playing troubled teens. Male roles, she complained, were now "mimed mostly by swishes." Powerful columnists Walter Winchell, Ben Gross, and Dorothy Kilgallen also blasted "gay" and "queer" television actors, and the tabloid *Confidential* ran an exposé on homosexuals in the industry, quoting network executives about a coming crackdown on what one called TV's "Fairyland." Television, they said, needed real men, not "semi-boys."[9]

Manliness complaints followed Dean from TV to the movies. To audition for a role as a youth being shipped off to war in the movie *Battle Cry* in December, Dean arrived unshaven, in dirty clothes approximating battle fatigues, and gave a full-throated performance. "He was goddamned *dressed* for the part!" Warner Bros. executive Bill Orr recalled. "And he gave the most fantastic reading I'd heard. It wasn't a reading, it was a performance!"[10] Orr championed Dean's cause as he had with Marlon Brando in 1947, but the studio had other ideas and gave the taller, more muscular Tab Hunter the part. A second test for a different picture that month ended with Warner

Bros. deciding Dean wasn't physically what they wanted for the role. And when Dean had screen tested for *Oklahoma!* back in September, the director praised his dramatic skills but said he lacked the "necessary romantic quality" to convincingly act like he loved a woman.[11]

To achieve the greatness he knew to be his, Dean intentionally set about remaking himself to be more like what Hollywood and New York considered a real man. He began affecting a masculine mumble like Brando. He looked at the photograph of Albert Camus on a paperback copy of one of

James Dean avoided traditional beefcake photos like this rare bare-chested shot as much as possible. He felt they made him look soft or vulnerable. *Photofest.*

the existentialist philosopher's books and admired the roguish way Camus's cigarette dangled from his lip, his creased face with slicked-back hair staring magnetically from behind an upturned overcoat collar. So Dean copied Camus's pose, dangling his own cigarettes perilously close to falling from his lip, to give the perfect masculine image of jaunty indifference. In the coming year, he would pose for hundreds of his new photographer friend Roy Schatt's pictures, constantly obsessing over the right angles and imagery to show the world the James Dean he wanted them to see.

He took his own photos, too, filled with odd angles, knives, and mirrors—surreal artistic experiments in symbolism understood only by him. A self-portrait on the set of a TV broadcast left his face out of focus in close-up while ornate French furniture stood in sharp relief. "Sometimes I feel that he was writing a biography at that time about himself, you know," Schatt recalled, "and that moment was entitled 'This Is the Way Jimmy Dean Prepared for His Role in. . . .' That's the feeling I got!"[12] The trouble was keeping track of the many roles Dean wanted to assume. One day it might be a TV job; another day, a dance class or a study of classical composers or endless hours focused exclusively on mastering the bongos.

Dean poured everything he had into each new role, losing himself for a few hours or a few days in his characters, his art, or his latest obsession, but none was greater than the ongoing role in which he cast himself. He had defined his life for so long through careful, calculated dualities. But the departure of his one truly close friend in a haze of romantic confusion reinforced his sense of being unworthy of love. All of his relationships ended in pain.

Now for the first time completely free of any man besides himself, in his loneliness he sought to remake himself as someone new, someone inviolable. He cultivated new friendships. He buddied up to the unabashedly straight young actor Martin Landau and loudly and frequently talked to him about girls to the point that Landau remained convinced until his death that Dean had been completely heterosexual. He ingratiated himself with the composer Leonard Rosenman, seven years his senior, using him to fill Bast's former role as an intellectual sounding board and a role model for bookish sophistication. Rosenman, condescending with avant-garde pretensions, unkindly dismissed Dean's efforts to digest the weighty tomes he himself breezed through.

Dean also threw himself into the pursuit of women, seldom without a girl on his arm though rarely in his bed. He told himself he could not be gay if

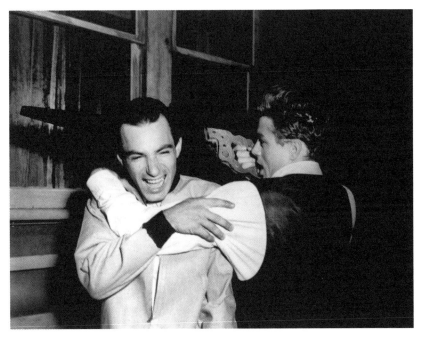

Leonard Rosenman (left) was one of several men James Dean sought, but failed to receive, emotional support from. Rosenman would instead spread disparaging rumors about Dean. *Photo by Floyd McCarty / Warner Bros. Pictures/Photofest © Warner Bros.*

he never sought or received "emotional support" from men, but when drunk he would tell his companions about his homosexual feelings and share crude drawings of men having gay sex.[13] Increasingly, he fed his infatuation for Barbara Glenn, and she, for him, but despite professions of love, they were never truly happy together. He loved the idea of her more than the reality, for he understood he could share his emotions with a woman in a way that was dangerous to do with men. However perilous his sexual desires might be, women would be safe. But Glenn was neurotic and frequently absent, and she blamed herself for his foul moods and the many breakups that followed.

"We would fight every time we were going to be separated," Glenn recalled.

Once I was going away to do stock and everyone decided to have a party for me, and it was going to be at Jimmy's apartment. And he said, "What the hell is all this party crap? She's only going away for two weeks." The night of the party he just got nastier and nastier and surlier and surlier. Jimmy just sat in the corner and sulked until eventually everyone went home. I was left there with a friend and Jimmy wouldn't talk to me, wouldn't relate to me. So I said, "Okay, Jimmy, if you're around when I'm back, I'll see you." He just grunted, so I walked out.

I walked down the street to Jerry's Tavern and we were sitting in the booth having a drink, tears streaming down my face, and, of course, in a few minutes Jimmy walked in. He didn't have much to say, but he held my hand and we sat there—and then we spent the night together and that was it. There was never very much said at our partings, but they were intense because there was a cutting off.[14]

While he played paramour in the drama of their lives and squired a parade of other young women through the motions of flirtation, the longing he could never bring himself to speak aloud banged as loudly as the bongos he practiced by night.[15] This time, however, there would be no older men pushing him beyond his comfort. He developed an intense attraction to a handsome young actor he met while out to breakfast one day that spring, Jonathan Gilmore, an eighteen-year-old who had come to New York in part to escape the sexual demands of Hollywood's lecherous elites, especially his agent, Henry Willson, and who, by coincidence, shared Dean's passion for bull-fighting. Gilmore recalled that they quickly became friends, and Dean found through Gilmore that he related more easily to younger men. Their innocence and inexperience were closer to his own immature emotions, and the awkwardness of their fumbling flirtations was endearing rather than humiliating. Above all, they were safe, unable to truly hurt him.

Over a few meetings, Dean began to flirt with Gilmore. He asked him about his homosexual experiences, drew out as many details as he could, listened intently to all the stories as though to learn from them, and offered little about himself in return. He suggested that they might explore a physical relationship. "His intense interest in gay sex seemed as intense as his passion for the heroics of bullfighting or sculpture," Gilmore recalled.[16] Dean told Gilmore that their shared experience of unwanted sex with producers had bonded them. He told Gilmore that what he liked sexually was the exact opposite of what they had known in those moments. To Gilmore's surprise, Dean wanted to kiss, cuddle, and be close more than to fuck. Gilmore became uncomfortable. Sex for him was a physical act, not an emotional one. He had never known a man to show affection during sex or knew that a man could. Their fumbling efforts at sex ended in failure, Gilmore said, because Dean was simply too well-endowed.[17]

Dean also used Gilmore in pantomime to replay the pain of his previous relationships, as though doing so might exorcise his longing for a friend, brother, and lover. At first Gilmore only understood Dean to be interested in "weird" things, though later he, too, came to feel that Dean had sought in him what he termed a "mother, brother, lover."[18] Dean shocked a Greenwich Village party when, in a scene straight out of a Bugs Bunny cartoon, he convinced Gilmore to dress as a woman and brought him as his date, "discovering" the deception to his "surprise" in an elaborately choreographed fake fight that ended in a passionate makeup kiss. Even he must have realized he was working out something half understood that kept resurfacing, a tension between the sex acts he had learned to mechanically perform and the intimacy he both craved and feared.

After a few months housesitting in a gay TWA purser's apartment on West Fifty-Second Street, where he perused his host's collection of gay pornography, Dean moved into a new apartment on West Sixty-Eighth Street, five floors up in an aging Victorian, into a room lit by two porthole windows, the only other notable feature a severely geometric wall of shelves surrounding a desk. He loved that the portholes looked a bit like the one in a magazine photo of Marlon Brando's apartment he had saved, and he pretended it was the same room. A folding regimental cot served as a bed. He filled the apartment with unmatched furniture and hung a bullfighting poster, his cape, and his horns on the walls. He stacked books everywhere in great piles as though building a wall of wisdom around him, expecting to someday find answers within.

He tried to drown his unresolved feelings in gin, and he wrote plaintive letters to the absent Barbara Glenn while drunk. They had the form of love letters but contained much more about him, his feelings, and the emptiness he couldn't fill. He told her how he would wander infernal streets, of the corruption and filth and misery he encountered, the sexual wantonness and the bottomless pit of his loneliness he found echoing in a nearby strip club:

In the pensiveness of night the cheap, monotonous shrill, symbolic, sensual beat of suggestive drums tatoos orgyistic images on my brain. The smell of gin and 90 cent beer, entwine with the sometimes suspenceful slow, sometimes labored static, sometimes motionless, sometimes painfully rigid, till finally the long awaited for jerks and convulsions that fill the now thick chewing gum haze with a mist of sweat, fling the patrons into a fit of supressed joy. The fated 7 days a week bestial virgin bows with the poise of a drunken pavlova. Rivilets of stale persperation glide from and between her once well formed anatomy to the anxious, welcoming front-row celebrities who lap it up with infamous glee. The Aura of Horror. I live above it and below it. . . . I did not ask for this; I did not seek it; it is. It is my Divine Comedy. The Dante of 52nd Street. There is no peace in our world. I love you.[19]

If he were Dante, then Glenn had become his Beatrice, an ideal loved more in the abstract than in the flesh. Yet it was not Beatrice but Virgil who guided Dante through the darkness to the gates of the ideal. Eventually, Dean would realize that Glenn could not fill that role. Dean had once preferred solitude, but now, less willing to be alone with his thoughts, he worked to fill his hours with hangers-on and acquaintances and square roots of zero who passed under the name of friends, wandering the circles of hell in search of the human. "Can't get along with nobody I guess," he wrote to Glenn. "Makes you feel good when you're not wanted."[20]

Drinking more frequently—"quite a bit lately," mostly imported beers, his favorite—his mind turned toward questions of the eternal, whether the strange and lonely world he could not fully embrace were truly real. "Lamas and scientists may fume and quander," he wrote to Glenn while drunk in August 1953, mirroring a line from an old Conan the Cimmerian story he once read. "Everything is not just illusion. You are my proof."[21] He clung to the idea that as long as she professed to care, then the world was not completely hostile, that he might find his way to the more perfect plane beyond the material: "In antiphonal azure swing, souls drone their unfinished melody. . . . When did we live and when did we not?" But his higher thoughts of metaphysics—which Glenn dismissed as schoolboy nonsense, unfit for the workaday world of jobs and money and struggle—clashed with the mundane truth that Dean sought in Glenn less an object of his love than a mirror to reflect himself back to him. "You think you need understanding?" he wrote to her only half in jest. "Who do you think you are? I could use a little myself."[22]

But who would understand him in a world he could not himself understand, that continually disappointed him with its venality, corruption, and madness? How could he open himself fully to anyone when they all left him, or he, them, in the end? If the world were mad, unreal, then he would take a lesson from his favorite Shakespeare play, *Hamlet*, and catch the world's conscience by turning his life into a performance. He would be mad north-northwest, wander about not in madness but mad in craft. And so late on October 4, 1953, as he walked down an empty Madison Avenue with Jessica Tandy and Mark Rydell after dancing to the song "Crazy Man, Crazy" in the *Omnibus* television production of "Glory in the Flower," he whipped off his coat and used it to play matador with a bus speeding headlong toward him at forty miles per hour. "This guy is going to kill himself," Rydell thought as he leaped back in shock. The bus touched Dean's shirt as it whipped by.[23]

Sensitive, wild, troubled boys like James Dean—they were the coming thing, or so movie executives at Warner Bros. believed. William Orr had championed Dean to his bosses at Warner, and though Dean did not land a role in *Battle Cry*, Orr continued to hold Dean in mind for some future part, seeing in him a reflection of the delinquent boys making news, boys whose stories Warner Bros. was certain they could turn into the next cinematic sensation.

In November 1953, New York City psychiatrist Fredric Wertham published in *Ladies Home Journal* and then again in the book *Seduction of the Innocent* in April 1954 his deep concern about a spiraling crime rate—up more than 30 percent since 1940, largely due to an increase in crimes by teenagers. He blamed comic books. He said comics enflamed sexual passions that made teenagers turn to crime as an outlet. Male superheroes were partly at fault, he said, for being too attractive: "The muscular male supertype, whose primary sex characteristics are usually well emphasized, is in the setting of certain stories the object of homoerotic sexual curiosity and stimulation." The disgusted doctor was horrified.[24]

In a lengthy diatribe, Wertham complained that Batman and Robin were a modern embodiment of the Classical Greek model of homosexual love between a man and a teenage boy. "It is like a wish dream of two homosexuals living together," he wrote of their warm relationship. Senator Estes Kefauver, a once and future candidate for the Democratic presidential nomination, took notice of Wertham's claims after members of the public began writing to the Senate about his work, and in an effort to appear tough on juvenile crime—arrests of teenagers had risen 40 percent in just five years—Kefauver's subcommittee investigating juvenile delinquency heard testimony from him during televised hearings in New York on the afternoon of April 21, just two days after *Seduction*'s publication. "I think from the public-health point of view something might be done," Wertham told Kefauver.[25]

Executives at Warner Bros. watched Kefauver's hearings—which dragged on intermittently until June—with great interest and realized that the time might be right for a new movie to dramatize the struggle of juvenile delinquents, the studio's first serious attempt since adapting *The Amboy Dukes* five years prior to a modest box office return. After all, Marlon Brando had made quite the impression less than a year ago as the leather-clad leader of a gang of delinquents on motorcycles in Columbia Pictures' *The Wild One*, inspired by a raucous motorcycle rally during the summer of 1947. Warner Bros. wanted a delinquency film of its own but one that appealed to an audience a little younger than Brando, who had just turned thirty: the teenagers reading comic books.

Indeed, Warner Bros. executives were in the process of searching for new, young talent attractive to the burgeoning teen audience, one who had doubled in size since the start of the postwar baby boom. Until now, the ideal Hollywood star of the 1950s was, well, in his fifties. A survey in the *Journal of Living* in 1953 found that Hollywood's most desirable men were all well into middle age. At fifty-one, Clark Gable topped women's list of best-loved screen lovers, and runners-up Spencer Tracy, Gary Cooper, Walter Pidgeon, and Charles Boyer were all in their early fifties. The experts that newspaper reporters called on to comment on older actors' popularity raved that mature men were more stable, more reliable, and had better judgment.[26]

Conventional wisdom was that few would be interested in a mere boy. However, movie studios could read the tea leaves. They saw the success of books like *Catcher in the Rye* and musicians like the emotional young singer Johnnie Ray and predicted the growing teen audience's next big star would be much younger. The new crop of actors their scouts had eyes on all seemed to look alike, less the gnomish Leo Gorcey of the Bowery Boys, at age thirty-seven still playing the same juvenile delinquent he'd played since 1937, and more Johnny Sheffield, the handsome but distinctly youthful twenty-three-year-old star of the *Bomba the Jungle Boy* movies so popular with young audiences. Paul Newman, Steve McQueen, Tab Hunter—boyish, sandy-haired young men, earnest, sensitive, and handsome—were the coming thing. With the right star, the half-finished scripts for *Rebel without a Cause* suddenly seemed fresh and exciting again. First, they needed a director to take on the film, and so far, no one wanted the project.

In Philadelphia in early January 1954, Jimmy Dean was decidedly less excited about the opening of his new play, *The Immoralist,* for a week of tryouts before its Broadway debut. The production adapted a semiautobiographical novel about a man's gay awakening at the hands of a teenage boy by the Nobel Prize–winning French novelist André Gide, a onetime friend of Oscar Wilde. In 1893, the pair had shared an Algerian adventure paying young boys for sex, sodomizing the barely pubescent boys in adjoining rooms, an experience of five orgasms Gide rhapsodized about in his autobiography as the greatest pleasure of his life, a "jubilation" he spent his remaining years trying to recapture.[27] He proudly proclaimed himself a "pederast" in his 1920 philosophical work *Corydon* and in his published journals, and like his friend Wilde, he thought romantic relationships between older men and adolescent boys were the highest form of human connection: "I maintain that it is good; each of the two finds exaltation, protection, a challenge in them; and I wonder whether it is for the youth or the elder man that they are more profitable."[28] When Gide died in 1951, the *New York Times* lauded him as the "greatest French writer of this century."[29] In reviewing *The Immoralist,* the *Motion Picture Herald* declared Gide "notably authoritative in the world of what are now politely called 'deviates.'"[30]

In late 1953, after a dazzling audition that wowed the producers, Dean had landed the role of Bachir, a wily young homosexual Arab who lures an unhappily married archaeologist into crisis when Bachir's attentions force him to confront his own homosexuality. But from the start, it was not the role he wanted. Dean had hoped to be the lead in Elia Kazan's 1953 production of *Tea and Sympathy*, Robert Anderson's frank new drama about Tom Lee, a teenage boarding school student. Lee's sensitive nature and bookish behavior lead his gruffer, more raucous classmates and even his own father to bully him and accuse him of homosexuality, sending him into a suicidal spiral that ends only when a sympathetic older woman beds him so he can prove his masculinity to himself and the other boys.

Dean saw much of himself in Tom. But while he looked the part of the slight, sensitive youth, the casting director felt a lifetime of performing the role of jock had given him too obvious an undercurrent of aggression and danger to embody a quiet innocent. That unstated edge, however, had convinced *Immoralist* director Herman Shumlin that the boy who showed up to his audition in torn blue jeans and boots would, with suitable brown makeup, make a fine Arab catamite. To the production team, Dean seemed a sweet kid whom the world had only started to make bitter, like wine turning to vinegar.

From the start, Dean was uncomfortable with the role. He worried that portraying a homosexual character might damage his career and suggest too much. He didn't like his costume—basically a bathrobe. "Hate this fucking brown makeup," he wrote to Barbara Glenn of the coloring needed to make him appear North African. The frequent rewrites to the script bothered him, too. The play "looks like a piece of shit to me," he added.[31] He made no secret of his indifference to the play's success. He put little effort into learning his lines and in rehearsal barely offered a performance—*that* he kept in reserve for actual show nights, when he gyrated with seductive moves audiences found almost shockingly sexual. "Jimmy played Bachir like a Third Avenue faggot," one of Rogers Brackett's friends complained after seeing the show.[32] Dean had buddied up to Shumlin, who found him fascinating to a point and tended to indulge his artistic temperament, but his castmates found him difficult and unpleasant, particularly his showboating improvisation and his perpetual lateness.

When Shumlin was replaced with the less-indulgent Daniel Mann six days before the play opened, Dean lost his protector and reacted with more aggressively off-putting behavior. "The little son of a bitch was one of the most unspeakably detestable fellows I ever knew in my life," the play's writer, Ruth Goetz, recalled.[33] Dean could not get along with Mann, disapproved of his directing style, and described him in a rage of expletives behind his back. Mann remembered how strange the boyish Dean seemed to him, trying so hard to project an image of masculinity that he slid into a parody of Brando's *Wild One*, as though fighting against the role of Bachir. He disliked Dean's gruff attitude, his penchant for revving the engine of the motorcycle that he bought in Harrisburg that December for $475 (to his agent's great financial dismay) and raced through the streets with wild abandon, and the large knife he carried everywhere.[34] Mann considered him "very, very disturbed," and soon enough the production broke down into arguments over Dean. Just before the New York opening, producer Billy Rose exploded at Dean over changes Rose had made that Dean felt undermined the artistic unity and emotional power of the play: "Okay, Dean, this is Billy Rose talking! Shape up or ship out of here!" Dean, with calculated indifference, replied to a fuming Rose, "What did you say your name was?"[35]

Louis Jourdan as Michel (top) attacks James Dean as Bachir (bottom) for awakening his homosexual feelings in *The Immoralist. Photofest.*

But Dean's recalcitrance was not random pique. It flowed from two competing sources. The more cerebral concerned his disapproval of the production and unwillingness to devote his time and talent to what he felt would now be an artistic failure. The more practical surrounded the excitement that Warner Bros. had shown for Dean. Warner executive William Orr had been enthusiastic about Dean's audition for *Battle Cry* but now informed Dean that he didn't get the part. Over the long years, Dean had grown attuned to the trumpeting of destiny, and in that rejection he nevertheless had heard the sound of blaring brass. And one could only bow before fate. He suspected from Orr's enthusiastic reaction to his audition that Orr planned great things for him, so he had laid the groundwork to ensure he could leave *The Immoralist* unencumbered should Warner Bros. come calling again, even if his methods betrayed an adolescent's idea of sophistication.

When the show opened, WNBC's breakfast-time radio talk show host Jinx Falkenburg issued an on-air warning advising her listeners to stay clear of *The Immoralist* because of its homosexual content.[36] But when screenwriter Paul Osborn saw Dean in the play, he called Elia Kazan to tell him he had found a potential star for their new Warner Bros. movie, an adaptation of John Steinbeck's biblically inspired *East of Eden*. Steinbeck had written a multigenerational saga of familial strife and redemption in early-twentieth-century California echoing the primeval history of the book of Genesis, but Osborn's script stripped the book down to a narrower narrative focusing on the anguished, self-tortured Cal Trask, a troubled youth struggling to do right in a fallen world that had written him off. The story would concern his uneasy relationship with his distant father, his rivalry with his better-loved brother, and his reunion with his prostitute mother—unsubtle reworkings of the biblical Cain and his family in Eden.

Kazan viewed Dean's *Battle Cry* screen test, then called Dean in for a meeting at Warner Bros.' New York offices, and found himself taken aback by the surly, unpleasant young man who slouched on his couch, staring at him in silence. Dean had tried being charming on other directors' couches, and now he wore unpleasantness as an armor—"I'm not going to let them do that to me again," he told himself, recalling his past experiences. "This time I'm going to make damn sure of it."[37] Finally he offered to take Kazan for a wild ride on his motorcycle that the director did not enjoy. Kazan took Dean to meet Steinbeck, and Steinbeck found Dean as unlikeable as Kazan had. There was, they thought, an anger beneath his quiet mistrust and pained suspicion.

Steinbeck thought Dean a Brando wannabe, but Kazan, who had vowed to go to any extreme, no matter how abusive, to push actors into the performance he desired, saw something else, a hurt the confident Brando lacked. Dean "has balls and eccentricity and a 'real problem' somewhere in his guts," Kazan wrote to Steinbeck in March. "Dean has got a real mean streak and a real sweet streak."[38] Kazan was delighted to diagnose Dean as "twisted and sick." His motto had long been to turn trauma into drama, and he saw an opportunity to salt Dean's wounds in order to bleed art from him.[39] Yes, Kazan disliked Dean, but he really *was* Cal Trask, wasn't he? Steinbeck had to agree. Dean, too, felt very close to the role and saw himself in Cal.[40]

Kazan brought Dean in for screen tests. Shooting a shirtless scene with Richard Davalos as his brother, full of tension bordering on the erotic, he reached a moment of sublimity, painfully lamenting his inability to connect with his father and to experience real love. Kazan and the executives at Warner Bros. were in awe. He had spoken truth with the voice of the gods. But his earlier screen test with Paul Newman was far from sublime. Playing with his switchblade and fumbling awkwardly for words, he and Newman traded improvised lines until Kazan suggested they discuss which of them the girls would go for. Dean instead asked Newman to "kiss me," to Newman's giggles as they stared at each other through Dean's insistently erotic gaze. "I know its [*sic*] a hell of a gamble and all on my shoulders," Kazan wrote after deciding to cast Dean that March. "But I'm delighted to take it."[41]

Despite Dean's best, if unintentional, efforts to alienate everyone, even his self-sabotage fulfilled the destiny he had so long believed was his. The gods had played a terrible joke, for the pain, the suffering, the loneliness, and the longing that had made him so miserable all had conspired to clothe him in the raiment of the chosen one, to prepare him for this moment. The prophecies he had imagined for himself about the great work to come, about his pilgrimage to New York, about working with Elia Kazan—they fell into place with an inevitability out of an Aztec myth. Dean had learned a dangerous lesson. Fate had marked him for success, and it mattered not what he did. Some things were simply destined to happen.

8
HARVEST

Perhaps James Dean felt sure Elia Kazan would give him the nod, or maybe his rage at Daniel Mann got the better of him, because he submitted his two weeks' notice from *The Immoralist* on February 9, 1954, one day after it opened for previews, the earliest his actors union rules allowed.[1] He resigned a week before Kazan screen-tested him and a month before Warner Bros. agreed to a nine-picture contract and a $1,200 weekly salary. Critics had singled out the brilliance of his performance at the play's Broadway debut, particularly the sensual dance of homosexual seduction he performed with a pair of scissors—just like Bugs Bunny had done in "The Rabbit of Seville." But he knew no one would fight his departure. He had made few friends among the cast or crew, beyond a professional and sometimes sexual relationship with its star, Geraldine Page, for whom he made a series of sexually suggestive drawings.[2] Although Page came to care deeply about Dean, he evidently was far less committed.

Castmate Vivian Matalon recalled that over those weeks Dean would invite him to his apartment for a drink and try awkwardly to seduce him, stage-managing each attempt like a little play where he could be director and star. In mid-February, Matalon agreed to spend the night. Dean tried so hard. He played soft music, dimmed the lights, and was entirely disappointed when Matalon told him he would do nothing more than sleep in Dean's bed. On February 20, his twenty-third birthday and the play's Broadway opening

night, Dean asked Matalon why their friendship had faltered. Matalon said
he didn't want to fall for Dean only to have him protest that he wasn't queer.
Confused, Dean told Matalon, just two years his senior, "But you must
remember what I told you about Rogers Brackett. Well, you remind me of
him."[3] After his attempted seduction of Matalon failed, he spent more time
in Page's brass bed, trying unsuccessfully over a two-week period of frequent
sex to assuage an unfulfilled longing for true intimacy. Page fell in love. Dean
thought nothing of abandoning her once a better opportunity arrived.

In some ways, he felt he deserved to be hated. Now twenty-three, he often
found himself feeling lonely and isolated, longing for a closeness he couldn't
quite feel. He surrounded himself with people, most of whom thought they
were close or even best friends with him, but he could not form a deep and
authentic connection with any of them. In his mind, he had no truly close
friends in New York, not the kind with whom he could share his inner world.
Even he recognized the growing gulf between his deep thoughts about art,
history, and fate and his shallow understanding of people.

Those who called themselves friends spoke of how terrible he was at conversation, all mumbles and false starts, desperately unable to find words that
connected to others and only coming to life when touching on one of his pet
subjects.[4] They often gawked in bafflement at his behavior. He would show
up at their homes at all hours, settle into a chair, and stare at them, motionless for hours. One night, when he called his understudy Bill Gunn, Gunn
joked that he and some guys and girls were having an orgy. When Dean
invited himself over, he found the group, comprised mostly of teenagers, had
stripped off their shirts as a gag and arranged blankets over themselves to
pantomime an orgy. Dean played along but took it too far. He unzipped his
pants, pulled out his penis, began waving it about, and said, "Okay, let's go!"
The others couldn't tell if he had been serious or in on the joke, and feeling
"like we'd just been fucked with," in Gunn's words, no one felt comfortable
enough to ask about what happened.[5]

All of Dean's attempts at love had ended in some degree of failure,
and his tempestuous relationship with Barbara Glenn quaked, by her own
account, before her frequent barrages of screaming, selfishness, and invective. He absorbed the abuse in sullen silence, her emotions seeming to
prove he was at least worth caring about enough to berate. Glenn had the
unfortunate feeling that Dean saw her less as a girlfriend than as a mirror

of his mother, whom he discussed frequently in their first months together and whom he told her she resembled. She noticed how angry he was that his mother had abandoned him by dying and that no one afterward had understood him enough to provide him with the same love and security. She worried that he was becoming reckless and destructive as his sadness and rage grew in tandem with his career.[6]

She was right. He was, as always, indifferent to physical danger and death, which were for him but the gateway to a transcendent peace. He tore about on his motorcycle without concern for his safety. He fantasized about leaving everything behind to become a bullfighter, to die gloriously in the ring. "God gave James Dean so many gifts to share with the world," he had written on page 348 of his copy of Hemingway's *Death in the Afternoon*, opposite a photo of a dead matador, "has he the right to throw them away in the bull ring?" He color-coded passages in the book—*death* underlined in red crayon, *disability* in green, *disfigurement* in blue, and *degradation* in yellow—as though to convince himself to give up his fantasy.[7] He met a teenage actress, Arlene Sax, at the Metropolitan Museum of Art and took her out a few times, assuaging his loneliness by reading her *The Little Prince* while they listened to music. She thought him a genius and fell instantly in love. "I told him I loved him, but he pretended not to hear," Sax remembered three years later. "And then he said: 'You can't love me. And I don't think anyone can yet.'"[8]

In March, Dean wrapped his clothes in brown paper tied with twine and departed New York on his first ever flight, the predawn TWA Flight 91, courtesy of Warner Bros., his blue jeans fastened with a safety pin where the button had fallen off.[9] He pressed his nose to the window of the airplane, watching the lights of the darkened world shrink below him. He left behind his so-called New York friends with hardly a thought, despite the big party the owner of Jerry's threw for him the night before. His friends complained that he had used them and dropped them, but who among them, other than perhaps Page, had tried to fight for him? Even Barbara Glenn became only an occasional pen pal after a year's relationship. She soon took up with another man without Dean noticing. "Must I always be so miserable?" he wrote to her when he got to Los Angeles and again found happiness elusive. "I try so hard to make people reject me. Why?" He had no real answer. All he could say was, "Wow! am I fucked up."[10]

Elia Kazan had left instructions for Dean to eat well, get sunshine, and fuck a lot.[11] He wanted him healthy and handsome for *East of Eden*. A scant forty-eight hours after he arrived in Los Angeles, Dean showed up at Bill Bast's apartment in a rented convertible, roused him from bed at an early hour, and hustled him into the car for a trip to the Anza-Borrego Desert south of Palm Springs to get a tan. They had spoken only a couple of times over the past year, but now, all smiles and teasing affection, it seemed as though no time had passed. During the drive, Dean, confident and safe with the adoring Bast, said that he saw *Eden* as a stepping stone toward the transcendent greatness that lay beyond acting, beyond movies, and a way to take back what powerful men had stolen from him, to "fuck 'em like they've never been fucked before."[12]

On the way to their hotel in the sandy wastes of Borrego Springs, their car hit a small bird, and Dean pulled over to find the creature. He comforted the dying bird, whispering to it and holding it until it passed, and then buried the tiny body by the side of the road. He and Bast drove on to the hotel—a collection of bungalows, really—and found themselves the only guests. They relaxed by the pool and wandered beneath the endless blanket of shining stars, and when they returned to their room, Dean invited Bast to join him in bed. Bast hesitated. "Nothin' to be scared about," Dean whispered as they embraced beneath the sheets. Here, in the desert to the east of Hollywood's false paradise, now the only two people in their world, they had found a true Eden.

When the dawn broke, the two boys were happier than they had ever been. They rode out into the desert on horseback and shouted and whooped until laughter caused tears to roll from Dean's eyes. "Hello, America!" Bast cried with uncharacteristic exuberance. Bast named his horse Pegasus and said he would ride him straight into the sun. "I *am* the sun!" Dean shouted in reply. They spent a week in Borrego Springs, the most relaxed, contented week of their lives, a moment of innocence and peace, a holiday from history and destiny in a world of their own. They wished this might last forever. And in that better world beyond the stars, it might have.[13]

James Dean's happiness was forever incomplete, and as happened whenever he surrendered to his desires, he hated himself for his weakness and ran from it. When he first landed in L.A., he met his new Hollywood agent, Dick Clayton, of Famous Artists Corporation in Beverly Hills, who had offered to

comanage Dean's West Coast activities after being impressed with his performance in "A Long Time till Dawn."[14] Clayton—a "prince of a guy," in Dean's
words—told Dean and his New York agent, Jane Deacy, "I . . . understand
him and all his problems," though what those were he discreetly chose not
to say out loud, having discussed them behind closed doors.[15] He made plain
that Dean needed to be seen with starlets to prove his manliness, and Dean
understood personal and professional fulfillment could not coexist. No matter how much pain it caused him, he had to keep pushing toward the great
work that fate had marked for him.

However, the interlude in Borrego Springs had left Dean "very brown and
healthy looking," he wrote to Deacy in a letter addressed to "Mom," putting a
happy face on his professional future.[16] "Kazan is pleased." He realized, he said
in another letter, how badly he had treated his body over the preceding year.
"I was really run-down. I'm fatter now and feel much better. Tear myself up
in New York. Build myself up in Calif. (health and maybe career, huh?)." But
he also told her that the men at Famous Artists, aside from Clayton, "think
I'm a weird one, of course," and he signed off as "your little monster." She
wrote back with cheering words, begging him not to feel "so despondent."[17]

Shortly after his return from the desert, he got drunk and wrote his former
girlfriend, now confidante, Barbara Glenn—still "my girl" to him, albeit only
in an emotional sense—a maudlin letter on Clayton's stationery dripping
with self-loathing and guilt, exorcising on paper emotions he couldn't let
himself feel, masking words he couldn't say behind fictions and lies. "I don't
want to write this letter," he said. "It would be better to remain silent." But the
feelings wouldn't stay quiet. He asked why he felt compelled to push people
away, though Glenn would never know whom he masked beneath the word
people. "I WANT TO DIE," he wrote in sloppy capital letters. He protested
that the actresses Clayton set him up with in Los Angeles were "sterile, spine-
less, stupid prostitutes" whose attentions he had rejected, and he lamented,
falsely, "I HAVEN'T BEEN TO BED WITH NOBODY," and wouldn't until
filming of *East of Eden* ended. "I'm sad most of the time," he said. But in
unintentional acknowledgment of the literary fiction that glazed the hidden
truths inside his letter, he added that "writing in capitals doesn't help either."
He signed it, with irony, as "Jim (Brando)(Clift) Dean."[18]

In a more sober moment, he assessed his problem as a fundamental skepti-
cism that anyone could truly love him. "I see a person I would like to be very

close to (everybody)," he wrote to Glenn, "then I think it would be just the same as before and they don't give a shit for me. Then I say something nasty or nothing. Or I walk away."[19] Dean decided he would quit drinking, and he vowed that he would start seeing a psychoanalyst as soon as *East of Eden* wrapped to get to the root of his misery.[20]

It did not help that shortly after writing the first few of these letters, an April 28 notice arrived from the Selective Service informing him that he had been recalled for a second induction physical, which must have prompted a sense of panic about having to once more assert his claim of homosexuality, now as a Hollywood star-to-be, with the press scrutiny that entailed.[21]

Over the next few weeks, Dean gradually started pushing Bast away, somewhat unkindly, even taking to calling Leonard Rosenman his only real friend and confidant and undertaking a successful effort to have Kazan hire him to score *Eden*. Barbara Glenn replied to Dean's missives with a letter announcing her marriage to another man, and Dean wished her well and told her he knew he could never marry her and would make a terrible husband.

Back in L.A., after a few weeks shooting on location in Mendocino and Salinas, he entered, at the instigation of his agent, Dick Clayton, into an arrangement with a starlet, the Sardinian-born actress Anna Maria Pierangeli, who acted under the name Pier Angeli, to stage a relationship for the gossip columnists to gush over.[22] According to the papers, he was the bad boy; she, the angelic princess; and her overbearing mother, Enrichetta, the force keeping them apart, but in reality they spent relatively little time alone together outside of visiting each other's movie sets and posing for photos. It was true, however, that Mama Pierangeli disliked Dean, not least because he wasn't Catholic, and tried to keep him from her daughter. Angeli claimed that by late summer they had had but one dinner date, and that was with Dean's father and stepmother.[23] They both enjoyed the farce and each other's company—though without sex, Dean insisted privately both to Bast and to gossip columnist Kendis Rochlen.[24] To Jonathan Gilmore, whom he liked to shock, he joked crudely that the Italian girl tasted like a pizza, and he took to calling her "Miss Pizza," even to the press.

Angeli gradually developed affectionate feelings for Dean, and she came to see the long, mostly silent walks they took on the beach and the quiet rental cottage they briefly shared there as romantic interludes. "We were made for

Warner Bros. promoted James Dean's relationship with Pier Angeli as an epic romance, but it was never the love affair depicted in publicity photos. *Warner Bros./Photofest © Warner Bros.*

each other like no other man and woman," she decided years later, though in the moment she insisted she was *not* in love with him. "I must grow up first before I fall in love," she told a reporter at the time.[25] Against the crashing waves, he would talk to her about death and immortality, and from her incomplete mastery of English, she imagined he was planning their eternal life together. He was, instead, talking mostly to himself about whether his soul deserved a place in heaven.

He was living so many lives now—a different person to everyone who met him, confident and shy, wild and quiet, man and boy, straight and queer—breaking himself into pieces that no longer locked together into a coherent whole. Could such a fractured soul achieve perfect peace in the world beyond?[26] He brought a revolver to the studio and kept it in a drawer in Dressing Room Q until someone at Warner Bros. quietly removed it.[27] He took to calling himself an "existential pencil"—seemingly solid but erasable at any moment.

For a time, Dean thought they might make something real of their relationship; he enjoyed her company and, in his way, had come to love her, or at least the idea of her, even if he got more of a thrill out of thwarting Mama Pierangeli's efforts to keep him away from Angeli than from their dates. So for the fifth time in five years, he considered proposing marriage to a woman he had known only briefly.[28] He filled in her name in a pamphlet outlining the Catholic rite for the solemnization of marriage and asked his agent, Jane Deacy, for advice. She told him not to get married just yet. He reconsidered. "I don't think I'm emotionally stable enough to do so right now," he confessed to a reporter that summer, perhaps thinking about his own conflicted sexual feelings, since he claimed to be "too neurotic" for marriage.[29]

But a darker concern stood behind his sudden change of heart. He sent a letter to Deacy that summer with an urgent query: Would a marriage void his claim of homosexuality and prevent him from receiving another 4-F exemption from service? He likely also wondered whether the newspapers would find out. "I don't know what to tell you," Deacy wrote in August after making inquiries. "I found out that if you get married, you have to advise your draft board, and whether they will re-examine you or re-classify you or what happens, I can't find out."[30]

But fortunately, the choice was made for him, for Angeli's infatuation was short-lived. She insisted that they were *not* going to get married. "I will get married only one time. So I must be sure," she told the press. "No, you cannot meet the first guy and fall in love right away and there you are. No, it is the wrong bit"—*bit* being theatrical slang for *way*.[31] By July they were already fighting frequently and loudly. They saw progressively less of each other in August, and Angeli officially ended things before September's end.[32] Within days, she was in the company of actor Vic Damone, becoming pregnant by him and marrying him in less than two months' time, with only a brief courtesy call to Dean. She told the press that she and Dean had only ever been "just friends." He pretended to be upset, adopting a hangdog attitude in public and writing to his father that he was hurt, but privately he told Bast that he felt nothing for her.[33]

Kazan was delighted. With a manipulative glee he barely concealed in recounting his actions in later years, Kazan had stripped away anything that he suspected might make Dean happy. Dean had bought a horse like the one he rode in the desert and jokingly called it his true love. Kazan sent it away. He bought a new motorcycle and a sports car, and Kazan moved Dean into accommodations on the studio lot so he wouldn't drive them. He tried to stop him from taking photographs, one of his artistic interests. He suspected Dean was sneaking off set to carouse with Angeli or other women and returning exhausted (he was actually suffering from insomnia and wandering the streets at night, drinking, smoking marijuana, and watching the whores ply their trade); therefore, Kazan tightened the leash and moved into a trailer next to Dean's on set so Dean could neither come nor go unnoticed. He plied Dean with chianti, employed unspecified "extraordinary means" to force him into Cal Trask's wounded and angry mindset, and stoked animosity with costar Raymond Massey, playing Cal's father, to realize their characters' estrangement until the two actors were at each other's throats. "Now I had Jimmy as I wanted him, alone and miserable," Kazan crowed.[34]

The director pretended to be Dean's friend, smiling and nodding through Dean's endless interest in the many photographs he took of himself and offering encouraging words, but privately he loathed Dean, thought him a narcissist, and gave no thought to the damage that his methods might inflict. Dean, who suspected enough not to trust Kazan, worried about the anger he kept trying to provoke in him to make Cal Trask real. He told Barbara Glenn that he feared his anger—that if he were to let it out, he might never be able to contain it again.

Kazan arranged for Marlon Brando to visit the set, ostensibly as a reward for Dean but really to intimidate him. Initially awestruck, Dean was all but unable to speak before his acting idol, and seeking Brando's favor, he let the actor believe that his new motorcycle was his first and bought in imitation of Brando's. Brando was unimpressed and thought Dean was mimicking him, in acting and in lifestyle. He, too, didn't care for Dean.[35] Privately, Dean groused that he was no mimic. He had been motorcycling for years before Brando ever bought a bike. "Brando drove a motorcycle for effect. I drive one because I know how," he later quipped.[36] But he nevertheless made something of a pest of himself that week trying to secure Brando's attention at a party.

Similarly, Dean tried to get closer to Rosenman, then scoring *Eden*, only to have Rosenman become cross at Dean's insistence that the two play basketball. "Why is it so important for you that I go out and play basketball with you?" he asked harshly. "Well, you know how a fellow feels," Dean said quietly. "It's like you want your father to play ball with you." Rosenman left Dean in tears by angrily rejecting the proffered role of surrogate father.[37]

Elia Kazan (left) arranged for James Dean (right) to meet Marlon Brando (second from left) as a clandestine tactic to intimidate Dean. Brando's dislike ended up making Dean angry. *Warner Bros./Photofest © Warner Bros.*

Dean wandered the Warner Bros. lot, sometimes when he was supposed to be shooting. In late July he found his way onto the soundstage where Judy Garland was filming the "Born in a Trunk" dance sequence for George Cukor's *A Star Is Born*, her first film in four years. There, standing in the shadows behind the lights shining down on Garland, a rising star on the brink of fame watched a fading one desperately trying to regain that glory.

On the last night of filming, Dean again broke down crying in his trailer.[38] "It's all over. It's all over," he sobbed. This thing that might have been his great work or at least the start of it was finished. Kazan had worked magic, and even Dean was in awe of the performance he gave, which captured a fallen angel, overflowing with a love that had no outlet in a world too harsh for him. The coming thing had finally come, and the struggle to fulfill fate's plan was now out of Dean's hands. But he also hated how much he resembled his character. He thought the sweet, misunderstood, damaged Cal "demonic," seeing only his own imagined inner evil.[39] He hated himself for his inability to let himself

James Dean lies on the Warner Bros. lot during the filming of East of Eden. Completing the film overwhelmed Dean and left him in tears, thinking his life's greatest work was now behind him. *Warner Bros./Photofest © Warner Bros.*

be loved, and he hated that placing his trust in someone inevitably ended in pain. He lamented that so many people thought him mean. "I'm really kind and gentle," he protested in a letter to Barbara Glenn.[40]

The burden of greasing the path to glory as handmaiden to destiny fell now to Warner Bros., which invested heavily in turning James Dean into the next

big star. He did not make it easy. He performed an obnoxious cartoon of his
adolescent models of masculine power—frat boys and jocks—and his anger
at the world transformed into contempt for life. He showed up to a formal
luncheon shirtless and in dirty blue jeans. He watered the Warner Bros. walls
with his urine. He tore about town on his motorcycle and collected a group of
sycophants and strays to accompany him, boys he called his "Night Watch,"
whom gossips whispered wildly were Satanists and cannibals.[41] He hired a
body double to ride by Pier Angeli's wedding on a motorcycle in full view of
the press.[42]

He joked crudely about sex, drank heavily, and appeared before photo-
journalists' cameras with a rotating parade of girls he neither cared for nor
remembered—Mamie Van Doren recalled how in their one brief encounter,
he took her out on his motorcycle, cupped her breasts, and promptly lost all
interest.[43] After attending a screening of Elia Kazan's *On the Waterfront*, he
intimidated Shelley Winters and Marilyn Monroe by dangerously circling his
roaring motorcycle around their car on the road to the Chateau Marmont, a
French-style residential hotel and celebrity gathering spot, and then spent an
awkward evening staring daggers at Monroe across a postscreening party and
muttering about what a vapid sellout he found her. She thought him shallow
and rude and dangerous. A frightened Winters, who had known Dean since
they attended the Actors Studio together, told him he was self-destructive,
demanded he see a psychiatrist, and offered to pay for a session with her and
Monroe's therapist, Judd Marmor, a prominent Freudian psychoanalyst.

Dean, now drunk, jokingly agreed, and he fulfilled the promise, techni-
cally. He spent the $25 hour sitting in complete silence. Unbeknownst to
Winters or Marmor, in late summer Dean had already started seeing Dr.
Carel Van der Heide, a Beverly Hills Freudian analyst fixated on uprooting
sexual anxieties. He soon added a second psychoanalyst, Dr. Bela Mittelmann, to continue analysis when in New York, but he stayed tight-lipped
about what he discussed in these sessions.[44]

In spite of his antics—or because of them—before *Eden* ever had its
premiere, Dean was already one of Hollywood's best-known new personalities, and he banked that his performance art—and it *was* all a performance,
however dangerous—would prove that his exceptional talent could force the
entertainment industry to bow before him no matter what. In "The Dark,
Dark Hour," a live episode of CBS's *General Electric Theater* broadcasted

just before Christmas, he tried to upstage the show's host and ostensible star, Ronald Reagan, outshining him with a histrionic performance as a young thug seeking a doctor's help for his dying buddy. "He seemed to go almost all out any time that he read his lines," an amazed Reagan noted.[45] In "Dark," Dean's character, Bud, holds Reagan at gunpoint before collapsing into a sobbing mess, offering what, in Dean's emotional delivery, became a dangerously homoerotic lament that the corpse he hugs tight was the only person ever to truly love him.[46]

Even in these months, at his wildest and earthiest, he still dreamed of higher things. He quoted Gerald Heard's *Pain, Sex, and Time* to friends and spoke of the transcendence that must inevitably come to him who masters the material and immaterial worlds.[47] As his thoughts swirled around death and immortality during the late nights that he held court with his "spooks" at Googie's, an angular, modernist coffee shop across from the Chateau Marmont, he became intrigued by an exotic older woman who slinked into his orbit. Maila Nurmi, a decade his senior, hosted a new KABC-TV showcase for horror and science fiction movies in the guise of Vampira, a busty, black-clad vixen somewhere between a Charles Addams cartoon and Dracula's daughter. She openly mixed pain, sex, and death into her beguiling and macabre on-screen persona, cracking jokes and skewering respectable society.

Dean met her through his new lapdog, Jack Simmons, a younger man who spent his nights at the Tropical Village gay club in Santa Monica dancing with men like Rock Hudson.[48] He had fallen in love with Dean at first sight, styled his clothes and hair after him, and offered himself in mind and body. Although Dean held his obsequiousness in bemused contempt—and pointedly refused Simmons's persistent requests for kisses and sex—he made use of his fawning devotion and repaid it by securing Simmons's first acting role, as Dean's beloved buddy in "The Dark, Dark Hour." Simmons had introduced Dean to Nurmi, and Dean found himself absorbed by the newspaper stories she had planted about her supposed supernatural powers and witchcraft. She found him attractive and thought he talked about death as a gag in her honor. She said they instantly felt a connection as outsiders because "we're both from other planets and didn't know our way around on Earth, you know."[49]

Although they became fast friends, they misunderstood each other. The unhappily married Nurmi wanted a sexual relationship. Dean did not. Nurmi thought Dean could help her rise from local television to movies, while Dean thought he had finally met his intellectual equal, someone who matched his deep interest in metaphysical questions of death and transcendence, who might see beyond the veil. She began to notice that his continued talk of death and the afterlife wasn't simply a put-on, and he quickly realized her feints toward cosmic understanding were just a performance. "I had studied *The Golden Bough* and the Marquis de Sade," he recalled shortly after, "and I was interested in finding out if this girl was obsessed by a satanic force. She knew absolutely nothing. I found her void of any true interest except her Vampira make-up. She has no absolute."[50] One night she asked him why he spoke so much about death. Was it a desire to reunite with his mother in heaven? No, Dean solemnly insisted, that wasn't it. Death was the "only way I'll ever know any peace."[51] She thought it a pompous answer, but he had sought in her feigned satanism a negative proof of divine grace and failed to find it. "It is necessary to arrive at goodness through a sense of the Satanic rather than the puritanic," he told a reporter around this time.[52]

As the new year dawned, the Reverend Edward L. R. Elson of the National Presbyterian Church in Washington, DC, the church that President Dwight Eisenhower attended, praised the commander-in-chief for revitalizing faith by "investing prayer with masculinity and religious action with a new manliness."[53] In Los Angeles, James Dean told Jonathan Gilmore, now a member of his "Night Watch," that he did not believe in the punitive morality of the Christian God. He believed only in freedom, and for him freedom—from society, from phony people, from his own pain—*was* God.[54]

9
A LONG TIME
TILL DAWN

In the fall of 1954, *Rebel without a Cause* author Robert Lindner prepared a two-part excerpt from his forthcoming book, *The Fifty-Minute Hour*, to run in the December 1954 and January 1955 issues of *Harper's*. He wrote of an extreme case of psychosis, his recent analysis of an important government researcher, whom Lindner masked under the name Kirk Allen. Allen worked on top-secret military projects and had become convinced he was in contact with space aliens and visited other worlds to live a heroic life akin to Buck Rogers or John Carter. The military had asked Lindner to cure Allen of his madness for fear that he posed a national security risk. Lindner traced the delusion to his governess raping him at the age of eleven, a trauma that filled him with feelings of evil and sin, which he repressed through a retreat into science fiction novels and pulp adventure stories and the esoterica of Charles Fort. This young man, now in his late thirties, had come to believe that space operas were his own biography; the characters, his other lives. "My everyday life began to recede at this point," the young man recalled. "In fact, it became fiction—and, as it did, the books became my reality."

Allen's distant father had died when he was a boy, his mother abandoned him, and all that remained were the stories. Isolated and alone, he found it impossible to make true friends at school, and his intellectual gifts set him further apart from the other boys. He came to believe that space and time had folded in on one another, that past and present had merged, and the books—the stories—recorded a future he lived in a parallel dimension on worlds beyond his own. This life on Earth was perhaps a punishment. Over the course of two decades, Allen wrote 12,000 pages of the "history" of his future life among the stars.[1] And for the second time, Lindner had accidentally recorded a twisted prophecy and mirror of James Dean, as he would soon realize himself. Lindner had recently found out that *Rebel without a Cause* was finally coming to the screen.

When Jimmy Dean arrived back in New York in January 1955, with twenty-six-year-old photographer Dennis Stock in tow to document his Manhattan lifestyle for *Life* magazine, he noted that a half-year mostly away from the city had left him an outsider, no longer a part of the crowd. It wasn't home anymore. No place was. When friends on both coasts asked about the heaps of clothes unhung in his closets, the beer cans and empty cups and piles of books on the floors of two apartments, he shrugged and said these rooms weren't home, so why bother? For him, an apartment was just a "wastebasket with four walls."[2]

Stock and Dean spent hours cleaning his New York place to make it presentable for pictures, but that just made it seem as cold and empty as the parties he faked his way through that month. He shot a couple of TV shows to air later in the year, including a piece for *Schlitz Playhouse of Stars* called "The Unlighted Road," playing a young man who confesses to causing the car accident that he thinks killed a state trooper, unaware that the man was already dead and not a police officer. The theme of guilt for an imagined sin was not unfamiliar, but television now seemed small compared to the movies. One evening, after several sleepless nights, a friend handed him an amphetamine pill to help him stay alert through a performance by his new friend Eartha Kitt.[3] By intermission, the pill had kicked in, and for the first time in his life, he felt good—so good he couldn't contain it. He called another onetime friend, Martin Landau, from a pay phone.

"It's Jimmy!" he shouted quickly and with excitement. "I feel just like you. *I feel terrific!* Jesus, is this the way you feel all the time?"[4] When he hung up, his unceasing laugher faded from Landau's ears. But Dean's question lingered.

On January 4, 1955, Warner Bros. announced that James Dean would star in a new picture, *Rebel without a Cause*, directed by Nicholas Ray. It was the culmination of Ray's months-long effort to attach the studio's most dynamic new star to Warner's least-desirable mothballed project. The forty-three-year-old director had spent the preceding year watching the Army-McCarthy hearings—which had brought down the Red-baiting, antigay Senator Joseph McCarthy—and Estes Kefauver's juvenile delinquency investigation and seeing in them a morality play with uncomfortable similarities to his own life.

Ray had come up through the theater and the movies, as an actor and then as a director, through the friendship and patronage of Elia Kazan. Like Kazan, Ray had been an indifferent member of the Communist Party in the 1930s, worked in left-leaning theater groups, and had been the subject of an FBI investigation. The bureau tracked him for years, consumed with the idea that he was secretly writing communist propaganda. J. Edgar Hoover personally signed off on secret orders to take Ray into custody as a subversive in the event of a war with the Soviet Union. Ray's name also appeared in the files of the House Un-American Activities Committee, but unlike Kazan, Ray was never called to testify because his then-boss, Howard Hughes, shielded him.

In the summer of 1954, Ray had begun to ponder the effects of an oppressive culture of paranoia on young people. He had a strained relationship with his own teenage son Tony. His wife, the boy's stepmother, had seduced Tony when he was just thirteen, and Ray had kicked them both to the curb, angrier at his son for allegedly instigating a seduction than with his wife for raping a child. By fall, Ray found inspiration in news reports inspired by Kefauver's efforts, especially a pair of early September pieces on "vicious young hoodlums" in *Newsweek* and a cover story on why teenagers "go wrong" in *U.S. News & World Report*, the latter article being an interview with a Kefauver staffer.[5] "I want to do a film about the guy next door," Ray told a friend a few days after the magazine pieces ran, someone who "could be one of my sons."[6] He tried to sell Warner Bros. on the idea, and the studio offered him *Rebel without a Cause*. Ray didn't like the story, but the studio told him that if he had an idea that they could at least hook to the book, then they'd give him a relatively free rein.

Two weeks after *Newsweek*'s cover story, Ray had his big idea. He wrote a sensational, wild treatment for a melodramatic extravaganza of three youths in crisis—a teenage hero in a knife fight, a teenage girl stripped and whipped, and a teenage psychopath consumed with rage—and of a suicidal car race, called a "blind run," that ended in flame and gore and death. Remarkably,

Jack Warner approved the project, contingent on more tasteful revisions and the use of the *Rebel* title, which Warner controlled. Ray attended a few lectures by Robert Lindner, who futilely encouraged Ray to use more of his book in the movie.

As Ray started to work on turning his idea into a filmable movie—with the unproductive help of *Amboy Dukes* author Irv Shulman—he became possessed of the idea that destiny guided the production, that this film would be his great work, a masterpiece that would stand athwart history, stand against McCarthy and Kefauver, stand for the young against a world that had failed them. Full of grandiosity, he rejected Warner Bros.' offer to put Tab Hunter in the lead role, and when Elia Kazan showed his friend a rough cut of *East of Eden*, he felt a thunderclap of inspiration: The boy playing Cal Trask would be his star, reprising the damaged, conflicted, loveable character in a modern setting.

He set about befriending Dean, inviting him to weekend parties at Bungalow 2, his home at the Chateau Marmont. He proudly introduced his star to agent Clancy Sigal, just twenty-eight but respected for his feel for young audiences' tastes. "The kid," Sigal replied after meeting a surly, barefoot, and unwashed Dean in Ray's Burbank office, "is monosyllabic, possibly retarded, and needs a bath."[7] But by then Ray had already developed a fixation on the boy who sat reading a book with his feet propped on the desk, ostentatiously ignoring them. He did everything he could to lure Dean into the picture, despite Dean's insistence that he was instead angling to be cast in George Stevens's production of *Giant*, a sprawling epic about the decades-long rivalry between a cattle man and an oil man in Texas.

To seal the deal, Ray traveled to New York and spent time with Dean in his fifth-floor apartment, listening to his grandiose lies about the room once being Brando's. The more he watched Dean, the more he felt that Dean possessed a "desperate vulnerability" born of a desire to belong, mixed with a fear of belonging. Ray introduced Dean to his son Tony, now seventeen but still in a long-running sexual relationship with his former stepmother. Ray encouraged the two to bond, and Dean took Tony Ray to a series of raucous musical parties with his New York acquaintances. Dean had already heard the scandalous stories about Ray's family but got along well with younger boys, and the gambit helped turn Dean's attention toward *Rebel*.

To secure James Dean's participation, Nicholas Ray (right) ceded extraordinary power to Dean, leading *Rebel without a Cause* to take on the shape of Dean's life. *Warner Bros./Photofest* © *Warner Bros.*

After the two young men charmed each other, Dean took the elder Ray to dinner at an Italian restaurant and showed off his mastery of the intricacies of his now-favorite cuisine. Over dinner, he staged a comedy of manners as a bit of black humor, a display of power, and a warning born of unpleasant memories. He put on a troubled air, as though he had something serious to say, and Ray anticipated him announcing he would be signing on to *Rebel*. Instead, at the key moment, in deadpan earnestness, he told Ray, "I got crabs. What do I do?" After watching Ray slink into a nearby pharmacy to buy him medicine for pubic lice, he smiled at the director. "I want to do your film," Dean told a humbled Ray as he walked away.[8]

The months Dean spent in New York from the late fall of 1954 to the upcoming premiere of *East of Eden* in March 1955, punctuated by regular business trips back to L.A., had the surreal quality of a personal apocalypse. His old, gray Manhattan, even his old self, were dying, and the eternally new Hollywood and his new life suddenly awaited his second coming. He pushed away Jane Deacy, leaving unanswered her pleading letters asking to hear from him. A December preview screening of *East of Eden* had been a smashing success, but the triumph of the crowd of young people cheering wildly for him at a theater in Huntington Park contrasted with Bill Bast's pained reaction.

Dean had asked Bast to sit with him to watch his debut feature, but Bast demurred, concerned that he might become emotional and cause a scene in front of the press. Once the movie ended, Bast fled the theater before Dean could find him. Dean slipped away from the gala audience and followed Bast home. When a knock at the door produced no response, he climbed in through an open window and found Bast crying in the bathtub, unable to control himself after seeing the soul of the boy he loved splashed across the screen, all of Dean's conflicts between his boundless desire for love and bottomless fear of inner evil laid bare. Dean kissed Bast softly and told him to let his feelings out. They sat together and quietly mourned what could not be, tears echoing off cold tiles, and then Dean left to rejoin the cheering crowd.[9]

In New York, he spent a sad party following Liz Sheridan around, looking for a connection no longer there. At another gathering, claiming to be bored with life, he carried a chair out into the street and sat in the busy road, daring traffic to hit him. "I just wanted to spark things, man," he said when the other guests tried to pull him back. At a dinner with people he had once considered close companions, he stopped midmeal, asked loudly, "Where are my friends?," and walked out.[10] In Los Angeles, Sammy Davis Jr. recalled how strange he found it that Dean had no interest in "chicks" or alcohol and would sit quietly alone at Davis's parties. Davis tried to pair Dean up with eager young women. "You a little shy? Is that it? You want me to fix you up with one of the chicks?" Davis asked. Dean smiled, shook his head, and responded, "Man, all I want is to be a good actor." Davis told him his lack of interest in women made him seem dead, and he walked away in a mixture of confusion and disapproval.[11]

In the weeks before the *Eden* screening, Rogers Brackett had come back into Dean's life, unbidden and unwelcome. Since November, Brackett had been calling Jane Deacy, "on the warpath" and demanding that Dean repay him $1,200 for the years he supported Dean.[12] Now, Foote, Cone & Belding had eliminated his position, and Brackett was short of cash as he planned a doomed opera with the eccentric Alec Wilder, his dear friend and fellow member of the Algonquin Hotel circle.[13] He imposed on Dean for a drink and, striking a more conciliatory tone, asked him for money—a loan, he called it. The brazenness of the request shocked Dean, who had come to believe his time "dancing" for Brackett's friends had been abusive. "Sorry, pops," he said to Brackett, refusing to give money. He told him that he had outgrown him, that he no longer wished to see him. But privately he was furious.

Wilder, twice Dean's age, reminded Dean that they were all friends for many years and he and Brackett had given him the help that launched his career. The undercurrent threatening public scandal should Dean refuse was obvious. He upbraided Dean for his unkindness, demanding Dean write a letter of apology and shouting that Brackett should sue Dean for all the support he had given him over the years. "I didn't know it was the whore who paid," Dean shot back. "I thought it was the other way around." He reluctantly signed his name to an apology Wilder drafted, likely to avoid the risk of bad press, and he pasted on a smile when Wilder unexpectedly staged a reunion with Brackett later in the week. But he vowed never to see or speak to Brackett again.[14]

Brackett still kept an old photo of Dean in his wallet, sitting unclothed in a tree, from a photo shoot Daniel Blum, the lecherous editor of *Theatre World* magazine, commissioned for his private collection of young male nudes. Whenever he looked at the picture, he cried.[15] But he still took Wilder's advice and on January 28 had his lawyer send Dean a formal legal demand for the $1,200 he had informally badgered Dean about for months, supposedly for hotel bills and living expenses from the time they met in 1951 until January 1, 1953, the date he considered the end of their relationship. The letter came with the implied threat of exposure should the rising star not "liquidate your obligation"—that is, pay Brackett off.[16]

Shortly after, Dean asked Barbara Glenn if he could meet her fiancé before they wed, and he charmed the new man during an amicable restaurant dinner. "He's good for you," Dean told Glenn sadly. He asked her—begged, actually—to speak privately, so Glenn visited his apartment the next day, with trepidation. She found him sitting beside a suitcase filled with cash, which he demanded she take, displacing the past weeks' sadness and rage onto a softer target. Confused, she asked if he were trying to repay her the money she had spent on him during their intermittent relationship. "You can't leave me, Barbara," he said. "You can't go. We can't end like this." She left, and he followed her down the five flights of stairs, yelling at her, angry that twice in two months a former girlfriend had married into bliss while he remained frozen in time, sad and alone. He threw fistfuls of money down the stairs at her—apparently wanting to ensure no one could again demand repayment from him—and as she left, he shouted from the landing, "And when I die, it'll be your fault!" She closed the door and walked away.[17]

Around the same time, Brackett filed suit for the slightly lesser amount of $1,100 in New York's Municipal Court, including $450 in hotel bills and the remainder in support and personal loans. Dean quietly agreed to an $800 settlement, in $100 weekly installments beginning March 28, to avoid a scandal when he could least afford one, just two days before the New York premiere of *East of Eden*. Dean agreed to compensate Brackett for the gifts of cash and goods, but he refused to pay the hotel bills. Shelter, he felt, couldn't reasonably be described as a loan. Brackett accepted the offer with one caveat: If Dean failed to pay him the full $800, the Municipal Court would hold him responsible for the full $1,100. After Dean paid all $800, apparently at least six weeks ahead of schedule, Brackett signed a form releasing his claim on Dean on April 6, 1955.[18] Jane Deacy quietly convinced Warner Bros. to pay Brackett a sizable "finder's fee" in addition to ensure his continued silence.[19]

Back in Hollywood, Shulman's script for *Rebel without a Cause* was proving unsatisfactory. Nicholas Ray had provided a rough outline from an earlier failed screenplay, and by the end of January, Shulman had written a violent, dark tale about four teenagers who leave a high school lecture at a planetarium. The youths commit a series of escalating crimes, culminating in one taking the others hostage in a fit of jealous rage over losing his best friend to a girl. He blows himself up with a grenade after the police shoot him

MUNICIPAL COURT OF THE CITY OF NEW YORK
BOROUGH OF MANHATTAN : FIRST DISTRICT

- - - - - - - - - - - - - - - - - - -- - - -x

ROGERS BRACKETT,

                     Plaintiff,

          -against-

JAMES DEAN,

                    Defendant.

- - - - - - - - - - - - - - - - - - - -x

       The parties have agreed and stipulated as follows:

       1. The defendant acknowledges the jurisdiction of this
Court and admits the debt as set forth in the complaint and
acknowledges the truth of the allegations of the complaint to the
extent of the sum of $1100.00.

       2. The defendant acknowledges the debt of $1100.00 plus
interest from the 1st day of January, 1953.

       3. The defendant agrees to make the following payments
in full payment and satisfaction of the debt:

March 28, 1955	$100.00
April 4, 1955	100.00
April 11, 1955	100.00
April 18, 1955	100.00
April 25, 1955	100.00

RIDER 3A

      Notwithstanding anything in this agreement herein
contained, the amount to be paid, in full settlement hereof,
by defendant to plaintiff is $800.00, and the sum of $1,100.00
is acknowledged only for the purpose of and is to be paid only
in the event of default. Further, default shall not be held
to have occurred on the dates specified unless defendant is
receiving weekly payments as a regular matter on his present or
any other theatrical motion picture contract, provided, however,
that if the payments are not made as specified for this reason,
then they shall be made as soon as regular theatrical motion

The settlement agreement in the case of *Rogers Brackett v. James Dean* provides a rare glimpse into a relationship Dean fought to keep secret. *Author's collection.*

during a standoff. Ray, however, did not like the draft, and tensions started to rise between the two men. Ray wanted the movie to end in the planetarium, beneath the artificial cosmos—a "suggestion of classical tragedy," he said— but Shulman found that pompous.

Ray also wanted Shulman to bond with and take inspiration from his star, James Dean, to make for a more authentic script. Ray hoped that a shared love of sports cars would bond writer and actor, but Dean disapproved of Shulman's MG because it lacked a racing-grade carburetor, and he considered Shulman an automotive dilettante. For his part, Shulman, who was Jewish, expressed his disgust, born of the war years, that Dean had recently purchased a *German* sports car, a white Porsche 356 Super Speedster. To judge from the negative shading Shulman imposed on the character meant to reflect Dean, he deeply disliked Dean. The dustup over sports cars was the last straw. Forced to choose between writer and star, Ray removed Shulman from *Rebel*, though Shulman maintained he voluntarily quit to focus on turning his failed screenplay into a novel.[20]

Dean had recently met a shy, bookish, young, Oscar-nominated screenwriter named Stewart Stern at Stern's cousin Arthur Loew's Christmas party (unable to make conversation, Dean had mooed like a cow, and the two bonded by trading animal impressions), and Ray gave Stern a shot at revising Shulman's script, at $1,250 per week. Stern had a stroke of inspiration and suddenly saw the whole movie at once, almost a divine vision. Stern immediately decided that the movie needed a classical gloss, with overtones of Greek mythology to ennoble the youths crippled by society's uncaring caprice, the planetarium serving as a temple to absent gods in their empty heavens. Ray loved the idea. From there, Stern took Aristotle for his model and structured *Rebel* as a Greek tragedy depicting a lifetime of pain in a single symbolic day, from one dawn to the next. The story would now be about three teenagers with flawed parents who form an ersatz family in an abandoned mansion on the edge of civilization, able to find in each other the love and support society denied them, until the forces of violence and adult disapproval destroy their bliss.

To craft his characters, Stern drew from the movie's star, now his friend, molding the movie around James Dean's personality, the weight of Dean's years of longing, sadness, and pain resolving themselves into an inky dew.[21] Slowly, under Dean's gravity, the elements Warner Bros. had wanted for the story—the delinquency, the violence, the gang wars—fell away, replaced with something sweeter and sadder. But the parts did not quite gel. Stern imagined the story as a love match—a *Romeo and Juliet* story, Ray requested—between a boy and a girl, Jim Stark and Judy, with a second boy, named Plato, who would idolize Jim and die, a "sacrifice on the steps of the temple."[22] But in classical tragedy, the sacrifice must be meaningful, something beloved and lost. What loss did this boy's death represent?

Two weeks before Stern delivered the final script, Dean was still uncertain whether it was good enough, and then he realized what was missing. "He believed that the cry of the world is for tenderness between human beings— all human beings—and he felt that to be tender requires more courage of a man than to be violent," Stern recalled. "Men are brave enough for war, but not yet brave enough for love."[23] This realization would inform Dean's approach to performing Stern's script and improvising as he acted. However, both Dean and Stern recognized that this gentleness—Dean's own gentleness—was "considered by society as unmanly."[24] Meanwhile, Ray proceeded to cast the movie as though it would still be a violent gang picture, staging bloody fights between potential actors to find the toughest boys for their roles.

James Dean spent a week in Fairmount with Dennis Stock, shooting photos for a *Life* magazine spread to promote *East of Eden* and film footage for a planned documentary. The trip had the uneasy air of a wake. Friends and family eulogized him to Stock, and Dean spent a surreal evening attending a Valentine's Day dance with the kids at his former high school, the ghost of his own teenage past. He climbed into a casket for sale at Hunt's General Store and insisted that Stock photograph him inside, eyes haunted and pleading. *Life* labeled him "moody" in its March 7, 1955, piece, and Dean seethed that *Life* refused to publish what he considered the best photos.[25] "Printed some stuff of me around the farm. Country boy—that routine," he scoffed in an interview afterward.[26] The brief text accompanying the photos told America that Dean's "incessant self-analysis" was "sincere, though it may seem to others like theatrical posturing."[27]

Readers might have been forgiven for thinking the many photos, and others like them, depicted different men. In some, like a sublimely sly shot of him posed in classical contrapposto next to a pig, Dean appears smooth-faced, boyish, years younger than his age. In others, his face is contorted, creased, a decade beyond the twenty-fourth birthday he celebrated on February 8. A sculptor he met that spring found the effect disconcerting. When Dean flashed him his full smile, the awkward, lanky youth erupted into a supernatural vision. "He smiled, his dimples appeared, and he suddenly transformed himself into the most beautiful person I had ever seen," Kenneth Kendall recalled, paralyzed before the angelic sight.[28] Gossip columnist Louella Parsons and screenwriter Andrew Solt both noted the same effect, astonished that the small, feral, almost-frail boy could inflate into a commanding presence on-screen or with just a smile.[29] Like the shifting vision of a half-formed memory of himself, Dean could seem physically, not just mentally, two men, both Dorian Gray *and* his picture.

Dean worked tirelessly to manage his image. He charmed the doyen of the gossip press, Hedda Hopper, whom he disliked, by appearing clean-cut and respectful and speaking expansively about longing to play Hamlet as a stumbling, searching youth.[30] He earned gossip columnist Joe Hyams's affection, by sharing regular pints of raspberry and coffee ice cream with his young son, and his respect, by confessing mostly false stories of nightly sexual conquests. He ritually denounced communism to the *Los Angeles Times*: "I hate anything that limits progress or growth. I hate institutions that do this," he said. "I hope this doesn't make me sound like a communist. Communism is the most limiting factor of all today."[31] Thinking undoubtedly of Rogers Brackett's legal claims, he told the *New York Times* that he was self-made, the product of no help. Reviewing proof sheets with the photographer Frank Worth, he drew an *X* over any picture that he thought made him look weak, vulnerable, or needy. "I don't want people to see me that way," he warned.[32]

Celebrity magazines listed him alongside Rock Hudson and Tab Hunter—both leading secret gay double lives—as one of Hollywood's most eligible bachelors, but he was well aware that unlike them, he had neither the military musculature nor experience to shield him from questions of masculinity. Publicity photos taken on the *Rebel* set with Hunter struggled to make the diminutive Dean appear an even match to the strapping, six-foot-tall Hunter.

Such natural advantages let Hudson and Hunter lead double lives with relative ease. Men like them could attend secret gay orgies unseen by the press and have boyfriends so long as a pretty girl accompanied them to movie premieres, but Dean had to indifferently date starlets, occasionally take them to bed, and lie, sometimes outrageously, about escapades with them to friends and colleagues to ensure the right kind of gossip—the right stories. "It had to do with the columnists, who he was seen with," Leonard Rosenman recalled.[33] Dean tended to wander away from his dates middinner to join his male friends, leaving the interchangeable actresses resigned to eating alone.

Nevertheless, many women told the gossip columnists how attractive they found his complete lack of interest.[34] When he did show interest, it sparked the wrong kind of gossip. He developed one of his infatuations for a young woman at Googie's who had lost a leg in a motorcycle accident. She subsequently described how he had helped restore her self-confidence, calling her special and showing no fear of her partial leg—"it's beautiful, and you're beautiful," he insisted. But the gossips, fearful of difference, tittered that he had become morbidly obsessed with mutilation, and they imagined the platonic friendship included perverted sex acts.[35]

Dean's idea of the *right* kind of gossip, however, exasperated his bosses at Warner Bros. That spring, he seemed to purposely tear about Los Angeles performing the part of daredevil loner, breaking all rules of social convention, offending anyone and everyone, and ensuring he was always in exactly the right place for his calculated outrageousness to make the papers. Introduced to one of Jack Warner's biggest investors, he performed a perfectly timed comic satire of his role as profit generator, tossing his pocket change at him and sauntering off. The best the Warner team could do was to extract a promise that he would stop urinating in public. He made a special point of eating at Barney's Beanery, a West Hollywood café with a sign over the bar in all capitals: "FAGGOTS—STAY OUT." With an impish smile, he declared, "That's why I like coming here."[36] He never did care to obey rules.

He nearly lost his life on Sunset Boulevard. When Warner Bros. ordered Dean to vacate his trailer on the Warner lot, Dick Clayton had given him his apartment on Sunset Plaza Drive, where Dean had once lived with Rogers Brackett.[37] When Dean sped through a red light near his apartment on his motorcycle, he missed crashing into a car by inches, spared by luck, skill, or the gold St. Christopher medal he wore on his belt. Separately, Bill Bast saw him driving drunk in his Porsche, careening with strangers before a race he had entered. Competitive auto racing was his newest momentary passion and one he mastered instantly, coming in second on his first try, to the amazement of his competitors but disappointing himself. He had expected to win.

This new, assertive James Dean seemed at such odds with the quiet, sensitive boy of a year or two earlier that some wondered if he had developed a split personality or if stardom had gone to his head. Brando had told him he needed a psychiatrist, which convinced Dean that Brando hated him, so in retaliation Dean called him in the middle of the night and blasted Big Mama Thornton's "Hound Dog" into the receiver, her lyrics telling Brando he was no friend.[38]

Those who looked closely noticed that at times he would seem to forget to cloak himself in his aggressive parody of masculinity and the softer boy inside the character wore through. The hunched brooding would give way to excited curiosity. Even his voice would change, thin and clear and eloquent, before he remembered himself and snapped back into a macho mumble.[39] Few looked so closely. There had always been two Deans, a public face and a private, though rarely were the two halves of his bifurcated life at such extremes. Dean shrugged and said that others saw only as much of him as they wanted to see. "People sit and listen to me until I say something that fits in with what *they* figure I'd be like," he told *Seventeen* magazine. "That's the part they write down. Then they say, 'Dean, hughh! That character!'"[40] Bast noticed something else: a deep fear, a fear of the moral and artistic compromises that becoming a star would require.

In his longing and his fear, he turned toward the spiritual, reading books of Eastern mysticism and the Western occult and thinking about this life and the next. He always felt an unease that the world was less than solid. Now, in his tireless search for whatever truth lay beyond reality, he latched onto "The Mysterious Stranger," a solipsistic fable by Mark Twain in which the angelic son of Satan reveals an electric truth about existence: that all people and their rules and beliefs are the "silly creations of an imagination that is not conscious of its freaks—in a word, that they are a dream, and you the maker of it. The dream-marks are all present; you should have recognized them earlier." Twain wrote, "It is all a dream—a grotesque and foolish dream. Nothing exists but you. And you are but a thought—a vagrant thought, a useless thought, a homeless thought, wandering forlorn among the empty eternities!"[41] So Dean's Hamlet now danced alone through a desolate Elsinore, overturning chairs and smashing windows, daring the uncaring cosmos to prove the world beyond him real.

The final *Rebel without a Cause* script late in March did little to assuage Dean's metaphysical concerns or his sense that his past was folding into his future. Stern had arranged the story as a Greek tragedy, and he layered onto it overtones of the End of Days—which must have seemed to Dean a surreal addition to a story built partly on his life. An early scene set in the planetarium featured a discussion of the death of the universe, the characters mirroring the zodiac circling the faltering heavens, their fates written in the stars. Plato asks Jim, "You think when the end of the world comes it will be at night?" Jim replies, "No. In the morning." The story revolves through a single day, ending at dawn. After a night that features Jim confronting his failed parents, watching a boy die during their drag race over a cliff's edge, and bonding with Plato and Judy in an abandoned mansion, the breaking dawn finds him comforting a suicidal Plato in the planetarium, where Plato has fled with a gun after wrongly thinking Jim had abandoned him to gang members attacking them. Jim talks him down gently, only for the police to shoot Plato dead anyway, leaving a devastated Jim to cry over his corpse. The tragedy bore a divine inevitability, indicting a world that had failed its youth at every level, from the dying cosmos emptied of its gods to impassive authorities and blinkered parents. But the structure of the story demanded an answer to its most pressing question: Why is Plato's death at dawn Jim's personal apocalypse?

"I wanted the role to have homosexual overtones," Stern later recalled of Plato.[42] Stern had taken inspiration from Shulman's draft script in which Plato became dangerously obsessed with Jim, but he stripped away many of the unsavory layers. He had in mind the close connections of intimacy he saw his fellow soldiers share during the war years, especially among the youngest, most inexperienced men—the kinds of relationships that had started the government's panic over homosexuality at war's end. "A lot of romantic attachments were formed before heterosexual encounters," he remembered. The same, he felt, applied to adolescent boys who sought affection wherever it might come until social pressure made it impossible. Plato would be, in his words, "that faggot character."[43] But he had stopped short of making those implications explicit in the script. Even his hints were too much for the studio. One suggested addition, possibly from Nicholas Ray, shocked Warner executives. "Jim kisses Plato?" read a horrified note from Warner production head Steve Trilling, who feared after reading a draft script that the two boys would kiss during a scene where Plato invites Jim to spend the night at his house. Stern denied writing any such kiss, and perhaps an audacious Ray had added it himself to Trilling's copy of the script, but Trilling nevertheless recommended that Jim instead stroke Plato's head. Warrner censor Geoffrey Shurlock went further and warned that nothing in their relationship should be allowed to imply a sexual connection. Even the word *punk* was excised because of its slang connotation of homosexuality.[44]

Dean not only disagreed but also seemed to take the notes as a personal challenge. Ray, too, sensed what was missing and took perverse pride in circumventing the Warner censors. For the story to work, for the climax to have meaning, Plato had to mean something serious and real to Jim. In Stern's script Jim's father is weak and emasculated, and his mother, shrill and domineering, which psychoanalysts insisted could cause a boy to develop homosexual feelings. It all started to come together. It was not enough for Plato to love Jim as Stern had planned. Jim would have to love Plato, as well. "Warners did not know what the hell I was doing," Ray said.[45]

Dean pushed Jack Simmons for the role of Plato, with all its loaded implications, but Ray thought him too effeminate, and not even Dean's best efforts to help him relax—which included staging a pissing contest over the wall of the old set of *A Streetcar Named Desire* where they were shooting screen tests—could help him butch up his performance.[46] Newly minted TV star Billy Gray was seriously considered. His first episodes of *Father Knows Best* that fall had revolved around his teenage character fretting about being seen as effeminate. But at the last minute, Ray found the right actor in fifteen-year-old Sal Mineo, who he felt looked rather like his own son Tony.

Mineo and Dean bonded over their shared love of New York City and fast cars, and both Ray and Dean saw what Mineo realized long after, that the young actor had developed a crush on Dean, bordering on love. "It was only years later that I understood I was incredibly in love with him," Mineo recalled. "But at the time, that feeling was something else. I never found men sexually attractive. No way. Couldn't even think about it. But I realized later that I was homosexually attracted to him. When he showed love to me, when he said it, that did it."[47] Ray seized on those feeling and instructed Mineo to play Plato as though Jim was the thing he most wanted in the world. Dean was blunter and advised Mineo to look at him the same way Dean looked at

Natalie Wood, the seventeen-year-old playing Judy. Theirs was to be a love story, albeit one cloaked just enough to elude the censors.

A test shot of the scene where the three characters take refuge from the world in an abandoned mansion took the theme farther than Ray knew the final film could show. As Wood remains mostly in the background on the *Streetcar* set, Dean and Mineo engage in horseplay, giggling uncontrollably

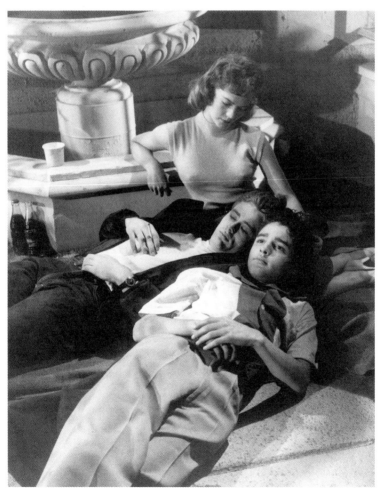

A screen test for Rebel without a Cause found James Dean and Sal Mineo displaying intimacy and attraction for each other as Natalie Wood (top) looked on, largely irrelevant. *Warner Bros./Photofest © Warner Bros.*

as they stalk each other around the set, intimately close, erotically charged, before collapsing into a pile of intertwined limbs. Another test shot found Mineo unable to keep his hands off Dean, who plays with Mineo's hand and gives him a kiss as Wood watches on Dean's other side. Many in the cast reacted negatively to what they saw as Mineo's obvious homosexuality, and they ostracized him. Dean, however, treated him with kindness, but he knew enough not to let Mineo's infatuation progress beyond friendly affection.[48] Meanwhile, Ray began having sex with Wood, three decades his junior, in violation of California's statutory rape laws.

Ray treated Dean as a beloved son, a replacement for Tony, indulging his rowdy troublemaking; lavishing him with praise; and giving Dean almost unprecedented control over the script, the blocking, and occasionally the direction of *Rebel*, so much so that his castmates would refer to it, with only minimal hyperbole, as "Jimmy's movie." In truth, it became two movies: the first, a story drawn from Ray's and Stern's lives about disaffected youths infantilized by bad parenting, and the second, a sympathetic, tender romance between two boys, animated by Dean's longing and thwarted desires.

But Dean seemed to realize that the story was a risk, and the thought of jeopardizing his career should it backfire scared him. As shooting began in Hollywood in late March, he fled to New York, called Stewart Stern, and threatened to leave the picture, saying he was uncertain whether he could trust Nicholas Ray.[49] His disappearance on March 28 coincided with the day his first payment to Rogers Brackett was due, and a little more than a week later, Brackett signed a note releasing Dean of further obligation, suggesting Dean used the trip to make financial arrangements that would free him to make *Rebel* the way he wanted. He returned a few days later, as though nothing had happened, confounding colleagues with absurdist humor and mercurial affections, an orphaned Marx brother. But unease was never far.

Both Dean and the movie grew during the month of shooting, as though Dean's life had become a supernova consuming everything orbiting him. Past and present merged in surreal, almost preternatural ways. The campus where Dean attended junior college became the façade for *Rebel*'s high school. The movie's climax occurred at Griffith Observatory, overlooking the place where Dean shot his first commercial. The future beckoned, too. When *East of Eden* opened, the spate of negative reviews savaging him as "sophomoric," "clumsy," "queer," and a "maniacal brat having tantrums" could not compete with a lavish ad campaign centered on his face, lifting the film to the top of the box office.[50] He delighted in being called the new Brando but chafed at many, including the *New York Times*, labeling him an imitation. "People were telling me I behaved like Brando before I knew who Brando was," Dean fumed in a *Los Angeles Times* interview ahead of *Eden*'s opening. "I have my own rebellions and don't have to rely on Brando's." He insisted that while he might have imitated Brando early on, "the more I work, the less I have the tendency to fall back on Brandoisms." He said that he had within himself expressions of emotion as or more "valid" than Brando's ready to come out.[51]

Critic Pauline Kael hailed him as a "beautiful, disturbed animal, so full of love he's defenseless," but warned against turning a "boy's agonies" into the "new and glamorous lyricism." She compared the viewer's "erotic gratification" in watching the alienation of Dean's gorgeous, broken boy to the "cult realities" of the homosexual cruising grounds of city parks and urban bath houses—an extravagant, unintentionally clairvoyant metaphor.[52] Young audiences reacted as Kael had so feared by cheering for *Eden*'s tortured protagonist, seeing in him an embodiment of the heroic tragedy of adolescence, a mythic figure somehow made flesh.

Elia Kazan hated watching Dean's performance overshadow his movie. "The goddamn kid became a legend overnight and the legend grew more intense with every showing," he groused. "It was a legend I didn't approve of." He thought Dean, like Cal, was "self-pitying, self-dramatizing, and good-for-nothing."[53] However, even he admitted that Dean spoke to young people in an almost telepathic way: "The audience didn't know who Dean was. But there was some kind of immediate recognition, the way two homosexuals can spot each other in a strange town."[54]

The girls screamed for Dean, and the boys wanted to be him, and Warner Bros. ordered Nick Ray to stop filming in black and white because *Rebel* would now be a prestigious widescreen CinemaScope *color* picture, in keeping with the status of its explosive star.[55] The switch to color necessitated a wardrobe change, and suddenly Dean's Jim no longer wore a black leather jacket like Dean himself. He now sported a flame-red nylon windbreaker over Dean's typical white T-shirt and blue jeans. The color was striking, lending an all-American gloss to a character originally conceived as a delinquent, and it made more visually dramatic the tender moment when Jim trades Plato his jacket for Plato's gun and Plato melts into it as though in a lover's embrace.

Dean poured into his performance all of the longing, the pain, the sadness, and the uncertainty he had experienced in life, and in his scenes with Plato, he made Jim's sparse dialogue suggest more than words could convey through gestures, glances, and tones. In scenes with Jim's parents, Dean played the alienated, confused kid, a ball of rage, but with Plato he embodied the classical

James Dean (right) advised Sal Mineo (left) to look at him with erotic longing, and Dean's body language signaled that the affection was mutual. *Warner Bros./Photofest © Warner Bros.*

ideal of father, brother, lover, and friend, that paradoxical, intoxicating combination, that highest ideal of love he had strived in vain to find for himself. Jim was gentle, protective, and sweet. When Jim zips the dead Plato into his jacket, into himself—so he wouldn't be cold in the hereafter—it becomes the perfect union of body, mind, and soul that Dean had longed to experience himself. Jim weeps uncontrollably for Plato, his deepest expression of love in the film, crying the tears of a father for his son, a husband for his wife, Achilles for Patroclus, a grief known only to heroes.

Against the power of Dean's grief, the film tacks on a brief epilogue in which Jim and Judy announce their union at dawn with halfhearted smiles

In trying to save a suicidal Plato, James Dean's Jim displays the ideal traits of father, brother, friend, and lover that Dean had sought for himself. *Warner Bros./Photofest © Warner Bros.*

as Jim's parents sputter in amazement that their son has taken up with a *girl*, an intentionally forgettable throwaway moment that closes the apocalyptic narrative.[56] Stern meant the final scenes with Plato and Judy to represent the end of boyhood. Dean played them as the end of the world. Something impossible had died, and inexorable, oppressive conformity held illimitable dominion over all.

10
THE UNLIGHTED ROAD

Dean's sense of metaphysical longing for some other world and his disappointment with this one eventually gave way to something like hope. He found the process of making *Rebel without a Cause* the most satisfying of his career, filled with a creative freedom he had never experienced, and he imagined himself becoming a director, starting a production company with Nicholas Ray, making movies meaningful to him.[1] He toyed with the idea of filming a biopic of his childhood idol Billy the Kid and adapting *The Little Prince.* He even hoped one day to transcend movies altogether and take on what he considered the hardest of creative jobs, to become a writer—"But I'm afraid of that one," he told a reporter.[2] First, though, he had another film already scheduled, having charmed director George Stevens into casting him in *Giant* after Alan Ladd declined the showy supporting role of Jett Rink, a driven young ranch hand corrupted by money and power. He had already started preproduction work while shooting *Rebel*, working with a coach to build his Texan persona and sometimes showing up on the *Rebel* set wearing his *Giant* cowboy gear.

But professional success invariably arrived in tandem with personal challenges. Late the previous year, Maila Nurmi tried to make use of Dean's growing fame to boost her own. She planted stories in the gossip columns that she and Dean were an item, infuriating him because she was so much older and in the midst of a divorce. The scandal was the wrong kind of gossip. He met with Hedda Hopper and via her column cut himself free from Nurmi in late 1954, denouncing her personally, professionally, and intellectually: "I have never taken Vampira out, and I should like to clear this up," he said. "I have a fairly adequate knowledge of satanic forces, and I was interested to find out if this girl was obsessed by such a force. She knew absolutely nothing! She uses her inane characterization as an excuse for the most infantile expression you can imagine."[3] Nurmi, angry that the blow came through *Motion Picture* magazine rather than in person, made her rebuttal in the gossip columns. "I'll challenge him to an intelligence contest any time," she said. She insisted that she wasn't "at all like the Vampira character. James Dean sought me out but was disappointed to see I'm not a character."[4]

Dean and Leonard Rosenman had another falling out when Dean showed up drunk at a party and announced Rosenman's infidelity with another woman in front of Rosenman's wife and friends. The infuriated Rosenman, also upset to owe his newfound Hollywood career to someone he considered untrustworthy and inferior, did not speak to Dean for a year and soon started spreading false stories. He spoke of Dean's lack of intelligence, scoffing that Dean "could believe he was an *intellectual*," and he darkly gossiped that Dean beat up his girlfriends.[5]

Dean found other rumors potentially more damaging, the curse that might destroy him. Persistent whispers murmured, "James Dean," alongside, "homosexual." The actor William Redfield recalled hearing that Dean had been involved with the gay actor Clifton Webb, which he assumed took a "sexual form."[6] Even the dialect coach Warner Bros. sent to train Dean to talk like a Texan for *Giant* had heard similar gossip and asked him about it. Dean tried treating it as a joke, offering witty half-denials. He also tried telling colleagues a limited version of the truth, burying sanitized confessions of his casting-couch traumas amid some truth and many lies about the girls he said he conquered. Though Dean had recently received a much-delayed second 4-F designation freeing him from military service, the letter he had sent to the draft board still hung over his head.[7] And even now in New York, Rogers Brackett was reading about Dean's "genius" in Hedda Hopper's column and telling the wrong people that he thought Dean had conned her worse than he had deceived him.[8]

Dean picked up a copy of Thomas Mann's *Death in Venice*, the story of a frustrated writer consumed with Platonic ideals of beauty whose life collapses into obsession and annihilation before his desire for a teenage boy. He knew it could all blow up at any moment. All April, he threw himself into ensuring the Swedish starlet Lili Kardell told all the right people about his sexual prowess, for as long as he could sustain the effort. She whispered to Joe Hyams that Dean had sex with her while holding his matador's cape, conquering her like a bull and using his penis as the bullfighter's sword.[9] Yet at the same time, he spoke vaguely to Bill Bast that when the summer's movie shoot ended and the publicity calmed down, they could share a place and live together again. It was as though Dean hoped to inhabit competing fantasies without needing to choose among them.

And then the thing he feared most happened, just not to him.

Robert Harrison, a former journalist with a blandly nondescript face, published men's magazines full of sadomasochistic sexual imagery. He also published *Confidential*, a self-proclaimed "uncensored" scandal magazine whose masthead boasted it "tells the facts and names the names." Under editor Howard Rushmore, a veteran of Joseph McCarthy's subcommittee staff, *Confidential* had twenty million readers, more than *Reader's Digest* or the *Saturday Evening Post*.[10] Rushmore devoted himself to exposing Hollywood communists and homosexuals when he wasn't drunk or high on amphetamines.

Harrison and Rushmore had heard rumors about Rock Hudson, now a major star on the heels of the previous year's *Magnificent Obsession* and the impending release of *All That Heaven Allows*. During a European tour in 1954, Hudson had shared a hotel room with his agent, Henry Willson, and it raised Harrison's eyebrows. By summer, Harrison knew there was a great story to exploit while the actor was up for the lead in *Giant*, a major prestige picture. He had already exposed matinee idol Van Johnson as a "lavender lad." Now, he and Rushmore assigned their best writer to the Hudson beat, and within weeks, Hudson's associates received lucrative lures. The reporter offered Hudson's former roommate, Bob Preble, $10,000. "We know this man is gay, Mr. Preble," the reporter said, "and we'll help fatten your wallet a little bit if you'll tell us everything you know about this gay bird."[11] Preble refused, but Harrison sent photographers to catch Hudson in the act, and soon enough one of Hudson's former boyfriends offered a photo of Hudson in flagrante, along with many stories.

Henry Willson stepped in to save Hudson's career—and his investment. Through backroom dealing, Willson secured Harrison's promise to kill the story in exchange for providing Harrison with dirt on the robbery conviction of Universal-International actor Rory Calhoun and the homosexuality of a star who had just fired Willson. Only weeks earlier, Tab Hunter, fresh off his star-making turn in *Battle Cry* (the role Dean lost to him), had publicly declared himself a perpetual bachelor because "marriage is for squares" in the pages of *Screenland*.[12] Now, the September 1955 edition of *Confidential* breathlessly reported that in 1950 Hunter had "landed in jail, along with 26 other good-looking young men, after the cops broke up a pajama party they staged—strictly for boys."[13]

Hudson had narrowly escaped disgrace, but even before the issue hit news-stands, the talk in Hollywood was that Hudson would need to marry, and soon, to avoid a repeat of the potential scandal. Henry Willson began casting about for a girl to become Hudson's wife. By late summer, he was officially "dating" Phyllis Gates, Willson's secretary, and speculation arose that they might be heading toward marriage. An obviously planted rumor swirled in fan magazines that they had secretly been married earlier in the summer.[14]

James Dean always had his ear to the ground and undoubtedly had heard enough to know what had befallen Hudson—it was well-known among both media and actors.[15] He certainly knew of the *Confidential* story about Hunter, on newsstands in late August 1955. Dean's agent, Dick Clayton, was Hunter's longtime friend, and the two actors vied for some of the same roles and went on fake publicity dates with some of the same women. The growing cry of tabloid features exposing public figures as secret homosexuals was swelling into a chorus through the pages of *Confidential*, *Hush-Hush*, *Uncensored*, and their rivals. Every week it seemed there was another: flamboyant pianist Liberace in March, automotive heir Walter Chrysler and movie star Marlene Dietrich in July, Tab Hunter in September. In its August 1955 issue, *Lowdown* launched a campaign to have the governor of Michigan pardon singer and teen idol Johnnie Ray for soliciting an undercover male cop, by arguing Ray couldn't really be sexually perverted because he was "nice" and had married a woman.[16] Similarly, Warner Bros. tried to forestall any speculation about Dean with planted features, like the one now on newsstands in *Motion Pic-ture*, "The Dean I've Dated," in which the studio had struggling starlet Lori Nelson, whom Dean once dated on his agent's advice, offer a lengthy and defensive portrait of the "hesitant" and "shy" Dean's very heterosexual dat-ing life.[17]

In August 1955, a magazine called *The Lowdown* launched a campaign to convince Michigan's governor to pardon singer Johnnie Ray for soliciting a male police officer, arguing that Ray couldn't be homosexual since he married a woman. *Courtesy J.D. Doyle.*

And yet the press kept hinting something was amiss. *Screenland* even groused that "brother Dean" was "unusual" after the magazine could find no woman he dated who considered him sexually robust, a "wolf," or "romantically aggressive." The magazine added that the "Theatre Arts set"—obvious code for *homosexuals*—was competing with America's women to embrace him.[18] It weighed on Dean. At lunch with his insurance agent, Lew Bracker, Dean said, seemingly out of nowhere, "You know, we have to get married." "To each other?" Bracker quipped, making a joke of it. Dean became upset. He did not find the joke funny. "No. We both have to get married and have families." It had become, he insisted, a necessity. "My days of fun are over," he told a reporter. "It's time to start being a man."[19]

On the set of *Giant*, Dean traded Leonard Rosenman's condescension for the warm encouragement of set photographer Sanford "Sandy" Roth, his wife Beulah, and their cat. Roth had earned Dean's trust by taking the wary young man aside and explaining that he wanted nothing but friendship, and neither would nor could do him harm. The Roths spent long nights discussing art and culture with him and welcomed him into their home and, too often, their refrigerator.

By contrast, his relationships with director George Stevens and costar Rock Hudson degenerated into recriminations and loathing. He thought them mediocre talents mechanically manufacturing a plastic product, not true artists. They thought him an unprofessional, self-involved jackass. Dean remembered every moment of working with Hudson for a day on *Anybody Seen My Gal?* a few years before, including Hudson making unwanted sexual advances toward him on set. Hudson had no memory of Dean but quickly grew to dislike him. Hudson called him a "prick," who was "selfish," "petulant," and "arrogant." In his darker moments, he thought Dean would steal the movie from him with his incandescent fame, and he wished him dead.[20]

In the lodgings they were forced to share, Dean reacted badly to the effeminate private behavior Hudson would put on for fun when relaxing from the performance of masculinity—girlish giggles; a swish to his hips; a campiness to his conversation; even, rumor had it, a penchant for wearing women's clothes. Dean still longed for a union of heroic equals, and even pretended effeminacy made him deeply uncomfortable. He quickly moved out but taunted Hudson as a "fairy" and one day pounced on him in revenge with an aggressive and unwanted kiss.[21]

Shooting exteriors in Marfa, Texas, Dean found himself isolated and alone, retreating into his character, and taking his meals by himself in a shed while the rest of the cast and crew dined together. He spent his off hours tramping out into the brush and shooting jackrabbits by the dozen.[22] He must have

On the set of *Giant*, James Dean (left) bonded with Elizabeth Taylor (center) but clashed with Rock Hudson (right), whose masculinity he considered a hypocritical false front. *Warner Bros./ Photofest © Warner Bros.*

flashed back to his childhood, the first time a friend handed him a gun and told him to kill a bunny. Back then, he missed on purpose several times, too sensitive to kill, and when a shot found its target, he wept for the poor creature. He, too, might have thought back to last year, when he comforted a dying bird on the road to Borrego Springs. But now he was a real man, and he blew away hares indiscriminately, and he felt nothing.

Even before they returned to Los Angeles in the second week of July to shoot interiors, Stevens had ordered his crew to keep a list of Dean's every infraction, no matter how small. "Wait for Dean 5:30 to 5:35," read a particularly petty July 2 entry. Dean responded in kind with growing frustration, urinating on and around the set, and his opinion of the movie fell in tandem with his mood, until he decided that it would be less a work of genius than just another melodrama.

Dean abandoned plans to rent a house in Laurel Canyon when tourists began surrounding it to get a glimpse of him, and instead he rented a furnished house in Sherman Oaks near the studio, a manly ersatz hunting lodge with an open floor plan, a bearskin rug, and no bedrooms, just a cavernous great room and a loft. He hung a noose from the ceiling, put his head in it as a gag, and told a reporter for *Modern Screen* it was all his "macabre sense of humor." He moved in with his beloved new Siamese kitten, Marcus, in the last week of July and within a week had already filled the house with stacks of books and boxes of records.[23]

Part of his displeasure stemmed from the challenge of the part he played, which exposed both his gifts and his shortcomings as an actor. Jett Rink ages thirty years in the film. Dean dominates his early scenes, playing a dark version of himself with an intensity that seemed to place him in a completely different film from his more traditionally theatrical costars. But his later scenes as an older, wicked man eluded his experience and thus his easy command of prior roles, despite the long hours of tireless preparation he put into each movement and line. His ability to channel the voice of the gods when actor and role merged translated into inchoate glossolalia when the union was less a marriage than a ball and chain. "He was brilliant as the young man," Rock Hudson said, "but he didn't know what to do with the old man."[24]

Consequently, he pushed too far. Dean got drunk to give authenticity to an inebriated banquet scene he did not feel worked in the film, but the impairment left him overestimating his delivery and lent the performance a misplaced comedic gloss. After three days of humoring Stevens's perverse desire to keep filming endless variations on a restaurant scene in which the older Jett Rink proposes to his rival's daughter, played by Carroll Baker—twenty-one hours of film for a scene lasting mere moments—Dean broke the repetition and ended the "great boxing match" between him and Baker that Stevens so enjoyed watching. He reached under the table, grabbed Baker's crotch, and squeezed. "I gasped," Baker recalled. "I wiped the tears of pain and humiliation from my glazed eyes." He silently apologized with a hug, and Baker could tell he felt bad about it. She forgave him.[25]

A saving grace became the relationship Dean formed with his costar Elizabeth Taylor. He purposely provoked Taylor early on by ignoring her, and when she demanded to know why, she proved to him she cared, and they became fast friends. She saw him as a wounded puppy, and he saw her as sensitive, caring, and (most importantly) safe. She described their bond as like siblings. They stayed up long nights talking, and Dean found that once he started to let slip bits of emotional truth, the words poured out.

He told Taylor that his minister—he almost certainly meant the Reverend DeWeerd—had sexually abused him, and Taylor felt that the trauma of that abuse had hurt him deeply and profoundly. "He would tell me about his past, his mother, minister, his loves, and the next day he would just look straight through me as if he'd given or revealed too much of himself, given too much of a part of himself away," Taylor recalled years later. As he shared more of his life, his loves, and his pain, Taylor developed the distinct impression that Dean was trying to tell her he was gay.[26]

Taylor often noted that most of her male friends were gay, but her close bonds with Montgomery Clift, Rock Hudson, and other men leading double lives made her more sympathetic than anyone Dean had confided in before. For the first time, he shared his deepest pain with someone who neither dismissed nor mocked nor blamed him. Yet even now, his discomfort and his fear prevailed. After baring his soul, he couldn't look Taylor in the eye and would sulk in silence for days, wracked with guilt or embarrassment, until he worked up the courage to share more of himself. Taylor wasn't wrong that Dean's wounds cut deep.

In August, Dean began dating a nineteen-year-old Swedish starlet, Ursula Andress, but the effort seemed to exhaust him. The gossips loved seeing Dean with the woman they dubbed "the female Marlon Brando," a moniker rich with symbolism, but when Leonard Rosenman saw them together at a party, he couldn't get over how closely the two resembled one another, much as the now-dismissed Jack Simmons had been a homunculus of Dean. "My gosh," he thought. "He's going with a mirror image."[27] Actress Joan Collins similarly expressed shock that Andress and Dean looked and dressed alike—similar hairstyles, wearing the same T-shirts and blue jeans.[28] And the observation was too true. In trying to see himself, he broke the mirror. "I don't really know who I am," he wrote to DeWeerd that summer, "but it doesn't matter."[29]

He and Andress fought constantly and loudly, and not always coherently, given her shaky command of English. She had known Jean-Paul Sartre in Paris and spoke expansively of existential philosophy. He could quote Sartre, too, but no one recognized his references. When Sandy Roth's wife, Beulah, noted Andress's existentialist leanings, Dean quoted Sartre's famous line,

"Existentialism? I don't know what that is," only to have her think it a serious question and patiently explain it to him.[30] He and Andress might have been an intellectual match, but Andress didn't think so, and he didn't care for the notes of condescension that crept into her philosophizing.[31] She decided he was nothing but a boy, and an inexplicable one, and left him to bang his bongos with the boys at Tablehoppers, a nightclub in West Hollywood, or spend his nights at home alone doting on his cat and recording on tape poems he composed about death and dying and being enclosed in a grave.[32] He drank a lot, and he studied *Hamlet* intently, hoping to play the title role on Broadway soon. "The time is out of joint," he read. "O cursèd spite. / That ever I was born to set it right!"

He refused a request the National Safety Council made to Warner Bros. for him to film a public safety announcement about the dangers of speeding until William Orr shoved him onto his dressing-room sofa on the *Giant* set and swore at him. "Listen to me, you little son of a bitch!" Orr shouted. "You've been nasty to a lot of people around here, but you're not going to be nasty to the whole country. You're going to go down and make this damned public service announcement, or I'll stand here until you do!"[33] Dean showed up, but he put in no effort, slouching and slurring his way through before offering a final kiss-off, altering the council's famous slogan, "The life you save may be your own," to "The life you might save might be mine."

Not only did Dean care little about speeding ("I'm not always in a rush!" he protested), but he also wanted a faster car so he could be a more competitive racer.[34] Dean ordered a Lotus Mark IX racing car from the United Kingdom, which was to be shipped without an engine or a paint job, to be customized and finished in the United States. Dean put down a deposit, but the car took too long to ship and wasn't scheduled to arrive until October at the earliest.[35] Therefore, in mid-September he traded his Porsche 356 Speedster for the new Porsche 550 Spyder on the advice of a mechanic he had recently befriended, Rolf Wütherich, and almost immediately got it banned from the Warner Bros. lot thanks to his wild driving. The new car was small, sleek, and silver, low to the ground, and streamlined into sensual curves that gave it the Atom Age flair of a flying saucer hovering just above the asphalt. Dean had it painted with his racing number, *130*, and the nickname studio chief Jack Warner had angrily bestowed on him, *Little Bastard*, a speeding billboard of performative offense. He lavished attention on the car, showed it off to anyone he could corral into looking at it, and referred to it only half in jest as his true love. In calling it by his nickname, he revealed too much.

He also resumed seeing Dr. Van der Heide, the psychoanalyst, who advised him with the blasé cruelty of a profession still mistaking Freud for fact that his real problem, the cause of all his traumas and sexual confusion, was anger at his father. According to the therapeutic notions then prevalent among high-profile therapists in the L.A. area, too many males like James Dean were emotionally immature due to flawed parenting, and in extreme cases, this could induce homosexuality. These perpetual adolescents wanted someone to care for and protect them instead of mastering their emotions to become more aggressive, dominant, and manly. Van der Heide reminded Dean of the reasons—excellent ones, Dean thought—that he had pushed his father away. Yet he told Dean he needed regular and sustained love from his father in order to heal. The thought left Dean depressed. "Jim and I—well, we've never had that closeness," his father Winton said around this time. In treating the wrong problem, therapy did more harm than good.[36]

At the end of the month, he entered a race to be held in Salinas, the town where the story of *East of Eden* had taken place, an hour and a half south of San Francisco.[37] In the days before the race, he spent an hour with Marcus and Ortense Winslow and his grandfather, visiting from Indiana, and, following his therapist's advice, his father. He also saw that Bill Bast was broke and miserable, living with rowdy roommates in a crowded apartment, struggling to write. After the *Confidential* Tab Hunter story, Bast had feared that his increasingly public gay lifestyle could harm Dean's career, so he stayed in the background, avoiding the galas Dean had begged him to attend with him.

But now Dean told Bast he wanted to repay him the $700 he estimated Bast had spent on him over the years and asked Bast to join him in his rented home, the one with no separate bedrooms, in which he had placed a miniature planetarium to fill the ceiling with stars, a reminder of the cosmic and the eternal.[38] In the same gentle tones he had used as Jim Stark to promise love to Plato in the planetarium in *Rebel without a Cause*, Dean told Bast that next week, in October, Bast would move in and it would be as it was before, but more so. They would live together, and Bast would write his great screen work, a modern *Jekyll and Hyde*. "Make me a promise," Dean said, both of the screenplay and the life Bast wanted for them, art and flesh swirling into one. "You know what you want," he added, speaking as much to himself as to Bast. "Stop putting it off. Like I told you," he said, echoing his words from Borrego Springs, "there's nothing to be scared of." Bast recalled feeling as though Dean had spoken to him as big brother, best friend, and lover—the Greek ideal Dean had so long sought for himself.[39]

Not long after, Dean received a strange phone call from a waiter at his favorite Italian restaurant, the Villa Capri, telling him that a postcard had arrived for him from Maila Nurmi showing her as Vampira sitting by an open grave with the words "wish you were here" written across it.[40] Dean called Nurmi on September 29 to ask if she wished him dead. She had intended the photo as a rejoinder to the *Life* magazine picture of Dean in a coffin and had sent it to the restaurant not knowing his address. But she told him only that it was a joke, without explanation, expecting to entice him into a renewed friendship. He hung up.

Some said they saw him that night in the Malibu Colony, a private, wealthy enclave, at an all-boy party of the kind where Burt Lancaster and Rock Hudson could sometimes be found. *Giant* bit player Dennis Hopper implausibly said Dean had told him he had been in Malibu a few days before to commune with Trappist monks. Or maybe he had really been in Santa Monica studying Hindu beliefs about immortality and piercing the veil of reality with the fifty-one-year-old gay author Christopher Isherwood and Isherwood's adolescent boyfriend, as Dean had told Bill Bast.[41] One man at the party, whenever it occurred, remembered hearing shouts in the early hours. A young man Dean had been quietly seeing off and on while he was publicly dating Andress had confronted him and berated Dean for living a lie. He demanded Dean admit to being gay and stop the charade of dating women, "except for publicity purposes."[42]

The story might have been true. Probably, it was just a legend. But those who passed it around didn't know that Dean had finally made his choice. When reporter Mike Connelly had asked him about marriage for an upcoming *Modern Screen* profile, he had changed his mind. He now had no intention of getting married, and he answered Connelly's questions with a remarkably studied ambiguity. Asked when he'd wed, he replied, "When I find the right companion." When asked if he were looking for a companion, he responded with a distraction: "Every man looks. But looking in itself is superficial. Looking can be an inward thing. It can have nothing to do with actual physical and emotional involvements. Oh sure, I'm looking." He told

Connelly, "It would be a very delicate setup—marriage I mean," because "I fall short in the 'human' department. I expect too much of people." Calling himself immature "where women are concerned," he said he'd consider marriage at thirty a "good age."[43]

Early on September 30, Dean threw a red windbreaker over a white T-shirt— copying his own mirror, Jim Stark, as reality folded into story—and joined Rolf Wütherich, Sandy Roth, and another friend for the trip up to Salinas for the race and then on to San Francisco. Dean called Bill Bast and asked him to join them, but Bast said he needed to finish packing for the move the next day. Dean had planned to tow the Porsche with his Ford station wagon, but instead he chose to drive it with Wütherich riding shotgun and the others following in the Ford. They drove all day, beneath the endless expanse of blue sky, until the sun grew low over the rolling hills. He dreamed of racing Little Bastard, of winning his first competition, as though if he could only go fast enough, he might finally break free to that absolute reality beyond this world.

Jimmy Dean drove down California's State Road 466, heading toward Paso Robles, basking in the final rays of the dying sun, the sky growing dim.

James Dean bestowed his own nickname, "Little Bastard," on his Porsche and saw it as an extension of himself. He is seen here driving the car a few hours before his death. *Photofest.*

Wütherich said he had never seen Dean happier. A few days earlier, Mark Twain's "The Mysterious Stranger" had again been on Dean's mind. The words had echoed in his head: "Strange, indeed, that you should not have suspected that your universe and its contents were only dreams, visions, fiction!"[44] Well, then, *here*, now, as Dean came to the intersection of routes 466 and 41 in Cholame, he could think only of winning his race, of the transcendent glory of triumph, of the great story he would make of it, the story he would tell Bill Bast back home—in *their* home.[45] A college student turning his two-toned Ford sedan into the intersection didn't see the low-slung silver Porsche.[46] "That guy's gotta see us—he'll stop," Dean shouted to Wütherich. But he didn't.

They collided, flinging Wütherich from the car and crushing the beautiful, fragile Porsche and its beautiful, fragile driver. The boy who wished with all his heart for someone to share a perfect melding of mind, body, and soul found in death an ironic fulfillment of his desire for a union of heroic equals. Smashed into the metal, pinned behind the wheel, as the constellations manifested in the growing darkness to pay their twinkling tribute, he had become one with the car that bore his name, his last true love, himself. In the end, there could be no other equal. When help came, too late, and men cleaved Dean from the wreckage, Wütherich said he heard a final cry escape the mangled body, the sound of a soul breaking free to join the immortal stars.[47]

James Dean, the little prince, the sweet prince, was dead, and all that remained were the stories. The rest was silence.

11
THE HOUND OF HEAVEN

William Bast was at his desk typing, his packed bags sitting beside him for the next day's move, when Beulah Roth called and told him Dean had died. Bast dropped the phone and fell from his chair, passing out on the floor. "So it was over," he thought when he came to. "All over."[1] At the same time, across town at the Warner Bros. lot, near the home Bast would never share with Dean, the security guard on duty at the gate took a call from the hospital where Dean's body had been received. He, in turn, called the studio's publicity department, which began relaying the news. Attendees that night at the Deb Star Ball honoring Hollywood makeup artists gasped when they saw in their programs an advertisement Dean had purchased to thank his makeup artist, a picture of his eyes staring intently from beyond the grave.

In New York City, Dean's costars from *Rebel without a Cause*, Sal Mineo, Natalie Wood, and Nick Adams, dined with Richard Davalos, the actor who played Dean's brother in *East of Eden*. They talked of their mysterious costar and his reckless lifestyle, speculating that his fast driving would inevitably lead to a serious injury, and Adams said he believed Dean would never live to see thirty. The others laughed, but as they left the restaurant, a Warner Bros. chaperone told Mineo and Adams the news and asked them not to tell Wood to avoid upsetting her before an early-morning call time.[2] Minutes later, the wire services pushed the first stories about Dean's death. Some California radio stations interrupted their programming to report the news.

Come morning, the news reached the set of *Giant*, where Elizabeth Taylor and Rock Hudson were scheduled to shoot some of the remaining scenes. George Stevens ordered production to continue, with no period of mourning.[3] Elizabeth Taylor was too overcome with grief to work, and even Rock Hudson broke down when he returned home to the woman he would soon marry, devastated not at Dean's death but that he had wished him dead.

In New York that morning, a group of Dean's friends entered his apartment to remove any evidence of homosexuality, fearing he had kept incriminating letters, like his draft board missive or correspondence with Rogers Brackett, and photographs that might become tabloid fodder if exposed.[4] Indeed, a tabloid, *Private Lives*, was about to print, over an unexceptional article prepared when Dean was alive, a sensational headline teasing that he might be gay.[5]

In Los Angeles, Lew Bracker filled a box with papers and detritus from Dean's desk. He found a scrapbook filled with clippings, poems, newspaper articles about loneliness, photographs of happy children and pleasant scenes of nature, and a few typewritten pages of "The Mysterious Stranger," all dating to February and March. The scrapbook read like an attempt at an autobiography by collage. Dean had saved newspaper columnist George Matthew Adams's February 6, 1955, reflection on the greatness, genuineness, and humility of Abraham Lincoln, and in the sentence "The mould disappeared after his humble birth," he crossed out the final three words and wrote in his own birthday.[6]

The Los Angeles papers treated Dean's death as major news, with large headlines about another Tinseltown tragedy. Syndicated columnist Walter Winchell told the nation that Dean had chosen "reckless hobbies" because he "lugged the torch" of love for Pier Angeli and only by challenging death itself could he end the "fiery burden" of heartbreak.[7]

The New York papers were less impressed. The *New York Times* ran a small notice, as did the *New York Herald*. Joe Hyams heard the news in the morning, in Mexico City, where he was reporting from a movie set. He called his editor at the *Herald* and offered to write a remembrance. "Dean was really not that well known," the editor replied, "to warrant much more space than we've already given him."[8] How wrong he was.

"Dean is even more alive with our audience than when he was alive," a magazine editor told the Associated Press a year after Dean's death. "We have to run a story on him every two or three months."[9] Steven Brooks, Warner Bros.' head of magazine publicity, tried to explain Dean's continuing popularity in terms of the existential uncertainty and pessimism of the Cold War: "It seems to be a sense of identification on the part of the young kids in America. That's the only explanation there can be. Why else would they embrace an actor who had been seen in only two fairly successful pictures?" Brooks said teenagers had developed a deep connection to Dean: "In 'East of Eden' and again in 'Rebel without a Cause,' Dean portrayed the kind of young person that many kids in this country think they are. They are confused and mixed up—and with good reason. In our youth, life was fairly simple; you could look forward to a reasonably certain future. What do the kids of today have to look forward to?"[10] Indeed, within days of Dean's death, a *Christian Science Monitor* editorial had already declared Dean a symbol of American youth from a generation that felt "the whole world is lost."[11]

In late 1955, Dean came out on top in the Committee of Motion Picture Organizations' first-ever Audience Awards poll of favorite movie stars, in which fifteen million Americans reportedly voted. Grace Kelly announced Dean's win at a star-studded gala at the Beverly Hilton hotel, only to have the crowd fall silent. Natalie Wood accepted the award on Dean's behalf, and the ceremony recognized Dean with a moment of silence. Many in the audience were crying during the tribute. Tab Hunter won the most promising male newcomer.[12] Dean's triumph arose from an unprecedented meeting of man and moment, from a death that hit teenage audiences like no other, followed by the release of *Rebel without a Cause*, prophecy and eulogy on celluloid.

In his most famous soliloquy, Hamlet asks who would suffer the "slings and arrows of outrageous fortune" were it not for the "dread of something after death," and in the hours and days and weeks after James Dean died, that undiscovered country seemed to be made manifest, in an ecstasy of grief and messianic yearning for an indescribable salvation that his young worshipers themselves barely understood even as they fell to their knees praying and begging for it to sweep over them and to carry them toward a more perfect world whose outlines they perceived but dimly.

In the days after Dean's death, the newspapers reported that teenage girls across the country fainted when they heard the news. Boys choked back tears. A letter Warner Bros. received from Durant, Ohio, informed the studio that the "boys in our high school workshop are making a statue of him." Another, from Dallas, said, "I am 25 and have never written a fan letter to any star or studio before. But I want to write to someone concerning the late James Dean. I think he is the greatest actor I have ever seen." From Chicago, a correspondent apologetically noted, "Oddly enough, his death was a personal loss to me."[13] Many letters were blatantly sexual, expressions of discontent and longing, offering to sacrifice marriages and virginity for Dean. Some fans spoke of "how good" they felt inside when thinking of Dean, how sharing that feeling with other fans "brings inner peace."[14] The old men stared in bafflement as the young cried and prayed for a boy they never knew, weeping for him as the women had wept for Tammuz. It hadn't been like this when Valentino died, they sneered.[15]

The adulation had already begun by the time the Reverend DeWeerd presided over James Dean's funeral in Fairmount on October 8 to a crowd of three thousand mourners and dozens of reporters, more than the entire

Thousands gathered for James Dean's funeral in Fairmount, Indiana. The number of attendees exceeded the population of the town. *Photofest.*

population of the town. The Reverend Xen Harvey delivered a melodramatic eulogy rhapsodizing over Dean's brief life and declaring in a strange, almost supernal allusion to the passion of Christ that in death his career had only begun. "And remember," he finished, "God himself is directing the production."[16]

The depth of mourning for Dean took Warner Bros. by surprise, and teams of publicists struggled to decide between minimizing his death or exploiting it. In macabre choice, with all of the marketing for *Rebel without a Cause* already produced for an October release and *Giant* still to come the next year, Warner Bros. chose to promote the new movie as though Dean were still alive, rolling out promotional materials, photographs, and interviews as they would for any other living star. And for his fans, he had become more than alive, something supernatural.

In those early days after Dean's death, he became the object of a battle between those who saw him as a saint, a demigod, or even a deity and those who condemned him as a demon in human form. Both images emerged from conscious efforts to mold from the raw material of Dean's life a mythological, supernatural character that might stand in place of the real man and deny or explain away the unsavory facts that, if known, might render him unacceptable or, worse, unprofitable. It was easier to imagine a fallen idol as an angel or a demon than queer.

The gossips reported that someone had broken open Dean's casket before his burial—Jack Simmons trying to steal a forbidden kiss, Bast bitterly suspected—but soon enough rumors spread in the press that Dean had become the victim of a necrophiliac cult. Seizing on Dean's claim to know about "satanic forces" and to have a "sense of the Satanic," stories spread that he had served as the head of satanic coven, a master of black magic.[17]

Teenagers tried to harness the occult arts to commune with the young man for whom in death they felt an undying love. Countless teens attempted séances to reach him in the beyond, and some thought they succeeded. Sal Mineo used a Ouija board to try to reach Dean and believed Dean sent back a message. A thirteen-year-old boy held a séance in the basement of his New York home with several of his friends and his ten-year-old sister. They sat around a table below a pipe where the boy's mother had placed a number of clothes hangers to hold laundry. They implored Dean's spirit to rattle the hangers to signal his presence. And then the hangers moved. "I felt the thrilling shock of it all," Joanne Milazzo remembered, "and my big brother and his friends scrambled upstairs to safety."[18]

But Dean did not speak simply through board games and household goods. In 1957, the traveling magician Kara Kum promised the "materialization of James Dean back from the grave" in a stage spectacular featuring "sadistic surgery," dancing skeletons, and an "attack" by "vampires" and "zombies."[19] Beneath a lurid cover painting by pulp artist Thomas Beecham depicting James Dean's death, the March 1957 issue of *True Strange* magazine carried a posthumous interview Robert De Kolbe allegedly conducted with Dean through psychic Anna M. van Deuseun. When van Deuseun began to speak in Dean's voice, Dean told his fans to "stop mourning me. I am very happy where I am."[20] He must have drunk from the waters of Lethe, however, because he had forgotten indelible moments from his own life, as though it were only van Deuseun pretending to be him. But who would doubt the word of the dead? Or of a god?

In Europe, where Dean quickly became more famous than any living American star, a Belgian intellectual and pederast, Raymond De Becker, compared him to Adonis, Mithras, Antinous, and other gods whose deaths the world mourned and called him the "god of American youth" who would restore the world—and who was, according to "some circles," gay. To French historian Pierre Gaxotte, Dean was Adonis or Tammuz, with a cult of ritual mourners, a sentiment echoed by filmmaker Tony Richardson. The French philosopher Edgar Morin wrote an essay declaring Dean a perfect "mythological hero" reconnecting humanity to the divine. A British youth who became famous in 1956 for resembling Dean, Daniel Winter, was more succinct in his appraisal of Dean's divine appeal: "It was like . . . looking on the face of God."[21]

The February 1956 edition of *Whisper* magazine ran an equally sensational story, declaring Maila Nurmi to have been Dean's "Black Madonna," a diabolical influence and demon lover, and all but accusing her of using witchcraft to end his life—"one of the most shocking stories to come out of Hollywood, U.S.A.," it proclaimed.[22] It printed the photo she had sent Dean of herself by an open grave and declared it a witchy curse placed on the hapless young hero, lured by a devil-woman into a satanic trap. Nurmi tried to launch a new show at Los Angeles's KHJ-TV, only to lose that gig when a late-July edition of the *American Weekly* newspaper supplement with a circulation of fifty million repeated the *Whisper* story implying her occult knowledge of Dean's impending death while adding an awful new wrinkle already widely believed among Dean's teenage fans: the "fantastic rumor—that Dean was not killed in the crash, but was so badly burned that his studio and family decided to tell the world that he died while he lives out his days in a sanitarium."[23]

Dean's fans wrote to him, begging him to show himself, even disfigured. "My true feeling is that you were horribly disfigured in that terrible car accident," one woman wrote. "I don't care. I know I should not be writing this, but I feel you are not dead. If you are dead, you will come back again."[24] A prophecy circulated in the gossip columns that when *Giant* was released,

Images like this set photo from *Giant*, in which Elizabeth Taylor and James Dean posed like Mary keeling before Jesus on the cross, encouraged Dean's fans to think of him in divine terms. *Warner Bros./Photofest © Warner Bros.*

Dean would return to life in glory, made beautiful and new.[25] After making a sidelong reference to the star's ongoing presence on his radio show, Walter Winchell was besieged with so many teenage letters that he broadcasted a rare correction: "I never, at any time, said that James Dean was still alive. This message is addressed to his fans, who have deluged my office with hundreds of letters. The physical James Dean is dead."[26] But the metaphysical Dean lived on.

In a morbid attempt to turn the scandal to her advantage, Nurmi embraced the ghoulish persona she previously claimed was merely a character, posed next to a satanic altar, and alleged that Dean's ghost had been her constant companion for the six months following his death. She said that when he was near, he would make ash in an ashtray burst into flame. She claimed that Dean spoke to her after his death by moving a photograph of his ear that he had once, in some strange act of unexplained symbolism or art, cut out and pinned to her wall. "Jimmy, was that you—were you talking to me?" she asked, imagining that songs on the radio carried his thoughts to her. She said he rang a disconnected phone at a séance she held. That Halloween, she attended a party with an actor dressed as Dean, his face covered in bandages, and she claimed him to be the resurrected, disfigured Dean, while she paraded about as a witch. "I didn't think it was bad taste," she said shortly after. "I just thought it was satirical of all this craze about Jimmy not being dead."[27]

"We took a bus trip to your grave and we are sure that an empty coffin was placed there," two young women wrote to Dean a few months earlier. "Jimmy, you can't fool us. Men like you never die. Men like you were placed on earth to make women happy."[28]

The resurrected Dean and his ghostly image made quite the career of pleasing women, and sometimes men, as an object of fantasy and desire. In North Carolina, a teenage girl presented herself as the new Virgin Mary, the new Danaë. She told a tabloid that James Dean had come to her as a beautiful, angelic spirit and made her pregnant from the celestial realm.[29] In California, Pamela Des Barres, just eight years old, had never heard of James Dean until she received the news in a radio bulletin while riding in her parents' truck, but she remembered that "the finality of James Dean's demise filled me with trepidation and a longing I didn't understand," and seeing his picture at the local drugstore's newsstand, she spent hours learning about him from the magazines, "gazing rapturously at his chiseled visage, aching to hear his voice, see him move, breathe, and come wildly back to life on the silver screen."[30] The movies became instruments of resurrection, a triumph over death.

And soon this restoration would have its sacred hymns. The Cheers had recorded a song about a motorcycle-riding tough guy, the "terror of Highway 101," who vanished supernaturally in the wake of a crash. Released a week before Dean's death, it now became an anthem of his mourning, reaching number six on the Billboard best-selling singles chart and sparking a morbid genre of songs crooning over the loss of the young and beautiful that persisted into the 1960s. Songs praising Dean followed, each more maudlin than the last. The folk singer Dylan Todd released the "Ballad of James Dean" in 1956, bidding farewell to the "Prince of Players" and imagining "the role you must play" in Heaven on Judgment Day, alongside the angels. "A star is born in the sky," he sang.

Around the time of *Giant*'s release, Roger Steven "Steve" Foster, a twenty-one-year-old welder from Oxon Hill, Maryland found himself mobbed by young James Dean fans wherever he went because of his strong resemblance to the late actor. People stopped him on the street to ask for autographs or even physically grabbed him for a better look. He would sign for them, but wrote "Steve Foster," not "James Dean." When he went to see a screening of *Rebel without a Cause* at an F Street theater in Washington, a group of girls, apparently believers in the conspiracy theory that Dean had not died, caught sight of him and shouted, "There's James Dean sitting there!" From Florida to Maryland, packs of girls mobbed him, and he indulged them by acting the part of Dean. "We all miss Jimmy so," one girl said, "but maybe now we have someone who can play his role." During National Guard training, half the soldiers called him "James." A friend convinced Foster to play up the resemblance, and he showed up at the offices of Washington, D.C.'s *Evening Star* dressed like Dean in *Rebel*. "It was like interviewing a ghost," reporter Fifi Gorska wrote in February 1957.[31]

Foster was far from the only young man to receive plaudits for his resemblance to Dean. Keith Thompson, twenty, a Cleveland painter, was swarmed by high schoolers who spent a week lusting after him as he painted their school because he looked like James Dean.[32] Bob Rickman, a Washington, D.C. disc jockey for WEAM, twenty-one, received similar treatment, even though the resemblance was slight. Another twenty-one-year-old, construction worker

Wes Bryan of Ohio, did the other boys one better. Bryan's picture appeared in the *Akron Beacon* when he crashed his motorcycle and readers wrote a barrage of letters praising the young man's similarity to Dean. Hollywood producer Clarence Greene swooped in and signed him to a movie contract, and he negotiated a recording deal for Bryan with United Artists Record Corp., where Bryan recorded a ballad and a novelty song about space aliens visiting Earth. "I'm not knocking it," Bryan said of owing his career to looking like James Dean. "But somehow it's like judging a book by its cover. A face, after all, isn't very important. It's what's inside a person that counts."[33] If a face was all you wanted, Hollywood Art Studios sold effigies of Dean's visage in "Miracleflesh," "full life size so real you'll tremble," they promised. "Send $10 now and James Dean will be yours." *Life* magazine reported that the studio produced three hundred of the supple faces per week, and correspondent Ezra Goodman attested that they felt "something like human flesh."[34]

Warner Bros. purposely encouraged the madness with a steady drip of planted stories about Dean. A publicity department memo advised that "columnists, fan magazines, all segments [of the] press and television" were "to be kept provided with all possible material on James Dean." Newspapers reported openly about the studio's "ultra-private" plans for planting stories and "keeping the Dean vogue 'hot.'"[35] Warner Bros. stoked a rivalry between NBC's Steve Allen and CBS's Ed Sullivan, who competed to stage the most lavish TV memorial to Dean at 7 p.m. on the same Sunday night, October 14, 1956.

Magazines and newspapers aimed at older audiences, also recipients of studio material, looked askance at Dean and his fanatical acolytes. Many newspapers ran a vicious column from *Saturday Evening Post* contributor Maurice Zolotow in late October attacking Dean as a "rotten idol," declaring him a "brutal," abusive monster and calling him "sexually sadistic."[36] *Look* magazine labeled him strange and derided his sense of masculine aesthetics as "grotesque." *Real* magazine called him America's "weirdest national hero." *Exposed* called him the "god of a weird and morbid cult." *On the QT* asked, "Was Jimmy Dean a psycho?" *Esquire,* in backhanded compliment, ran a photograph in December 1956 of James Dean behind cracked glass with a mocking headline scoffing at "The Apotheosis of Jimmy Dean."[37] And yet the choice of words was far from wrong. Fans lit candles to his memory and chiseled chunks from his gravestone and treasured them as holy relics.

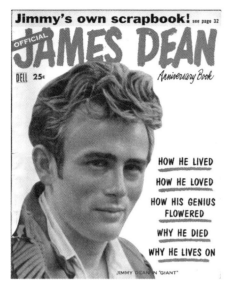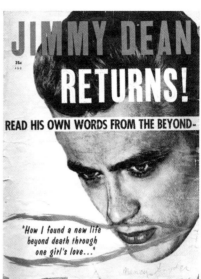

So-called one-shot magazines devoted entirely to James Dean generated massive profits for publishers and sold well over a million copies in the first year after Dean's death. *Author's collection.*

A disturbed young man pretended to be one of Dean's friends, charmed his way into living in the Winslows' Fairmount home in the spring of 1956, slept in Dean's old room, and propositioned a visiting Bill Bast, asking him to have sex among Dean's adolescent mementos.[38]

"It is definitely a sickness," one psychologist told *Lowdown* magazine, adding that when people become "disappointed in life," they can lose touch with reality and "seem to want more than mortal men can give them—and so they build up an imaginary picture of an immortal man who can give them the satisfaction they seek."[39] John Steinbeck's ex-wife, Gwin Steinbeck, echoed the sentiment, telling *Picture Post*, "For many of these youngsters without emotional roots, without a basic faith, Dean has become a substitute Christ. As such, they are even trying to resurrect him."[40]

The release of *Rebel without a Cause* in late October 1955 galvanized the teenage love of James Dean. Jim Stark's on-screen anguish transformed into a passion play and prophecy whose culmination was the actual death of James Dean, actor and character seamlessly merging into a Greek myth of the agony and anguish of being young. In less than a year, four hundred fan clubs formed around the world and still more in the year that followed. One estimate put membership at 3.8 million people. Warner Bros. could not keep up with the flood of fan letters that arrived for Dean—five thousand per month, half from abroad—and Dean's family and friends received similar entreaties, begging for scraps of information, to connect with hands that touched the divine.[41] Fans issued threats to George Stevens, demanding that no frame of Dean be excised from *Giant* before its 1956 release.[42] In Indonesia, roving gangs of teenage boys dressed as Jim Stark, rebelled against the oppression of traditional society, and held secret services to "idolize" their demigod and hero.

The Academy of Motion Picture Arts and Sciences twice nominated Dean for Oscars, for *Eden* and *Giant*, the first posthumous Best Actor nominations. European academies awarded him honors, and Princeton University placed a bust of Dean by Kenneth Kendall in its hall of fame, alongside Beethoven and Keats, the youngest man ever so memorialized "among the immortals of art," in the words of a newspaper report.[43] The gay poet Frank O'Hara published several nearly romantic odes to Dean, whose death had devastated him. In the journal *Poetry*, he begged the gods to give Dean peace and claimed to be "this dead man's voice." A letter to the editor in *Life* magazine highlighted the poem and complained that Dean worship "has penetrated even the upper echelons of culture."[44]

And yet, when *Rebel without a Cause* arrived in theaters, the critics did not know what to make of it. *Variety*'s Robert J. Landry watched the whole film and barely registered that the character of Plato had played a role in what he saw as an epic about the effects of bad parenting. Although Sal Mineo would receive a Supporting Actor Oscar nomination for the role, Landry devoted twice the space to considering Judy's "bosoms, lipstick and sex feelings," which he saw as central to the story.[45] The *Hollywood Reporter*'s Jack Moffitt similarly considered Judy the fulcrum of the film, conflating actors with characters and arguing that its true climax occurred when the "love of Dean for Natalie is at last viewed sympathetically by their parents." So intent was he to duck the implications of the movie that not only did he avoid mentioning any connection between Plato and Jim, but he also invented a Romeo-and-Juliet

A year after Dean's death, *Modern Screen Magazine* struck this gold-toned brass commemorative medallion, which was meant to be worn on a bracelet, necklace, or key ring. *Author's collection.*

ending that doesn't exist in the film, because Jim's and Judy's parents never disapproved of their union.[46]

Bosley Crowther of the *New York Times* repeated his disappointment in Dean as a secondhand Brando but this time went further than his anger at *Eden*, stopping just short of demanding censorship of a film he called a "desperate and dangerous distortion" of the real causes of teen delinquency.[47] He, too, ignored the character of Plato except in passing, claiming the best element of the film was the approval Jim's parents gave to Judy as his girlfriend. Their powerful romance could only be summed up in Jim's minimal response to Judy's confession of love: "Well, I'm glad."

Warner Bros. had helped ensure critics wouldn't see the film for what it was. Based in part on discarded elements of Irving Shulman's early draft of the *Rebel* script, before Dean and Ray pushed the film in a very different direction during shooting, the studio marketed the film deceptively as the story of a "teen-war" rooted in "juvenile violence." In the fall of 1955, even after seeing the finished film, they circulated to newspapers prewritten sample news stories incorrectly describing Jim as a violent thug who "seeks to become a member of a juvenile gang." They offered exhibitors newspaper ads showing Dean, with arms upraised, and the caption "Look, Ma! No handcuffs—yet!"

And they distributed to exhibitors and the media a strictly not-for-publication plot summary of the movie that bore little relation to the finished film. Again, they described Jim as an "unruly" aspiring gang member, Plato as a "gun-crazed" murderer, and the death of Jim's "buddy" Plato as the impetus to renounce gang life and reconcile with his parents. Warner Bros. effectively shaped perceptions through misleading marketing.[48]

Nevertheless, most critics recognized some sort of animating power in the movie beyond the surface story, and they sensed that something was happening beyond their perception. America's movie critics had no trouble recognizing what *Time* called the "repressed homosexuality" of *The Strange One* in 1957, a film about a sadistic military academy cadet who abuses his classmates.[49] (Its director, Jack Garfein, even claimed James Dean helped develop the stage play that preceded it.)[50] Nor did Crowther fail to notice the accusations of homosexuality only thinly veiled in the film adaptation of *Tea and Sympathy* in 1956. But in both cases, the gay themes conformed to the popular notion of gay men as monstrous, effeminate, or undesirable. No matter how blatantly *Rebel* framed Plato as gay—he had a pinup of heartthrob Alan Ladd in his school locker—most critics in 1955 could not conceive of a story where the love of one boy for another might be treated with sympathy or grace, an impossibility beyond comprehension. Even the National Legion for Decency, the powerful Catholic group that rated films for moral purity, gazed uncomprehendingly at *Rebel*. They gave it an A-II rating, "morally unobjectionable."[51] Only one critic, for *Presbyterian Life*, thought he saw a "suggestion of a latent homosexuality."[52] And so what was essential became invisible, as Dean liked to say in quoting from *The Little Prince*.

Most watching *Rebel* remained blind to the invisible, but those with eyes to see understood, particularly the boys who saw themselves on the screen. Vito Russo was nine years old when *Rebel* was first in theaters, but in later years he recalled how Jim Stark's mourning for Plato spoke to boys like him, allowing them to see, "even before they knew the words for what they were, something on the screen that they knew related to their lives in some way, without being able to put a finger on it." He especially recalled the "tone in James Dean's voice as he zipped up the jacket of the dead Sal Mineo" and the "sense of longing" Dean conveyed.[53] Martin Greif, then seventeen and in high school, was blunter, recalling that "anyone with half a brain knew that it should have been

Mineo's Plato and Dean's Jim who embraced at the climax."[54] Jack Fritscher, then sixteen years old, felt a deep love for Dean, a young man he had never met. "I found my first lover in James Dean," he recalled, remembering the grief he experienced when Dean died and how he learned to read the subtext in *Rebel* that fall to see gay boys like himself on-screen. "James Dean was masculine; he was blond; he was hot; he was California; he was American; he was gay. I wanted James Dean. I wanted to be him."[55]

Gay boys and men watched the movie, and a "surprising number of boys," as *People Today* reported in 1956, sent the dead Dean love letters filled with longing for something that seemed just out of reach, a way to share fantasies that could barely be spoken aloud. One such letter, printed in the scandal rag *Lowdown* in 1957, read,

> SWEET JIMMY: I wrote you tonight because I see before me vividly the curly locks of your hair and your sweet body. Your limbs and mine—Oh, I cannot go on.
>
> I know you never knew real love for you were snuffed out before you had the chance. Studying your pictures in the movie magazines, I know you would have come over to our side, to the world of men that hates [*sic*] women.
>
> I know you would have allowed me to serve you breakfast in bed and to kiss you full on the lips as you lie there on OUR pillow, sleepy and drowsy. And then . . .

The remainder of the letter, *Lowdown*'s editor informed readers, was unprintable.[56]

Yet even as *Rebel* burned its way through American theaters in the fall of 1955, there were unpleasant reminders of the pressures and the threats from which Dean's death had freed him. In its October 3 cover story, *Life* magazine said fans had pointedly demanded Rock Hudson explain why he wasn't married.[57] He wed Phyllis Gates two weeks after *Rebel*'s premiere, on November 9. That same month, a man who attended an all-boy party at a millionaire gay man's New York City home rushed to the FBI's New York office to report that Burt Lancaster had been in attendance, and a sailor made the same confession to the Office of Naval Intelligence after seeing Lancaster at another party in Beverly Hills a few months later.[58]

Just after New Year's, with Warner Bros.' permission, Irving Shulman published the novel he made from his failed *Rebel without a Cause* script. *Children of the Dark* followed the movie's rough outline but turned Plato into a bespectacled psychopathic murderer with a fatal attraction to Jim, now called Steve but still transparently modeled on James Dean. Plato orchestrates a violent effort to murder the "witch-bitch" Judy in order to seize the dim, confused Steve for himself. A scheming Judy rallies the police against Plato in a final shootout when it looks like she might lose Steve to Plato's enticements, and Plato kills himself with a grenade, leaving a confused Steve to wonder if he will ever be manly enough for Judy. Shulman prefaced the novel by warning of a coming "national disaster" of teenage crime, but the book made plain that this disaster was a failure of masculinity and the threat that boys might be led away from their proper manly roles by domineering women and homosexuals.

Bill Bast had seen enough to feel nauseated and sad and angry in the early months of 1956. The boy he loved had become both angel and demon, hailed as a giant of the arts and condemned as a prince of Satan. Surely, this was madness. "The real James Dean, the Jimmy I knew, was getting lost in all the hype and hysteria," he said. So Bast decided he needed to memorialize the real James Dean before the strange, supernatural creature that bore his face utterly replaced the flesh-and-blood man. At a friend's suggestion, he decided to write a biography of Dean, though there would be impossible challenges. "And what about our 'relationship'?" he asked himself. "Just how candid could I be about the intimacies?"[59] Bast's editor at Ballantine advised him to write whatever he could as fast as possible, and they would cut and prune until it was suitable.

Bast did not wait for the pruning. He censored himself and even falsified some facts about Dean's life to conform to a socially acceptable mold. His was the literary version of the awkward coda tacked on to *Rebel without a Cause* to render the essential invisible. Nevertheless, after experiencing a frightening dream of Dean and a sense of supernatural guidance, he wondered—seriously, not merely metaphorically—if Dean's spirit had not stage-managed the project. He often felt Dean's presence from beyond the veil.

Tabloids and gossipmongers were already starting to close in. *Uncensored* teased the "truth" about the James Dean "whispers" in the fall of 1956.[60] In a major but heavily sanitized and partially falsified *Redbook* biographical feature in September, Joe Hyams wrote that Dean "was sought by homosexuals"

William Bast self-censored his memoir-cum-biography of James Dean to obscure Dean's homosexual experiences. Nevertheless, many read between the lines anyway. *Author's collection.*

in the New York arts scene due to his beauty and promised opportunities.[61] A few weeks later, *Rave* directly addressed "slimy insinuations" among Dean's detractors that Dean had been a "sex pervert"—code for *homosexual*—who had patronized "certain Greenwich Village hangouts": that is to say, the neighborhood's well-known gay bars.[62] For a tabloid to robustly rebuke such stories was to concede how widespread and widely believed they were. Indeed, European publications were far less reticent to assert directly that certain groups spoke of Dean's "homosexual relations."[63] Britain's *Picture Post* wrote that in life his "personal magnetism" had "captivated . . . sexually maladjusted men."[64] Even the respectable *New Republic* ran a highly critical article heavily implying that James Dean's lack of a strong core identity could too easily slide into homosexuality.[65] Overshadowing the rumors, Bast's 35¢ paperback and $2.75 hardcover biography, expurgated and sanitized, arrived in bookstores on November 29, stripped of the most controversial moments of Dean's life, though not as thoroughly as Bast imagined. W. Somerset Maughan, himself discretely gay, told Bast that he could read between the lines and see how deeply he had loved Dean. Less-discreet members of the literary and artistic elite asked Bast to describe Dean's penis and how he was in bed.

Stripped of the context that made Dean's life meaningful, the remaining fragments seemed alternately capricious, cruel, and crazy—but Dean was now a robustly heterosexual hero driven by Freudian yearning for parental affection. The new James Dean, a fictional figure built from selected moments of real life, the characters in his movies, and Bast's intentional distortions, developed a messianic power. This Dean was no longer ambitious, anguished, and awkward. He was now a confident but sensitive rebel, an agent of destiny, Milton's Satan by way of Holden Caufield. Comic book artists drew his face on the idealized boyfriends of love stories in *Girls' Romance* and *Falling in Love*. A bowdlerized documentary directed by Robert Altman and George W. George, *The James Dean Story*, followed in 1957, touted grotesquely as featuring Dean "portraying" himself through a very spare use of photographs and film clips.

Young people showed up at Bast's New York home, sometimes hysterical, often lost in religious reverie. His unlisted number would ring in the middle of the night with plaintive calls from Dean's fans. Letters arrived in such volume that Ballantine sent overflowing filing boxes to Bast each week. "They believed he was the One," Bast marveled, "who would surely have understood their anguish, their yearning, their unfulfilled dreams, their loneliness, their sense of alienation, whatever." They also wanted, Bast said, to come close to the person who was closest to Dean. Their desire for salvation and earnest hopes contrasted with the reaction of adults, who asked after Dean's penis size and his performance in bed. He even found that the young men he took to bed wanted not him but Dean: "Imagine how off-putting it is to have a sexual partner on the point of orgasm gasp in your ear 'Oh, Jimmy!' when in fact your name is Bill."[66]

One night at a pub in London shortly after *James Dean* hit bookstores, the boyishly bespectacled enfant terrible of British letters Colin Wilson, the same age as James Dean and Bill Bast, his eyes half-hidden beneath a mop of disheveled sandy hair, cornered Bast and pumped him for information about Dean. He suspected Dean's life fit the mold of the lonely, disaffected artists, like Franz Kafka, Albert Camus, and William Blake, whom he had profiled in his best-selling 1956 book *The Outsider*, an existentialist mirror of Bast's biography of Dean. Together, they talked of James Dean, homosexuality, movies, and alienation in the same language Wilson would later use to ennoble science fiction with philosophy and raise it to literature. Wilson's future work on the occult was, his publisher would proclaim, "for those who would walk with the gods," and Bast was even now an apostle of a secular saint. Bast admitted to Wilson that Dean had been "queer," and he bragged that he had been sexually involved with him.[67] It was all of a piece, really. Wilson would come to believe in psychics and ghosts and the mysteries of the pyramids, and Bast already believed James Dean pulled supernatural strings from the other side of the veil. Both had faith in the power of an artist to transcend the limits of reality, and both knew themselves to be some kind of outsider, like James Dean or space aliens, forever beyond the golden circle of acceptance that marked a man as normal, healthy, and sane.

Still more among the famous felt the desire to connect with the departed through the living. Elvis Presley, age twenty, found himself entranced by *Rebel without a Cause* in the fall of 1955. He memorized the script and would act out Dean's scenes from the film for friends. He modeled some of his stage persona on Dean and dreamed of starring in a Dean biopic. When a TV interviewer asked if he were another James Dean, Presley replied, "I would never compare myself in any way to James Dean, because James Dean was a genius at acting, although I'll say that, uh, that, uh, I sure would like to [be]."[68] In 1956, he attempted to befriend Nick Adams, who had taken to describing himself as one of Dean's closest friends. When Presley met Maila Nurmi, he wanted to bed the woman he wrongly thought had been the last to sleep with James Dean. Now twenty-one, he told Nurmi, twelve years his senior, "I know you're getting old and all, but if you'd like to come back after the show, I'd be proud to take you back to my bungalow."[69] She declined, and

Presley settled for becoming her friend and attaching her to his entourage. Whatever magic he hoped to gain from Dean worked. Presley surpassed Dean in popularity among America's teenagers in 1957, a new and living teen idol.

Things worked out less well for Maila Nurmi. Presley dropped her once he reached the heights of fame. She could not find work in television. In 1956, she accepted an offer from the talentless director Ed Wood to appear in his new low-budget flying-saucer movie *Plan 9 from Outer Space*. Nurmi claimed Dean's ghost came to her less often now, but perhaps it was only because she had replaced his tragedy with an uncomfortably resonant farce.

Plan 9 made its way into theaters three years later, in July 1959, four weeks after the execution of Charles Starkweather, a young man who wanted to be James Dean and sought transcendence through murder. Starkweather was sixteen years old when *Rebel without a Cause* first played in Lincoln, Nebraska, and his friends and neighbors thought he looked a lot like James Dean. Both young men had the same faraway, nearsighted gaze and the same mouth. Bullied over misshapen legs and a speech impediment, Starkweather saw himself as an outsider. He idolized Dean, dressed like him, combed his hair the same way, obsessed over *Rebel*, and imagined that delinquency and crime could yield rebellion and freedom. His sister remembered seeing him posing like James Dean, complete with cigarette, trying to perfect the smile to match the hair. He quit school and went to work, and following a fight with his father that resulted in expulsion from his home, he went on a murder spree with his underage girlfriend, killing eleven people over a two-month period from December 1957 to January 1958, including most of his girlfriend's family. Police captured him in Wyoming when a sheriff's bullet shattered the windshield of the car Starkweather was driving. He thought he was bleeding to death from the cuts, so he surrendered rather than die. "That's the kind of yellow son of a bitch he is," the local sheriff said.[70]

That year, John Dos Passos, the great writer of the *U.S.A.* trilogy and a friend of Ernest Hemingway, thought the worship of James Dean had gone too far. He hated the "sinister" Dean for his "thwarted maleness," calling him "girl-boy almost" in the pages of *Esquire* and later in his novel *Midcentury*, because to express emotion was to be effeminate. He noticed that young men now tore through the streets in blue jeans and piled their hair high and sneered at their betters. He thought it distasteful that young men would emulate one of their own, especially someone unmanly. He saw in their worship shades of Narcissus, a vanity unbecoming of real men. Dos Passos, once a socialist but now an angrily conservative former supporter of Joe McCarthy, wrote mockingly in *Esquire* of their blue jeans and leather jackets, their big deep eyes and pouting mouths, the young men who "look at themselves and see James Dean," the "lost cats in love with themselves just like James Dean." Dos Passos believed the future salvation of America would come at the hands of powerful old men like Richard Nixon, not young men like the "demonic" Dean, and that men should be hard and tough and burly and old, like Hemingway. He took pleasure that "James Dean was dead sure enough."[71]

Even patrons of New York gay bars in the later 1950s complained that young men didn't want to be drag queens anymore but instead dressed like James Dean and became "male impersonators" affecting Dean's half-formed masculinity.[72] Half a century later, the young men who modeled themselves on James Dean, straight and gay alike, still acted like him. "So completely did I incorporate what I borrowed from Dean," the novelist Jaime O'Neill recalled in 2010, "that even now, edging toward my own more natural rendezvous with death, I occasionally catch myself in a gesture of his expropriated more than half a century ago."[73]

On Halloween night, 1958, the promising but moody young actor Tom Pittman, aged twenty-five, crashed his Porsche into a ravine in the Hollywood Hills. It took weeks to find his body, and the newspapers compared his death to that of his idol, James Dean—in fact, the first three paragraphs of the wire service report of his death all began with some variation of the words *Like Dean* and listed the ways Pittman emulated him. A rumor circulated that Pittman had secretly been gay, and some speculated that he had purposely crashed his car to die like Dean, though no evidence beyond Dean's shadow supported either story.[74] There was little doubt about the artist John Minton, a thirty-nine-year-old gay man who had come to identify himself with Dean in the year after Dean's death. He completed a painting he titled *The Death of James Dean* in January 1957 and then took his own life with sleeping pills.

In Los Gatos, California, Constance Chase, seventeen, and Jerrell Morris, sixteen, died in separate crashes in 1958, both driving their cars at high speeds into the same oak tree. Authorities suspected one or both belonged to an alleged suicidal "James Dean Death Club" at their high school. Afterward,

Many older men complained that teenage boys, like these young men on Nantucket in 1957, had become too casual, too surly, and too emotional because of James Dean. *Library of Congress, Prints and Photographs Division, Toni Frissell Photograph Collection, LC-DIG-tofr-07961.*

a newspaper columnist joked tastelessly that the club's ceremonies must involve "burning incense on an altar of blue jeans."[75] Two girls in Hamburg, West Germany, aged eighteen and twenty-one, committed suicide in November 1959 to join Dean in the afterlife, the older girl writing in a letter to the younger that Dean had called out from the grave and was prepared to receive them in death: "At the very end, Jimmy sits and smiles as he follows our path to him. He raises his head when he hears a soft, 'Jimmy, come get me.' He has already realized that it was two different voices. With a powerful jerk, he pulled himself up and shouted out into space with all his might, 'I am waiting for you!'" They were said to have offered in reply, "Jimmy, we're coming!" as they plunged to their doom from a fourteenth-story window.[76]

12
GLORY IN THE FLOWER

A decade after James Dean died, the real man had faded away until he had become a flickering image in revival theaters and evening television reruns, a set of faded photographs of a taciturn but sensitive rebel, a movie character who had somehow once been flesh. Magazines like *Modern Teen* ran occasional pieces to explain who James Dean had been to a new generation of teens who knew only the name. Even the legends had taken on a spectral air. The Greater Los Angeles Safety Council sent the wreckage of Dean's Porsche on tour for four years, ostensibly to promote road safety but more as a sacred relic for fans to sit in, at 50¢ apiece, and imagine themselves one with the dead. And then one day in 1960 the broken chassis vanished, never to be seen again. The engine and other working parts had been salvaged and used in other cars, and stories swirled that a "jinx" caused every recipient to crash, sometimes with fatal ends. A few of the stories were even true.[1] Some claimed to see Dean's ghost in his red jacket, standing at the intersection where he had died or driving down the road and vanishing into the night.[2] A vicious but fabricated rumor even said that Dean's spirit scrawled his name on Sal Mineo's car windshield and then turned Mineo gay.[3] He was less divinity now than a haunting memory.

But that memory held an almost totemic power. From the moment of Dean's death, Andy Warhol—who considered Dean the perfect embodiment of the "damaged but beautiful soul of his time"—began a series of pieces transfiguring Dean's image into a symbol of gay male identity, culminating in a half-hour film of an actor styled as James Dean receiving the titular *Blow Job*.[4] The openly gay avant-garde filmmaker Kenneth Anger had grown up in Santa Monica, not far from where James Dean spent his early years, and in 1937, at the age of ten, he made a short home movie playing a matador and roping his Boy Scout troop into serving as bulls. In high school he became an occultist, and after college he became close friends with Alfred Kinsey, whom he considered a father figure. Anger had once been arrested by vice cops in a gay sting, and he made artsy films suffused with homoeroticism and the occult, one of which went to California's Supreme Court on obscenity charges. He, too, had wept for James Dean, on whom he had had a crush.[5]

In 1959, Anger published in France a wild—and false—claim that Dean engaged in sadomasochistic sex and had the "underground" nickname "The Human Ashtray" due to the cigarette burns he purposely received.[6] In 1963, his short film *Scorpio Rising* mixed imagery of motorcycle gangs, Nazism, Catholicism, and the occult with homosexuality, clips of Brando's *Wild One*, and a shrine to James Dean, a phantasmagoria openly comparing the cult of James Dean to that of Christ and both to a gay orgy—all embodiments of the ecstasy and freedom of rebellion that at any moment could cross into violent oblivion. Anger styled his lead actor, Bruce Byron, with Dean's distinctive hairdo and posed him in profile beside a parallel pinup of Dean.

The film served as proud rejoinder to a growing chorus of authors condemning Dean for his rumored homosexuality. Walter Ross, the former head of press relations for Warner Bros. in New York who had met—and disliked—Dean, knew the stories about James Dean's sexuality circulating down Broadway and sought to publicize them under the guise of fiction.[7] His 1958 novel *The Immortal* used these rumors of Dean's sexual involvement with powerful older men to depict a lightly fictionalized version of Dean diabolized into a heartless psychopath driven to destruction by the evils of homosexuality.[8] Ross offered almost impossibly accurate descriptions of homosexual incidents from Dean's life, including his experiences with Rogers Brackett and Lemuel Ayers, with only minimal disguise; the words used to talk about his homosexual "dabbling" ("Why rule out a whole big sex?") were virtually identical to those Dean's friends would attribute to him in their own accounts.[9] Warhol drew the cover image of a Dean-like young man, which publisher Simon & Schuster blew up into a forty-foot-by-twenty-foot billboard in midtown Manhattan, the first such advertisement to promote a novel.[10]

Mainstream reviewers treaded lightly in condemning Dean's memory. Some pointed out resemblances to Dean, but many only implied them. The *New York Times* hinted at some superficial connection to the "disquieting" story; *Billboard* declined to name any influence on the novel's "sick, sick, sick" bisexual hero. *Newsweek* none too subtly reminded readers James Dean would have perfectly played the "grotesque" protagonist in a hypothetical movie.[11] Screenwriter Whitney Bolton, however, recognized the hero easily. In the *New York World Telegram*, he wrote that the book was absolutely about Dean, included previously unpublished facts about Dean known to him, and contained an accurate and unspeakable truth about him.[12] Though he did not identify this truth, the context made plain it was homosexuality.

One, the most important gay magazine of the time, was more explicit, writing that Ross was clearly disgusted by the homosexuality of his hero, whom reviewer Robert Gregory had "no difficulty" identifying as James Dean, and therefore sought to posthumously punish him. "The traits about him that seemed good in the eyes of others are obliterated; every intention is made to seem dishonorable, and his attractions for others placed on the level of a modern Svengali," Gregory wrote. He added that it read like a case study for Edmund Bergler, the famed psychoanalyst who claimed homosexuals were perverted masochists stuck in an arrested state of development.[13]

New York and Hollywood elites were "agog" over the scandalous book.[14] MGM bought the film rights for $50,000 several months before publication and soon after announced an adaptation of the massive best-seller with a script by Rod Serling. Two years later, George Hamilton was set to star, with Paul Gregory directing, but nothing came of it.[15] Some speculated Warner Bros. pressured MGM to kill the project to protect their star's reputation.

Without the superficial veil of fiction, Royston Ellis, a twenty-two-year-old gay British novelist, openly declared Dean a "bisexual psychopath" with a "strong homosexual streak" in his 1962 Dean biography *Rebel*, and like Ross, he accurately—surprisingly so—described some of Dean's encounters with older male producers and with younger men.[16] In 1964, actor Gene Ringgold published an acid-laced tribute to Dean in *Screen Facts* that condemned Dean's involvement with a "street-corner clan of homosexual would-be actors" that Ringgold blamed for introducing Dean to the "midnight pick-up" libertine lifestyle of the "sadist and masochist perverts, damned to the slavery of their half-world hell."[17] In 1966, when Fe-Be's, San Francisco's first Folsom Street gay leather bar, commissioned a sculpture from Mike Caffee to represent the bar's patrons, he delivered a recreation of Michelangelo's David modeled on a leather-clad James Dean.

Two decades after James Dean died, his long-awaited resurrection finally occurred, after a fashion. The teenagers who had mourned for him in 1955 were now staring down middle age, amid a collapsing culture and a broken country. Vietnam had ended with an inglorious scramble from Saigon, and Richard Nixon proved not savior but villain. A backward glance at adolescence provided some relief but an incomplete escape, tinged with darkness dancing a pose of maturity.

In 1973, the National Enquirer ran a sensational, if recycled, story alleging James Dean yet lived, disfigured and secluded in a sanitarium, a nostalgic Watergate-era callback to a more innocent age. As the twentieth anniversary of Dean's death approached, nostalgia turned him into a profitable commodity. Posters, photos, books, comic books, T-shirts, and merchandise of every kind flew off shelves, an onslaught of marketing that would never end.

Dean's estate, managed first by his father, Winton, and later by his cousin Marcus Winslow Jr., took in millions, and still today Dean routinely nears the top of the annual Forbes list of most profitable dead celebrities. His name appeared in more pop songs than almost any other person living or dead, save perhaps Jesus. By most measures, in the 1970s and 1980s, his was among the most widely recognized celebrity faces on Earth, rivaled only by Elvis Presley and Marilyn Monroe. But what that face meant had bifurcated in death as it had in life, dividing into the Dean of straight men and of queer men.

"Everyone knows about Jimmy," Sal Mineo said of Dean's sexuality in 1972, but he meant everyone in Hollywood and the media, not the general public.[18] For a few more months, the rest of America knew only the image Hollywood had sold them. And then the image cracked.

Starting in 1974, a slate of books sought to expose the "real" James Dean, to deface the legend and strip away the veneer of manliness. In the hands of a new generation of biographers, the boy once heralded as a pagan god who would restore the world would become a shattered idol, an unwelcome alien hiding behind an angelic vision. In 1975, Jonathan Gilmore, now writing under the name John Gilmore, published his first book about Dean as a "lover of men as well as women," as its pink-accented front cover declared.

Not long before, the playwright and screenwriter Venable Herndon published *James Dean: A Short Life*. Having read that Dean had homosexual relationships, he prowled Manhattan's gay S&M clubs, interviewing aging patrons, who indulged him with fantastical—and false—stories claiming to have witnessed Dean performing public acts of extreme sadomasochistic sex in the fall of 1951. They said he served as a gay prostitute specializing in the outer limits of S&M for the "fist-fuck set." Herndon dutifully reported these claims—inspired, no doubt, by Kenneth Anger, whose allegations about Dean Herndon had also read—alongside the truth that Dean had had a relationship with Rogers Brackett that included sex.[19] But even when wallowing in the depths of imagined debauchery, Herndon couldn't shake the feeling that Dean possessed a spark of the divine. He commissioned an astrological chart for Dean and professed to be amazed that Dean's life and fate had been written in the stars.

The writer Ronald Martinetti published a "myth-shattering" biography the next year, *The James Dean Story*, with Rogers Brackett's first and only interview about his relationship with Dean. The "myth" of the "cult idol" Martinetti wanted to shatter was the fiction of heterosexuality. The teaser on the book's first edition back cover loudly asked, "Was he a closet homosexual? Was he a ruthless manipulator? Was he a petulant, spoiled trouble-maker?" John Howlett's *James Dean: A Biography* from that same year described Dean's gay experiences as the desperate acts of a heterosexual man seeking to exploit powerful men for any advantage. The unspoken undercurrent remained a certain degree of unmanliness, a failure of manhood caused by sex with men. Some went so far as to describe Dean—who spent his life pursuing a masculine ideal—as "androgynous," an acknowledgment of an unpleasant assumption that art and emotions belonged to women and sissies. Straight men knew only anger.

Together, these books cracked open fault lines in Dean's posthumous image and made space for gay cultural critics like Parker Tyler and Jack Babuscio to adopt Dean as a gay icon, his sexuality indivisible from his appeal. "We all know that the late James Dean's rather hard, but very pretty, physical shell was a homosexual parody of Marlon Brando," Tyler wrote in an overstated 1972 study of homosexuality in film, calling him a "fetish of boy-man

James Dean's version of masculinity often created discomfort in older straight men and appealed to younger queer men because it walked up to the edge of parody. *Photofest.*

homosexualism."[20] His rebellion, Tyler said, had a real cause: homosexual desire, his movies an exultation of queer S&M relationships.

Dean's photograph graced the walls of hundreds of gay bars, and gay men wore T-shirts emblazoned with his face. His name appeared somewhere in virtually every issue of the *Bay Area Reporter*, San Francisco's gay newspaper, for more than two decades. The *Advocate*, a major gay magazine, published a photograph of an erect penis in 1976 that writer Donald von Wiedenman falsely claimed to be Dean's, and the Legend Gallery, a New York sex shop, falsely advertised in gay newspapers an "uncensored" photo of a nude seventeen-year-old Dean for $2 by mail order.

Dean became a hero of the burgeoning gay rights movement, growing up in the wake of the Stonewall riot, someone who, like the newly liberated men fighting for new rights, had stood against an oppressive system, lived by his own rules, and had also been queer. "A reminder, then, to future biographers: James Dean was a homosexual. This fact was crucial to the development of his personality and his art," Babuscio wrote in *Gay News* in 1975. "Furthermore, as a member of an oppressed sexual minority, his orientation adds further psychological significance to his life experience and creative output. If this is not understood, then no sense can ever be made of the life of James Dean."[21] But many tried.

All the other 1970s books faded before the most popular of the Dean biographies, *James Dean: The Mutant King*, an idiosyncratic, scattershot 1974 account by *Rolling Stone* editor David Dalton, then twenty-nine. Dalton presented Dean as a somewhat ethereal presence and dismissed his "insinuated" homosexuality by claiming Dean affected androgyny because it was expected of an actor and that he merely collected sexual experiences to fulfill an "auto-erotic" desire for himself. Instead, Dalton focused on his bizarre occult belief that Dean embodied the dying-and-rising gods of *The Golden Bough* and had become a modern Osiris, whose Egyptian cult of resurrection he claimed presaged Dean's own. He wrote, with imagined profundity, "Like Osiris, James Dean was linked with Lucifer as both a god of youth and rebellion, king of the dead and god of light," and he declared Dean the soul and messenger of America's core myth, the only person to have embodied the history and future of the United States simultaneously, the inventor of adolescence and a young mythic hero like Perseus, Jason, or Theseus.[22] No homosexual could serve in the role of savior; no sexual deviant could truly be a hero. Thus, sexuality became mythology, to save the legend by denying the man.

Dalton understood what the other 1970s biographers had missed. Americans of the mid-1970s weren't looking to prove, as *Time* magazine had famously asked in 1966, whether God was dead and all idols smashed. They wanted to know that gods and heroes had once been flesh and blood, real, and

Dalton had made it possible for adults to idolize James Dean again by proving the demigod of their youth had truly walked the Earth before ascending
to the pantheon of the stars. They wanted myth and reality entwined, a world
enchanted.

Bill Bast tried to straddle these extremes in 1976 when NBC commissioned
an adaptation of his James Dean biography as a television movie, with Bast
writing the script. In a late 1974 ABC *Wide World Special*, "James Dean
Remembered," Peter Lawford openly discussed Dean's homosexual activity
with a skeptical Leonard Rosenman before a national audience, albeit at 11:30
p.m., and Bast felt such claims had cast a pall over his friend's reputation. He
told the *Advocate* he signed on to the movie to refute homosexual rumors and
allegations about Dean, and he told Tom Shales of the *Washington Post* that
Dean was merely a "dabbler" in homosexuality out of curiosity as an actor.[23]

The film aired to strong ratings and critical acclaim in February 1976, but
middle American audiences saw a very different depiction of the 1950s than
the anodyne nostalgia of *Happy Days*. Despite his stated intentions, Bast
produced a startlingly homoerotic film that included an unexpected scene in
which Stephen McHattie's James Dean speaks of experimenting with gay sex
and encourages Michael Brandon, playing Bast, to visit a gay bar. The movie
did not use the words *homosexual* or *gay* because NBC strictly limited any
direct references to homosexuality and had even placed a viewer advisory
on the broadcast warning of its gay content. But it was the last more-or-less
direct acknowledgment of Dean's complex sexuality on film until the twenty-
first century.[24]

After the 1976 *James Dean* broadcast, a young man wrote rambling letters
and sent a ranting audiotape to Bast, claiming to be the reincarnation of Dean
and begging to meet Bast to prove a supernatural connection to his fallen idol.
Bast ignored the letters but also remained far too protective of Dean's image.
He insisted publicly that Dean had been "heterosexually inclined," if sometimes bisexual. "Maybe he did some experimenting," he told David Dalton.
"But to say he was gay? That's ridiculous." Three more decades passed before
Bast would finally find the moral courage to write that Dean's queer sexuality
was "a given" and tell publicly the story he had so long kept invisible.[25]

Bast's efforts to "protect" Dean's reputation failed, and the onetime Dean
fans looking to define manhood anew in an unmoored world grew angry and

scared. The sandy-haired boy a generation had worshiped as the best of them revealed himself to be homosexually inclined, and the straight men who modeled themselves on him in youth and hung his picture on their dorm room walls and in their bachelor pads felt betrayed that the real man was not quite their celluloid hero.[26] Artists like the Beach Boys and the Eagles had once crooned longing odes to Dean, "too fast to live, too young to die," but in 1989 the Goo Goo Dolls, on the brink of stardom, now told of how young men wished to be James Dean, wild and free, until "you found out Dean was gay." And so, Johnny Rzeznik sang, "I don't want to be James Dean anymore."[27]

The producer of a 1995 documentary special, *James Dean: A Portrait*, claimed the Disney Channel ordered references to Dean's queer sexuality removed during production on the dubious premise that "in all the other bios on Dean, the subject was never mentioned."[28] Glossy new biopics would revise Dean into a robustly heterosexual figure, a cardboard caricature for the age of the culture wars, Rush Limbaugh, and Jerry Falwell. In film, among many examples, 1997's *James Dean: Live Fast, Die Young* presented his life as enthusiastically heterosexual, as embodied by a well-muscled, square-jawed Casper Van Dien, while 2001's cable TV movie *James Dean*, starring James Franco, hinted only obliquely at possible bisexuality while crafting a narrative of intense heterosexual romance. Producer Marvin Worth said in preproduction that he didn't want to sully the film with gay distractions, as though being queer were simply an unnecessary affectation or a weird hobby: "We'll try to make a good movie—not one of innuendo and rumor."[29] And yet as stories of Dean's sexuality circulated anew, the project declined from a star-studded prestige film for theatrical release to a TV movie, with news reports suggesting that several big-name actors had refused a role they feared might associate them with homosexuality.

Queer people had achieved greater prominence, sometimes unwanted, as tragic figures in AIDS-era America. Rock Hudson's deathbed revelation of homosexuality as he succumbed to AIDS in 1985 marked a seismic shift in Hollywood, the first marquee name publicly identified as gay. Paul Alexander, a journalist born the year Dean died, responded by depicting Dean as a tragic, doomed gay man in his 1994 sex-focused, pornographic, and uncritically sourced biography *Boulevard of Broken Dreams*.[30] He received intense criticism from all quarters and a libel suit from Bill Bast, who disingenuously objected to being called Dean's lover.[31] The celebrated feminist film critic

Molly Haskell, writing in a *New York Times* review, condemned Alexander for "proudly exposing" what should be "allowed" to "remain hidden." She said that calling the emotional pain Dean suffered in life "tragic" was "arrant nonsense, the hyperbole of gender politics." She cheerfully wrote that Dean's transactional relationships and unwanted sex were not problems if "he could keep himself in sports cars with a $100,000-per-picture contract." Instead, she viewed Dean as a feminist ideal, imagining him—motorcycles and race cars, knives and guns, and leather and blue jeans—as "androgynous," a woman by other means, because he dared to feel.[32] Nora Sayre, a former *New York Times* film critic turned academic, made the same case a decade earlier. His sobbing and screaming, she said, were an emotional release familiar to women: "In the best sense, Dean was unmanly, and an adolescent girl or young woman could identify with him, as I did."[33] Marie Cartier, a feminist academic, went still further, claiming in 2003 that Dean was essentially transgender, living as a "butch," a masculine lesbian constrained by having a penis.[34] Only "sissies," even feminists believed, had emotions. He couldn't be that awful thing, a *man*.

Echoes of that angry hurt, that suspicion of what Dos Passos called "thwarted maleness," lingered. Many who knew Dean would only cooperate with writers or filmmakers who agreed not to discuss homosexuality.[35] At a 1995 ceremony in Fairmount to commemorate the fortieth anniversary of Dean's death, the crowd of middle-aged Dean fans nodded like congregants praising a pastor when Lew Bracker proudly proclaimed Dean to be straight. Hollywood reporter Joe Hyams's 1992 Dean biography saw Dean as an unknowable cypher, a perpetual adolescent unsure of his own desires but ultimately consumed by love for Pier Angeli. Val Holley's 1995 *James Dean: The Biography* presented Dean's sexual experiences with admirable frankness but muddled the message in a flurry of contradictions and steadfastly refused to draw even the most obvious of conclusions. In his 1996 Dean biography *Rebel*, celebrity biographer Donald Spoto, himself gay, conceded Dean was bisexual but allowed himself an escape, arguing that *all* of Dean's relationships were failures, little more than experimentations, with little or no impact on his art. He spent pages on the consumer price index and crime statistics, as though to bury Dean beneath sociological data, historical materialism made flesh. He threw up his hands in the end. "No one could be quite sure just what James Dean wanted—a pliable man, a strong woman, a man who cradled him like a woman, a woman who acted like a man. . . . It was all very confusing," he wrote.[36]

Dean's fault, aging authors all agreed, was his failure to conform to mid-century masculine stereotypes, to embody their childhood idea of a real man. Or, absent that, to enact the homosexual stereotype, to be flamboyant and effeminate and campy. Existing between categories, to be masculine and queer, sensitive and strong—that was beyond the comprehension of minds raised in the twentieth century's polarized world of absolutes. And yet, in his enigmatic ambiguity, Dean remained the "gay man's Mona Lisa," the highest achievement of queer artistry, in the 1996 words of Richard Martin of the Metropolitan Museum of Art.[37]

Even in the more open and liberated twenty-first century, there was no consensus on how to handle James Dean. Books stinging with wounds of betrayal still rolled from publishers' presses, declaring Dean to be a malevolent, psychopathic prostitute. Literature professor Don Graham's 2018 study of *Giant* made Dean the villain of his narrative, emphasizing what he saw as the vicious, sociopathic egocentricity of a heterosexual man who eagerly entrapped powerful men in a web of sex-for-work favors. Scandal-mongering celebrity biographers Darwin Porter and Danforth Prince self-published an influential biography of Dean in 2016 comprised of seven hundred pages of sexual rumors, innuendo, and gossip, suffused with an iconoclast's vengeful glee at toppling an idol. They alleged without evidence that Dean had been a prostitute since high school, painted him as an opportunist using gay sex as a weapon, and repeated their own claim from their 2006 biography *Brando Unzipped* that he had been the submissive for years in an S&M relationship with Brando that involved Brando inflicting humiliations and injuries on Dean.[38] Newspapers like the *New York Post* couldn't get enough of the fabrication, despite being chronologically impossible and without documentary evidence, and online articles and podcasts still widely repeat the false claims. In 2012, the motion picture *Joshua Tree: 1951* depicted Dean as uncompromisingly bisexual by dramatizing the most salacious lies about Dean's alleged S&M gay sex life.

Alongside the cartoonish claims, the respectable press slowly began to change how they talked about James Dean, albeit in fits and starts, and to move beyond the limits Bast established for Dean in 1976, anachronistic echoes of the fear and oppression that had marked so much of twentieth-century life. In

writing about *Rebel without a Cause* for the National Society of Film Critics'
2002 list of essential films, *Boston Globe* critic Jay Carr noticed the "unmistakable" homoeroticism of the film but was unable to reason from it why Natalie
Wood's character was so underwritten, her romance with Jim so tacked-
on.[39] The great film critic and lifelong liberal humanist Roger Ebert did not
acknowledge the homoeroticism of *Rebel* until 2005, half a century after the
film's release, ultimately failing to see any real message in the movie: "The
film has not aged well. . . . Like its hero, 'Rebel Without a Cause' desperately
wants to say something and doesn't know what it is."[40]

Lawrence Frascella and Al Weisel's 2005 book *Live Fast, Die Young: The
Wild Ride of Making Rebel without a Cause* discussed sexuality openly and
praised the film for its subversive and sensitive depiction of same-sex desire
at the height of the homophobic 1950s. Bill Bast, who had spent the twentieth
century defending James Dean's honor by insisting he was "heterosexually
inclined," published a revision of his 1956 biography as a 2006 memoir focusing on his and Dean's journeys through Hollywood's gay underground. But
only a small press published the book, and it passed largely unnoticed by the
mainstream media.

And yet, even in recent years, older interpretations still dominated outside
of the limited world of explicitly queer media. Dean's own family rejected half
a century of research and commissioned an "official" biography from film
writer George Perry for the fiftieth anniversary of Dean's death. Perry, just
four years Dean's junior, sought to reinforce the family's preferred view of
Dean as robustly heterosexual. Perry asserted that Dean used Rogers Brackett
merely as a "convenient means to an end" and that Dean's homosexuality
was a "persistent myth." Perry claimed all young male actors experimented
with homosexuality out of curiosity, but after Dean's "ruthless" efforts to
exploit Rogers Brackett with feigned homosexuality, he returned to full heterosexuality and would eventually have "found a satisfying female love" had
he lived.[41] Dean's heirs would rather we see him as an amoral monster than
as queer.

In 2015's movie *Life*, a dramatization of Dennis Stock's James Dean
photo shoot for *Life* magazine, director Anton Corbijn reverted to the 1950s
Esquire and *Look* caricature of Dean, with actor Dane DeHaan playing him

as an indifferently heterosexual collection of verbal tics, unpleasantness, and disaffection, with no trace of whatever magic drew so many to him. In various works published between 2012 and 2021 that became the novel *Widespread Panic*, James Ellroy, who hated James Dean with the burning passion of the betrayed, depicted Dean as a villainous stooge and homosexual prostitute working for *Confidential*, wantonly jerking off on the set of a porn shoot.[42] In early 2024, several editions of *Vogue* magazine worldwide published a story that attempted to refute the "poisoned rumors" of Dean's homosexuality or bisexuality by celebrating Dean's failed romance with Pier Angeli as the "best possible denial" of his sexual deviance.[43]

Through it all, CMG Worldwide, the company Marcus Winslow Jr. hired to license and exploit Dean's image, kept the endorsement machine running, plastering Dean's name and face on everything from cookie jars to postcards, from restaurants to dolls, from fountain pens to T-shirts, generating as much as $8.5 million for the estate and its beneficiaries each year, according to *Forbes* estimates. Winslow, who was a small boy when Dean died, tirelessly asserted Dean's absolute heterosexuality and dismissed any claims otherwise as scurrilous lies. It was in the estate's interest to ensure a Dean acceptable to the largest possible audience, and into the first decades of the twenty-first century, corporate America still considered queer people to have only niche appeal. Few of the officially licensed products boasted any great quality; many "collectibles" bore little resemblance to the real Dean. The sculptures were often cartoons of masculinity, some generic, hard-boiled stud, often uncomfortably well-muscled, identifiable only by a hairstyle and a red jacket.

It didn't matter, of course. The "James Dean" offered for sale was a celluloid saint, a memory of manhood carved from fantasy, a depiction of "cool" unmoored from the messiness of life. By 2019, Winslow and CMG planned to digitally resurrect Dean using deepfake and motion-capture technology to star in new projects, ranging from movies to video games, a CGI demon lover finally able to fulfill any fan's every fantasy, and in 2024, CMG licensed a computer recreation of Dean's voice to a mobile app to read books and articles aloud. CMG and its digital partner Worldwide XR planned a science fiction movie called *Back to Eden* in which the

James Dean so fully defined what it means to be a cool, young male that, seven decades after his death, he remains a model that nearly every young man either follows or reacts against. *Photofest.*

digital Dean would portray the real Dean being reborn in the twenty-first century.[44] It was everything Dean never wanted, to be rendered powerless, compliant, a puppet on a string dancing mechanically for whoever paid the bill. "James Dean" had become a franchised brand. Jimmy Dean would have wept.

EPILOGUE

Near 11:00 p.m. on September 18, 1998, Texas police burst into the Harris County apartment near Houston shared by Tyron Garner, aged thirty-one, and John Lawrence, fifty-five, at the instigation of Robert Eubanks, a friend of both men and sometime lover of Garner. An inebriated Eubanks, in a fit of jealousy, called police from a pay phone and told them falsely that Garner had a gun and had gone crazy. Eubanks waited for the Harris County sheriff's department to arrive, and he directed officers to unit 833 of the Columbia Club Apartments, on the complex's second floor. When officers burst into the apartment's bedroom, guns drawn, they claimed to find Garner and Lawrence naked, having sex on the bed, unwilling to stop, even at gunpoint. The two men insisted police made up the story, out of disgust for gay men and contempt at Garner for being Black and effeminate. One officer called him a "naggy little bitch" and crudely imitated a queerly accented voice in falsetto. Cops arrested both men for violating a Texas law against "homosexual conduct," which criminalized same-sex sodomy. Police called the men "faggots" as they placed them under arrest. As they did, something caught their eye on the bedroom wall: two drawings of James Dean that Lawrence had acquired from an artist in a gay bar in the early 1990s.

These were "two pencil sketchings of James Dean, naked, with an extremely oversized penis on him," sheriff's deputy Joseph Quinn reported. Quinn recalled being disgusted that the two images were hung in such a way as to be visible from the bed. "It was like his fixture, his art manifesto up there on the wall," Quinn said. Another deputy stopped to gawk at the pictures. "Did you see that sketching in there?" he asked Quinn. They spent several minutes examining the pictures. "Well it did look like James Dean," the second deputy said, "well, facially it looked—it was a pretty good sketch of his facial." They laughed. One of them joked, "This is the kind of thing I would have in my house!" They then remarked that it was obvious where the "faggots" trained their eyes. They made some unspecified homophobic remarks about the pictures to Lawrence as they handcuffed him.[1]

Working with gay-rights advocates, Lawrence challenged the Texas law against gay sex, and the case against Texas made its way to the Supreme Court. In 2003, the court ruled 6–3 in *Lawrence v. Texas* that laws criminalizing gay sex were unconstitutional. Americans, Justice Anthony Kennedy wrote on behalf of the court, "are entitled to respect for their private lives. The State cannot demean their existence or control their destiny by making their private sexual conduct a crime."[2]

Traditionally, the epilogue draws the story to a close and offers catharsis, if not a note of triumph. In that better, more perfect world that James Dean imagined might someday exist, *Lawrence v. Texas* would be that triumph, a fitting moment of finality. No young man would ever again have to live in fear. I would be able to write joyfully of the steady progress of our culture, from gay liberation in the 1970s to gay marriage in the 2010s, of the revolution in Americans' understanding of masculinity, sexual orientation, and gender roles. But just as James Dean lived an incomplete life, the story of sexuality and masculinity in America is unfinished, the triumphant conclusion still just beyond the horizon.

In that better, more perfect world, we would celebrate a Gallup poll released in early 2024 that found one in five young adults, 22 percent, identified as LGBTQ+, a generational shift doubling from even my own cohort born in the preceding generation. Among those still surviving from Dean's generation, the number is just 1 percent.[3] There is no reason to suspect more people are queer today than in the past, but more people, especially young people, feel safe and empowered identifying themselves that way.

In that better world, I would point to the end of formal government prohibitions of gay people in public service in the 1960s and the more recent integration of queer people into the military as a steady march of progress. I would write at length of the new push in Hollywood, however inconsistent, to represent queer stories and empower queer creators. In 2022, 12 percent of all series regular characters on American TV were queer, though most were lesbians, and the gay men were too often flamboyant. In 2016, *Moonlight*, a coming-of-age story that dealt frankly with themes of masculinity and homo-sexuality in depicting the life of a young queer man, won the Academy Award for Best Picture, something no one who made *Rebel without a Cause* could have imagined possible.

In that more perfect world, I would write of the generations of actors who took their inspiration from James Dean. I would write of Martin Sheen, who brilliantly played his murderous *Badlands* character in 1976 as if James Dean were playing Charles Starkweather playing James Dean, and Nicolas Cage, who attributes his uneven career to a revelation gained in the light of Dean's movies. I would write of contemporary stars like Jacob Elordi and Austin But-ler who still cite Dean as a guide, seven decades after his death. I would write, too, of young Americans' embrace of less-confining forms of masculinity, the kind of freer, more open, and loving forms of manhood that James Dean tried to live in a world that insisted emotion was a failure of manliness. And I would write of the connection between the stories of young men the Dean-inspired actors put on the screen and the way young men came to think about them-selves. More than any other twentieth-century star, James Dean paved the way for a radical reimagining of what it means to be a man. He made it acceptable, even admirable, to cry and shout and to feel. And we are all better for it.

But we don't live in a perfect world. It is a better one, one that has grown more accepting and more tolerant and more open, becoming unrecognizable from the world of my youth, in the 1990s, which was much closer in spirit to that of the 1950s than to today. I didn't feel comfortable being gay or coming out when I was a teenager. I can still remember the day in middle school when an older boy threatened to kill me because he perceived me to be unmanly and gay, the lunches in the high school cafeteria when friends would joke about the reasons gay people deserved death, and the gathering of friends in my college dorm room when a football player turned red with rage and punched a hole in the wall after a fellow player's roommate announced his bisexual-ity to the group. Such experiences leave deep scars. The vast improvement in attitudes I have witnessed over my lifetime, however imperfect, is astonishing.

Yet all of the triumphs and the progress in creating the world that James Dean hoped to inhabit, the one where people like him could live without labels, free from pain and judgment, are under threat. Across America, reactionaries have once again turned sex and gender into culture wars, intent on resurrecting the world of absolutes, returning to the 1950s, when "men were men." State legislatures across the country enact legislation to negate LGBTQ rights, to brand queer kids as vectors of some invisible contagion, to symbolically restore "FAGGOTS—STAY OUT" signs. A sitting justice of the U.S. Supreme Court openly encouraged in 2022—2022!—the restoration of gay marriage bans and the criminalization of gay sex. The persistence of pederasty and sexual exploitation, especially among the powerful, from Boy Scout campgrounds to the executive suite of Abercrombie & Fitch, made possible by twentieth-century America's culture of secrecy and oppression, left generations of boys and young men vulnerable to abuse, with little recourse and less sympathy. It also led inevitably to a resurrection of the smear that queer men were inherently vampiric "groomers," preying on boys to convert them.

All the while, the leaders of one of America's two great political parties actively sought to purify gender roles, to make men manly again. "I want to talk with you about the Left's attempt to give us a world beyond men," Republican senator Josh Hawley of Missouri told a conference of conservatives in late 2021. "The Left want to define traditional masculinity as toxic. They want to define the traditional masculine virtues—things like courage, and independence, and assertiveness—as a danger to society." The destruction of "manly virtues," Hawley said, is a "crisis for the republic." To save America and manhood, "we need men who will shoulder responsibility, men who will start and provide for families, men who will enter the covenant of marriage and then honor it."[4]

Representative Madison Cawthorn, a North Carolina Republican, was blunter. Boys, he said, must be raised to be monsters. "Our culture today is trying to completely de-masculate all of the young men in our culture," he said in a 2021 speech. "If you are raising a young man, please raise them to be a monster."[5] But he really meant "beast," something animalistic and uncivilized, aggressive and untamed. In 2022, the nation's most-watched cable news host, the effete conservative pundit Tucker Carlson, then of Fox News, produced a documentary on *The End of Men*, claiming that American men had become less aggressive, less powerful, and less manly than their forebears.

"Hard times make strong men," the *End of Men* proclaimed amid homoerotic imagery of idealized muscular men lifting heavy things, while "weak men make hard times."[6]

Fearful that the growing numbers of young men identifying as queer threatened traditional masculinity, conservative politicians in states like Alabama, Arkansas, Florida, Indiana, Iowa, Kentucky, and North Carolina passed restrictions on discussing LGBTQ+ issues in schools in the early 2020s, and right-wing advocacy groups like Moms for Liberty demanded and often achieved removal of books with queer characters and themes from school and public libraries. Media companies, including Warner Bros. Discovery, cancelled an unprecedented number of shows with queer characters or themes in 2022 and 2023, while the Justice Department reported a rising number of hate crimes motivated by sexual orientation or gender identity. After the U.S. Supreme Court overturned *Roe v. Wade* in 2022, conservative groups began applying legal arguments and strategies that had succeeded in ending national abortion protections in a quest to overturn decisions legalizing gay marriage and gay sex, and at least two Supreme Court justices seemed to encourage such efforts.

I sincerely hope they fail and that when future readers pick up this book ten or twenty years from when I write, this dark moment will be remembered, like the antigay panic of the 1950s, as a shameful aberration. Instead, what I hope readers remember from this book is that the biggest star in Hollywood, once the most famous man in the world, the man who defined what a man was supposed to look and act like for seven decades, the very model of young manhood, was himself queer. His face is everywhere, his name synonymous with America, manliness, and cool. And that can't be erased.

The renewed panic over masculinity and gender purity and the vicious assault on LGBTQ people reflect America's polarized, binary understanding of life, our country's intolerance for ambiguity. Those who fall somewhere between the extremes become monsters, and the villagers come for them with torches. No matter how sympathetic the monster, the threat of violence is never far. Traditional movie monsters occupy the liminal space between categories, the vampire between the living and the dead, the werewolf between beast and man. So, too, do the monsters of sex and gender live between the categories. The reason the figure of James Dean remains both attractive and troubling, reassuring and threatening, is that he existed in the space between absolutes—not a boy but not quite a man; not straight but not gay enough; not effeminate but not quite fully masculine; not living but not yet safely dead.

The battle over masculinity and sexuality that began in the mid-twentieth century remains unfinished today. We have been here before. All of this played out in the 1950s, and we know the results of oppressive policies, degrading media messages, and censorship. Yet the longing for transcendence outshines every effort to snuff out the flame. The faithful still ignore the grave men, their blind eyes blazing like meteors, who claim unearned truths and tell them that being different is evil. Each fall, the true believers gather in the thousands in Fairmount to honor James Dean with the rites usually afforded to a Catholic saint or an ancient Greek hero.[7] The annual memorial service for Dean mixes the solemnity of a religious service, held at the Back Creek Friends Church, with the camaraderie of a street fair. Fans stand in the pulpit to testify to Dean's life-changing power, his face projected behind them on the off-white wall of the blue-carpeted church, side by side with a mural of Jesus as the Good Shepherd. People who view themselves as outsiders come together as one in their longing and their hope and place their trust in an absent icon, imagining a salvation that will never come in this world—only, perhaps, in the one beyond. Wherever James Dean's influence is felt in the arts, there, too, a little something of that better, more perfect world can still be glimpsed, a world less confining, less oppressive, less rigid—liberated in the truest sense of freedom. No wonder angry old men still think him a monster.

The rebels and the queers, the alienated and the outsiders, the ones who were different, persecuted, hated, hunted, afraid—in the terror and wonder of infinity, they found a cause for hope, a moment of grace and joy in knowing someone had gone this way before, had felt for a moment the cold winds of the unlighted road, and had glimpsed something secret beyond the veil of time and space and the stifling tyranny of reality. In the life and art of a single man they could see themselves, burning with an eternal flame, immortals unbroken beneath a boundless heaven. "A real star carries its own illumination, an inward brightness," James Dean once said.[8] And for a glorious moment, James Dean had been the brightest star of all.

Acknowledgments

I am fortunate to have had the opportunity to write about as rich and fascinating a character as James Dean. My previous books tended to focus on much drier subjects, and it was a bit of culture shock to plunge into writing about a subject that felt, even at a distance of seven decades, so vital and so alive. However, while James Dean came to life in my research, nearly everyone who knew him is no longer with us, and most of the research for this book necessarily involved published sources, almost all of which are readily available.

Anyone writing about James Dean is both blessed and cursed by the sheer volume of material available. Thanks to unprecedented interest in Dean in the 1950s and 1970s, his is among the best-documented and most thoroughly discussed lives of the twentieth century, particularly given its brevity. Where in past decades, I might thank a laundry list of librarians for working with me to uncover these texts, in today's digital world, my thanks must go to the anonymous staffers who populated a variety of research databases, which I am not paid enough to give free publicity here. Special thanks, however, go to the Harry Ransom Center, University of Texas at Austin, for access to Royston Ellis's working notes and to the Clark Art Institute Library for access to the rare French edition of Kenneth Anger's *Hollywood Babylon*.

I also thank my family for putting up with the inconvenience of too much of my time going to research, writing, and revision. My most important professional thanks go to my agent, Lee Sobel, who believed in this book when no one else did and found it a home, and to my editor at Applause Books, Chris Chappell, whose insightful editorial notes, given with grace and good humor, sharpened my manuscript, excised distracting material, and helped focus the narrative. Thanks to Dave Holmes and Kelly Stout at *Esquire* magazine for taking a chance on me, letting me write about James Dean as a queer icon in *Esquire*'s august pages, and launching me on the path to this book. Thanks, too, to Ronald Martinetti for discussing Dean's life and his own adventures writing Dean's biography with me. Similar thanks go to those who, under their own names or screen names, shared information, thoughts, and ideas with me on social media and in comments on my online articles about James Dean during the writing of this book.

I confess that I am often taken aback by the number of people thanked in book acknowledgments, and I fear my list looks less impressive by comparison. James Dean once claimed to be self-made and to have done everything on his own. That was never true for him or me, but unlike so many writers, I did not have research assistants to collect documents for me or interns to write my drafts. The research in this book is mine, and I obtained and read every book, article, and document in it. Indeed, Dean was never shy about criticizing those he felt had wronged him, and if I followed his example, I might include a page to disacknowledge the many people who refused help or who actively tried to hinder my project, from those who withheld research materials to powerful media figures who insisted this book could not be published because the topic was inappropriate, offensive, or unwelcome in a conservative political climate. One very famous network news personality even advised me to write a different book and sneak the thesis of this one into it because my topic was so incendiary. I am not quite as willing as Dean to burn every bridge, but like him, I won't let this pass unacknowledged.

Finally, my thanks must go to James Dean himself, who was, even in death, both my best collaborator and my most unfailing research source. Dean was self-dramatizing and lived his life like a story. As a result, he littered his life with material meant for some imagined future biography, and frequently, to my immense surprise, he left behind some quotation or another that not only confirmed a conclusion I had drawn but, in several cases, used nearly the same words I had. I fear I will never again have such a cooperative subject for a book. And, yes, I borrowed for my chapter titles the names of episodes from Dean's less-known television appearances.

James Dean was among the first movie stars to build a personal brand that was bigger than his film work. As such, he was obsessed with his image and controlling how others saw him, talked about him, and thought about him. Given how readily he lied about his own biography, I can only imagine how he would have reacted in 1955 to a book that revealed the man behind the myth. I would hope that had he lived into his nineties, he would have eventually approved of my effort to depict him honestly and to strip away the hypocrisies of Hollywood that he so hated.

A Note on Sources

The historiography of James Dean is almost impossibly convoluted. Primary sources are scarce, and Dean himself was often cagey or deceptive in his own letters. Important documents were accidentally or purposely destroyed. Most information about Dean comes from three problematic groups of sources: contemporary media coverage, memories from Dean's acquaintances, and the work of earlier biographers. The first group is problematic for all the reasons journalism is not history, including biases, incompleteness, and a lack of perspective. Media of the 1950s and 1960s worked much more closely with movie studio publicists than they do today, and much of what was published was studio-approved public relations more than an accurate description of events.

The second group is still more problematic for all the reasons that memory is not history. Memories change and fade over time, and many of Dean's acquaintances changed their stories, sometimes markedly, over the course of decades. Some of this is due to the natural memory drift of aging, but too often changes seem to reflect a personal or political agenda. Also it is not always the case that the earliest version of an anecdote is the most accurate; as with many queer narratives, many sources bowdlerized or suppressed references to homosexuality, sometimes for decades, before offering a more complete account, too often when memory had faded. William Bast's 2006 revision of his own 1956 James Dean biography to reintroduce the queer content omitted from the original is perhaps the most dramatic but certainly not a unique instance.

The third group of sources, the third-party biographies, is similarly problematic for the reasons discussed earlier and for three more: First, most biographers of James Dean (and other celebrities) were not historians by trade, and their research methodology varied greatly in quality from writer to writer, frequently relying mostly on previously published material and interviews with Dean's friends. Far too few clearly cited sources, and where these could be traced, many errors occurred in the copying from one magazine or book to the next. Second, the major Dean biographies were written in the previous century, and they bear the hallmarks of their time, with heavy-handed Freudianism and outdated attitudes toward homosexuality coloring both what facts were admitted and how they were interpreted. Third, and most importantly, because most biographers hung their narratives on access to Dean's celebrity friends and his family, there is little critical analysis of anecdotes and claims, even when they appear prima facie false. Earlier writers needed to please both their sources and their audience, and they faced great pressure to simply publish what people said without angering them by offering critical analysis or asking them difficult questions. Now that almost everyone Dean knew is dead, I face no such pressure, though at the cost of not having direct access to the people involved.

Finally, and perhaps unique to Dean in volume if not in quality, is the problem of fabrication. Falsification was present right from the beginning, when Dean himself lied about his biography and Warner Bros. rewrote his life story for promotional purposes. Much of what was written about Dean was fake. Whether this be entire books, like the hoax biography *I, James Dean*, or magazine articles by alleged confidants who never met Dean or anecdotes and stories in otherwise reputable books that never happened or even nonexistent "friends" cited as sources, Dean's historiography is rife with fabrications that have continued to fool even serious writers. Some of this was opportunistic, from profiteers looking for fortune or fame by claiming a piece of Dean's notoriety. Some of it was out of misguided "protection." Early biographers, like William Bast and Joe Hyams, falsified material to protect Dean's reputation from accusations of homosexuality, as Bast later admitted.

Sporadically, writers would attempt to correct some fabrication or another only to see the next book repeat the false claim. For this book, I have started anew and systematically applied a rigorous scholarly analysis of sources, tracing each claim back to its primary source or as close as I could come to it and collating claims against official documentation and records and independently verifiable chronology. I cannot guarantee that I rooted out every fabrication, but I have turned over, as close as I could come, every scrap of relevant paper known to exist to find the truth. In the chapter notes, I provide specific detail on the reasoning behind rejecting specific claims as hoaxes, as well as an analysis of variations and contradictions between sources. I have chosen to keep the main narrative focused on James Dean rather than the people who wrote and spoke about him; therefore, the interested reader is invited to review the messy, under-the-hood work of historiography in the notes.

Notes

EPIGRAPH

1. The first two sentences of the quotation are condensed from Edwin Miller, "An Actor in Search of Himself," *Seventeen*, October 1955, 114, and the last three are from "The Little Things That Made a Myth," in *Official James Dean Anniversary Book* (New York: Dell, 1956), 34. The popularly repeated version, running these lines together uncredited, appeared in Royston Ellis's *Rebel* (London: World Distributors, 1962, 57) before becoming the epigraph to John Howlett's influential 1975 James Dean biography, again uncredited.

INTRODUCTION

1. *Giant* premiere booklet, Warner Bros. and Roxy Theatre, 1956; "'Giant' to have Roxy Premiere," *Brooklyn Daily*, September 21, 1956, 17; H. Viggo Andersen, "World Premiere of 'Giant' Gives New Yorkers Thrill," *Hartford Courant*, October 14, 1956, 13E; Frances Smiley, "Premiere of 'Giant' Was Outsized Race for Quotes from Stars of Picture," *St. Louis Globe-Democrat*, October 15, 1956, 1B; Kaspar Monahan, "'Giant' Premiere Stirs Big Crowd," *Pittsburgh Press*, October 11, 1956, 12.
2. *Tex and Jinx*, WRCA-FM, October 11, 1956.
3. Gertrude Trawick, "Jett Rink, Not Davy Crockett Is Latest Hero of Teenagers," *Macon* [GA] *News*, January 31, 1957, 19; Eugene Gilbert, "They Still Like Movies . . . and Boys Prefer Blondes," *Meriden* [CT] *Journal*, January 17, 1957, 14.
4. John Dos Passos, "The Death of James Dean," *Esquire*, October 1958, 121–23; John Dos Passos, *Midcentury* (Boston: Houghton Mifflin, 1961), 479–86.
5. Nell Dodson Russell, "The Way I See It," *St. Paul Recorder*, April 14, 1950, 3.

6. Boze Hadleigh, *Celluloid Gaze* (New York: Limelight Editions, 2002), 13. Some have accused Hadleigh of fabricating parts of his interviews, though he claimed to have almost all of them on tape. (See, e.g., talk show host Woody McBrearity's 1987 interview with Boze Hadleigh [Woody McBrearity, "Woody McBrearity Interviews Boze Hadleigh," YouTube video, 6:05, January 19, 2010, https://www.youtube.com/watch?v=YpKn362MoQU].) Parts of the interviews were published without contest during the subjects' lives, and to my knowledge no one has argued that the previously unpublished portions of Hadleigh's 1972 Sal Mineo interview were fabricated.

7. Review of *Rebel without a Cause*, *Variety*, October 26, 1955, 6; Jack Moffitt, review of *Rebel without a Cause*, *Hollywood Reporter*, October 21, 1955.

8. Martin Mayer, "The Apotheosis of Jimmy Dean," *Esquire*, December 1956; Jason Colavito, "It's Time We Let James Dean Be the Queer Icon That He Is," *Esquire*, September 30, 2021.

9. Val Holley, *James Dean: The Biography* (New York: St. Martin's Press, 1995).

10. William Bast, *James Dean: A Biography* (New York: Ballantine, 1956); Joe Hyams, "James Dean," *Redbook*, September 1956; George Scullin, "James Dean: The Legend and the Facts," *Look*, October 16, 1956.

11. Walter Ross, *The Immortal* (New York: Simon & Schuster, 1958). Ross specifically refers to his Dean analog's homosexual life as "immoral" on page 237.

12. The Deacy family sold the collection piecemeal at auction in May 2023. A representative for the family told me the documents were Deacy's complete file on Dean, but the content of the letters indicates that additional documents, including several letters from Dean, once existed. Many of these were likely destroyed after his death as part of an effort to protect Dean from accusations of homosexuality, as Dean's friends previously stated. I purchased two of the documents that most closely confirmed stories about Dean's homosexuality in order to ensure that they did not disappear from the public record forever.

13. Headlines on the covers of *Real* for July 1957 and *Look* for October 16, 1956.

14. Joe Hyams and Jay Hyams, *James Dean: Little Boy Lost* (New York: Warner Books, 1992), 5.

15. Edmund Bergler, *One Thousand Homosexuals: Conspiracy of Silence, or Curing and Deglamorizing Homosexuals?* (Paterson, NJ: Pageant Books, 1959), 152; B. Richard Peterson, "Homosexuals Can Be Cured!" *Confidential*, May 1957, 38.

CHAPTER 1

1. Emily Post, "Are Gentlemen Sissies?" *Evening Star* [Washington, DC], January 5, 1947, 14.

2. Hedda Hopper and James Brough, *The Whole Truth and Nothing But* (New York: Doubleday, 1963), 172.

3. "Spotlighting James Dean," in *The New Film Show Annual* (Great Britain: LTA Robinson, c. 1955), 61.

4. Biographer Val Holley claims that in early childhood Dean suffered nosebleeds and black-and-blue bruises indicative of child abuse, presumably at the hands of his

father, but the underlying sources offer no indication of the cause, and I could find no independent confirmation that the bruises were the result of abuse (Holley, *James Dean*, 17).

5. Donald Spoto, *Rebel: The Life and Legend of James Dean* (New York: HarperCollins, 1996), chaps. 2–3; many of the anecdotes of Dean's youth first appeared in posthumous magazine reminiscences, such as Emma Woolen Dean, "James Dean—The Boy I Loved," *Photoplay*, March 1956, 57, 84–85.

6. Hyams and Hyams, *James Dean*, 18.

7. My characterization of Dean's feelings is based on descriptions of Dean's autobiographical conversations to friends later in life and recollections from friends of his attitudes as a teenager. I have read these in combination with Joe Hyams's 1992 account of Dean's involvement with the Reverend James DeWeerd (see later) and the conversations Hyams describes them having about Dean's discomfort with what Hyams interprets as references to homosexuality. I have taken the small liberty of assuming that the understanding of his feelings and desires he expressed in college were not entirely unknown to him in the preceding years and did not emerge ex nihilo.

8. David Dalton was the first to give the quotation (David Dalton, *James Dean: The Mutant King: A Biography* [New York: Dell, 1974], 171; David Dalton, *James Dean: The Mutant King: A Biography* [Chicago: Chicago Review Press, 2001], 150–51), but he cited no source, and when asked about it by anthropologist James F. Hopgood, he was unable to recall the origin, speculating Natalie Wood may have been the source (James F. Hopgood, *Adoration and Pilgrimage: James Dean and Fairmount*, Kindle ed. [Eugene, OR: Luminare Press, 2022], 86). Later writers altered the quotation to have Dean explicitly deny being gay, and many, starting with Mick St. Michael in 1989, claimed Dean used the line in answer to a reporter's question about sexuality, though I have found no evidence of this, and it seems unlikely that the image-conscious Dean would have openly courted sexual controversy.

9. Jack Ricardo, "A Different Kind of Coming Out," *Record* [Hackensack, NJ], November 27, 1972, A18.

10. Francis Sill Wickware, "Psychoanalysis," *Life*, February 3, 1947, 104; Howard Whitman, "Is Psychoanalysis at War with God?", *Cosmopolitan*, June 1947, 110.

11. Marx Kaye, "Mystery of the Peruvian Giants," *Amazing Stories*, June 1947, 162–63. On the popularity of pulps, see Anita P. Forbes, "Combating Cheap Magazines," *English Journal* 26, no. 6 (June 1937): 476–78.

12. "Homosexuals in Uniform," *Newsweek*, June 9, 1947, 54.

13. "Homosexuals in Uniform," 54.

14. Hyams and Hyams, *James Dean*, 14.

15. Lynne Brennan, "The Legend of Jimmy Dean," *Indianapolis Star Magazine*, December 10, 1967, 27.

16. "Mental Aid Found Deficient in Kings," *New York Times*, July 6, 1947, 15.

17. E. B. Henderson, "Athletics Help Keep Males Normal Men," *Minnesota Spokesman*, February 21, 1947, 6.

18. Ronald Martinetti, *The James Dean Story* (New York: Pinnacle Books, 1975), 15.

19. Spoto, *Rebel*, 36.

20. Ernst Jacobi, "The Lonely One," in *The Real James Dean Story* (New York: Fawcett, c. 1956), 64.

21. Hedda Hopper, "Hollywood's Rebellious Genius," *Hartford Courant*, March 27, 1955.

22. Brennan, "Legend of Jimmy Dean," 27; Hopper and Brough, *Whole Truth*, 173.

23. Thomas M. Pryor, "Jerry Wald, the Big Idea Man," *New York Times*, January 19, 1947, X5.

24. Robert M. Lindner, *Rebel without a Cause: The Hypnoanalysis of Criminal Psychopath* (New York: Other Press, 2003 [1944]), 2.

25. Lindner, *Rebel without a Cause*, 13.

26. Lindner, *Rebel without a Cause*, 14.

27. Dalton, *James Dean* (2001), 223–24.

28. Paul Hendrickson, "Remembering James Dean Back Home in Indiana," *Los Angeles Times* (*Calendar* insert), July 22, 1973, 22.

29. DeWeerd took issue with journalist Joe Hyams for wrongly stating he preached in Fairmount because he did not serve in a church there. See "Letters to the Editor," *Redbook*, December 1956, 10.

30. "Murphy Tells How Degenerates Ruin Lives of Many Youngsters," *Evening Star* [Washington, DC], August 23, 1947, A12.

31. Evelyn Washburn Nielsen, "The Truth about James Dean," *Chicago Tribune Magazine*, September 9, 1956, 22–23, 48–49.

32. Dalton, *James Dean* (2001), 37.

33. Hyams and Hyams, *James Dean*, 20; a truncated and sanitized form of the quotation first appeared in Joe Hyams, "James Dean," *Redbook*, September 1956, 73.

34. Joe Hyams, who knew Dean, heavily implies that sexuality was meant, though he offers no evidence for his conclusion. Elizabeth Taylor said that Dean spoke to her of his sex life and DeWeerd, suggesting a connection.

35. Joe Hyams, "James Dean," 73.

36. "The Truth behind the Rumors That James Dean Committed Suicide!" *Photoplay*, November 1956, 111.

37. Dalton, *James Dean* (2001), 38; George W. George and Robert Altman (prods.), *The James Dean Story* (Warner, 1957).

38. Undated diary page titled "Great Friends I've Known." DeWeerd lists nine under the subheading "Closest Friends." Seven appear in the left column, and "Jim Dean" appears at the top of the second column.

39. Hyams and Hyams, *James Dean*, 19–20, 223; Peter L. Winkler, "James Dean: The Hungry Matador," in *Real James Dean: Intimate Memories from Those Who Knew Him Best*, ed. Peter L. Winkler, electronic ed. (Chicago: Chicago Review Press, 2016). Public speculation about DeWeerd's relationship with Dean began after DeWeerd's death in the 1970s, though there are indications of earlier rumors. In 1992 Joe Hyams reported the rumor as fact in a passage widely interpreted as implying DeWeerd had confessed to Hyams in 1956. Many subsequent biographers (Spoto, Holley, etc.) dismissed the story as unlikely and accused Hyams of fabricating the interview. However, Hyams never actually says DeWeerd confessed, and the sexual-contact claim occurs only on Hyams's own authority. Throughout his work, Hyams's general pattern was to collate multiple sources without clearly acknowledging them to create a composite narrative. The quotations from DeWeerd alongside the claim are not

explicitly incriminating, and many had previously been published in Hyams's 1956 *Redbook* piece.

Elizabeth Taylor seemed to confirm the molestation story in a 1997 interview, in comments about secrets Dean had told her on the set of *Giant*. This material was not published until 2011, after Taylor's death, but see notes in chapter 10 on misquotations in the published version. When read in combination with her comments to Hyams confirming she discussed Dean's confession with Hyams (Hyams and Hyams, *James Dean*, 223, in which Taylor closely echoes the parallel version, which she frequently repeated, quoted in Randall Riese, *The Unabridged James Dean: His Life and Legacy from A to Z* [Chicago: Contemporary Books, 1991], 519–20), and the pair's long social and professional relationship and mutual love for Dean (Bast says Hyams gave Taylor a copy of *The Little Prince* he removed from Dean's apartment after his death as a "gesture of kindness" in their shared grief [William Bast, *Surviving James Dean* (Fort Lee, NJ: Barricade Books, 2006), 240]), I believe Taylor, not DeWeerd, was likely the unacknowledged source into which Hyams added suggestive material from his DeWeerd interview.

40. Hyams and Hyams, *James Dean*, 20. Many writers dispute the authenticity of the quotation. As the surrounding quotations are reasonably accurate (though often stripped of the original context), I accept the authenticity, but it is unlikely DeWeerd was speaking explicitly of sexual relations as Hyams implies but rather more broadly about their close friendship, which would have raised eyebrows for a clergyman or a movie star.

41. William Kostlevy, "DeWeerd, James A.," in *Historical Dictionary of the Holiness Movement* 2nd ed., ed. William Koslevy, Historical Dictionaries of Religions, Philosophies, and Movements, no. 99 (Lanham, MD: Scarecrow Press, 2009), 94. Kostlevy implies that rumors about sexuality played a role. DeWeerd married when he changed faiths.

CHAPTER 2

1. Various origin stories for the nickname exist, some referring to tennis rackets, others to racking billiard balls.

2. Venable Herndon, *James Dean: A Short Life* (New York: Signet/New American Library, 1974), 1–2.

3. Bast, *Surviving James Dean*, 14; William Bast, *James Dean: A Biography* (New York: Ballantine, 1956), 13. Dalton wrongly claims Dean told this to DeWeerd (Dalton, *James Dean* [2001], 342).

4. Bast, *Surviving James Dean*, 14; Bast, *James Dean*, 13.

5. Bast, *Surviving James Dean*, 15; Bast, *James Dean*, 13–14.

6. Holley, *James Dean*, 9, 30, 34; Hyams and Hyams, *James Dean*, 21. Impetuously proposing marriage before a woman could develop doubts about him became a pattern. Dean repeated the dinner scene years later with Dizzy Sheridan and Rogers Brackett.

7. Charles Dickens, *The Posthumous Papers of the Pickwick Club*, vol. I (Boston: Ticknor & Fields, 1866), 148.

8. Spoto, *Rebel*, 48; Hyams and Hyams, *James Dean*, 22–25; David Dalton gave a less dramatic version in Dalton, *James Dean* (2001), 44, involving a punch to the mouth in class. As with so many memories, the truth seems to reside in the teller.

9. Dalton, *James Dean* (2001), 52.

10. Hopper and Brough, *Whole Truth*, 173. Here he spoke of his adolescence, but he said something similar in *Parade* magazine about acting: "In this business, nobody helps you. You can be grateful to somebody for opening your eyes to certain things. And in return you can open somebody else's. But you do it all yourself" (Lloyd Shearer, "Dizzy? Not This Dean," *Parade*, May 13, 1955, 22).

11. E.g., Howard Thompson, "Another Dean Hits the Big League," *New York Times*, March 13, 1955, X5.

12. David K. Johnson, *The Lavender Scare: The Cold War Persecution of Gays and Lesbians in the Federal Government* (Chicago: University of Chicago Press, 2004), 154. Lafayette Park was a notorious gay cruising ground in the postwar era and the site of frequent police and vigilante activity.

13. Dalton says he traveled by bus (Dalton, *James Dean* [2001], 57); Spoto, by train (Spoto, *Rebel*, 53). Spoto places this on June 14, but Dean sent a letter to his former high school from California dated June 6 requesting transcripts (James Dean to F. Stanton Galey, June 6, 1949).

14. Frank O'Leary, "How to Keep Your Kid off Queer Street U.S.A.," *Whisper*, November 1963, 35. I base the speculation on Dean's fantasies in college classmate John Holden's account of Dean's collegiate curiosity about gay bars and efforts to acquire information about gay life (Holley, *James Dean*, 51).

15. Marynia F. Farnham, "The Unmentionable Minority," *Cosmopolitan*, May 1949, 51; "Queer People," *Newsweek*, October 10, 1949, 52.

16. The 1948 version has the protagonist murder the man who rejected his advances. In the 1965 revision, Vidal softened the climax to rape.

17. James Baldwin, "Preservation of Innocence," *Zero* 1, no. 2 (1949): 21.

18. The quoted language is from a January 7, 1953 contract between James Dean and NBC preserved in Jane Deacy's records for an appearance on *The Kate Smith Hour*, but similar language was standard in contracts for radio, TV, and movie roles.

19. Alfred C. Kinsey, Wardell B. Pomeroy, and Clyde E. Martin, *Sexual Behavior in the Human Male* (New York: W. B. Saunders, 1948), 639.

20. Oscar Wilde, *De Profundis: Unabridged*, edited by Vivian Holland (New York: Philosophical Library, 1960), 66, 82–83.

21. James Dean to F. Stanton Galey, June 6, 1949; Dalton, *James Dean* (2001), 60.

22. See, e.g., "Spotlighting James Dean," 61, where Dean claims falsely to have spent two years at UCLA. Dean's agent included the false claim in a set of 1954 biographical notes, "James Dean—Biography," provided to Warner Bros.

23. Literally, according to the rather unkind recollections of a classmate, "He was shy and awkward, and he peered through big horn-rimmed glasses at a world that baffled him. But somehow he knew exactly what he wanted, and he was learning quickly what strings to pull to get it" (Spoto, *Rebel*, 63).

24. Gene Nielson Owen, "The Man Who Would Be 50: A Memory of James Dean," in *Real James Dean: Intimate Memories from Those Who Knew Him Best*, ed. Peter L.

Winkler, electronic ed. (Chicago: Chicago Review Press, 2016). In her piece, first published in 1981, Owen claimed that Dean was a poor reader, contributing to the legend that Dean struggled with reading. What she actually observed is that a half-educated eighteen-year-old unsurprisingly had difficulty with Shakespeare's early-modern English. Friends, teachers, and mentors watched Dean read in great volume with no difficulty, as his own marked-up books testify.

25. Joe Hyams, "James Dean," 74; Hyams and Hyams, *James Dean*, 30.
26. Hopper and Brough, *Whole Truth*, 173. However, Edward Harris of the *Post-Dispatch* claimed Dean said it to him. Perhaps it was a rehearsed phrase Dean used with each interview. Edward A. Harris, "Young Man in a Hurry," *St. Louis Post-Dispatch*, October 9, 1955, 2G.
27. Selective Service Classification Record, Indiana Local Board no. 38, National Archives. Several friends testified to Dean's fear of being drafted.

CHAPTER 3

1. Holley, *James Dean*, 51.
2. Russell, "Way I See It," 3.
3. Holmes Alexander, "A Delicate Touch," *Los Angeles Times*, June 21, 1950, pt. 2, 5.
4. Ralph H. Major Jr., "New Moral Menace to Our Youth," *Coronet*, September 1950, 101–8.
5. "Novel Poses Study in Abnormality," *Sunday Star* [Washington, DC], January 11, 1948, C3; "Gore Vidal's Vivid New Novel Proves He Is an Author to Be Reckoned With," *Evening Star* [Washington, DC], October 8, 1950, C3.
6. James Polchin, *Indecent Advances: A Hidden History of True Crime and Prejudice before Stonewall* (Berkeley, CA: Counterpoint, 2019), chap. 4.
7. L.A. police annual reports for 1947 and 1950, as cited in Lillian Faderman and Stuart Timmons, *Gay L.A.: A History of Sexual Outlaws, Power Politics, and Lipstick Lesbians* (New York: Perseus Books, 2006; rpt., Berkeley: University of California Press, 2009), 376n19.
8. Bruce Cory, "The Lowdown on That . . . 'Disorderly Conduct' Charge against Tab Hunter," *Confidential*, September 1955, 18, 19, 60.
9. Hunter's account changed over the years. In his final statement on the matter, he admitted to attending the party on purpose but claimed not to know it was a party for queers until he arrived. See Tab Hunter and Scott Feinber, "Tab Hunter on (Almost) Being Outed in 1955: 'I Thought My Career Was Over,'" *Hollywood Reporter*, August 13, 2015.
10. Milton E. Hahn and Byron H. Atkinson, "The Sexually Deviate Student," *School and Society* 82 (1955): 85–87; Beth Baily, *Sex in the Heartland* (Cambridge, MA: Harvard University Press, 1999), 61–62.
11. Thompson, "Another Dean," X5.
12. Thompson, "Another Dean," X5.
13. Thompson, "Another Dean," X5.

14. Alfred McClung Lee, *Fraternities without Brotherhood: A Study of Prejudice on the American Campus* (Boston: Beacon Press, 1955), 93–94. At the 1954 Sigma Nu convention, the West Coast chapters, including UCLA's, argued that their "campus prestige" derived from racial discrimination.
15. Spoto, *Rebel*, 51.
16. Bast described this rather plainly in 2006 (Bast, *Surviving James Dean*, 5–8, 11–14), revising his allusive 1956 account (Bast, *James Dean*, 6, 8, 11–12). Royston Ellis stated in 1962 that the fraternity members thought Dean was gay (Ellis, *Rebel*, 120), but his working notes show he was merely drawing conclusions from Bast's suggestive references to the fraternity's dislike of theater and sensitivity.
17. Dalton, *James Dean* (2001), 63.
18. As with so many stories about James Dean, the truth of the more colorful anecdote isn't clear. Dalton tells the drowning story in great detail without any sources (Dalton, *James Dean* [2001], 67–68), but William Bast has Dean saying, "I didn't like the stuff they wanted me to do for initiation" (Bast, *James Dean*, 12, and Bast, *Surviving James Dean*, 12), implying he refused to participate. Venable Herndon's sources agreed with Bast that Dean objected to a set of special humiliations they planned for him (Herndon, *James Dean: A Short Life*, 43).
19. Ronald Martinetti, *The James Dean Story: A Myth-Shattering Biography of an Icon* (Citadel Stars, 1995), 21.
20. Bast, *Surviving James Dean*, 5.
21. Holley, *James Dean*, 52–53; Bast, *James Dean*, 11; Bast, *Surviving James Dean*, 6. Bast repeated the story from 1956 down to 2006, and it served as the basis for most later accounts. Draesemer eventually explained what had actually occurred, but by then the myth had set like concrete. A third version, told by James Bellah, claimed Bellah had secretly convinced Draesemer to sign Dean as a personal favor and had arranged for the backstage meeting to make it seem spontaneous. Victory has a thousand fathers.
22. Bast, *James Dean*, 8, 9, 12; Bast, *Surviving James Dean*, 7–8; Dalton, *James Dean* (2001), 68. Dalton paraphrases the exchange as involving the word *fruit* but gives no source. That it was connected to accusations of effeminacy and homosexuality had been known since 1956, despite some later authors minimizing the connection (e.g., Holley, *James Dean*, 56, attributing the incident to a dinnertime food-fight prank). Dalton seems to be paraphrasing in his imagined college patois the account given in Joseph R. Marshall, "Dean Seemed No Different than Other College Boys," *Shreveport* (LA) *Journal*, September 19, 1956, B6.
23. Bast, *Surviving James Dean*, 12–13; Bast, *James Dean*, 12.
24. Patrick McGilligan, *George Cukor: A Double Life* (New York: St. Martin's Press, 1991), 186–89. Remarkably, despite hosting weekly gay sex parties for years, known widely throughout Hollywood, almost no one spoke of the "open secret" on the record beyond a telling allusion in a gossip column or an occasional joke from Rock Hudson.
25. On George Cukor's "quick, cold efficiency," see Scotty Bowers with Lionel Friedberg, *Full Service: My Adventures in Hollywood and the Secret Sex Lives of the Stars* (New York: Grove Press, 2012), 50–51.
26. Bast, *Surviving James Dean*, 11–16; Bast, *James Dean*, 13–14.

CHAPTER 4

1. I cannot begin to parse out how biographers have them living in two different apartments, in two different parts of Los Angeles County, at the same time. Most say they lived on Comstock Avenue, a mile east of UCLA, but Bast, who was there, places them in Santa Monica.
2. Holley, *James Dean*, 46. Others claimed to have taught James Dean fencing, and it is not clear whether he let them believe that or they were mistaken or they simply made up the claims.
3. Bast, *James Dean*, 63–64; Dalton, *James Dean* (2001), 38. Bast places this during the pair's stay in New York, while Dalton places it at UCLA. As the letters from DeWeerd were most numerous in Dean's first years away from Indiana, UCLA is more likely, though he probably continued the habit into his New York years.
4. Bast gives the story this way (Bast, *Surviving James Dean*, 34; Bast, *James Dean*, 23), but other accounts, from people not there, said Dean displayed the candle to the boys' girlfriends, causing one to flee in tears. The less directly a writer experienced events, the more that writer seems to accept the harshest version of events.
5. Henry Miller, *Sextus: The Rosy Crucifixion, Book One* (New York: Grove Press, 1965), 13. Bast remembered the book being *Sextus*, then newly published. Other biographers assert, probably inaccurately, that it was Miller's more famous *Tropic of Cancer*, published two decades before.
6. Albert Maisel, "The Smut-Peddler Is after Your Child," *Women's Home Companion*, October 22, 1951.
7. Miller, *Sextus*, 206–7.
8. J. D. Salinger, *The Catcher in the Rye: A Novel* (Boston: Little, Brown, 1951), 186.
9. This reading of the book is indebted to Pia Livia Hekanaho, "Queering *Catcher*: Flits, Straights, and Other Morons," in *J. D. Salinger's* Catcher in the Rye, ed. Sarah Graham (London: Routledge, 2007), 89–97. Her queer reading goes much farther than my presentation and attempts to make the case that Holden is a closeted gay teenager in the process of coming out.
10. Nash K. Burger, "Books of the Times," *New York Times*, July 16, 1951, 32. The "queer" moniker appears in James Stern, "Aw, the World's a Crumby Place," *New York Times*, July 15, 1951, B23. The adjectives describing Holden were used in Mary McGrory, "Story of Adolescent Steers away from Mawkish into Something New," *Sunday Star* [Washington, DC], July 15, 1951, C2. Only three critical academic essays on *Catcher* were published before 1956. Following James Dean's death, scholars reassessed the novel, and seventy essays followed between 1956 and 1960.
11. Vito Russo, *The Celluloid Closet: Homosexuality in the Movies*, rev. ed. (New York: Harper & Row, 1987), 99.
12. James Dean was a Method actor, and I am a Method writer, so, dear reader, I ate the concoction, and it was surprisingly edible. It could have used some fresh apple, though.
13. Bast, *Surviving James Dean*, 46. Bast gives much lengthier and more explicit descriptions of his various incidents of sexual arousal than I have summarized here. But discretion is the better part of valor. Cf. expurgated version in Bast, *James Dean*, 29–30.

14. Gene Ringgold, "James Dean," *Screen Legends*, May 1965, 18, reprinted from *Screen Facts*, no. 8 (1964).
15. Beverly Wills, "I Almost Married Jimmy Dean," *Modern Screen*, March 1957, 82.
16. Bast, *James Dean*, 42.
17. Philip K. Scheuer, "Jimmy Dean Says He Isn't Flattered by Being Labeled 'Another Brando,'" *Los Angeles Times*, November 7, 1954, pt. 4, 3; variations of the quotation appeared in many magazines, either from copying, Dean's reuse of stock lines, or Warner Bros. publicity. See, e.g., "Kazan's Steinbeck," *Newsweek*, March 7, 1955, 91, and Sidney Skolksy, "Demon Dean," *Photoplay*, July 1955, 78.
18. Bast, *Surviving James Dean*, 64–68.
19. Bast, *James Dean*, 30.
20. Bast, *Surviving James Dean*, 53–55. Alternately, one might read these events with the speculation Bast wondered about but never asked after: that Dean was prostituting himself for money, a rumor that dogged his memory for decades. But Dean's chronic lack of cash would suggest otherwise, unless he was very, very bad at it. Others have suggested that Dean was waiting for an actor or producer to solicit him in order to parlay the sex into a job. Strangely, Royston Ellis has a somewhat garbled version of this story in his 1962 biography *Rebel* half a century before Bast published it officially (Ellis, *Rebel*, 120).
21. Bast, *Surviving James Dean*, 75–79. The earlier expurgated version (Bast, *James Dean*, 44–48) merely claimed a dispute over Wills and minimized Dean's reaction to Bast abandoning their home. In that version, Dean coldly acknowledges Bast's departure with a formal handshake.
22. This was sometime in late June or early July. Rogers Brackett remembered meeting Dean on a Saturday, which was the day he oversaw *Alias Jane Doe* (Ronald Martinetti, *The James Dean Story* [New York: Pinnacle Books, 1975], 43). Spoto claims it occurred on a weekday prior to July 4 when Brackett recorded commercials, but he provides no source. It could not have occurred prior to Dean starting work at the parking lot at the end of June, nor can it be later than July 21 because Dean appeared on at least four episodes of *Jane Doe*, starting July 28. Bast was ambiguous about these events in his first account (Bast, *James Dean*, 49–54), where he implies months had passed and discusses Brackett only in expurgated terms as a "friend" who had taken Dean in as a roommate. Dalton went further than Bast in minimizing Brackett's role in Dean's life, making only two direct references to their friendship, apparently in order to limit gay implications, as Brackett was by the 1970s fairly well-known as an out gay man.
23. Biographer Venable Herndon claims Dean spent these weeks bumming free meals from gay men who dropped off their cars and Brackett was the last in line, but there is little evidence to support the claim besides John Gilmore's assertion that in 1955 Dean told him that on his way to stardom, he had had "my cock sucked" by five big Hollywood names who offered nothing but dinner in return (Herndon, *James Dean*, 64; John Gilmore, *The Real James Dean* [New York: Pyramid, 1975], 94). Gilmore also claimed, almost certainly falsely, that Dean met Brackett at a party for gay men in the industry to find and trade young one-night stands, a party attended by Rock Hudson and Liberace (John Gilmore, *Live Fast, Die Young: Remembering the Short Life of James Dean* [New York: Thunder Mouth's Press, 1997], 66–67). Bast claimed

that CBS stars and executives were famously big tippers, which accounted for Dean's spending money (Bast, *Surviving James Dean*, 80–81).

24. James Dean, handwritten acting résumé, c. 1952. Four pay stubs survive, but Brackett remembered him appearing in six episodes. No recordings survive.

25. On Brackett's character, see Ed Sullivan, "Radio Award," *Modern Screen*, November 1946, 26. Sullivan's description of Brackett is a marked contrast to Bill Bast's (see note 27 below).

26. Wills, "I Almost Married Jimmy," 83, with Bast, *Surviving James Dean*, 81–82. Authors sympathetic to Dean suggest Wills enjoyed riling him up by flirting with other boys, while those sympathetic to Wills depict her actions as an innocent invitation interrupted by rage. Cf. Bast, *James Dean*, 49, which relates the events from Dean's perspective, emphasizing his heterosexual bona fides. Venable Herndon quotes Isabelle Draesemer as believing, based on her experience with other gay actors, that Dean staged the breakup to justify pursuing gay directors in the CBS parking lot (see later; Herndon, *James Dean*, 62).

    Val Holley quotes her final version, much expanded and probably untrue, in which she claimed Dean came to her for advice on whether to marry Wills or move in with Rogers Brackett (see later), and she dismissed Dean as a "leech" (Holley, *James Dean*, 72). Each successive account becomes more detailed and attributes greater perspicacity to Draesemer, sometimes with contradictory details, suggesting a degree of fantasy creeping in. Wills seems to place the events just after her eighteenth birthday, leading to some confusion among writers due to conflation of her actual June 7 birthday with her early August annual gala birthday bash. According to Bast, Dean attended Wills's August birthday party, and the *Los Angeles Times* confirms the date in an August 9, 1951 notice.

27. Brackett, in his only interview on the subject, said he believed that their love was mutual (Martinetti, *James Dean Story* [1975], 45). Less-sympathetic writers have suggested Dean coldly traded sex for professional favors, but the evidence argues against this as the exclusive motivation. Bast, with characteristic jealousy of Dean's various lovers, wrote in 2006 that Brackett was a "bitchy queen" and portrayed him as a "foppish," sunburned predator with unlovely birdlike features and a too long neck (Bast, *Surviving James Dean*, 82–83). Bast claimed Dean and Brackett mutually exploited each other. Liz Sheridan, also angry at Brackett, similarly and incorrectly described Brackett as resembling a "woman made-up to look like a man" (Gilmore, *Life Fast, Die Young*, 82). She labeled him a "predator" (Sheridan, *Dizzy & Jimmy: My Life with James Dean: A Love Story* [Boston: G. K. Hall, 2000], 163).

28. Spoto, *Rebel*, 87, in which Draesemer repeats more explicitly similarly worded claims she made twenty years prior to Herndon (Herndon, *James Dean*, 62). To Val Holley, researching around the same time as Spoto in the early 1990s, she instead claimed Dean was rather blunt about their relationship and asked her advice on pursuing it before he moved in (Holley, *James Dean*, 62). As with so many sources about Dean, her contradictory testimony makes her a somewhat unreliable witness. As the oft-repeated "twin bed" line cannot easily be squared with her late-in-life claims, I judge her earlier version the more plausible.

    Val Holley gives a completely different timeline of events than other authors (Holley *James Dean*, 67–72), stating that Dean dated Brackett while living with Bast and never bunked with Avery, only moving in with Brackett after breaking up with Wills. He provides no direct source, and the notes for other facts on those pages refer only to the same sources I have used here, Bast's first book and Martinetti, whom Holley contradicts. I have followed the order of events in Bast's unexpurgated account in Bast, *Surviving James Dean*, chaps. 8 and 9, which among all differing versions is best supported by independent documentary evidence.

CHAPTER 5

1. Martinetti, *James Dean Story* (1975), 48.
2. See descriptions throughout Bowers with Friedberg, *Full Service*, and cf. Bast's description of being invited to similar orgies after Dean's death made him famous (Bast, *Surviving James Dean*, 261–62). Government records of such orgies appear in an FBI memorandum from M. A. Jones to Cartha DeLoach re: Burton Stephen Lancaster; Tony Fanciosa, July 12, 1963; and "Hollywood Vice," FBI memorandum from SAC Los Angeles to J. Edgar Hoover re: CRIMDEL—CRS (Current Developments in Criminal Matters, Central Research Section), February 16, 1960.
3. Martinetti, *The James Dean Story* (1995), 40. The quotation does not appear in the 1975 edition of Martinetti's biography.
4. Brackett believed Dean didn't know the word, and he believed Dean to be uneducated. But after years of high school art classes and showing his mobiles to everyone who visited his apartment in college, that seems a stretch. It is not dissimilar to the many mentors Dean let believe that they were all the first to introduce him to Shakespeare. More directly relevant, Bob Hinkle recalls Dean performing the exact same bit in Texas, pretending not to know the word *gun* (Bob Hinkle, "My Friend, Jimmy," in *The Real James Dean Story* [New York: Fawcett, c. 1956], 61).
5. Winkler, "James Dean." The date of this event, where he got the cape, and every other detail vary from source to source. Most place this in 1951, but Boetticher thought it happened in late 1952, facilitated not by Brackett but by Anthony Quinn. Most say it happened in Mexico, but Boetticher said it occurred in his Universal Studios office in L.A.
6. Tommie Walters, "In Tune with the Times," *Victoria* [BC] *Daily Times*, April 14, 1951, 27. Contrary to news accounts, Madison Musser told Val Holley that Brackett did not get the rights because Hedy Lamarr owned them (Holley, *James Dean*, 72).
7. "Said Fort," *Fortean Society Magazine*, Autumn 14 F.S. (1945), 141.
8. Quoted in "Spotlighting James Dean," 61. Various sources put the date Dean read *The Little Prince* anywhere from high school to adulthood, but Brackett told Martinetti that he had given Dean the book, and none of his friends mention it prior to that time. Although Dean was widely known as a voracious reader in the 1950s (see, e.g., "James Dean," *Motion Picture*, December 1955, 29), later writers, building from Leonard Rosenman's 1956 criticism of Dean's intellect and his 1990s recollection that Dean struggled to read even brief selections from Kierkegaard's *Fear and Trembling*,

suggested that Dean did not read any books, merely skimming them, mining quotations to make himself look smarter.

Jonathan (later John) Gilmore claimed in 1997 that Dean told him he read slowly and had a reading disability, though his report seems colored by later, secondary research. However, surviving bills from Doubleday Book Shops in New York document Dean's significant spending on books, an unlikely expense for someone who didn't read. Because so much of what Dean said and did mirrored what he read and his books were marked up with his handwritten notes, I would guess he read the books he found valuable and skimmed those that proved unsatisfying. Not every nonfiction book is worth reading cover to cover, except, of course, this one.

9. Frank Harris, *Oscar Wilde: His Trial and Confession* (New York: Author, 1918), 275–76. An abbreviated version taken from the shorthand transcript appeared in *The Trial of Oscar Wilde* (Paris: privately printed, 1906), 58–9.

10. John Addington Symonds, *A Problem in Greek Ethics* (London: privately printed, 1901); Hans Licht, *Sexual Life in Ancient Greece*, trans. J. J. Freese (London: Routledge & Keegan Paul, 1932), 411–98. For a more contemporary view on the historiography of homosexuality and the distinction, not typically observed prior to the 1960s, between homosexuality, pederasty, and effeminacy, see David M. Halperin, *How to Do the History of Homosexuality* (Chicago: University of Chicago Press, 2002). Cf. Scotty Bowers's accounts throughout *Full Service* of wealthy gay men patronizing barely legal high school boys.

11. Martinetti, *James Dean Story* (1975), 38. Brackett's mother reported a similar encounter.

12. Gerald Heard, *Pain, Sex, and Time: A New Outlook on Evolution and the Future of Man* (New York: Harper & Brothers, 1939), especially chapters 2 and 3 and 283–86. Of course, Heard also believed flying saucers were piloted by super-intelligent bees from Mars, so take him for what he's worth.

13. Martinetti, *James Dean Story* (1975), 37.

14. In Bast's telling (Bast, *Surviving James Dean*, 89–94), Dean was indirectly admitting to performing sexual favors for one or more men to advance himself, but the ambiguity of the language used by two closeted men speaking past each other made it unclear even to Bast. Bast assumed Dean meant Brackett specifically, not multiple men, but this incident became the foundation for later assertions that Dean prostituted himself widely for acting roles. More charitably, the reported conversation suggests that Dean resented being treated by Brackett's friends as their amusing dancing monkey and by Brackett as a son rather than as an equal, a situation he considered undignified. See especially Dean's monologue about Caligula and court jesters in Bast, *James Dean*, 51–53, and Bast, *Surviving James Dean*, 91.

15. Various sources provide widely divergent accounts of *Fixed Bayonets*. Several writers claimed Dean filmed the movie before meeting Brackett, which Dean's pay stub refutes. His agent, Isabelle Draesemer, took credit for all of Dean's 1951 film roles, though Brackett attributed Dean landing these roles to his own influence. The movie's director, Samuel Fuller, wrongly claimed in his autobiography to have chosen Dean for his looks after Dean arrived in Hollywood from New York.

16. Winkler, "James Dean."

17. Martinetti, *James Dean Story* (1975), chap. 3.

18. Martinetti, *James Dean Story* (1975), chap. 3; Bast, *Surviving James Dean*, 142–43; Laura Owen Miller and Anna Kendall, "Smoldering Dynamite," *Movie Screen*, June 1955, 70; Joe Hyams, "James Dean," 74–75. This incident later became conflated with Dean's 1949 Selective Service registration, leading to the rumor that at age eighteen he had registered as a "homosexual" to avoid the draft. Brackett placed the draft letter in 1951 in Los Angeles, but Bast places it in 1952 in New York. James Bellah claimed Dean told him of the deferment in Los Angeles in 1951. Dean's Selective Service record proves it occurred in the fall of 1951.

    Bast was unaware of Brackett's intervention and thought Dean's letter alone secured the deferment. Dean himself (or Warner Bros.' PR department) falsely claimed he was declared 4-F due to poor eyesight, a story Hyams repeated in 1956 (despite knowing it was false, as he admitted in his 1992 biography of Dean), but his vision would not have been disqualifying at the time because it was correctable with glasses, per military guidelines. The National Archives, at my request, searched for Dean's letter but reported no such correspondence survived the routine destruction of records not "appraised to be of permanent legal or historical value." Records indicate the U.S. government destroyed Dean's correspondence on or after October 5, 1970. Hyams confirmed Dean attended a few psychoanalytical sessions in what he implies was New York in 1952 and suggested strongly that these were to discuss his sexuality.

19. Bast, *Surviving James Dean*, 89. Dean was in the habit of bragging to Bast, so the tale may be exaggerated. Bast places this in his narrative in the summer or early fall of 1951, which is belied by production records.

20. Rock Hudson and Sara Davidson, *Rock Hudson: His Story* (New York: William Morrow, 1986), 17.

21. Jonny Whiteside, *Cry: The Johnnie Ray Story* (New York: Barricade Books, 1994), 98.

22. On Hudson, see Mark Griffin, *All That Heaven Allows: A Biography of Rock Hudson* (HarperCollins E-Books, 2018), chaps. 1–5; cf. Hudson and Davidson, *Rock Hudson*, chaps. 2–3.

23. "Radio-TV Briefs," *Los Angeles Evening Citizen-News*, August 24, 1951, 20; "Radio News and Reviews," *Buffalo News*, August 22, 1951, 8; Tommie Walters, "In Tune with the Times," *Victoria* [BC] *Daily Times*, December 8, 1951, 21. Brackett did not mention these plans in his interview with Martinetti, and no friend of Dean's recalls hearing tell of them, yet they were published in syndicated newspaper columns across the United States and Canada.

24. Martinetti, *James Dean Story* (1975), 48.

25. Hyams and Hyams, *James Dean*, 45–46. So Martin Landau said he told him in early 1952 when Landau noted that they were the same age but he looked like a full-grown man while Dean sill resembled a teenager.

26. Bast, *James Dean*, 54; *Surviving James Dean*, 94.

27. Desmond Stone, *Alec Wilder in Spite of Himself: A Life of the Composer* (New York: Oxford University Press, 1996), 99. Wilder remembered Dean coming by train, but Dean stated in interviews that he went by bus (presumably to cover up Brackett's help) and told Beverly Wills he went by car with a "friend," referring to Brackett driving him the first leg.

28. Ringgold, "James Dean," 19. Quoted in most Dean biographies; Dean offered variations of the same sentiment in many interviews.
29. Holley, *James Dean*, 85.
30. Schatt quoted in Spoto, *Rebel*, 92. Herndon claims Dean prostituted himself at gay bars during these months, citing "oral history" among aging New York gay club patrons in the 1970s that Dean submitted to fisting and other extreme S&M acts for cash. I find the claim unbelievable, however popular it has been in gay culture, because the first S&M leather bar had yet to open; however, this may be a half-remembered echo of Dean accompanying Brackett's friends to gay bars (Herndon, *James Dean*, 64).
31. Dalton, *James Dean* (2001), 194. Dean allegedly said this to Dennis Hopper in 1955, who recalled it two decades later and offered variations on the story thereafter.
32. Christine White, an actress of Dean's acquaintance and a Deacy client, claimed she connected Dean with Deacy (Holley, *James Dean*, 108). Dean's correspondence suggests he was meeting with multiple agents at the time (undated letter to James DeWeerd on YMCA stationery, c. late 1951), so it is possible he sought and received help from several acquaintances.
33. Dorothy Kilgallen, "So Suite of Bob!" *Washington Post*, March 20, 1955, J5; Erskine Johnson, "In Hollywood," *Dixon* [IL] *Evening Telegraph*, March 30, 1955, 4; Natalie Wood, "You Haven't Heard the Half about Jimmy," *Photoplay*, November 1955, 82. Wood (or rather the Warner publicity agent writing for her) claims the show was *Break the Bank*, but the NBC quiz show did not feature stunts.
34. James Dean, undated letter on to James DeWeerd on YMCA stationery, c. December 1951.
35. Most biographers assume Dean sought in her a surrogate mother, but the correspondence between Deacy and Dean indicates this was more of an affectionate rather than a maternal relationship. Dean shared few details of his personal life with Deacy, who often pleaded for him to offer more, and he routinely ignored her for weeks at a time. Okay, so maybe like a mom. Four hundred lots of Deacy's James Dean files, including letters, business documents, legal documents, and other ephemera from 1952 through Dean's death were published online by Nate D. Sanders Auctions shortly before Deacy's heirs auctioned them off in May 2023.
36. Martinetti, *James Dean Story* (1995), 52–53.
37. James Dean, undated letter to James DeWeerd on YMCA stationery, c. December 1951.
38. Hyams and Hyams, *James Dean*, 48–50; Martinetti, *James Dean Story* (1975), chap. 4. Sheridan, in her memoir *Dizzy & Jimmy* (1–74), remembered their meeting and subsequent falling in love as occurring over one week in late fall 1951, though evidence would seem to argue otherwise. As best I can tell from cross-referencing facts, Sheridan conflated some genuine events from December 1952 with December 1951, before they met, and created a composite but false account of their early days together. Additional details in the book show she worked from a later Dean biography, as they contradict the documentary record in Jane Deacy's archive. Her first account, which implied their relationship developed over time in late January and early February 1952, was published as "In Memory of Jimmy," *Photoplay*, October 1957, 70, 102–5,

but was partly falsified to disguise the socially unacceptable practice of an unmarried woman living with an unmarried man.

39. Wills, "I Almost Married Jimmy," 83.

40. Bast, *Surviving James Dean*, 131. Bast, who did not recognize the Platonic references, wrote that he felt like a "dunce" because he couldn't understand what he was going on about.

41. Sheridan, "In Memory of Jimmy," 104. Dean's cooking is reminiscent of the bizarre meals featured in food advertisements of the era, which were heavy on strange combinations of cheap canned goods and gelatins, and it's likely he took inspiration from recipes he saw in magazines. A processed cheese and jelly omelet he was known to make is nearly identical to one that had previously appeared in a 1949 Velveeta advertisement, for example.

42. So he wrote on a photograph of himself in midair that he sent to Barbara Glenn during the filming of *East of Eden*, adding, "You think I have to come down from up here don't you[?]" Cf. his alleged musings on space aliens as superior beings in Sheridan, *Dizzy & Jimmy*, 103–4. His analysis of *The Little Prince* is quoted in Hopper and Brough, *Whole Truth*, 170.

43. Spoto, *Rebel*, 100. Sheridan's story changed over time. In Sheridan, *Dizzy & Jimmy*, 160, she claimed they repeatedly had the best sex of her life. Sheridan claimed that the difference was due to her own reticence to discuss their relationship. However, the memoir is self-evidently largely invention, as it is told primarily in dialogue that is neither shown to be contemporary with events nor reads true to life. (The expository dialogue is particularly obvious.) It's rather clear from the progression of Sheridan's views from 1957 to 2000 that nostalgia colored her memories.

44. Martinetti, *James Dean Story* (1995), 128. Dean echoed that moment in *Rebel without a Cause* when Judy (Natalie Wood) declares her love for him. However, Sheridan, *Dizzy & Jimmy*, 56–58, claims Dean professed his love first and long before, after knowing her only a few days, when they began a year of incessant, orgiastic sex in which she details specific ejaculations. Frankly, the scene she describes reads like pure fantasy and does not align with any of her previous accounts nor any other partner's account of sex with Dean.

45. Spoto, *Rebel*, 96, quoting a 1995 letter.

46. Sheridan, *Dizzy & Jimmy*, 144–47, 162–70.

47. Dalton, *James Dean* (2001), 85.

48. Sheridan claims they continued living together until she left for summer stock (Sheridan, *Dizzy & Jimmy*, 172–73). As always, the sources don't agree. Most biographers say he had a room at the Iroquois while with Brackett, but Bast said he was living full-time with Brackett and had even hung his bull's horns on Brackett's wall. Martinetti, drawing on Brackett, said Dean was living with Brackett. There are still other stories from other people claiming he was living with them some or all of the time. They can't all be true, and no surviving documents list his address (he used his agent's address on contracts and correspondence during 1952).

49. Sheridan, *Dizzy & Jimmy*, 161.

50. Sheridan's story changed over time. In accounts published in the 1970s through the 1990s, she claimed to have known about Dean and Brackett's ongoing relationship,

but later in the 1990s, she presented herself as having been an innocent duped by Dean's duplicity. Similarly, her view of Dean's sexuality changed from claiming he was conflicted over his sexuality to asserting that he was robustly heterosexual. Nostalgia seems to have changed her views. Cf. Martinetti, *James Dean Story* (1975), chap. 4; Hyams and Hyams, *James Dean*, 50; Spoto, *Rebel*, chap. 6; Sheridan, *Dizzy & Jimmy*, 139–70. In *Dizzy & Jimmy*, Sheridan claims Brackett disappeared from Dean's life after her meeting with him, but this does not accord with Dean's work history. He may have simply stopped talking to her about him.

CHAPTER 6

1. Jack Shafer, "What Jimmy Dean Believed," *Modern Screen*, October 1957, 24. Ellipses in original.
2. Bast, *Surviving James Dean*, 100, 116–18.
3. Bast, *Surviving James Dean*, 113–21; Sheridan, *Dizzy & Jimmy*, 176–79. There is really no reconciling Sheridan's claim not to know Dean was still involved with Brackett with Bast's claim that Dean was living with Brackett while seeing her, but while both witnesses are biased, it seems logical that she was encouraging Dean to leave Brackett by pushing him toward Bast, whose sexuality she did not know.
4. Brackett and McDowall had worked together on theatrical productions in Santa Barbara and Tucson in the late 1940s. McDowall and Clift became friends in 1949 and remained close until Clift's death. Scotty Bowers reported the never-married McDowall's "fussy" sexual preferences in Bowers with Friedberg, *Full Service*, 218.
5. The group's acquaintance is confirmed in court records for *Wilder v. Ayers*, 2 A.D.2d 354 (N.Y. App. Div. 1956).
6. Holley, *James Dean*, 153; Hyams and Hyams, *James Dean*, 86. Arlene Sax quotes the phone conversation, but she attributes it to a movie star and "idol" of Dean's, implying that he spoke to Montgomery Clift or Marlon Brando, an impossibility that contradicts the historical record. While the call's content is consistent with facts, Sax's account is mixed with fabrication and exaggeration.
7. Matthew Rettenmund, "Late Director James Sheldon on James Dean and Affairs with Men," *Hollywood Reporter*, July 9, 2020. Sheldon said Stevens offered Dean a part on *Suspense*, a show he both produced and directed, though the episode or episodes are not among the 90 surviving from the series' 260-episode run.
8. Bast gives Dean's bravado-laced account of the incident in Bast, *Surviving James Dean*, 133–34, including the fly. The language I use echoes Dean's later phrasing to John Gilmore and contemporary phrasing to Liz Sheridan, and the description of his feelings I extrapolated from earlier and later statements about sexual encounters he regretted. He gave a sanitized description to Bob Hinkle in 1955, burying truth amid some rather bald-faced lies about his sexual prowess, claiming to have had an affair with Natalie Wood, then seventeen (Robert Hinkle and Mike Farris, *Call Me Lucky: A Texan in Hollywood* [Norman: University of Oklahoma Press, 2015], 136). There is no way to know which director Bast hid beneath a cloak of anonymity, but James Sheldon's recollections of Robert Stevens (1920–1989), who held a great deal of power

as producer and director of *Suspense*, match very closely the description and the time period in which Bast placed the unwanted encounter. Given Dean's spotty work history in this period, candidates are relatively few.

9. Bast, *Surviving James Dean*, 137; *James Dean*, 65.

10. I keep trying to give Bast the benefit of the doubt, but I can't fathom how he never asked Dean about this nor for fifty years made any connection between *The Moon Is Blue* and the events of that night except to note that the play had something to do with sex (Bast, *Surviving James Dean*, 134–38; cf. expurgated and abbreviated account in Bast, *James Dean*, 65).

11. Holley, *James Dean*, 108, states that Fabrikant was a jewelry store owner, but the newspaper records, telephone books, and city directories of the time indicate the only Fabrikant named Louis was a textile merchant. His name appears in Jane Deacy's files as leaving a message for Dean and stating they were "good friends."

12. Margaret Henderson to James Dean, March 13, 1953, reporting a check from Brackett's firm for Dean's appearance on the February 24, 1953, episode of *Aunt Jenny's Real-Life Stories* radio soap opera.

13. Just as he had done with William Bast, Dean choreographed a stage-managed play for his scene partner, Christine White, the night before the audition. At the home of Louis Fabrikant, he brought in four girls and planned some elaborate scene involving White and Dean performing their Actors Studio audition skit, but White walked out without finding out what Dean expected the girls to do or how he expected the performance to go (Holley, *James Dean*, 108–10).

14. Bast originally bowdlerized the line as "sterilize me" in 1956 but gave the unexpurgated reading in 2006.

15. Bast reports this (Bast, *Surviving James Dean*, 149), but many of Dean's friends claim he never expressed a political opinion. McCarthy's line about "cocksuckers," widely quoted, is apparently secondhand, remembered by reporter Charles Seib in a 1976 interview. See Edwin R. Bayley, *Joe McCarthy and the Press* (New York: Pantheon, 1982), 73. Seib recalled the reporters gathered in McCarthy's office all laughing along with the senator as he spoke. McCarthy's "earthy language" about gay men, though without the exact slurs, was reported in Alexander, "Delicate Touch," 5.

16. "Alec Wilder Show Listed; New Ryan Play Due in March," *New York Daily News*, January 20, 1950, 71; Si Steinhauser, "Radio and Television News and Views," *Pittsburgh Press*, August 26, 1951, 70. *The Impossible Forest* did not successfully reach the stage until 1958.

17. Bast, *Surviving James Dean*, 149–50, with Holley, *James Dean*, 134–35, but contrast Bast's first expurgated account in Bast, *James Dean*, 73, where he says it was "obvious" Dean "enjoyed himself." Bast and Holley suggested Dean set sail with the intention of trading sex for a role, but Bast's description of Dean's upset response to the trip, so different from the "no big deal" attitude he had previously tried to affect regarding transactional sex, suggests he was unprepared for what occurred. The official line Dean and Warner Bros. later put out was that Dean "talked himself into" a deckhand's position when in need of money and by dumb luck chanced upon a friend of a Broadway producer who discovered him. See, e.g., Miller and Kendall, "Smoldering Dynamite," 70.

Yves Salgues, a French journalist, got the story partly right in 1957, when he claimed that Dean got the role after "bathing" (i.e., having sex) with a male one-night stand ("*un marin d'un soir*") on Fire Island (a notorious retreat for libertines, especially gay men and theater people) who brought him aboard the unnamed Ayers's yacht. Salgues, however, claims that the sex partner was a crew member on the yacht and that Dean met him while playing Fire Island slot machines. Presumably the confusion stemmed from a Warner Bros. publicity story that Dean knew the skipper of the yacht who secured his audition. See Yves Salgues, *James Dean ou le mal de vivre* (Paris: Editions Pierre Horay, 1957), 119. That the Dean-Ayers encounter was well-known gossip at an early date can be seen from its inclusion in Walter Ross's fictionalized account of Dean's life, *The Immortal* (New York: Simon & Schuster, 1958), and others' later recollections of hearing the gossip all over New York in 1952 (Holley, *James Dean*, 134–35).

18. John Gilmore, "The Great White Way," in *Real James Dean: Intimate Memories from Those Who Knew Him Best*, ed. Peter L. Winkler, electronic ed. (Chicago: Chicago Review Press, 2016). Gilmore's recollections have a rather artistic gloss that suggest they are as much a literary construct as they are an accurate reporting of events. I have drawn from them sparingly. Sheridan, in her memoir, claimed to have turned a blind eye and purposely ignored Dean's trip with Ayers (Sheridan, *Dizzy & Jimmy*, 193–94). While it seems Bast and Sheridan were his best friends in this period, Martin Landau also claimed that Dean was his best friend. Dean kept his life so compartmentalized, so Landau knew nothing of any of this and indeed later claimed to be certain Dean was completely heterosexual and girl-crazy.

19. Scheuer, "Jimmy Dean Says," 3; Mark Dayton, "James Dean: Excitement for the Lovelorn?" *Screenland*, July 1955, 70; Harris, "Young Man," 2G; "Spotlighting James Dean," 61. Given the widespread publication of Dean's claim to read five or six books at once, skipping between them, it was clearly a line he practiced for reporters, probably in consultation with Warner Bros. publicity, which marketed him as a genius.

20. Dalton, *James Dean* (2001), 79.

21. Liz Sheridan claimed in *Dizzy & Jimmy*, 34, that Dean was already playing the recorder prior to December 1951, but this contradicts every other account. He purchased his first recorder for Christmas in December 1952. She seems to have conflated Christmas 1951 and Christmas 1952 in her memory.

22. Shafer, "What Jimmy Dean Believed," 24. The story of the Aztecs surrendering after mistaking Cortes for Quetzalcoatl was Spanish propaganda but widely repeated as historical truth down to the twentieth century. For whatever reason, the Aztec book made an impression on Dean, who kept it with him for years and mentioned it to reporters regularly right up until his death.

23. Nick Adams, "Jimmy's Happiest Moments," *Modern Screen*, October 1956, 78. Dean spent time with Adams in 1950 and 1955, so he would have said this sometime in 1955.

24. Dalton, *James Dean* (2001), 85. According to Sheridan, she, Dean, and Bast got a ride back home with a wealthy Texas oilman en route to New York City (Sheridan, "In Memory of Jimmy," 104). The only such oilman I could find who was likely traveling to New York that week was Raymond Lee Tollett, the president of Cosden Petroleum

and a former Hollywood-based FBI agent en route to the annual meeting of the Society of Former Special Agents of the FBI in New York. Tollett was a fan of André Maurois, whose 1949 *Maurois Reader* Tollett owned in an autographed edition. Dean purchased a copy in the weeks after his return to New York. I happen, by bizarre coincidence, to own Tollett's copy. Decades later, Sheridan changed her description of the man from a wealthy oilman to a drunk (Sheridan, *Dizzy & Jimmy*, 226).

25. Dalton, *James Dean* (2001), 105.
26. Dalton, *James Dean* (2001), 151. Dalton read this as a funny joke about lighthearted experimentation.
27. Holley, *James Dean*, 162–63; Holley, as is a pattern with Dean biographers, did not recognize the reference and assumed Dean was pretentiously imitating "intellectual friends" with odd words and Latin.
28. George Henry and Alfred Gross, "Social Factors in the Case Histories of One Hundred Underprivileged Homosexuals," *Mental Hygiene* 22, no. 4 (1938): 591–611.
29. Bast tells the story in Bast, *Surviving James Dean*, 165–66, but John Gilmore gives the details of Dean's sleep habits in Gilmore, *Real James Dean*, 97, focusing weirdly on whether Dean's hands touched his penis.
30. The English translation of *Harpies* changes the name of the dead man, Jérôme in the original. Apparently, none of Dean's later biographers read the story, which seems baffling. Spoto, who clearly did not read it, complained that there was "something both immature and sad about the feeble attempt to sound enlightened and erudite" in Dean's allusion (Spoto, *Rebel*, 119), though nothing is mythologically or poetically incorrect. The verse incidentally is not from the story but was Dean's own line, probably modeled on Horatio's lament for Hamlet.

CHAPTER 7

1. Truman Capote, "The Duke in His Domain," in *The Dogs Bark* (New York: Plume, 1973), 338.
2. Um, yes.
3. Patricia Bosworth, *Montgomery Clift: A Biography* (New York: Harcourt Brace Jovanovich, 1978), 259–60.
4. Holley, *James Dean*, 151–53. Diamond's diary makes clear he and Cuomo had been together for more than a year. See excerpts in Virginia Spencer Carr, *The Lonely Hunter: A Biography of Carson McCullers* (Garden City, NJ: Anchor Press, 1976), 385.
5. The amounts are recorded in contracts and pay stubs Dean's agent, Jane Deacy, kept on file. His smallest television paycheck was his $200 fee for his brief appearance in "The Hound of Heaven" on *The Kate Smith Hour* on January 15, 1953, and his most lucrative contract, for the November 13, 1953, broadcast of "Padlocks" on CBS's *Danger*, came with a $1,000 payout.
6. Spoto, *Rebel*, 127.
7. "Tele Follow-Up Comment," *Variety*, September 2, 1953, 26.
8. Dalton, *James Dean* (2001), 100.

9. Edith Glynn, "Hollywood," *Los Angeles Mirror*, April 7, 1953; Brooks Martin, "The Lavender Skeletons in TV's Closet," *Confidential*, July 1953, 34–35.
10. Dalton, *James Dean* (2001), 135.
11. Hugh Fordin, *Getting to Know Him: A Biography of Oscar Hammerstein II* (New York: Da Capo, 1995 [1977]), 317.
12. Dalton, *James Dean* (2001), 122–24.
13. Gilmore, *Live Fast, Die Young*, 114; Holley, *James Dean*, 165–66. Gilmore took the "emotional support" claim as proof of heterosexuality, but in context it reads sadder.
14. Dalton, *James Dean* (2001), 141.
15. Alice Denham, then an aspiring writer (she would write *The Ghost and Mrs. Muir*) and later a *Playboy* model, claimed in her 2006 memoir to have had casual sex with Dean around this time, alleging that he enjoyed nuzzling her breasts, smelled of vanilla, and called her "Mommy." She also claimed his penis size was unimpressively average and that he was decisively "*not* gay." Her account, however, reads like a literary invention, with dialogue and details closely echoing, sometimes nearly verbatim, Barbara Glenn's account quoted in Dalton, *James Dean* (2001), 7–8, but differing from Dean's other lovers' accounts primarily when discussing sex details not covered in Dalton's biography. My judgment is that she may have met Dean through mutual friends but likely fabricated (or exaggerated) their sexual relationship (Alice Dunham, *Sleeping with Bad Boys* [self-published, 2006], 28–30).
16. Spoto, *Rebel*, 134.
17. Spoto, *Rebel*, 133–35; Gilmore, *Live Fast, Die Young*, 119–22. Gilmore's discomfort speaks to the distortions social opprobrium imposed on same-sex relations, as does his conclusion, following their romantic and erotic interlude, that they would "surely" have fallen in love "if either one of us had been a girl." However, it is unclear whether Gilmore's account is entirely reliable. "Bill Dakota" (a.k.a. William Cern), himself a tabloid publisher of dubious gay celebrity allegations, claimed in his memoir *The Gossip Columnist* (Studio D, 2010) that Gilmore was a serial exaggerator who fabricated some of his claims and rewrote other people's experiences as his own. My feeling is that Gilmore's account has a core of truth, but his later memoirs, which grow increasingly explicit, seem to have a greater proportion of fantasy.
18. Gilmore, *Real James Dean*, 115.
19. Dalton, *James Dean* (2001), 141–42.
20. Dalton, *James Dean* (2001), 142.
21. Cf. Robert E. Howard, "Queen of the Black Shore": "Let teachers and priests and philosophers brood over questions of reality and illusion. I know this: if life is illusion, then I am no less an illusion, and being thus, the illusion is real to me. I live, I burn with life, I love, I slay, and am content." The 1934 story appeared in *The Coming of Conan* from Gnome Press in 1953 but seems to have been published too late in the year to have been Dean's source. He probably read it in the *Avon Fantasy Reader*, no. 8, published in 1948. The line must have meant a lot to him to stick in his mind, perhaps since high school. If not, it is a hell of a coincidence. *Pace*, Spoto, *quander* is a real word, and Dean used it correctly.
22. Dalton, *James Dean* (2001), 141.

23. *Larry King Live*, CNN, December 3, 2005; cf. Holley, *James Dean*, 233, about a similar incident with taxicabs.

24. Fredric Wertham, *Seduction of the Innocent* (New York: Reinhart, 1954), chap. 7.

25. *Juvenile Delinquency (Comic Books)*, Hearings before the Subcommittee to Investigate Juvenile Delinquency in the U.S., of the Senate Committee on the Judiciary, 83rd Cong., 2nd sess., on Apr. 21, 22, and June 4, 1954 (Washington: United States Government Printing Office, 1954), 91.

26. "Men over 50 Rate High in Sex Appeal," *Detroit Tribune*, February 21, 1953, 5. Hollywood's highest-paid actor, and in 1943 the highest-paid man by salary in the whole United States, *Double Indemnity* star Fred MacMurray, looked just as old. Only in his midthirties at the height of his fame, he already looked well into middle age (Herb Howe, "Laziest Man in Town," *Photoplay*, December 1947, 64–65, 84).

27. André Gide, *If It Die: An Autobiography*, new ed. (New York: Random House, 1935), 288.

28. André Gide, *The Journals of André Gide*, vol. 2: *1914–1927* (New York: Alfred A. Knopf, 1948), 246–47.

29. "Andre Gide Is Dead; Noted Novelist, 81," *New York Times*, February 20, 1951, 25.

30. Terry Ramsaye, "Terry Ramsaye Says," *Motion Picture Herald*, February 27, 1954, 16.

31. Holley, *James Dean*, 185.

32. Brackett's friend quoted in Holley, *James Dean*, 12. On Dean's sexualized performance, see references to his "interesting sexual gyrations" in Maurice Zolotow, "The Season on and off Broadway," *Theater Arts*, November 1954, 87.

33. Herndon, *James Dean*, 89; four decades after Dean's death, Goetz still autographed Dean biographer Val Holley's copy of *The Immoralist*, which I have inspected, with an inscription calling Dean a "bad boy."

34. "I am sorry you are buying the machine." Jane Deacy to James Dean, addressed to him at the address of the Capital City Motorcycle Club, the residence of motorcycle dealer Edward Hunsicker, in Harrisburg, December 8, 1953. However, other sources claim the motorcycle was his childhood bike, shipped back from Indiana.

35. Spoto, *Rebel*, 142. Vivian Matalon gives the same story in different words in Holley, *James Dean*, 187.

36. "Homo-Theme 'Immoralist' 'Embarrasses' Chapman; Jinx's Stay-Away Pitch," *Variety*, February 10, 1954, 2. *Tex and Jinx* aired at 8:45 a.m. weekdays on WNBC in early 1954.

37. Bast, *Surviving James Dean*, 177.

38. Elia Kazan to John Steinbeck, March 1954, in Elia Kazan, *The Selected Letters of Elia Kazan*, ed. Albert J. Devlin and Marlene J. Devlin (New York: Alfred A. Knopf, 2014), 259.

39. Andy Griffith recalled Kazan's tactical use of humiliation, ostracism, and verbal abuse to provoke a vicious performance from him for *A Face in the Crowd* and how psychologically damaging it was for him and his wife, on whom he took out his growing anger. In any other industry, Kazan's methods would be labeled abuse. See J. W. Williamson, *Hillbillyland: What the Movies Did to the Mountains and What the Mountains Did to the Movies* (Chapel Hill: University of North Carolina, 1995), 168–70.

40. Scheuer, "Jimmy Dean Says," 3.

41. Kazan to Steinbeck, March 1954, in Kazan, *Selected Letters*, 259.

CHAPTER 8

1. James Dean to Billy Rose, February 9, 1954. Contrary to most accounts that state Dean quit after being cast in the third week of February, Dean's letter indicates he quit before Kazan had formally screen-tested him the following week, apparently sure of his casting.

2. Page's daughter claims Page had a three-month affair with Dean, culminating in two weeks of nightly sex in late winter 1954. Page wrote allusively of it in her journal, decades later, in response to rumors of Dean's homosexuality: "Jimmy was not gay. At least not while I was around. I don't think we slept once in those two weeks before Jimmy went off to Hollywood." She was unaware he was attempting to seduce a male costar at the same time. See Michael Riedel, "Rip Torn's Daughter Salutes Her Actress Mother," *New York Post*, March 2, 2017.

3. Spoto, *Rebel*, 151. In 1957, the photographer's model Lynne Carter told an almost identical seduction story, including the repeated assignations stretching from Phila-delphia in December to New York in February and even the romantic lighting, set during the exact same period, down to the week. Given the lack of corroborating evidence that Carter had an actual relationship with James Dean, the close similari-ties in their stories and the genuine, if distorted, information about Dean's encounter with a gay producer embedded in the article make one wonder if Carter wasn't build-ing her story from anecdotes she had heard directly or indirectly from Matalon. Like other articles from the many women who discovered relationships with Dean after his death, the overarching purpose of Carter's piece was to reinforce Dean's heterosexual image, though she did so by indirectly acknowledging rampant speculation about Dean's sexuality. Most of the claims in her article, however, could have been gleaned from prior magazine pieces and William Bast's 1956 biography of Dean, which she had read. See Lynne Carter, "I Was a Friend of Jimmy Dean," *Rave*, January 1957, 30–34; Lynne Carter, "I Learned about Love from Jimmy Dean," *Rave*, April 1957, 24–27.

4. See, e.g., Richard Moore, "Lone Wolf," *Modern Screen*, August 1955, 28; Wood, "You Haven't Heard," 84.

5. Dalton, *James Dean* (2001), 138–39; Hyams and Hyams, *James Dean*, 86. Gunn said the incident took place at an unnamed girl's home, but Hyams specifies it was Arlene Sax's apartment. Sax's version, which seems to be textually dependent on Gunn's rather than an independent account, specifies that Dean was masturbating. Sax's account substitutes Sax for Gunn as the instigator of the incident but is otherwise nearly verbatim, though with less detail. I judge her account a fabrication.

6. Dalton, *James Dean* (2001), 7, 8, 140–41.

7. David Browne, "Proof, in His Own Handwriting, That James Dean Knew He Had a Date with Death!" *Confidential*, January 1958, 12–13, 46. Dean gave the marked-up book to Rod Steiger when they met during an audition for *Oklahoma!* in September 1953, indicating the markups occurred prior to that time. Steiger still had the book decades later, suggesting Steiger must have been *Confidential*'s source.

8. Joe Hyams, "James Dean," 74–75; "Why Kazan Made Him a Star," *Picturegoer*, December 14, 1957, 16; Hyams and Hyams, *James Dean*, 86. Sax later performed as Arlene Martel. In the 1990s, she claimed that Dean was seeing Rogers Brackett at this

time and described the pain from their anal sex to her, but I find it doubtful that he would have so bluntly discussed with a teenager he hardly knew names and details he could barely share with his best friends. Sax's claims about Dean expanded over the decades, with her eventually asserting implausibly that they had had a long, deep, and passionate sexual romance.

9. Jane Deacy to Dick Clayton, undated Western Union telegram, c. late March/early April 1954.

10. James Dean to Barbara Glenn, April 26, 1954. Dalton's and Spoto's published transcripts both differ from the autograph original, which places this phrase in quotation marks, suggesting Dean was making a reference to something whose context is now lost. Similarly, the published versions capitalize the *a* in *am*, though the manuscript does not, in keeping with the Victorian literary conventions Dean learned from his books.

11. Elia Kazan to Jack Warner, March 1954, in Kazan, *Selected Letters*, 260; Kazan left written instructions to engage in "fucking," using that word.

12. Bast, *Surviving James Dean*, 177.

13. Bast, *Surviving James Dean*, 182–84; cf. Bast, *James Dean*, 100–103, which rather clumsily omits any discussion of what occurred in Borrego Springs while offering rich detail on the trip there and the days after.

14. Dick Clayton to Jane Deacy, December 17, 1953, and December 31, 1953. Clayton's letters imply that Deacy had met with Clayton during a West Coast trip and discussed obtaining Hollywood representation for Dean to market him as a potential film star after MGM scuttled plans to sign Dean to their studio through their New York office. Contrary to his 1953 letters, Clayton later claimed he took on Dean because he remembered him from a brief meeting on the set of *Sailor Beware* in 1951, where both had bit parts, but film logs show they were not on set on the same day. Clayton filmed on September 6, and Dean, on September 29.

15. Dick Clayton to Jane Deacy, May 7, 1954.

16. Marvin "Monty" Roberts, eighteen in 1954, a rancher with a small part in *East of Eden*, asserted Dean lived with him after visiting the desert and notably showed no interest in local girls. Starting in the 1990s, he claimed Elia Kazan had hired him to give Dean the lay of the land. His story grew with the telling. Hyams concluded in 1992 that Dean had spent a week with Roberts on his father's ranch, but by 1996 Roberts had expanded this to three months, a claim belied by Jane Deacy's documents, *East of Eden* production records, and the recollections of Dean's friends. Dean's letter to Barbara Glenn of April 26, 1954, makes no mention of any such trip despite outlining his itinerary around California for the month of April, and Roberts's brother Larry said his "bare-faced liar" brother made up the claim: "We slept in the same room, and if somebody's going to be sleeping in my bed for four months, I'd know about it." Roberts did not claim to have had a friendship with Dean when interviewed in the *Lompoc Record* in November 1988, and the details of his story are inconsistent with established facts. His claim that Rolf Wütherich called him with a broken jaw to inform him of Dean's death minutes after arriving at the hospital seems at odds with logic. See Hyams and Hyams, *James Dean*, 121; Monty Roberts, *The Man Who Listens to Horses: The Story of a Real-Life Horse Whisperer* (New York: Random House, 1997),

102–4; Eric Brazil, "Book Rebuts 'Horses' Claims," *San Francisco Examiner*, July 19, 1999, A7.

17. James Dean to Jane Deacy, two undated letters on Dick Clayton's stationery, circa mid-April 1954; Jane Deacy to James Dean, April 30, 1954.

18. James Dean to Barbara Glenn, April 26, 1954. Due to intentional falsifications in published versions, I quote here from a scan of the autograph original. While it is not certain he was drunk when writing the letter, the handwriting is significantly looser and less legible than his usual style, and the sloppy prose resembles a letter he admitted to writing while drunk.

19. James Dean to Barbara Glenn, c. June 1954, in Dalton, *James Dean* (2001), 171, and Hyams and Hyams, *James Dean*, 125. Hyams and Hyams and Dalton print different but overlapping excerpts from the same letter, with Hyams and Hyams selectively editing out lines and words with ellipses for no obvious reason. Some minor transcription differences also exist between the two. Dalton gives "and walk away," which changes the meaning. I have not seen the autograph original of this letter.

20. James Dean to Jane Deacy, undated letter c. late April 1954. Sometime around this point, future actor and writer Michael St. John (a.k.a. Sandy Lewis) claimed to have befriended Dean, watched him have sex with a woman (at Dean's invitation), and sat beside him as Dean masturbated in a car. St. John's account is quite confused. He places it in an ahistorical period that is simultaneously before 1952 (the year *Inner Sanctum Mysteries*, on which Dean was working, left the air), the summer of 1954 (when Dean was dating Pier Angeli), and "nearly the end of the fifties," at which point Dean was dead. St. John claims he witnessed Dean experience many intense infatuations that summer, which is not supported by Dean's correspondence from the period or other friends' accounts. Given the close parallels with wording and imagery from John Gilmore's Dean memoirs and the fact that no one else ever mentioned St. John in connection with Dean, my judgment is that the account as written is likely fiction (Michael St. John Lewis, *Hollywood through the Back Door* [Bloomington, IN: Xlibris, 2019], chap. 5).

21. Selective Service Classification Record, Indiana Local Board no. 38, National Archives. Val Holley misread the file and claims Dean had a physical examination on April 28, 1951 (Holley, *James Dean*, 66), but Dean's Selective Service file indicates a date of 1954. While the crossbar in the 4 is malformed, the pattern in the record is to list examinations in reverse chronological order, so the topmost exam must have occurred last. Joe Hyams says that Dean received a renewed 4-F classification in the spring of 1955, a year later (Hyams and Hyams, *James Dean*, 215–16), but Dean's Selective Service record has no information either way, as it was closed out with his September 30, 1955, death, before the 1956 annual update, which would have listed the outcome.

22. Dick Clayton confessed to the staging but insisted it turned into a real romance. See Jerry Krupnick, "The Truth about Jimmy Dean: His Magnetism Had Women Fascinated," *Des Moines Register*, January 2, 1957, 7. Val Holley claims the pair met when Angeli decided to stroll across the Warner lot to get a look at him, but that is almost certainly a publicity story, as Holley quotes it from a publicity piece (Holley, *James Dean*, 204).

23. Alice Hoffman, "Change of Heart," *Modern Screen*, December 1954, 76.

24. Elia Kazan claimed in his memoir to have heard them having sex in Dean's dressing room on the set of *Eden*. Bast took this to mean a soundstage dressing room on the Warner lot and said this was acoustically impossible given the distance involved and the thickness of the walls. At other times, Kazan said he couldn't imagine Dean ever had sex with a woman. Kazan's memoir contains several obvious untruths about Dean and the making of *East of Eden*, and my feeling is that Kazan's story isn't trustworthy. Dean's friends agreed that their love was "spiritual" and lacked "mad passion," and decades later columnist Kendis Rochlen recalled Dean insisting that he had not had sex with Angeli. In late 1954, Angeli claimed to have merely been friends with Dean and only later claimed in the *National Enquirer* that they "fool[ed] around" but that it was "innocent." However, her final story came at the end of a *National Enquirer* paycheck in 1968, at a time when her second marriage was failing and she had every incentive to portray a lost romance as her true love. Joe Hyams twice claimed Dean thought Angeli's baby to be his own and had cried in Hyams's arms about it, but Hyams placed the story at the wrong time. I doubt Dean shared his deepest feelings only with his second-favorite gossip columnist, but he might have faked it for Hyams's benefit. Hedda Hopper, "Actress Pier Angeli Engaged to Vic Damone," *Los Angeles Times*, October 5, 1954; Hedda Hopper, "Vic Damone Will Wed Pier Angeli This Fall," *Chicago Daily Tribune*, October 9, 1954; "To Repair a Battered Heart—An Oil Filter," *Screen Album*, August 1955; Louella Parsons, "Art Lovers Hope for the Best," *Washington Post*, November 13, 1954; Benjamin Lewis, "Jimmy Dean's Hidden Heartbreak," *Hollywood Love and Tragedy*, November 1956, 40; Roger Langley, "James Dean's Ghost Wrecked My Two Marriages, Says Pier Angeli," *National Enquirer*, September 1, 1968; Elia Kazan, *Elia Kazan: A Life* (New York: Da Capo, 1997 [1988], 537); Hyams and Hyams, *James Dean*, 232; Holley, *James Dean*, 206; Bast, *Surviving James Dean*, 195–96.

25. Hoffman, "Change of Heart," 76.

26. I have woven here Angeli's romanticized 1968 recollections with her 1954 claims and slightly later statements Dean made to Vampira (Hoffman, "Change of Heart," 53, 76–77; Langley, "James Dean's Ghost").

27. Nicholas Ray, "From Rebel—The Life Story of a Film," *Daily Variety*, October 31, 1956. Dean claimed the revolver had been a gift but did not say from whom.

28. The five women were Bette McPherson (1950), Beverly Wills (1951), Dizzy Sheridan (1952), Barbara Glenn (1953), and Pier Angeli (1954).

29. Hyams and Hyams, *James Dean*, 262; Martinetti, *James Dean Story* (1975), 100–101, quoting a 1955 *Motion Picture* column; Hoffman, "Change of Heart," 77; Jane Deacy to James Dean, June 30, 1954.

30. Jane Deacy to James Dean, August 12, 1954. While Dean's letter to Deacy is lost, its contents can be inferred from her reply. Marriage had no legal effect on draft status in 1954 under the Selective Service Act of 1948, as amended in 1951, except in one specific circumstance, so the only reason Dean could have been concerned was if he had (1) been drafted previously and (2) secured 4-F status due to homosexuality. A marriage, even a sham one, would be prima facie proof of heterosexuality, draft eligibility, and even perjury if he could not prove homosexuality. The Selective Service

Act of 1948 also made men eligible for the draft until the age of twenty-six. Dean later suggested he would marry later, after age thirty, when he was no longer draft eligible.

31. Hoffman, "Change of Heart," 76.

32. *Daily Variety* announced the split on October 1, and Dean referenced being over it in an undated letter to his father announcing his appearance the following week on CBS's *Danger*, which aired November 9.

33. Bast, *Surviving James Dean*, 194–97. Bast says Dean's only reaction was anger that Mama Pierangeli had won the "game." Cf. Kendris Rochlen's recollection, in which Dean told her that he did not care that Angeli had left him but was fuming mad that Vic Damone, a much lesser talent, had bested him (Holley, *James Dean*, 214).

34. Kazan, *Elia Kazan*, 537.

35. Marlon Brando with Robert Lindsey, *Songs My Mother Taught Me* (New York: Random House, 1994), 348; "Marlon Brando: Unaccustomed as I Am . . ." *Modern Screen*, October 1955, 47; Capote, "Duke in His Domain," 338–39.

36. Aline Mosby, "James Dean, New Movie Sensation," *Daily Iberian* [New Iberia, LA], April 5, 1955, 5.

37. "James Dean Remembered," *ABC Wide World Special*, ABC-TV, November 13, 1974. Spoto, *Rebel*, 171–72, gives a slight variation from a 1995 letter by Rosenman. I have elected to use the earlier and possibly more accurate version.

38. Julie Harris, "How I Remember James Dean," *Picturegoer*, June 16, 1956, 10; Derek Marlowe, "Soliloquy on James Dean's Forty-Fifth Birthday," *New York*, November 8, 1976, 45.

39. Scheuer, "Jimmy Dean Says," 3; Louella O. Parsons, "James Dean—New Face with a Future," *Cosmopolitan*, March 1955, 44.

40. James Dean to Barbara Glenn, c. June 1954, in Dalton, *James Dean* (2001), 171, and Hyams and Hyams, *James Dean*, 125.

41. Bast recalled tabloid magazines making these claims (Bast, *Surviving James Dean*, 212). I have not been able to find contemporary articles stating such things, and Bast may have misremembered oral gossip.

42. Speculation about whether Dean tried to disrupt the wedding raged for decades. Bast claimed that Dean told him he wasn't dumb enough to pull a stunt like that in person and had hired a double for publicity and deniability (Bast, *Surviving James Dean*, 197).

43. Mamie Van Doren, *Playing the Field: My Story* (New York: Putnam's, 1987), 127–28.

44. Shelley Winters, "Drawing Blood," in *Real James Dean: Intimate Memories from Those Who Knew Him Best*, ed. Peter L. Winkler, electronic ed. (Chicago: Chicago Review Press, 2016); Hyams and Hyams, *James Dean*, 179. Van der Heide was Nicholas Ray's therapist, as well. Dean did not share his therapy sessions with many people, so various friends had wildly different impressions of whether and when he saw a therapist. Hyams quotes from a letter billing Dean for sessions, which he must have obtained after raiding Dean's New York apartment following his death. Dean's therapy is confirmed in a letter from Jane Deacy to James Dean of September 27, 1954, inquiring as to the name of his therapist, and a therapy bill from Bela Mittelmann forwarded to Deacy on March 8, 1955. Hyams quotes a letter to Dean from Van der Heide speaking of Dean continuing care in New York with another therapist.

45. Martinetti, *James Dean Story* (1975), 104.

46. The similarity between this scene and Dean's parallel lament for Plato in *Rebel without a Cause*, filmed a few months later, is remarkable. Few biographers or critics have commented on the close repetition because "Dark" was thought lost after its original broadcast until the kinescope was uncovered in 2010.

47. Gilmore quotes Dean as paraphrasing a line about pain being misdirected energy, which is a distillation from the second chapter of Heard's book. Dean specifically named *Pain, Sex, and Time* after delivering the line (John Gilmore, "Blindside," in *Real James Dean: Intimate Memories from Those Who Knew Him Best*, ed. Peter L. Winkler, electronic ed. [Chicago: Chicago Review Press, 2016]; Heard, *Pain, Sex, and Time*, 24–41).

48. For what it's worth, unlike most other young Hollywood men, Dean claimed to have an aversion to nightclubs ("Spotlighting James Dean," 61).

49. Maila Nurmi, "The Vampire Monologues: Vampira," interview with Sandy Clark and Michael Monahan, in Michael Monahan, *American Scary: Conversations with the Kings, Queens and Jesters of Late-Night Horror TV* (Parkville, MD: Midnight Marquee Press, 2011), 17–18.

50. Hopper and Brough, *Whole Truth*, 171.

51. Riese, *Unabridged James Dean*, 136, quoting from an unidentified source, presumably a magazine. Despite this, in an interview with Matt Berry late in life, Nurmi, heavily influenced by popular literature, insisted Dean was a "little boy in search of his mother." Her niece went further, claiming that Dean saw Nurmi as a mother figure and she saw him as a son—an odd claim, given her eagerness to date him. See Matt Berry, "The Lady Is a Vamp," *Vampire Show* (blog), 2013, https://the-vampira -show.tumblr.com/post/40421642839/matt-berry-interview; Sandra Niemi, *Glamour Ghoul: The Passions and Pain of the Real Vampira, Maila Nurmi* (Port Townsend, WA: Feral House, 2021).

52. Scheuer, "Jimmy Dean Says," 3.

53. "Elson Chides Trend to Grab Straws for Peace of Mind," *Evening Star* [Washington, DC], January 12, 1955, B16.

54. Gilmore, "Blindside."

CHAPTER 9

1. Robert Lindner, "The Jet-Propelled Couch, Part 1," *Harper's*, December 1954, 49–57; Robert Lindner, "The Jet-Propelled Couch, Part 2," *Harper's*, January 1955, 76–84. Many have speculated that the name *Kirk Allen* papers over Paul Linebarger, a Pentagon Asia expert who later wrote science fiction as Cordwainer Smith, though no conclusive evidence exists.

2. Jeanne Balch Capen, "The Strange Revival of James Dean," *American Weekly*, July 29, 1956, 5. Dean also described his living spaces as the "scene of a hurricane" ("Spotlighting James Dean," 61).

3. In a tale widely repeated across social media, Darwin Porter and Danforth Prince claim Kitt, Dean, and Paul Newman had a threesome around this time, quoting what they say is Kitt's extremely detailed description. They did not publish the allegation, allegedly made to Porter in 1979, until after Kitt's 2008 death, when Kitt, who

repeatedly denied having had a sexual relationship with Dean, could no longer sue for libel. The account, part of the pair's penchant for discovering posthumous confessions unknown to any other writer, is almost certainly false (Darwin Porter and Danforth Prince, *James Dean: Tomorrow Never Comes: A Myth-Shattering Tale about America's Obsession with Celebrities* [New York: Blood Moon, 2016], 416–18).

4. Dalton, *James Dean* (2001), 210.

5. "Our Vicious Young Hoodlums: Is There Any Hope?", *Newsweek*, September 6, 1954, 43–44; Richard Clendenen, "Why Teen-Agers Go Wrong," *U.S. News & World Report*, September 17, 1954, 80–84, 86, 88. Intentionally or not, the posters for *Rebel without a Cause* depicted James Dean leaning against a red brick wall colored just like the one on the *U.S. News* cover.

6. Lawrence Frascella and Al Weisel, *Live Fast, Die Young: The Wild Ride of Making Rebel without a Cause* (New York: Touchstone, 2005), 10–11.

7. Clancy Sigal, *Black Sunset: Hollywood Sex, Lies, Glamour, Betrayal, and Raging Egos* (Berkeley, CA: Soft Skull Press, 2016), 194. Sigal claimed erroneously in his memoir that Jack Warner hated *Rebel* as a "subversion of American values," and Sigal places his meeting with Dean after his client, Stewart Stern, was hired to work on the *Rebel* script, though Dean had already been attached to the film and had a falling out with Irv Shulman by that point. Sigal alleges that he met with Dean to determine whether Dean should be hired, but because Dean was announced for *Rebel* on January 4, 1955, and Stern wasn't hired until February, Sigal's account is chronologically impossible. Whatever the true order of events, they occurred between December 1954 and February 1955.

8. Ray, "From Rebel." Ray assumed Dean was serious, but the staging has all the hallmarks of one of Dean's jokes. However, as was typically the case, no one but Dean realized the humor.

9. Bast, *Surviving James Dean*, 199–200. Cf. Bast's original bowdlerized version in Bast, *James Dean*, 112–13.

10. Hyams and Hyams, *James Dean*, 103; Martinetti, *James Dean Story* (1975), 111.

11. Sammy Davis Jr., Jane Boyar, and Burt Boyar, *Yes I Can: The Story of Sammy Davis, Jr.* (Scotts Valley, CA: CreateSpace, 2012 [1965]), chap. 15. An oral account allegedly originating with John Gilmore, who said he heard it from Sammy Davis Jr., claims Dean cooked for Davis his signature omelet: eggs with jam, processed cheese, and marijuana.

12. Jane Deacy to James Dean, November 29, 1954.

13. The opera was *The Long Way*, which opened June 3, 1955, in a high school auditorium. The plot concerned a thirteen-year-old girl who has three fantastical daydreams that lead her to better understand her parents. Now known as *Ellen*, the opera was a failure, though it had a London production in 1956.

14. Martinetti, *James Dean Story* (1975), 113; with editorial notes in "Life with Rogers," in *Real James Dean: Intimate Memories from Those Who Knew Him Best*, ed. Peter L. Winkler, electronic ed. (Chicago: Chicago Review Press, 2016); Stone, *Alec Wilder*, 99–100. Wilder's friends and biographer portray this as a triumphant moment for him, getting one over on Dean, whom he considered an ungrateful con artist. But Dean had come to feel abused and exploited, and it is hard to read his reluctance to honor his own exploitation as a fault.

15. Holley, *James Dean*, 73. An alleged nude photo of Dean masturbating in a tree circulated in the 1970s but was later shown not be Dean, though not before it gained traction in the gay community.

16. Albert Heit to James Dean, January 28, 1955; Jane Deacy to Ted Kupferman, February 28, 1955.

17. Dalton, *James Dean* (2001), 210–11.

18. *Brackett v. Dean* settlement agreement of March 1955 (now in my collection) and letters of Jane Deacy to Ted Kupferman of February 14, 1955; Ted Kupferman to Jane Deacy of March 7, 1955; and Margaret Henderson to Carl Coulter of September 23, 1955, retained in Jane Deacy's papers. Brackett's opera with Wilder failed in June, and he instead staged a successful touring revival of S. N. Behrman's *No Time for Comedy* with his *Hallmark Hall of Fame* collaborator Sarah Churchill later that summer. He eventually became a restauranteur in Santa Monica, serving vichyssoise and his other beloved French fare at his Continental-style establishment, Le Cognac, built in the former Santa Monica Library, which he claimed was imbued with children's supernatural energy, leading to uncanny occurrences (Lois Dwan, "Roundabout," *Los Angeles Times*, October 24, 1971, E8).

19. Martinetti, *James Dean Story* (1995), 113.

20. Martinetti, *James Dean Story* (1975), 123; Irving Shulman, *The Children of the Dark* (New York: Henry Holt, 1956), vii. Shulman used his treatment and unfinished script as the basis for his novel *The Children of the Dark*. Ironically, his publisher advertised the book as a novelization of the movie to capitalize on Dean's fame.

21. Stern claimed the influence was involuntary, likening it to an infection.

22. Frascella and Weisel, *Live Fast, Die Young*, 53.

23. Natalie Wood, "Natalie Wood Reviews 'The James Dean Story,'" *Photoplay*, October 1957, 102.

24. Robert Wayne Tysl, "Continuity and Evolution in a Public Symbol: An Investigation into the Creation and Communication of the James Dean Image in Mid-Century America" (PhD thesis, University of Michigan, 1965), 106.

25. "Moody New Star," *Life*, March 7, 1955.

26. Moore, "Lone Wolf," 75.

27. "Moody New Star," 127. It is remarkable that his sincerity came across as fake, considering Dean was engaged in psychoanalytical therapy at the time.

28. Spoto, *Rebel*, 204.

29. Parsons, "James Dean—New Face," 44; Frascella and Weisel, *Live Fast, Die Young*, 93. Elia Kazan also noted how Dean could appear younger or much older than his age, seemingly at random (Elia Kazan to Margaret Day Thatcher, July 5, 1954, in Kazan, *Selected Letters*, 265).

30. Hopper and Brough, *Whole Truth*, 168–71; Hedda Hopper, "Liz and Mike to Work in Same Movie," *Washington Post*, February 6, 1955, H6. From the newspaper column: "I feel only a young man should play the part. When older actors play him, they anticipate the answers and substitute technique and sonority of voice for youth. The gauche, stumbling, feeling, searching boy that Hamlet was is lost." The version given in *The Whole Truth* is longer and more formal:

I want to do *Hamlet* soon. Only a young man can play Hamlet as he was—with the naïveté. Laurence Olivier plays it safe. Something is lost when older men play him. They anticipate the answers. You don't feel Hamlet is thinking—just declaiming. Sonority of voice and technique the older men have, but this kind of Hamlet isn't the stumbling, feeling, reaching, searching boy he really was. They compensate for the lack of youth by declamation. Between their body responses and reaction on one hand and the beauty of the words on the other, there is a void.

Hopper's reconstructed quotations make determining the more accurate impossible.

31. Scheuer, "Jimmy Dean Says," 3.
32. Dalton, *James Dean* (2001), 193–94.
33. Spoto, *Rebel*, 205.
34. Frank Campbell, untitled column, *Dig*, April 1957 (rpt. from June 1956), 17; Louella Parsons, "Preminger Snaps Up Prize French Shocker," *Washington Post*, April 29, 1955, 48; Imogene Collins, "The Secret Love That Haunts Jimmy Dean," *Modern Screen*, August 1955, 79; Sheila Graham, "Get These Men!" *Photoplay*, September 1955, 82; Cal York, "Inside Stuff," *Photoplay*, September 1955, 93. How he inspired nearly every woman he met to declare him her true love without returning the favor or, often enough, making more than a minimal effort is an insoluble mystery but an enviable talent.
35. Many biographers imply a sexual relationship. According to Bast, Toni Lee Scott, as she was later known, told him Dean was interested in touching her leg but had declined to have sex with her. Scott told a romanticized version of the same story in her autobiography *A Kind of Loving*, ed. Curt Gentry (New York: World, 1970), and in interviews for a half century after. She claimed the friendship lasted eighteen months rather than the few weeks standard biographies assign and included chronologically impossible details. She said she helped Dean after his breakup with Pier Angeli, an event that by her own account occurred before he befriended her. She had been a regular at Googies since 1954 and had a passing acquaintance with Dean for a year until he befriended her after the premiere of *East of Eden*.
36. Hinkle and Farris, *Call Me Lucky*, 46–47. Hinkle misunderstood the joke, thinking Dean aggressively homophobic.
37. Hyams and Hyams, *James Dean*, 149. Clayton turned over the lease when Jack Warner kicked Dean out of his accommodations on the Warner Bros. lot.
38. Bob Thomas, "Strange Genius James Dean in Role of Death," *Valley Times* [Hollywood, CA], October 4, 1955, 9; Capote, "Duke in His Domain," 338–39. The anecdote about "Hound Dog" appears in a quotation from Leonard Rosenman in Dalton, *James Dean* (2001), 195, where Elvis Presley's version is specified; however, Presley did not record his cover until July 1956. Thornton recorded the song in August 1952 and her record went on sale in February 1953. Rosenman's memory of this incident is obviously confused and almost certainly referred to Thornton's version, assuming it is not completely fictitious.
39. Don Graham, *Giant: Elizabeth Taylor, Rock Hudson, James Dean, Edna Ferber, and the Making of a Legendary American Film* (New York: St. Martin's Press, 2018), 163; Don Allen, "James Dean: The Man Behind the Camera," *Film Life*, September, 1955, 23–27, 62–64.

40. Miller, "Actor in Search," 114.

41. Mark Twain, *The Mysterious Stranger: A Romance* (New York: Harper & Brothers, 1916), 151. Dean used "The Mysterious Stranger" to describe his spiritual enlightenment to Dennis Hopper a few weeks later, but Hopper remembered only the author and a partial title. Joe Hyams reported that in Dean's papers were three pages from chapter XI (Hyams wrongly gives it as IX) which Dean had typed out, underlining "Life itself is only a vision, a dream." Twain's "Mysterious Stranger" as Dean knew it was cobbled together posthumously from Twain's unfinished drafts with some additional text by the editor, Albert Bigelow Paine.

42. Tysl, "Continuity and Evolution," 106.

43. Russo, *Celluloid Closet,* 110; cf. Tysl, "Continuity and Evolution," 106. Tysl interviewed Stern in August 1959, and at that early date he already openly admitted to intentionally making Plato gay, a claim he made more explicit when talking to Vito Russo two decades later. However, in the 1995 film version of Russo's *Celluloid Closet,* Stern instead claimed his "intention" was not to imply a "homosexual relationship" between Jim and Plato but to depict their "intimacy" and "tenderness," since, like many twentieth century men, he defined homosexuality primarily as a sex act not an emotional connection. Stern, oddly, thought Jim and the briefly encountered Buzz, the antagonist who dies in the car race, shared the deepest male intimacy in the film. Of course, he thought he was writing a picture about gang violence and thuggish warrior boys.

44. Paul Alexander relates both of these long-rumored anecdotes as though they were obvious fact, but without evidence (Alexander, *Boulevard of Broken Dreams* [New York: Viking, 1994], 210). A decade later, Frascella and Weisel uncovered the only surviving proof in Trilling's handwritten notes in the Warner Bros. Archive (*Live Fast, Die Young,* 171–72), but they found no reference to a kiss in any surviving script and were unable to determine what Trilling was responding to. It is possible that Ray added it to Trilling's draft copy, perhaps to draw fire away from homoerotic scenes he hoped to slip past the censors. Replacing *punk* with *chicken* to avoid homosexual implications was not necessarily an ideal solution, since chickens are, quite literally, lovers of roosters, which is to say, cocks.

45. Stern based Jim's parents on his own. On parents' gender roles as homosexual vectors, see: Robert Coughlan, "Changing Roles in Modern Marriage," *Life,* December 24, 1956, 112. Nick Ray's words are quoted in Frascella and Weisel, *Live Fast, Die Young,* 172 from a CBS-TV interview.

46. Tysl, "Continuity and Evolution," 106.

47. Marlowe, "Soliloquy," 46.

48. "But we never became lovers. We could have—like *that,*" Mineo said in late 1975 (Marlowe, "Soliloquy," 46). But like most people who knew Dean, his story changed repeatedly. Only a few weeks earlier, he claimed not to have been close to Dean ("We weren't that close friends, actually") and to have been unaware of "what his sex trip was" (Donald MacLean, "Meet Sal Mineo," *Bay Area Review* [San Francisco, Calif.], November 1975). Yet, in 1972 Mineo told Boze Hadleigh that "everybody knows about Jimmy" and that consequently the homosexual attraction between Jim and Plato in *Rebel* became obvious (Hadleigh, *Celluloid Gaze,* 13).

49. Hyams and Hyams, *James Dean*, 199–200.
50. Bosley Crowther, "The Screen: 'East of Eden' Has Debut," *New York Times,* March 10, 1955; Bosley Crowther, "Right Direction: The 'East of Eden' of Elia Kazan Has That But Not Much More," *New York Times,* March 20, 1955; Mae Tinee, "'East of Eden' Has Some Sins as Film Art," *Chicago Daily Tribune,* April 13, 1955; "National Box Office Survey," *Variety,* April 20, 1955.
51. Scheuer, "Jimmy Dean Says," 3. Of course this wasn't strictly speaking true. One of his favorite striped sweaters, in which he was frequently photographed in 1955, was identical to one Brando was photographed wearing. Brando may have had this in the back of his mind when he complained about Dean's performance in *East of Eden* by saying Dean was "wearing my last year's wardrobe, and using my last year's talent" ("Marlon Brando: Unaccustomed as I Am," 47).
52. Pauline Kael, *I Lost It at the Movies* (New York: Bantam, 1965), 49. I suppose Kael would have disapproved of this book, too.
53. Kazan, *Elia Kazan*, 538.
54. "Dean Legend Still Lives," *Yuma* [AZ] *Daily Sun*, October 10, 1975, 52.
55. Various other explanations for the shift to color have been proposed, including financial deals (specifically an overlooked contract clause) with CinemaScope and an effort to differentiate the film from the competing *Blackboard Jungle*.
56. Indeed, when Jim Backus mouths, "You mean he's . . ." one feels almost compelled to fill in "heterosexual." It's hard not to register that he is conveying Mr. Stark's surprise that his son is now sexually interested in women.

CHAPTER 10

1. Dorothy O'Leary, "Hollywood Love Life," *Screenland*, September 1955, 74; Bob Thomas, "Hollywood Builds Dean into Legend," *Dixon* [IL] *Evening Telegraph*, October 18, 1955, 12.
2. "James Dean," *Motion Picture*, 29.
3. Hedda Hopper, "A Friend, a Fan, a Fighter," in *The Real James Dean Story* (New York: Fawcett, c. 1956), 60, excerpting her May 1955 *Motion Picture* magazine column; a somewhat different version of the same sentiment appears in Hopper and Brough, *Whole Truth*, 171, which I quote at the end of chapter 12. It is unclear why the two versions differ or which is the more accurate. Based on Hopper's other variant quotations that differ between her periodical reporting and her later book, it seems that both versions contain parts, only partially overlapping, of what was really said and both have been selectively edited.
4. Aline Mosby, "Glamour Ghoul to Be Good Fairy as Well," *Lawton* [OK] *Constitution*, April 28, 1955, B1; Riese, *Unabridged James Dean*, 366.
5. Hyams and Hyams, *James Dean*, 146–47; Mayer, "The Apotheosis of Jimmy Dean." Rosenman spent half a century disparaging Dean's intelligence and mocking his interest in history and literature. It makes one wonder what might have been different had Dean looked up to someone who encouraged his curiosity instead. Rosenman, alone, claimed that James Dean told him he physically abused Pier Angeli while

drunk. He told two not entirely compatible versions of the story to Venable Herndon and David Dalton. Rosenman claimed Dean had a "reputation" for beating women. Neither Angeli nor any of Dean's other partners ever alleged physical abuse, but the journalist Maurice Zolotow implied it in a 1956 article discussing the "brutal" Dean's largely verbal "abuse" of Pier Angeli among many disparagements. The article's close similarity to Rosenman's later contempt for Dean suggests he was Zolotow's unnamed source within Dean's inner circle. My sense is that Rosenman, whose antipathy toward Dean persisted for decades after Dean's death, cast literally Dean's figurative language about berating Angeli in their frequent arguments. See Maurice Zolotow, "Legend Is Seen Based on Lies, Nonsense," *Detroit Free Press*, October 28, 1956, B3; Herndon, *James Dean*, 113; Dalton, *James Dean* (2001), 198.

6. Marlowe, "Soliloquy," 42. Whatever rumor Redfield heard seems to be exaggerated from Webb's excited statement to Hedda Hopper that she would be (and therefore he was) "crazy about this boy Jimmy Dean" after seeing a preview screening of *East of Eden* (Hopper and Brough, *Whole Truth*, 169) and Dorothy Kilgallen's March 16, 1954, column claiming Dean as Webb's protégé. Webb knew Dean's agent, Dick Clayton, and may have met Dean when he recommended a dentist for Dean (Dick Clayton to Jane Deacy, May 7, 1954).

7. Hyams and Hyams, *James Dean*, 215–16. Hyams claimed in 1992 that Dean was rejected (due to what Dean allegedly called "flat feet, bad eyes, butt-fucking, who knows?") in May or June 1955, and he said he saw a letter to prove it. The classification notification does not appear in Dean's Selective Service record, which was closed with his death before it could be updated. The government subsequently destroyed their copies of the correspondence, in keeping with document-destruction policies of the time. None of Dean's friends or colleagues were aware of any induction or draft board action in 1955 until they read it in the press. The movie press reported Dean's induction physical a year after it happened, along with Dean's confident claim that he was ready to serve if needed. His bravado was that of a man who already knew he wasn't going, and it seems likely Warner Bros. arranged a round of publicity claiming nearsightedness kept Dean out of the Army to help explain the government's long-delayed second declaration of his 4-F status (Moore, "Lone Wolf," 76).

8. Martinetti, *James Dean Story* (1995), 104. Hopper labeled Dean a "genius" in a March 27, 1955, profile.

9. Hyams and Hyams, *James Dean*, 209–10. Starlet Lili Kardell kept a diary filled with asterisks that Joe Hyams claimed stood for the sex acts she performed, marking several with Dean in April 1955. In September 1955, she called him "her only love" in her diary, and she was apparently one of his favorites, not least because she gossiped about him the right way.

10. As asserted by its attorney at a 1957 libel trial.

11. Griffin, *All That Heaven Allows*, chap. 7.

12. Paul Benedict, "Tab Hunter: 'Marriage Is for Squares,'" *Screenland*, July 1955, 42–47.

13. Cory, "Lowdown on That."

14. Griffin, *All That Heaven Allows*, chap. 7; O'Leary, "Hollywood Love Life," 74. Many versions of these events have been told over the years. Most assign Willson the role of suppressing the story, but other candidates have been proposed, including Universal's

publicity director Jack Diamond. *Confidential* also reported Rory Calhoun's 1940 stint in jail, believed to be another story Willson traded at the same time to protect Hudson. For simplicity, I present a streamlined narrative in the text.

15. References to the events, though omitting Hudson's name, show up in Hollywood journalism and must therefore have been in circulation. See Ezra Goodman, *The Fifty-Year Decline and Fall of Hollywood* (New York: Simon & Schuster, 1961), 52.

16. "Lowdown Demands Michigan Governor Pardon Johnny Ray," *Lowdown*, August 1955, 8–13, 48.

17. Lori Nelson, "The Dean I've Dated," *Motion Picture*, September 1955, 27, 62.

18. Dayton, "James Dean," 70.

19. Spoto, *Rebel*, 6; Hyams, "James Dean," 78; O'Leary, "Hollywood Love Life," 74; Charles Hamblett, "Early Life Explains Triumph, Tragedy of Hollywood Actor," *Australian Women's Weekly*, October 31, 1956, 13. Bracker retold the story far and wide through the decades, with various wording, including at a 1995 Dean memorial, where he told an approving crowd that the anecdote was proof positive that Dean was straight. The "days of fun" quote is given in various close paraphrases by different reporters. The text I use collates multiple versions.

20. Griffin, *All That Heaven Allows*, chap. 7. In 2002, costar Noreen Nash claimed Rock Hudson and Elizabeth Taylor bet on who could bed Dean first and Hudson won. Given Hudson's attitudes, the story is almost certainly false. "Noreen Nash, Actress Who Appeared in Giant, James Dean's Final Film," *Telegraph* [London], August 23, 2023.

21. Peter L. Winkler, *Dennis Hopper: The Wild Ride of a Hollywood Rebel* (Fort Lee, NJ: Barricade Books, 2011), 40. The rumors of Rock Hudson's cross-dressing were widely repeated but rarely committed to print prior to Hudson's death and the end of libel risk. See Ron Larsen, "Trash," *Bay Area Reporter* [San Francisco, CA], December 29, 1988, 26, reporting on *Hollywood Scandals and Tragedies*, an exploitative 1988 direct-to-VHS gossip documentary. Graham, *Giant*, 162, claims an acquaintance said Hudson propositioned Dean on set, citing C. David Heymann, *Liz: An Intimate Biography* (New York: Atria Paperbacks, 2011), 136. Heymann was an unreliable biographer and serial fabulist, and I could find no independent confirmation of the claimed source. Dean biographer Paul Alexander (*Boulevard of Broken Dreams*, 214, 217) attempts a speculative analysis of Hudson's and Dean's clashing "camps of the homosexual world" but offers no facts. Only Hopper's recollection provides factual support for Dean's disapproval of Hudson's effeminacy, in keeping with his repeatedly stated preference for masculine-presenting men (even if belied by his actions).

22. Elston Brooks, "James Dean Shoots Rabbits along Highway." *Fort-Worth Star-Telegram*, June 17, 1955; Bob Hinkle, "My Friend, Jimmy," in *The Real James Dean Story* (New York: Fawcett, c. 1956), 10.

23. Mike Connelly, "This Was My Friend Jimmy Dean," *Modern Screen*, December 1955, 53, 77–78; Martinetti, *James Dean Story* (1975), 152. The house burned down a few years later. Bast says Dean told him he gave the cat away in September 1955 out of concern for his peripatetic lifestyle and possible demise, but this is belied by a witness who saw him doting on the cat at a veterinarian's office and the instructions he left for its follow-up care while he was to be away in Salinas (Hedda Hopper, "Hollywood,"

New York Daily News, October 5, 1955, 77). Dean's words to Bast were more likely one of his jokes, funny only to him, riffing on his friends' warnings that week that he would die in his new Porsche. A magazine later claimed the cat vanished the day Dean died ("Little Things That Made," 36).

24. Hudson and Davidson, *Rock Hudson*, 59.
25. Carroll Baker, *Baby Doll: An Autobiography* (New York: Arbor House, 1983), 139. In a 2000 interview with *Media Funhouse*, Baker reversed herself and said filming the restaurant scene was "great fun" (Media Funhouse, "Caroll Baker on Working with James Dean," YouTube video, 1:23, November 9, 2008, https://www.youtube.com/watch?app=desktop&v=iDhYEttDbnQ).
26. Riese, *Unabridged James Dean*, 519–20; Winkler, "James Dean"; Hyams and Hyams, *James Dean*, 223; read with Taylor's 2000 GLAAD Awards speech. In statements to Joe Hyams and others, Taylor said Dean told her about the important people in his life, including his mother and minister. It is hard to read the minister as anyone other than DeWeerd. Similarly, she briefly and allusively said Dean told her of his loves. In a widely publicized 2011 *Daily Beast* essay, journalist Kevin Sessums revealed an out-take from a 1997 *POZ* magazine interview in which Elizabeth Taylor told Sessums that Dean had confessed to her that he had been molested by his minister after his mother died and that the abuse haunted him (Sessums, "Elizabeth Taylor Interview About Her AIDS Advocacy, Plus Stars Remember," *The Daily Beast*, March 23, 2011). Sessums further quoted Taylor as saying the secret could not be published before her death. However, in 2018 Sessums released the raw audio recording of his interview, which did not match the comments he published in the *Daily Beast*. On the raw recording, Taylor can be heard saying, "We used to sit up and . . . [pause] Off the record? He was eleven when his mother died. He was molested by his minister" (Sessums, "Elizabeth Taylor: Part Three," *Sessums Magazine*, August 27, 2018). There are no further comments about the molestation or that it "haunted" Dean, and Taylor did not link the molestation to Dean being eleven, as Sessum alleged, nor necessarily to having heard it directly from Dean, though it is a reasonable inference. (Sessums did not respond to my requests for clarification about the discrepancies.) Instead, Taylor goes on to say in response to a question about whether Dean was gay that he was "fascinated by women," loved Pier Angeli, and that she (Taylor) and Dean "twinkled," by which she apparently meant flirted, in contrast to earlier comments about their sibling bond.

    Three years later, Taylor revised her appraisal of Dean. In a speech at the 2000 GLAAD Awards, Taylor identified Dean as one of many "gay men" Taylor had known and loved, alongside Rock Hudson and Montgomery Clift. When read in conjunction with Taylor's earlier, more guarded comments about her conversations with Dean during the filming of *Giant*, which she long said had involved discussions of his minister and his love life, and the shame she said he felt after these conversations, we can approximate what was said despite Taylor's changing (and in my estimation progressively more honest) views and the inaccurate quotations attributed to Taylor.

27. Riese, *Unabridged James Dean*, 19.
28. Joan Collins, *Past Imperfect: An Autobiography* (New York: Berkley Books, 1984), 72.
29. Martinetti, *James Dean Story* (1995), 158.

30. Despite the context of their discussion manifestly indicating this was a joke, Roth maintained for the rest of her life that Dean, who had read Sartre and Camus, wasn't aware of existentialism until she told him about it.

31. Andress has continued to belittle Dean's intelligence over the decades, telling *Mandate*, a gay porn magazine, in 1991 that Dean was "not so very smart" and constantly walking into furniture. Her only praise was that Dean "had a big cock." Ursula Andress, interview with Boze Hadleigh, *Mandate*, October 1991, quoted in Daniel Mangin and Kevin Davis, "Out There," *Bay Area Reporter* [San Francisco, California], October 17, 1991, 30.

32. "Truth behind the Rumors," 112. The tapes were erased after Dean's death, ostensibly to protect his reputation.

33. Spoto, *Rebel*, 243.

34. "Spotlighting James Dean," 61.

35. Variously reported as Mark VIII, IX, or X. Made from an array of parts used in the *VIII*, *IX*, and *X*, the man who bought it from the Dean estate raced it as a Mark X, and it sold at auction in 1987 as a Mark IX.

36. Hyams and Hyams, *James Dean*, 179; Bast, *Surviving James Dean*, 231; Lewis, "Jimmy Dean's Hidden Heartbreak," 37–38, relying almost certainly on William Bast as the anonymous "friend" quoted at length. Although presented in biographies as a private revelation, Dean's agent had already disclosed a version of the facts to a gossip columnist only weeks after Dean's death, suggesting this was not much of a secret. See York, "Inside Stuff," 17. For therapeutic concepts prevalent among Los Angeles analysts, see Coughlan, "Changing Roles," 108–18, and for transcripts of Freudian sexual "therapy" see Bergler, *One Thousand Homosexuals*. Winton Dean's words are quoted in Moore, "Lone Wolf," 76.

     Royston Ellis implied Dean saw the psychoanalyst to overcome his "homosexual" urges, but his working notes show his source was the unreliable, semifictionalized 1957 biography *I, James Dean*, which was extrapolating from Joe Hyams's 1956 *Redbook* article, in which Hyams attempted to characterize Dean's psychotherapy as a homophobic effort to recover his masculinity after too many gay men hit on him. *I, James Dean*, published under the pseudonym of T. T. Thomas, was the work of screenwriter and novelist Jay Dratler, who dramatized (with fictitious dialogue) Dean's life into an unending Freudian quest to bed a mother replacement, terminating in a death wish. See Ellis, *Rebel*, 122; Royston Ellis Papers, Harry Ransom Center, University of Texas at Austin, MS-01307, Box 5, folder 6; T. T. Thomas, *I, James Dean* (New York: Popular Library, 1957), 95–96.

37. Monty Roberts claimed Dean was traveling to Salinas to buy a ranch. He told Joe Hyams in 1992 that he had purchased a property for Dean, who planned to go into escrow the next week and install Roberts as manager. However, in his own memoir a few years later, Roberts claimed Dean was merely planning to look for property in the area when he died. There is no documentary evidence to support either version of the claim. See Roberts, *Man Who Listens*, 104; Hyams and Hyams, *James Dean*, 241–42.

38. Harold Heffernan, "Filmdom's Big Debate: A Posthumous Oscar?" *Evening Star* [Washington, DC], February 12, 1956, E2.

39. Bast, *Surviving James Dean*, 229–30. Bast was certain Dean meant that they would be more than mere teammates, though Bast's account may be somewhat romanticized. Cf. the 1956 version (Bast, *James Dean*, 143–44), where Bast has Dean tell him he would mostly be in New York and Bast's stay would be temporary, thus avoiding an implication of cohabitation. The revised 2006 version has Dean insist that Bast still be in residence when he returns from New York, if he goes, so they can live and work together. A literal reading of Dean's words as applying only to the screenplay is of course possible, though it would imply a callous disregard of Bast's feelings out of step with his previous, albeit halting, romantic overtures. The callback to their Borrego Springs interlude seems a bit too neatly literary, but whether that was Bast's indulgence or Dean's, it is impossible to say. Both self-dramatized like that. Some contemporary support for Bast's later account can be found in statements from Colin Wilson in 1960, derived from a conversation with Bast in 1956, about Bast knowing Dean was "queer" and claiming to have had a long "affair" with him (Royston Ellis Papers, Harry Ransom Center, University of Texas at Austin, MS-01307, Box 5, folder 6).

40. Pasquale "Patsy" D'Amore, who first ran a pizzeria at the farmers market, opened the Villa Capri in 1954 but moved to a new location in 1957, which afterward he considered the restaurant's founding date. Confusingly, he celebrated its tenth anniversary in 1966.

41. "Truth behind the Rumors," 112; Martinetti, *James Dean Story* (1995), 169; Bast, *Surviving James Dean*, 228; Bast, *James Dean*, 142. Isherwood was a friend of Gerald Heard and part of a circle of gay and bisexual intellectuals studying eastern philosophy and spirituality. Martinetti asserts Dean never met Isherwood and lied to Bast about knowing him; Isherwood had attended an *East of Eden* screening with Dean and kept a biography of Dean with him until his death. The references to Isherwood do not appear in the 1975 Pinnacle edition of Martinetti.

42. Herndon, *James Dean*, 164.

43. Connelly, "This Was My Friend," 80.

44. Twain, *The Mysterious Stranger*, 150.

45. Now the intersection of routes 46 and 41. In 2022, officials announced plans to eliminate the dangerous junction after decades of bloodshed by replacing it with a flyover connection. The California Department of Transportation broke ground in April 2023, with completion scheduled for fall 2024.

46. The official police investigation concluded Dean was speeding at seventy-five to one hundred miles per hour and was therefore at fault, spawning decades of moralizing attacks on Dean's supposedly self-destructive love of speed, but a 1990s investigation for NBC's *What Happened?* by Exponent using more sophisticated modern techniques determined Dean was traveling at fifty-five miles per hour and the other driver, Donald Turnipseed, was to blame. The investigation attracted relatively little attention because NBC had already canceled *What Happened?* and burned off the episode on a random Tuesday (*What Happened?* NBC-TV, March 16, 1993).

47. Rolf Wütherich, "Death Drive," *Modern Screen*, October 1957, 77; David Myers, "The Last Story about Jimmy Dean," *Modern Screen*, October 1957, 75; Spoto, *Rebel*, 249. In his written-for-profit 1957 account for *Modern Screen*, brokered by an agent

shopping it around, Wütherich said the death sigh sounded like a man facing God but also sounded like a boy crying for his mother, an all-too-Freudian reading clearly influenced by Bast's biography and Freudian media coverage of the time.

CHAPTER 11

1. Bast, *Surviving James Dean*, 232. However, in Bast, *James Dean*, 147–48, Bast claimed the call came from someone whose name he does not report and only after receiving that call did he ring Beulah Roth. Presumably the later version was meant to clarify the implication that Roth called first with the news and hung up, and Bast then tried to return the call.
2. Sal Mineo and Larry Thomas, "The Dean I Know," in *The Real James Dean Story* (New York: Fawcett, c. 1956), 58.
3. Hopper and Brough, *Whole Truth*, 176.
4. Hyams and Hyams, *James Dean*, 256, with discussion in Bast, *Surviving James Dean*, 251. As there was no evidence of a break-in, as it is sometimes described, the friends likely entered using the spare set of apartment keys Dean left with Jane Deacy, who obviously was aware of what might be found.
5. "Is James Dean a Dandy?" *Private Lives*, December 1955. Fan magazines and gossip publications were often prepared months before their cover dates and delivered up to six weeks ahead of those dates, leading to a number of magazines writing about Dean as though he were alive into early 1956. The lag time also makes establishing chronology challenging because gossip could be four or five months old by the cover date of such magazines.
6. Hyams and Hyams, *James Dean*, 260–62; "Jimmy's Own Scrapbooks," in *Official James Dean Anniversary Book* (New York: Dell, 1956), 32–33. On one page, Dean had pasted a notice reading, "Wanted: Writers," suggesting perhaps that he saw the collection as an effort at memoir in search of a writer.
7. Walter Winchell, "Broadway and Elsewhere," *Indianapolis Star*, October 9, 1955, sec. 4, 3. Winchell changed his mind in revisiting (and largely reprinting) his Dean story in 1958, altering his 1955 text to now assert Dean's recklessness was due to success making him "lonely and bitter" (Walter Winchell, "The Tragic Romeos," *Scranton* [PA] *Tribune*, November 21, 1958, 17). Whether in tribute or from laziness, Winchell again recycled the opening lines of his Dean obituary for Jeff Chandler in 1961.
8. Hyams and Hyams, *James Dean*, 4.
9. Bob Thomas, "James Dean, in Death, a Film Idol beyond Sweep of Even Valentino," *Sunday Star* [Washington, DC], August 26, 1956, E1.
10. Thomas, "James Dean, in Death," E3.
11. Richard D. MacCann, "Straining toward Maturity," *Christian Science Monitor*, October 5, 1955, 18.
12. Bob Thomas, "James Dean and Jennifer Jones Are Movies' Best," *Nome* [AK] *Nugget*, December 7, 1955, 1.
13. Thomas, "James Dean, in Death," E1.

14. Herbert Mitgang, "The Strange James Dean Death Cult," *Coronet*, November 1956, 114.

15. Robert J. Landry, "Dean—Dead Star Who 'Lived,'" *Variety*, August 1, 1956, 5; Thomas, "James Dean, in Death," E3; George Stevens was among those comparing Dean to Valentino, claiming Dean's death cult was greater and more relevant because it was true to life rather than an "oriental fantasy."

16. Ezra Goodman, "Delirium over a Dead Star," *Life*, September 1956, 76.

17. Specifically, gossips took literally and exaggerated from Nicholas Ray's flippant summary in *Daily Variety* of Dean's comments to Hedda Hopper, which Ray wrongly condensed into saying Dean "had been studying magic." Ray had mistaken Dean's religious knowledge of "satanic forces" gained from the Reverend DeWeerd for the practice of (black) magic (Ray, "From Rebel"). It is often said that tabloids made such allegations, but I have not found contemporary evidence, only later accounts of people remembering such stories.

18. Spoto, *Rebel*, 2.

19. Printed advertisement for the July 15, 1957 performance of Kara Kum's International Mystery Show.

20. Robert De Kolbe, "James Dean Speaks from the Grave." *True Strange*, March 1957, 10.

21. For Dean as god of youth and world savior, see Raymond De Becker, "James Dean ou l'Aliénation Signifiante," *Tour Saint-Jacques*, nos. 9 and 10 (March–April, May–June 1957). For Dean as survival of the Adonis, Mithras, and Antinous cults, see Kenneth Anger, "L'Olympe ou le Comportement des Dieux," *Cahiers du Cinéma*, no. 76 (November 1957): 10, dismissively citing De Becker. On Dean as Adonis, see Roger Caillois, *Man, Play, and Games*, trans. Meyer Barash (Urbana: University of Illinois Press, 2001 [1961; original French edition, 1958]), 195, citing Pierre Gaxotte, writing in *Le Figaro* on Dean as mythological hero. See also Tony Richardson, "The Method and Why: An Account of the Actors' Studio," *Sight and Sound* 26, no. 3 (Winter 1957): 136. For Dean as hero connecting heaven and earth, see Edgar Morin, "The Case of James Dean," *Evergreen Review*, no. 5 (Summer 1958): 5–12. On Dean as contemporary myth, see Max Lerner, *America as a Civilization: Life and Thought in the United States Today* (New York: Simon & Schuster, 1957), 803; Jerome S. Bruner, "Myth and Identity," in *Myth and Myth-Making*, ed. Henry A. Murray (Boston: Beacon Press, 1968 [1960]), 284. For Daniel Winter, see Gavin Lyall, "Dean Worship in Britain," in *The Faber Book of Pop Culture*, ed. Hanif Kureishi and Jon Savage (London: Faber and Faber, 1995), 62, reprinting from *Picture Post*, October 22, 1956. Winter would also say that he considered plastic surgery to avoid incessant attention from Dean fans. While he was reported in American papers to be French, Winter was British ("In Death, James Dean a Hero to the French," *Variety*, July 11, 1956, 2).

22. Sam Shaeffer, "James Dean's Black Madonna," *Whisper*, February 1956, 13.

23. Capen, "Strange Revival," 4–6.

24. Perry Tausig, "Revealed: James Dean's Torrid Love Letters," *Lowdown*, January 1957, 43.

25. Mitgang, "Strange James Dean," 112.

26. Charles Hamblett, "Star They Won't Let Die," *Australian Women's Weekly*, November 7, 1956, 18.

27. Capen, "Strange Revival," 5; Berry, "Lady Is a Vamp"; Maila Nurmi, "The Ghost of James Dean," *Borderline*, January 1964, 19–23; Erskine Johnson, "Cashing in on James Dean Memory Hits Low Point," *Sacramento Bee*, November 28, 1956, C6.

28. Tausig, "Revealed," 43.

29. Bast, *Surviving James Dean*, 236. Bast reported that a tabloid ran the story sometime in early 1956. I have been unable to locate the specific tabloid that carried the story, but the supernatural pregnancy is referenced in Mayer, "Apotheosis of Jimmy Dean," 166. Mayer compared Dean to an incubus rather than an angel, in keeping with the thesis that Dean was demonic.

30. Pamela Des Barres, "Dancing with the Ghost of James Dean," *Please Kill Me*, February 19, 2019, https://pleasekillme.com/pamela-des-barres-james-dean/.

31. Fifi Gorska, "He Looks like James Dean," *Sunday Star* [Washington, DC], February 10, 1957, *Teen* insert, 1, 6.

32. "Shades of James Dean," *Sunday Herald* [Utah County, UT], June 2, 1957.

33. Harry Bakas, "Wes Bryan Cashes in on Dean Resemblance," *Sunday Star* [Washington, DC], December 29, 1957, *Teen* insert, 3.

34. Goodman, "Delirium over a Dead Star," 75, 80; "James Dean Can Be Yours Forever in 3-D Miracleflesh!" advertisement, *Photoplay*, November 1956, 112. *Life* gave the price as $5, but contemporary advertisements listed it at $10. *Life*'s Goodman disapproved of the excessive reaction to Dean's death. Maila Nurmi, in turn, disapproved of Goodman's skeptical take on the Dean cult and sent him a hex by telegram (Goodman, *Fifty-Year Decline*, 291).

35. Memo regarding campaign ideas for *Giant*, Warner Bros. Archives, School of Cinematic Arts, University of Southern California; "James Dean Bandwagon Rolls On," *Washington Post*, August 10, 1956, 36; Hedda Hopper, "Frankie's Time All 'Dated' Up," *Washington Post*, October 21, 1956, H6. Warner Bros. attempted to manage damage by denying exploitation and asserting its concern for young people. See Robert J. Landry, "Dean—Dead Star," 5; see also Lisette Dufy, "The Amazing James Dean Hoax!" *Inside Story*, February 1957, 14–16, 49–52. Dufy's tabloid pastiche of prior reporting alleges a conspiracy to "resurrect" the dead Dean for profit, based on the claims of an unnamed "executive" who disapproved. This was most likely Walter Ross, the future author of *The Immortal* and the disapproving Warner head of New York media relations (1953–1957), who at the time described himself as an "executive" publicist.

36. Zolotow, "Legend Is Seen," B3.

37. Scullin, "James Dean: The Legend and the Facts," photo caption on 121; cover of *Real*, July 1957; "James Dean: The God of a Weird and Morbid Cult," *Exposed*, September 1956; "Was Jimmy Dean a Psycho?", *On the QT*, March 1957; Mayer, "The Apotheosis of Jimmy Dean."

38. Bast, *Surviving James Dean*, 245–47.

39. Tausig, "Revealed," 43.

40. Charles Hamblett, "James Dean: The Name Goes Marching On," *Picture Post*, October 8, 1956, 19. When the article was reprinted, some news outlets edited out

Steinbeck's supposed blasphemy, changing "substitute Christ" to "a teenage god." See the reprint version, Charles Hamblett, "Star They Won't Let Die," 18.

41. Fan club membership: Caillois, *Man, Play, and Games*, 195. Letter estimates vary widely, ranging up to 1,000 per day (30,000 per month). The 5,000-per-month figure is the most commonly cited in the magazines and newspapers of the era. *Picture Post* in the United Kingdom reported in 1956 that half came from outside the United States (Lyall, "Dean Worship in Britain," 62). By 1965, Warner Bros. said it was still receiving 1,000 per month.

42. Krupnick, "Truth about Jimmy Dean," 16.

43. *Arizona Republic*, April 8, 1956, 52.

44. "Letters to the Editor," *Life*, October 15, 1956, 19.

45. Review of *Rebel without a Cause*, *Variety*, October 26, 1955, 6.

46. Jack Moffitt, review of *Rebel without a Cause*, *Hollywood Reporter*, October 21, 1955. Whether by coincidence or not, Moffitt's fantasized romantic storyline resembles Irving Shulman's abandoned script.

47. Bosley Crowther, "Juvenile Misfits: 'Rebel without a Cause' Depicts Another Set," *New York Times*, October 30, 1955, Drama 1.

48. Warner Bros., *Your Campaign*, 1955 exhibitors' marketing guide for *Rebel without a Cause*.

49. "Cinema: The New Pictures," *Time*, April 22, 1957, 108, 110–11.

50. Gary Lippman, "Life and Acting," *Paris Review*, February 9, 2016. The play, in turn, was based on a 1947 Calder Willingham novel, *End as a Man*, which had faced a court trial over its gay overtones. See Holley, *James Dean*, 164–65, for Dean's minimal involvement in workshopping the play.

51. *Motion Pictures Classified by the National Legion of Decency* (New York: National Legion of Decency, 1959), 191.

52. J. C. Wynn, review of *Rebel without a Cause*, *Presbyterian Life* [Dayton, OH], November 26, 1955, 42.

53. Russo, *Celluloid Closet*, 92. Russo wasn't entirely clear whether he was speaking for himself personally or only others of his generation in general when referencing *Rebel without a Cause*, but his tone suggests he selected this example to illustrate his point because it meant something to him.

54. Martin Greif, *The Gay Book of Days: An Evocatively Illustrated Who's Who of Who Is, Was, May Have Been, Probably Was, and Almost Certainly Seems to Have Been Gay during the Past 5,000 Years* (Secaucus, NJ: Carol, 1989 [1982]), 21.

55. Jack Fritscher, *Gay San Francisco: Eyewitness Drummer*, vol. 1., ed. Mark Henry (San Francisco: Palm Drive, 2008), 133–35.

56. Tausig, "Revealed," 43; "Jimmy Dean: A Cult Is Born," *People Today*, October 1956, 45. According to rumor, Winton Dean later had most of the letters sent by male fans destroyed to protect James Dean's image. Warner Bros. did not share their letters from male fans, either. However, the existence of letters from men is confirmed by contemporary reporters who noted them. In addition to the cited articles, see e.g., Krupnick, "Truth about Jimmy Dean," 16. A much less explicit letter from a male admirer was retained in Jane Deacy's files. The biographical details of the author match the obituary details for a then thirty-four-year-old confirmed bachelor who died in 2019 (Edward E. Lupton to James Dean, September 6, 1954).

57. "The Simple Life of a Busy Bachelor: Rock Hudson Gets Rich Alone," *Life*, October 3, 1955, 129.
58. FBI memorandum from M. A. Jones to Cartha DeLoach re: Burton Stephen Lancaster; Tony Fanciosa, July 12, 1963; "Hollywood Vice," FBI memorandum from SAC Los Angeles to J. Edgar Hoover re: CRIMDEL—CRS (Current Developments in Criminal Matters, Central Research Section), February 16, 1960. In February 1960, the Office of Naval Intelligence (ONI) raided the Los Angeles home of a "notorious homosexual" millionaire and seized stacks of files and secret photographs he had kept about the men he invited to his all-boy parties—"orgies," the ONI had called them—over the preceding years. Local base commanders had told ONI that more than 250 Marines had visited the millionaire's mansion, and when ONI hunted for evidence, they found Lancaster and Hudson among the men named in the secret dossiers. ONI provided the information to the FBI, which added it to their Sex Deviate files. I certainly hope the 250 Marines attended over months or years and not all together, or else the Marines had a much bigger problem than homosexuality.
59. Bast, *Surviving James Dean*, 237.
60. The bait-and-switch article was actually about his allegedly "atrocious" personal habits.
61. Hyams, "James Dean," 75. Hyams quoted Arlene Sax as saying Dean claimed to be disturbed by same-sex attention and worried it would compromise his masculinity.
62. Carter, "I Was a Friend," 35.
63. The words belong to pederast Raymond De Becker, among other francophone writers quoted in Serge Talbot [Paul Hillairet], "James Dean, ou l'avènement d'un archetype," *Arcadie*, no. 47 (November 1957): 14–23.
64. Hamblett, "James Dean," 21.
65. Sam Astrachan, "The New Lost Generation," *New Republic*, February 4, 1957, 17–18.
66. Bast, *Surviving James Dean*, 253, 274.
67. Bast claims Wilson never asked about "delicate" areas (Bast, *Surviving James Dean*, 282), but Royston Ellis's notes on a conversation with Wilson record Wilson asserting that Bast volunteered to him that Dean was "queer" and that Dean and Bast had been in a years-long relationship (Royston Ellis Papers, Harry Ransom Center, University of Texas at Austin, MS-01307, Box 5, folder 6).
68. *Hy Gardner Calling*, July 1, 1956.
69. Berry, "Lady Is a Vamp."
70. Joe McGowan, "Youth Who Slew Ten Captured in Wyoming," *Alton* [IL] *Evening Telegraph*, January 30, 1958, 1.
71. Dos Passos, "Death of James Dean," 121–23; Dos Passos, *Midcentury*, 479–86.
72. Ned Rorem, *The New York Diary of Ned Rorem* (New York: G. Braziller, 1967), 13–14.
73. Jaime O'Neill, "James Dean, the Epitome of Cool," *Los Angeles Times*, September 30, 2010.
74. "Actor, Missing 20 Days, Found Dead in Wreck," *Evening Star* [Washington, DC], November 20, 1958, B16; Sally Kellerman, *Read My Lips: Stories of a Hollywood Life* (New York: Weinstein Books, 2013), 49; Dalton, *James Dean* (2001), 336.
75. "Girl Dies like James Dean," *Los Angeles Mirror*, January 14, 1958, pt. 1, 1; Lee Belser, "James Dean's Fans Still Write to Him," *Los Angeles Mirror*, September 30, 1960, pt.

2, 6; Gael Greene, "Foreverness in Hollywood," *Cosmopolitan,* November 1961, 76; Dick Shippy, "Dick Shippy's Mailbag," *Akron* [OH] *Beacon Journal,* November 26, 1961, 102. Most later writers, including academics, wrongly claim the deaths occurred in 1960 because Dalton, *James Dean* (2001), 311, from whom they copied, misunderstood Belser's 1960 retrospective as current news.

76. *Internationale Verbrechens Bekämpfung* (Wiesbaden, Germany: Bundeskriminalamt, 1960), 255; "Jimmy, Wir Kommen!" *Der Spiegel,* June 26, 1995. The translations are my own.

CHAPTER 12

1. The only verified part still in existence is the transaxle assembly, now in a paranormal museum in Las Vegas. The myth of the "curse" of the Dean's Porsche originated in October 1956, when William Eschrich crashed his Lotus during a race in Pomona after installing the engine from Dean's Porsche in it. Another driver, Troy McHenry, who borrowed two small parts from Dean's engine, died in a separate crash at the same race when he lost control turning around a bend. Although the motor wasn't to blame in either case (and a third mishap, which injured another driver, had no connection to Dean's car at all), Dean fans in attendance labeled it a "jinx." See Aline Mosby, "Doctor Buys Engine from James Dean's Death Auto," *Belleville* [IL] *News-Democrat,* October 27, 1956, 3.

The story took on new life when car customizer George Barris, who owned the car's chassis before it vanished in 1960, alleged many more incidents of misfortune occurred around it (and claimed to believe in "psychic sciences"!) in the book he wrote with Jack Scagnetti, *Cars of the Stars* (Middle Village, NY: Jonathan David, 1974). The "jinx" achieved popular fame and the title of "curse" when DC Comics adapted the story as "James Dean's Curse on Wheels" in *Ghosts,* no. 44 (December 1975), and claimed a malign supernatural force worked through the car.

Afterward, paranormal enthusiasts took the fabricated fantasy for fact, culminating in an influential 1990 *Robb Report* story—a hoax, actually—asserting, among many other fabrications, that a Viennese professor had traced the steel used in Dean's Porsche to the destroyed Gräf and Stift double phaeton in which Archduke Franz Ferdinand was assassinated in 1914, an obviously untrue story, as the archducal death car still sits complete in a Vienna museum. See Ron Smith, "The Car, the Star—and the Curse That Linked Them," *Robb Report,* August 1990, 34–41.

The associated story Alec Guinness frequently told of his psychic premonition of Dean's death in September 1955 and his subsequent prophecy that Dean would die within a week is almost certainly Guinness's ex post facto fabrication. At the time, Guinness merely said Dean had told him that all his friends had begged him not to buy the car because they feared he would drive it too fast. See Louella Parsons, "Anne Baxter Signs for 'The Come On,'" *San Francisco Examiner,* October 4, 1955, I19.

2. Sam Shaeffer, "James Dean—The Ghost Driver of Polonio Pass," *Whisper,* December 1957, 8–11, 56–57.

3. Hadleigh, *Celluloid Gaze*, 25; Greif, *Gay Book of Days*, 21. The homophobic rumor obviously was a diabolizing response to stories about Dean's sexuality, attributing to it a supernatural, predatory evil. It was based on a supposedly true event reported in 1969, when Mineo held a séance to channel James Dean's spirit at a party and another guest who doubted Dean's foul-mouthed ghost had visited the gathering via the Ouija board allegedly crashed his Jaguar into a tree when the letters *J.D.* etched themselves into his windshield in indelible red. See Dick Kleiner, "Sal Mineo's Séance on Red-Letter Day," *Pittsburgh Press*, November 5, 1969, sec. 3, 8. The "séance" was a practical joke Mineo often played.

4. Written in "James," his cover story on James Dean for the March 1972 edition of *Interview: Andy Warhol's Movie Magazine*, 18, and widely quoted, usually without citation, thereafter. Warhol, however, was not wholly uncritical of Dean. In his diary, he confessed that while he found *Rebel without a Cause* sad and moving, Dean's old-age performance in the second half of *Giant* was the "worst thing" (Andy Warhol, *The Warhol Diaries* [New York: Warner Books, 1989], entries for January 11, 1981, and January 12, 1983).

5. Later in life, Anger claimed to have been one of a "select few" men to have had sex with Dean and to have paid $500 to view Dean's corpse. The stories are almost certainly false, and they blatantly contradict his other lies in *Hollywood Babylon*. Kenneth Anger, "Kar Krash Karma," in *Car Crash Culture*, ed. Mikita Brottman (New York: Palgrave, 2002 [2001]), 6.

6. Anger made the claim in the 1959 French edition of *Hollywood Babylon*: "Jimmy was also mourned by the homosexual, who thought he recognized one of his own, and he was especially grieved by the sadomasochistic set, who affirmed that Jimmy obtained his enjoyment only with belts, blows of the riding crop, and skillful cigarette burns: hence his nickname, the Ashtray of Flesh" (Anger, *Hollywood Babylone* [Paris: Pauvert, 1959], 11, my translation). A truncated translation (as "Human Ashtray") appeared in the 1965 first (and pirated) English edition (Anger, *Hollywood Babylon* [Phoenix, AZ: Associated Professional Services, 1965], 181, 270), but it did not appear at all in the standard 1975 English edition put out by Straight Arrow. Anger greatly expanded on the reference in 1984's *Hollywood Babylon II* (New York: Plume, 1985 [1984], 135–46) with material from later biographies of Dean. The name *Human Ashtray* is likely derived from the title of Dean's college-era painting of a human ashtray, though the French phrase Anger used (*Le Cendrier de Chair*) mirrors the title of surrealist Achille Chavée's 1936 poetry collection.

    Anger's discussion of Dean's S&M proclivities may be a somewhat garbled version of an observation made by the gay composer Ned Rorem. In a spring 1956 diary entry, Rorem wrote that young gay men looking to feel more masculine dressed up like the "divine James Dean" and practiced S&M in the backrooms of Third Avenue gay bars, writing that Dean "would not have existed without them," meaning that Dean was part of a culture of young "male impersonators" in New York City affecting unearned masculinity. Rorem was a close friend of Anger in Paris that year. They undoubtedly discussed Dean, a subject of Anger's fascination. See Rorem, *New York Diary*, 13–14. If one were so inclined, some support for Dean's S&M interests might be found in Ursula Andress's claim that Dean had frequent unexplained bruises in September

1955, though she attributed these to him bumping into furniture, likely due to walking around without his glasses. See Andress, interview with Hadleigh, quoted in Mangin and Davis, "Out There," 30.

7. "Walter Ross Joins WB," *Variety*, January 7, 1953, 86; "BMI Sets P.R. Post to Tell Its 'Story'; Taps Ross," *Variety*, March 20, 1957, 55.

8. Ross insisted his book was not based on any person living or dead but later admitted to Ronald Martinetti that he had known Dean at Warner Bros. and disapproved of his lack of conversational skill and his unfriendliness. Ross served as one of Martinetti's sources, per the acknowledgments of his 1975 biography (Martinetti, *James Dean Story* [1975], 136, 176). In his 1995 revision, Martinetti explicitly adds that Ross modeled his book on Dean's relationships with Rogers Brackett and Lemuel Ayers (see following note; Martinetti, *James Dean Story* [1995], 136).

9. Most notably, chapter 9, the account of a connected older man who violently seduces an unwilling Johnny Preston into a sexual relationship, is closely informed by Dean's experiences with Rogers Brackett, from the specific instances of help provided to Preston right down to the man giving Preston many of the same books. Ross, however, heightens the dynamic by having the older man engage in violent physical abuse of a younger exploitative gold digger. The chapter also contains a surprisingly clear account of Dean's encounter with Lemuel Ayers aboard his yacht (Ross, *Immortal*, 195–227). Martinetti told me that he asked Ross how he gleaned his information, but Ross would only say, "It was in the air" (personal communication, September 20, 2023). That gossip columnists of the era knew Ross's story was mostly true can be seen in a Louella Parsons column from 1960 in which she explicitly identifies the novel as the "story of Jimmy Dean" and refers to the novel's hero as Dean (Louella Parsons, "'The Immortal' Tells Dean Story," *Pittsburgh Sun-Telegraph*, January 6, 1960, 17).

10. Pauline Bloom, "New York Market Letter," *Writer's Digest*, August 1958, 74, 76. Bloom says the billboard was placed in Times Square. However, columnist Alice Hughes, in her "A Woman's New York" syndicated column for April 24, 1958, says the billboard was on Broadway between Forty-Sixth and Forty-Seventh Streets. I think Bloom conflated Simon & Schuster's press release with Ross's boast that his book deserved full-page ads and a Times Square billboard, while Hughes saw the ad in situ (Alice Hughes, "Exposes Hero Worshippers," *Muncie* [IN] *Star*, April 28, 1958, 10). The cover image by Andy Warhol was based on a 1956 Edward Wallowitch photograph of an unidentified young man.

11. Rex Lardner, "Human Meteor," *New York Times Book Review*, April 27, 1958, 34; "A Monster's the Hero," *Newsweek*, May 5, 1958, 117; "Reviewed in Brief," *Billboard*, May 12, 1958, 8.

12. Whitney Bolton, review of *The Immortal* by Walter Ross, *New York World-Telegram and Sun*, April 1, 1958. International coverage was even more explicit. An Australian paper devoted a full page to excerpting the book, declaring Ross had accurately reported James Dean's life and claiming its hero's "sexual misconduct" and "perversion" were Dean's and therefore a death blow to Dean's reputation and legend ("Story Seen as Blow to Legend," *Sun-Herald* [Sydney, Australia], October 26, 1958, 13).

13. Robert Gregory, review of *The Immortal* by Walter Ross, *One*, August 1, 1958, 27. Ironically, Bergler did later write a case study of men who cited *The Immortal* to

explain how they had been "seduced" into homosexuality, claiming it as an accurate illustration of gay men and bisexuals seeking out masochistic pleasure. See Bergler, *One Thousand Homosexuals*, 89–91, 153–55.

14. Sara Hamilton, "Inside Stuff," *Photoplay*, August 1958, 22; "Was James Dean the Man in the Book?" *Sun-Herald* [Sydney, Australia], October 26, 1958, 13.

15. Parsons, "'Immortal' Tells Dean Story," 17; Bloom, "New York Market Letter," 76; "Fame-after-Death Ross Novel to M-G," *Variety*, March 5, 1958, 3.

16. Ellis, *Rebel*, 117–18. Ellis's account of Dean's gay "side" is surprisingly accurate, if slightly garbled, and remarkable for appearing more than a decade before any other. His information came from Colin Wilson, who related that Bill Bast had told him the unexpurgated story. According to Ellis's handwritten notes, presumably from Wilson's account, Dean understood and accepted his orientation but "sometimes" pursued women to find a replacement mother, though this more plausibly disguises under Freudian readings an effort to find emotional support men denied him. The phrase *bisexual psychopath* is Ellis's attempt to harmonize Bast's gay Dean with the "psychopathic" heterosexual mother-fetishist of his other source, *I, James Dean*. Ellis originally conceived of Dean as gay in his notes but revised his assessment to bisexual after mistaking the fictitious *I, James Dean* for true (Royston Ellis Papers, Harry Ransom Center, University of Texas at Austin, MS-01307, Box 5, folder 6; Thomas, *I, James Dean*, 88).

17. Ringgold, "James Dean," 6, 18.

18. Hadleigh, *Celluloid Gaze*, 13.

19. Herndon acknowledges reading Anger's *Hollywood Babylon* in Herndon, *James Dean*, 48. The allegation of public fist-fucking appears on page 64 and is attributed only to gay S&M "oral history," the same source Anger had given in 1959. While underground S&M clubs existed in the early 1950s, the first gay leather bar only opened in Chicago in 1958, and it is unclear that fisting was regularly practiced prior to the 1960s, achieving popularity among gay men only in the 1970s. See Gayle Rubin with Judith Butler, "Sexual Traffic: Interview," in *Feminism Meets Queer Theory*, ed. Elizabeth Weed and Naomi Schor (Bloomington: Indiana University Press, 1997), 102. (*Fist-fucking* was also then slang for masturbation, but that does not seem to be Herndon's intended meaning.) The only point in favor of Herndon's allegation is Ned Rorem's 1956 diary entry about Dean's debt to gay S&M culture referenced in note 6, which suggests that a Dean-inspired gay S&M scene gave rise to anachronistic rumors about Dean's participation—or one might argue that gay men had read Anger and took his claims to heart.

20. Parker Tyler, *Screening the Sexes: Homosexuality in the Movies* (New York: Anchor Books, 1972), 143–44.

21. Jack Babuscio, "James Dean—A Gay Riddle," *Gay News* 79 (1975): 17–18.

22. Dalton, *James Dean* (2001), 337–41. Even my most purple prose can't do justice to Dalton's bizarre New Age hero worship. He literally provides Egyptian hieroglyphics to try to link Osiris and Dean as one. When Marcus and Ortense Winslow read the book, they were aghast. "We just weren't very pleased with the book," Ortense said. "Jimmy just didn't deserve that sort of thing" (Brian Knowlton, "Legend of Fairmount's Phenomenon Revived Again," *Anderson* [IN] *Herald*, November 24, 1974, 24).

23. Tom Shales, "Dean Lives . . . in Books, Records, and a TV Movie Tonight," *Democrat and Chronicle* [Rochester, NY], February 18, 1976, 4C.

24. Bob Martin, "James Dean: Legend, Idol and Rebel," *Press-Telegram* [Long Beach, CA], February 19, 1976, C18; Harry Harris, "Whitman Special Leads Flock of 'Gay' Programs," *Philadelphia Inquirer*, March 9, 1976, D5. Published reviews quoted more explicit references to homosexuality than appear in the available version of the film. I am unsure whether reviewers interpolated by seeing what was intended or whether edits occurred later. See, e.g., quoted dialogue in "McHattie Shines as 'Deaner,'" *Herald-News* [Passaic, NJ], February 19, 1976, 36.

25. Dalton, *James Dean* (2001), 151; Bast, *Surviving James Dean*, 301.

26. Journalists of the 1970s attributed the decline of the "James Dean cult" to revelations about homosexuality. See Norman Mark, "James Dean: The Cult Is Almost Dead," *Corpus Christi Times*, September 30, 1975, 9A.

27. Goo Goo Dolls, "James Dean," track 14 on *Jed*, Metal Blade Records, 1989, compact disc.

28. Producer Gary Legon of *James Dean: A Portrait*, quoted in the wraparound to the May 15, 1996, Australian Broadcasting Corporation *Wednesday World* broadcast of the documentary. Legon said Disney was initially okay with mentioning Dean's queer sexuality until they reviewed past biographies of Dean and failed to find prior references to homosexuality. The ABC noted that many American viewers found the David Dalton–scripted documentary "coy" about Dean's sexuality. The documentary notably falsified parts of Dean's biography to present a hagiographic—and heterosexual—account of a heroic figure. However, Legon had "unlimited access" to the Dean estate, raising the possibility that the estate asked Disney to cut the references. See Michael Starr, "Disney Documentary Examines the Dean of Tragic Heroes," *Herald and News* [Passaic, NJ], September 29, 1995, 15.

29. Army Archerd, "'Lies' Convinces H'w'd to Invest," *Variety*, July 19, 1994. More than a decade after the 2001 film aired, James Franco returned to James Dean in a group show for L.A.'s Museum of Contemporary Art. Franco's show revolved around *Rebel without a Cause*, and he used pornographic actor James Deen (whose screen name, obviously, was a nod to Dean) as a body double for a hard-core sex scene in "Rebel Dabble Babble," a short film depicting Dean having sex with Natalie Wood, which would have been statutory rape in 1955.

30. Also published under the title *James Dean: Boulevard of Broken Dreams*.

31. Lance Loud, "Boulevard of Broken Hearts," *Advocate*, December 27, 1994, 71. Alexander, who is not gay, marketed his book as a "serious" and "revealing" examination of homosexuality. Alexander's gossipy biography set back consideration of Dean's sexuality for three decades due to its salacious and often false claims and sexually graphic descriptions of Dean's sex acts and ejaculations. When pressed on his sources, Alexander provided nothing more than hearsay and betrayed a lack of knowledge about the history of the previously published allegations he accepted uncritically. See Lance Loud, "Too Fast to Live," *Advocate*, May 3, 1994, 68.

32. Molly Haskell, "Outing James Dean," *New York Times Book Review*, August 7, 1994, 11–12.

33. Nora Sayre, *Running Time: Films of the Cold War* (New York: Dial, 1982), 111.

34. Marie Cartier, "The Butch Woman inside James Dean or 'What Kind of *Person* Do You Think a Girl Wants?'" *Sexualities* 6, nos. 3–4 (2003): 449–64.

35. Holley, *James Dean*, 7. As I discovered in my research for this book, such attitudes persist even after those who knew Dean directly have mostly died.

36. Spoto, *Rebel*, 135.

37. Writing in *Out* magazine, quoted in Ted Anthony, "In Toughness, Vulnerability, James Dean Was Cooler than Even He Knew," *Napa Valley Register*, September 29, 1996, 2C.

38. Porter and Prince, *James Dean*, especially 314–19 for the account of Dean's alleged S&M relationship with Brando.

39. Jay Carr, "Rebel without a Cause," Library of Congress, 2002, https://www.loc.gov/static/programs/national-film-preservation-board/documents/rebel.pdf.

40. Roger Ebert, "The Young and the Restless," *Chicago Sun-Times*, June 19, 2005.

41. George Perry, *James Dean* (London: DK, 2005), 76, 216–19. Perry's outdated attitudes can be seen in his penchant for referring, rather offensively, to various men as "a closet homosexual."

42. This was not merely a literary conceit. Ellroy spoke about his incandescent "hate" for James Dean while accepting the Robert Kirsch Award for lifetime achievement at the *L.A. Times* Festival of Books in April 2023. Ellroy's novel is rooted in a claim *Confidential* fixer Frank Otash made in his 1976 memoir that he caught James Dean shoplifting caviar at the Hollywood Ranch Market, after which Dean joined him in hunting shoplifters. The story is almost certainly false because Dean preferred the Farmer's Market and was in college at the time Ostash's working notes state he recognized Dean as a screen idol. Otash, whom Ellroy admits was unreliable, likely modeled his story on the false claim that Dean ate at the Hollywood Ranch Market on his last day of life because the market was visible in a photo taken shortly before his death. He drove by it but had eaten at the Farmer's Market. See Frank Otash, *Investigation Hollywood!* (Chicago: Henry Regnery, 1976), 9–10.

43. Giacomo Aricò, "James Dean amò soltanto una donna: era italiana, la voleva sposare ma lei lo rifiutò portandolo all'autodistruzione," *Vogue Italia*, February 8, 2024, published in English as "James Dean and Anna Maria Pierangeli's Tragic Love Story," *Vogue*, February 10, 2024. The English version removes the author's explicit denial of Dean's queer sexuality and softens some of the rhetorical excess, but his overall conclusion about Dean's robust heterosexuality remains clear.

44. Alex Ritman, "James Dean Reborn in CGI for Vietnam War Action-Drama," *Hollywood Reporter*, November 6, 2019; Stav Dimitropoulos, "James Dean May Be Resurrected for a New Film, Decades after He Died," *Fortune*, September 30, 2021; S. J. Velasquez, "How AI Is Bringing Film Stars Back from the Dead," *BBC*, July 18, 2023; William Earl, "AI Firm ElevenLabs Sets Audio Reader Pact with Judy Garland, James Dean, Burt Reynolds and Laurence Olivier Estates," *Variety*, July 2, 2024.

EPILOGUE

1. Dale Carpenter, *Flagrant Conduct: The Story of* Lawrence v. Texas (New York: Norton, 2012), chap. 6.
2. *Lawrence v. Texas*, 539 U.S. 558 (2003), 578.
3. Jeffrey M. Jones, "LGBTQ+ Identification in U.S. Now at 7.6%," Gallup, March 13, 2024, https://news.gallup.com/poll/611864/lgbtq-identification.aspx.
4. "Senator Hawley Delivers National Conservatism Keynote on the Left's Attack on Men in America," Josh Hawley, U.S. Senator for Missouri, November 1, 2021, https://www.hawley.senate.gov/senator-hawley-delivers-national-conservatism-keynote-lefts-attack-men-america.
5. Daniel Villareal, "Madison Cawthorn: Society 'De-masculates' Men, Parents Should Raise Sons to Be 'Monsters,'" *Newsweek*, October 18, 2021.
6. *Tucker Carlson Originals: The End of Men*, Fox Nation, October 5, 2022.
7. The events surrounding the annual Fairmount Museum Days include both a memorial service for Dean and a celebration of Garfield the cat, whose creator was, like Dean, also born in Marion, Indiana and grew up in Fairmount. The sublime and absurd are never far apart.
8. "James Dean Not Star, nor Is He 'Brando,'" *Dayton* [OH] *Daily News*, April 9, 1955.

Bibliography

NEWSPAPERS

Akron Beacon Journal
Alton [IL] *Evening Telegraph*
Anderson [IN] *Herald*
Arizona Republic
Bay Area [San Francisco, CA] *Review*
Belleville [IL] *News-Democrat*
Brooklyn Daily
Buffalo News
Chicago Daily Tribune
Chicago Sun-Times
Christian Science Monitor
Corpus Christi Times
Daily Iberian [New Iberia, LA]
Daily Record [Dunn, NC]
Dayton [OH] *Daily News*
Democrat and Chronicle [Rochester, NY]
Des Moines Register
Detroit Free Press
Detroit Tribune
Dixon [IL] *Evening Telegraph*
Evening Star [Washington, DC]
Fort-Worth Star-Telegram
Hartford Courant
Herald-News [Passaic, NJ]
Indianapolis Star

Lawton [OK] *Constitution*
Los Angeles Evening Citizen-News
Los Angeles Mirror
Los Angeles Times
Macon [GA] *News*
Meriden [CT] *Journal*
Minnesota Spokesman
Muncie [IN] *Star*
Napa Valley Register
New York Daily News
New York Post
New York Times
New York World-Telegram and Sun
Nome [AK] *Nugget*
Philadelphia Inquirer
Pittsburgh Press
Pittsburgh Sun-Telegraph
Presbyterian Life [Dayton, OH]
Press-Telegram [Long Beach, CA]
The Record [Hackensack, NJ]
Sacramento Bee
San Francisco Chronicle
San Francisco Examiner
Scranton [PA] *Tribune*
Shreveport [LA] *Journal*
Smyrna [DE] *Times*
St. Louis Globe-Democrat
St. Paul Recorder
Sunday Star [Washington, DC]
Sun-Herald [Sydney, Australia]
Sunday Herald [Utah County, UT]
The Telegraph [London]
Valley Times [Hollywood, CA]
Victoria [BC] *Daily Times*
Washington Post
Yuma [AZ] *Daily Sun*

ARTICLES

Adams, Nick. "Jimmy's Happiest Moments." *Modern Screen*, October 1956.
Allen, Don. "James Dean: The Man behind the Camera." *Film Life*, September 1955.
Anger, Kenneth. "L'Olympe ou le Comportement des Dieux." *Cahiers du Cinéma*, no. 76 (November 1957).
Archerd, Army. "'Lies' Convinces H'w'd to Invest." *Variety*, July 19, 1994.

Aricò, Giacomo. "James Dean amò soltanto una donna: era italiana, la voleva sposare ma lei lo rifiutò portandolo all'autodistruzione." *Vogue Italia*, February 8, 2024.

———. "James Dean and Anna Maria Pierangeli's Tragic Love Story." *Vogue*, February 10, 2024.

Astrachan, Sam. "The New Lost Generation." *New Republic*, February 4, 1957.

Babuscio, Jack. "James Dean—A Gay Riddle." *Gay News*, no. 79 (1975).

Baldwin, James. "Preservation of Innocence." *Zero* 1, no. 2 (1949).

Benedict, Paul. "Tab Hunter: 'Marriage Is for Squares.'" *Screenland*, July 1955.

Berry, Matt. "The Lady Is a Vamp." *Vampire Show* (blog), 2013. https://the-vampira-show .tumblr.com/post/40421642839/matt-berry-interview.

"Big Day for Bards at Bay." *Life*, September 9, 1957.

Bloom, Pauline. "New York Market Letter." *Writer's Digest*, August 1958.

"BMI Sets P.R. Post to Tell Its 'Story'; Taps Ross." *Variety*, March 20, 1957.

Brennan, Lynne. "The Legend of Jimmy Dean." *Indianapolis Star Magazine*, December 10, 1967.

Browne, David. "Proof, in His Own Handwriting, That James Dean Knew He Had a Date with Death!" *Confidential*, January 1958.

Capen, Jeanne Balch. "The Strange Revival of James Dean." *American Weekly*, July 29, 1956.

Carr, Jay. "Rebel without a Cause." *Library of Congress*, 2002. https://www.loc.gov/static/ programs/national-film-preservation-board/documents/rebel.pdf.

Carter, Lynne. "I Learned about Love from Jimmy Dean." *Rave*, April 1957.

———. "I Was a Friend of Jimmy Dean." *Rave*, January 1957.

Cartier, Marie. "The Butch Woman Inside James Dean or 'What Kind of *Person* Do You Think a Girl Wants?'" *Sexualities* 6, nos. 3–4 (2003): 449–64.

"Cinema: The New Pictures." *Time*, April 22, 1957.

Clendenen, Richard. "Why Teen-Agers Go Wrong." *U.S. News & World Report*, September 17, 1954.

Colavito, Jason. "It's Time We Let James Dean Be the Queer Icon That He Is." *Esquire,* September 30, 2021.

Collins, Imogene. "The Secret Love That Haunts Jimmy Dean." *Modern Screen*, August 1955.

Connelly, Mike. "This Was My Friend Jimmy Dean." *Modern Screen*, December 1955.

Cory, Bruce. "The Lowdown on That . . . 'Disorderly Conduct' Charge against Tab Hunter." *Confidential*, September 1955.

Coughlan, Robert. "Changing Roles in Modern Marriage." *Life*, December 24, 1956.

Dayton, Mark. "James Dean: Excitement for the Lovelorn?" *Screenland*, July 1955.

Dean, Emma Woolen. "James Dean—The Boy I Loved." *Photoplay*, March 1956.

De Becker, Raymond. "James Dean ou l'Aliénation Signifiante." *Tour Saint-Jacques*, no. 9 (March–April 1957).

———. "James Dean ou l'Aliénation Signifiante." *Tour Saint-Jacques*, no. 10 (May–June 1957).

De Kolbe, Robert. "James Dean Speaks from the Grave." *True Strange*, March 1957.

Des Barres, Pamela. "Dancing with the Ghost of James Dean." *Please Kill Me*, February 19, 2019. https://pleasekillme.com/pamela-des-barres-james-dean/.

Dimitropoulos, Stav. "James Dean May Be Resurrected for a New Film, Decades after He Died." *Fortune*, September 30, 2021.

Dos Passos, John. "The Death of James Dean." *Esquire*, October 1958.

Dufy, Lisette. "The Amazing James Dean Hoax!" *Inside Story*, February 1957.

Earl, William. "AI Firm ElevenLabs Sets Audio Reader Pact with Judy Garland, James Dean, Burt Reynolds and Laurence Olivier Estates." *Variety*, July 2, 2024.

"Fame-after-Death Ross Novel to M-G." *Variety*, March 5, 1958.

Farnham, Marynia F. "The Unmentionable Minority." *Cosmopolitan*, May 1949.

Forbes, Anita P. "Combating Cheap Magazines." *English Journal* 26, no. 6 (June 1937): 476–78.

Goodman, Ezra. "Delirium over a Dead Star." *Life*, September 1956.

Graham, Sheila. "Get These Men!" *Photoplay*, September 1955.

Greene, Gael. "Foreverness in Hollywood." *Cosmopolitan*, November 1961.

Gregory, Robert. Review of *The Immortal* by Walter Ross. *One*, August 1, 1958.

Hahn, Milton E., and Byron H. Atkinson. "The Sexually Deviate Student." *School and Society* 82 (1955): 85–87.

Hamblett, Charles. "Early Life Explains Triumph, Tragedy of Hollywood Actor." *Australian Women's Weekly*, October 31, 1956.

———. "James Dean: The Name Goes Marching On." *Picture Post*, October 8, 1956.

———. "Star They Won't Let Die." *Australian Women's Weekly*, November 7, 1956.

Hamilton, Sara. "Inside Stuff." *Photoplay*, August 1958.

Harris, Julie. "How I Remember James Dean." *Picturegoer*, June 16, 1956.

Haskell, Molly. "Outing James Dean." *New York Times Book Review*, August 7, 1994.

Henry, George, and Alfred Gross. "Social Factors in the Case Histories of One Hundred Underprivileged Homosexuals." *Mental Hygiene* 22, no. 4 (1938): 591–611.

Hoffman, Alice. "Change of Heart." *Modern Screen*, December 1954.

"Homosexuals Answer Back." *Dare*, August–September 1956.

"Homosexuals Are Made, Not Born." *Dare*, November 1952.

"Homosexuals in Uniform." *Newsweek*, June 9, 1947.

"Homo-Theme 'Immoralist' 'Embarrasses' Chapman; Jinx's Stay-Away Pitch." *Variety*, February 10, 1954.

Hunter, Tab, and Scott Feinber. "Tab Hunter on (Almost) Being Outed in 1955: 'I Thought My Career Was Over.'" *Hollywood Reporter*, August 13, 2015.

Hyams, Joe. "James Dean." *Redbook*, September 1956.

"In Death, James Dean a Hero to the French." *Variety*, July 11, 1956.

"Is James Dean a Dandy?" *Private Lives*, December 1955.

"James." *Interview: Andy Warhol's Movie Magazine*, March 1972.

"James Dean." *Motion Picture*, December 1955.

"James Dean: The God of a Weird and Morbid Cult." *Exposed*, September 1956.

"James Dean's Curse on Wheels." *Ghosts*, no. 44 (December 1975).

"Jimmy, Wir Kommen!" *Der Spiegel*, June 26, 1995.

Jones, Jeffery M. "LGBTQ+ Identification in U.S. Now at 7.6%." Gallup, March 13, 2024. https://news.gallup.com/poll/611864/lgbtq-identification.aspx.

"Kazan's Steinbeck." *Newsweek*, March 7, 1955.

Landry, Robert J. "Dean—Dead Star Who 'Lived.'" *Variety*, August 1, 1956.

Langley, Roger. "James Dean's Ghost Wrecked My Two Marriages, Says Pier Angeli." *National Enquirer*, September 1, 1968.

Lewis, Benjamin. "Jimmy Dean's Hidden Heartbreak." *Hollywood Love and Tragedy*, November 1956.

Lindner, Robert. "The Jet-Propelled Couch, Part 1." *Harper's*, December 1954.

———. "The Jet-Propelled Couch, Part 2." *Harper's*, January 1955.

Lippman, Gary. "Life and Acting." *The Paris Review*, February 9, 2016.

Loud, Lance. "Boulevard of Broken Hearts." *Advocate*, December 27, 1994.

———. "Too Fast to Live." *Advocate*, May 3, 1994.

"Lowdown Demands Michigan Governor Pardon Johnny Ray." *Lowdown*, August 1955.

Maisel, Albert. "The Smut-Peddler Is after Your Child." *Women's Home Companion*, October 22, 1951.

Major, Ralph H., Jr. "New Moral Menace to Our Youth." *Coronet*, September 1950.

"Marlon Brando: Unaccustomed as I Am . . ." *Modern Screen*, October 1955.

Marlowe, Derek. "Soliloquy on James Dean's Forty-Fifth Birthday." *New York*, November 8, 1976.

Martin, Brooks. "The Lavender Skeletons in TV's Closet." *Confidential*, July 1953.

Mayer, Martin. "The Apotheosis of Jimmy Dean." *Esquire*, December 1956.

Miller, Edwin. "An Actor in Search of Himself." *Seventeen*, October 1955.

Miller, Laura Owen, and Anna Kendall. "Smoldering Dynamite." *Movie Screen*, June 1955.

Mitgang, Herbert. "The Strange James Dean Death Cult." *Coronet*, November 1956.

Moffitt, Jack. Review of *Rebel without a Cause*. *Hollywood Reporter*, October 21, 1955.

"A Monster's the Hero," *Newsweek*, May 5, 1958.

"Moody New Star." *Life*, March 7, 1955.

Moore, Richard. "Lone Wolf." *Modern Screen*, August 1955.

Morin, Edgar. "The Case of James Dean." *Evergreen Review*, no. 5 (Summer 1958).

Myers, David. "The Last Story about Jimmy Dean." *Modern Screen*, October 1957.

"National Box Office Survey." *Variety*, April 20, 1955.

Nelson, Lori. "The Dean I've Dated." *Motion Picture*, September 1955.

Nurmi, Maila. "The Ghost of James Dean." *Borderline*, January 1964.

O'Leary, Dorothy. "Hollywood Love Life." *Screenland*, September 1955.

O'Leary, Frank. "How to Keep Your Kid off Queer Street U.S.A." *Whisper*, November 1963.

"Our Vicious Young Hoodlums: Is There Any Hope?," *Newsweek*, September 6, 1954.

Parsons, Louella O. "James Dean—New Face with a Future." *Cosmopolitan*, March 1955.

Peterson, B. Richard. "Homosexuals Can Be Cured!" *Confidential*, May 1957.

Preble, Bob. "Bachelor's Bedlam." *Photoplay*, September 1952.

"Queer People." *Newsweek*, October 10, 1949.

Ramsaye, Terry. "Terry Ramsaye Says." *Motion Picture Herald*, February 27, 1954.

Ray, Nicholas. "From Rebel—The Life Story of a Film." *Daily Variety*, October 31, 1956.

Rettenmund, Matthew. "Late Director James Sheldon on James Dean and Affairs with Men." *Hollywood Reporter*, July 9, 2020.

"Reviewed in Brief." *Billboard*, May 12, 1958.

Review of *Rebel without a Cause*. *Variety*, October 26, 1955.

Richardson, Tony. "The Method and Why: An Account of the Actors' Studio." *Sight & Sound* 26, no. 3 (Winter 1957).

Ringgold, Gene. "James Dean." *Screen Legends*, May 1965.

Ritman, Alex. "James Dean Reborn in CGI for Vietnam War Action-Drama." *Hollywood Reporter*, November 6, 2019.

"Said Fort." *Fortean Society Magazine*, Autumn 14 F.S. (1945).

Scullin, George. "James Dean: The Legend and the Facts." *Look*, October 16, 1956.

Sessums, Kevin. "Elizabeth Taylor: Part Three," *Sessums Magazine*, August 27, 2018.

———. "Elizabeth Taylor Interview about Her AIDS Advocacy, Plus Stars Remember." *Daily Beast*, March 23, 2011.

Shaeffer, Sam. "James Dean—The Ghost Driver of Polonio Pass." *Whisper*, December 1957.

———. "James Dean's Black Madonna." *Whisper*, February 1956.

Shafer, Jack. "What Jimmy Dean Believed." *Modern Screen*, October 1957.

Sheridan, Elizabeth. "In Memory of Jimmy." *Photoplay*, October 1957.

"The Simple Life of a Busy Bachelor: Rock Hudson Gets Rich Alone." *Life*, October 3, 1955.

Skolksy, Sidney. "Demon Dean." *Photoplay*, July 1955.

Smith, Ron. "The Car, the Star—and the Curse That Linked Them." *Robb Report*, August 1990.

Strecker, Edward A. ". . . Sex and Your Child's Happiness." *This Week*, March 15, 1953.

Sullivan, Ed. "Radio Award." *Modern Screen*, November 1946.

Talbot, Serge [Paul Hillairet]. "James Dean, ou l'avènement d'un archetype." *Arcadie*, no. 47 (November 1957).

Tausig, Perry. "Revealed: James Dean's Torrid Love Letters." *Lowdown*, January 1957.

"Tele Follow-Up Comment." *Variety*, September 2, 1953.

"The Truth behind the Rumors That James Dean Committed Suicide!" *Photoplay*, November 1956.

"To Repair a Battered Heart—An Oil Filter." *Screen Album*, August 1955.

Velasquez, S. J. "How AI Is Bringing Film Stars Back from the Dead." *BBC*, July 18, 2023.

Villareal, Daniel. "Madison Cawthorn: Society 'De-masculates' Men, Parents Should Raise Sons to Be 'Monsters.'" *Newsweek*, October 18, 2021.

"Walter Ross Joins WB." *Variety*, January 7, 1953.

"Was Jimmy Dean a Psycho?" *On the QT*, March 1957.

Whitman, Howard. "Is Psychoanalysis at War with God?" *Cosmopolitan*, June 1947.

"Why Kazan Made Him a Star." *Picturegoer*, December 14, 1957.

Wickware, Francis Sill. "Psychoanalysis." *Life*, February 3, 1947.

Wood, Natalie. "Natalie Wood Reviews 'The James Dean Story.'" *Photoplay*, October 1957.

———. "You Haven't Heard the Half about Jimmy." *Photoplay*, November 1955.

Wütherich, Rolf. "Death Drive." *Modern Screen*, October 1957.

York, Cal. "Inside Stuff." *Photoplay*, September 1955.

———. "Inside Stuff." *Photoplay*, January 1956.

Zolotow, Maurice. "The Season on and off Broadway." *Theater Arts*, November 1954.

BOOKS

Alexander, Paul. *Boulevard of Broken Dreams.* New York: Viking, 1994.

Anger, Kenneth. *Hollywood Babylon.* Phoenix, AZ: Associated Professional Services, 1965.

———. *Hollywood Babylon.* San Francisco, CA: Straight Arrow, 1975.

———. *Hollywood Babylon II.* New York: Plume, 1985 [1984].

———. *Hollywood Babylone.* Paris: Pauvert, 1959.

Baily, Beth. *Sex in the Heartland.* Cambridge, MA: Harvard University Press, 1999.

Baker, Carroll. *Baby Doll: An Autobiography.* New York: Arbor House, 1983.

Barris, George, and Jack Scagnetti. *Cars of the Stars.* Middle Village, NY: Jonathan David, 1974.

Bast, William. *James Dean: A Biography.* New York: Ballantine, 1956.

———. *Surviving James Dean.* Fort Lee, NJ: Barricade Books, 2006.

Beath, Warren Newton. *The Death of James Dean.* New York: Grove Press, 1986.

Beath, Warren Newton, with Paula Wheeldon. *James Dean in Death: A Popular Encyclopedia of a Celebrity Phenomenon.* Jefferson, NC: McFarland, 2005.

Bergler, Edmund. *One Thousand Homosexuals: Conspiracy of Silence, or Curing and Deglamorizing Homosexuals?* Paterson, NJ: Pageant Books, 1959.

Bosworth, Patricia. *Montgomery Clift: A Biography.* New York: Harcourt Brace Jovanovich, 1978.

Bowers, Scotty, with Lionel Friedberg. *Full Service: My Adventures in Hollywood and the Secret Sex Lives of the Stars.* New York: Grove Press, 2012.

Brando, Marlon, with Robert Lindsey. *Songs My Mother Taught Me.* New York: Random House, 1994.

Brottman, Mikita, ed. *Car Crash Culture.* New York: Palgrave, 2002 [2001].

Caillois, Roger. *Man, Play, and Games.* Translated by Meyer Barash. Urbana: University of Illinois Press, 2001 [1961; original French edition, 1958].

Capote, Truman. *The Dogs Bark.* New York: Plume, 1973.

Carpenter, Dale. *Flagrant Conduct: The Story of* Lawrence v. Texas. New York: Norton, 2012.

Collins, Joan. *Past Imperfect: An Autobiography.* New York: Berkley Books, 1984.

Dakota, Bill. *The Gossip Columnist.* Studio D, 2010.

Dalton, David. *James Dean: The Mutant King: A Biography.* New York: Dell, 1974.

———. *James Dean: The Mutant King: A Biography.* Chicago: Chicago Review Press, 2001.

Davis, Sammy, Jr., Jane Boyar, and Burt Boyar. *Yes I Can: The Story of Sammy Davis, Jr.* Scotts Valley, CA: CreateSpace, 2012 [1965].

DeAngelis, Michael. *Gay Fandom and Crossover Stardom: James Dean, Mel Gibson, and Keanu Reeves.* Durham, NC: Duke University Press, 2001.

Dickens, Charles. *The Posthumous Papers of the Pickwick Club,* vol. I. Boston: Ticknor & Fields, 1866.

Dos Passos, John. *Midcentury.* Boston: Houghton Mifflin, 1961.

Dunham, Alice. *Sleeping with Bad Boys.* Self-published, 2006.

Ellis, Royston. *Rebel.* London: World Distributors, 1962.

Ellroy, James. *Widespread Panic: A Novel.* New York: Alfred A. Knopf, 2021.

Faderman, Lillian, and Stuart Timmons. *Gay L.A.: A History of Sexual Outlaws, Power Politics, and Lipstick Lesbians.* New York: Perseus Books, 2006; rpt., Berkeley: University of California Press, 2009.

Fordin, Hugh. *Getting to Know Him: A Biography of Oscar Hammerstein II.* New York: Da Capo, 1995 [1977].

Frascella, Lawrence, and Al Weisel. *Live Fast, Die Young: The Wild Ride of Making* Rebel without a Cause. New York: Touchstone, 2005.

Fritscher, Jack. *Gay San Francisco: Eyewitness Drummer.* Vol. 1. Edited by Mark Henry. San Francisco: Palm Drive, 2008.

Gide, André. *If It Die: An Autobiography.* New ed. New York: Random House, 1935.

———. *The Journals of André Gide.* Vol. 2, *1914–1927.* New York: Alfred A. Knopf, 1948.

Gilmore, John. *Live Fast, Die Young: Remembering the Short Life of James Dean.* New York: Thunder Mouth's Press, 1997.

———. *The Real James Dean.* New York: Pyramid, 1975.

Goodman, Ezra. *The Fifty-Year Decline and Fall of Hollywood.* New York: Simon & Schuster, 1961.

Graham, Don. *Giant: Elizabeth Taylor, Rock Hudson, James Dean, Edna Ferber, and the Making of a Legendary American Film.* New York: St. Martin's Press, 2018.

Graham, Sarah, ed. *J. D. Salinger's* Catcher in the Rye. London: Routledge, 2007.

Greif, Martin. *The Gay Book of Days: An Evocatively Illustrated Who's Who of Who Is, Was, May Have Been, Probably Was, and Almost Certainly Seems to Have Been Gay during the Past 5,000 Years.* Secaucus, NJ: Carol, 1989 [1982].

Griffin, Mark. *All That Heaven Allows: A Biography of Rock Hudson.* New York: Harper-Collins E-Books, 2018.

Grundmann, Roy. *Andy Warhol's* Blow Job. Philadelphia: Temple University Press, 2003.

Hadleigh, Boze. *Celluloid Gaze.* New York: Limelight Editions, 2002.

Halperin, David M. *How to Do the History of Homosexuality.* Chicago: University of Chicago Press, 2002.

Harris, Frank. *Oscar Wilde: His Trial and Confession.* New York: Author, 1918.

Heard, Gerald. *Pain, Sex, and Time: A New Outlook on Evolution and the Future of Man.* New York: Harper & Brothers, 1939.

Herbert, F. Hugh. *The Moon Is Blue.* New York: Random House, 1951.

Herndon, Venable. *James Dean: A Short Life.* New York: Signet/New American Library, 1974.

Heymann, C. David. *Liz: An Intimate Biography.* New York: Atria Paperbacks, 2011.

Hinkle, Robert, and Mike Farris. *Call Me Lucky: A Texan in Hollywood.* Norman: University of Oklahoma Press, 2015.

Holley, Val. *James Dean: The Biography.* New York: St. Martin's Press, 1995.

Hopgood, James F. *Adoration and Pilgrimage: James Dean and Fairmount.* Kindle ed. Eugene, OR: Luminare Press, 2022.

Hopper, Hedda, and James Brough. *The Whole Truth and Nothing But.* New York: Doubleday, 1963.

Howlett, John. *James Dean: A Biography.* London: Plexus, 1975.

———. *James Dean: A Biography.* London: Plexus, 2005.

Hudson, Rock, and Sara Davidson. *Rock Hudson: His Story.* New York: William Morrow, 1986.

Hyams, Joe, and Jay Hyams. *James Dean: Little Boy Lost.* New York: Warner Books, 1992.

Internationale Verbrechens Bekämpfung. Wiesbaden, Germany: Bundeskriminalamt, 1960.

Johnson, David K. *The Lavender Scare: The Cold War Persecution of Gays and Lesbians in the Federal Government.* Chicago: University of Chicago Press, 2004.

Juvenile Delinquency (Comic Books). Hearings before the Subcommittee to Investigate Juvenile Delinquency in the U.S., of the Senate Committee on the Judiciary, 83rd Cong., 2nd sess., on Apr. 21, 22, and June 4, 1954. Washington: United States Government Printing Office, 1954.

Kael, Pauline. *I Lost It at the Movies.* New York: Bantam, 1965.

Kashner, Sam, and Jennifer MacNair. *The Bad and the Beautiful: Hollywood in the Fifties.* New York: Norton, 2002.

Kazan, Elia. *Elia Kazan: A Life.* New York: Da Capo, 1997 [1988].

———. *The Selected Letters of Elia Kazan.* Edited by Albert J. Devlin and Marlene J. Devlin. New York: Alfred A. Knopf, 2014.

Kellerman, Sally. *Read My Lips: Stories of a Hollywood Life.* New York: Weinstein Books, 2013.

Kinsey, Alfred C., Wardell B. Pomeroy, and Clyde E. Martin. *Sexual Behavior in the Human Male.* New York: W. B. Saunders, 1948.

Kostlevy, William, ed. *Historical Dictionary of the Holiness Movement.* 2nd ed. Historical Dictionaries of Religions, Philosophies, and Movements, no. 99. Lanham, MD: Scarecrow Press, 2009.

Kureishi, Hanif, and Jon Savage, eds. *The Faber Book of Pop Culture.* London: Faber and Faber, 1995.

Lee, Alfred McClung. *Fraternities without Brotherhood: A Study of Prejudice on the American Campus.* Boston: Beacon Press, 1955.

Lerner, Max. *America as a Civilization: Life and Thought in the United States Today.* New York: Simon & Schuster, 1957.

Lewis, Michael St. John. *Hollywood through the Back Door.* Bloomington, IN: Xlibris, 2019.

Licht, Hans. *Sexual Life in Ancient Greece.* Translated by J. J. Freese. London: Routledge & Keegan Paul, 1932.

Lindner, Robert M. *Rebel without a Cause: The Hypnoanalysis of a Criminal Psychopath.* New York: Other Press, 2003 [1944].

Marois, André. *Marois Reader: Novels, Novelettes and Short Stories.* New York: Didier, 1949.

Martinetti, Ronald. *The James Dean Story.* New York: Pinnacle Books, 1975.

———. *The James Dean Story: A Myth-Shattering Biography of an Icon.* Secaucus, NJ: Citadel Stars, 1995.

McGilligan, Patrick. *George Cukor: A Double Life.* New York: St. Martin's Press, 1991.

Miller, Henry. *Sextus: The Rosy Crucifixion, Book One.* New York: Grove Press, 1965.

Monahan, Michael. *American Scary: Conversations with the Kings, Queens and Jesters of Late-Night Horror TV.* Parkville, MD: Midnight Marquee Press, 2011.

Motion Pictures Classified by the National Legion of Decency. New York: National Legion of Decency, 1959.

Murray, Henry A., ed. *Myth and Myth-Making.* Boston: Beacon Press, 1968 [1960].

Niemi, Sandra. *Glamour Ghoul: The Passions and Pain of the Real Vampira, Maila Nurmi.* Port Townsend, WA: Feral House, 2021.

Official James Dean Anniversary Book. New York: Dell, 1956.

Otash, Frank. *Investigation Hollywood!* Chicago: Henry Regnery, 1976.

Perry, George. *James Dean.* London: DK, 2005.

Polchin, James. *Indecent Advances: A Hidden History of True Crime and Prejudice before Stonewall.* Berkeley, CA: Counterpoint, 2019.

Porter, Darwin, and Danforth Prince. *James Dean: Tomorrow Never Comes: A Myth-Shattering Tale about America's Obsession with Celebrities.* New York: Blood Moon, 2016.

Quinn, Charles P., with Martin Landau. *The Photography of James Dean: New York City 1954.* Self-published, 2019.

The Real James Dean Story. New York: Fawcett, c. 1956.

Riese, Randall. *The Unabridged James Dean: His Life and Legacy from A to Z.* Chicago: Contemporary Books, 1991.

Roberts, Monty. *The Man Who Listens to Horses: The Story of a Real-Life Horse Whisperer.* New York: Random House, 1997.

Rorem, Ned. *The New York Diary of Ned Rorem.* New York: G. Braziller, 1967.

Ross, Walter. *The Immortal.* New York: Simon & Schuster, 1958.

Russo, Vito. *The Celluloid Closet: Homosexuality in the Movies.* Rev. ed. New York: Harper & Row, 1987.

Saint Exupéry, Antoine de. *The Little Prince.* New York: Harcourt, Brace & World, 1943.

Salgues, Yves. *James Dean ou le mal de vivre.* Paris: Editions Pierre Horay, 1957.

Salinger, J. D. *The Catcher in the Rye: A Novel.* Boston: Little, Brown, 1951.

Sayre, Nora. *Running Time: Films of the Cold War.* New York: Dial, 1982.

Scott, Toni Lee. *A Kind of Loving.* Edited by Curt Gentry. New York: World, 1970.

Sheridan, Liz. *Dizzy & Jimmy: My Life with James Dean: A Love Story.* Boston: G. K. Hall, 2000.

Shulman, Irving. *The Children of the Dark.* New York: Henry Holt, 1956.

Sigal, Clancy. *Black Sunset: Hollywood Sex, Lies, Glamour, Betrayal, and Raging Egos.* Berkeley, CA: Soft Skull Press, 2016.

"Spotlighting James Dean." In *New Film Show Annual.* Great Britain: LTA Robinson, c. 1955.

Spoto, Donald. *Rebel: The Life and Legend of James Dean.* New York: HarperCollins, 1996.

Springer, Claudia. *James Dean Transfigured: The Many Faces of Rebel Iconography.* Austin: University of Texas Press, 2007.

Stone, Desmond. *Alec Wilder in Spite of Himself: A Life of the Composer.* New York: Oxford University Press, 1996.

Symonds, John Addington. *A Problem in Greek Ethics.* London: Privately printed, 1901.

Thomas, T. T. [Jay Dratler]. *I, James Dean.* New York: Popular Library, 1957.

The Trial of Oscar Wilde. Paris: privately printed, 1906.

Twain, Mark. *The Mysterious Stranger: A Romance* (New York: Harper & Brothers, 1916), 151.

Tyler, Parker. *Screening the Sexes: Homosexuality in the Movies.* New York: Anchor Books, 1972.

Tysl, Robert Wayne. "Continuity and Evolution in a Public Symbol: An Investigation into the Creation and Communication of the James Dean Image in Mid-Century America." PhD diss., University of Michigan, 1965.

Van Doren, Mamie. *Playing the Field: My Story.* New York: Putnam's, 1987.

Warhol, Andy. *The Warhol Diaries.* New York: Warner Books, 1989.

Weed, Elizabeth, and Naomi Schor, (eds.). *Feminism Meets Queer Theory.* Bloomington: Indiana University Press, 1997.

Wertham, Fredric. *Seduction of the Innocent.* New York: Reinhart, 1954.

Whiteside, Jonny. *Cry: The Johnnie Ray Story.* New York: Barricade Books, 1994.

Wilde, Oscar. *De Profundis: Unabridged.* Edited by Vivian Holland. New York: Philosophical Library, 1960.

Williamson, J. W. *Hillbillyland: What the Movies Did to the Mountains and What the Mountains Did to the Movies.* Chapel Hill: University of North Carolina Press, 1995.

Willis, Shannon. "Forging Divinity: Warner Bros.' Role in the Creation of the James Dean Icon." Master's thesis, Emory University, 2009.

Winkler, Peter L. *Dennis Hopper: The Wild Ride of a Hollywood Rebel.* Fort Lee, NJ: Barricade Books, 2011.

———, ed. *Real James Dean: Intimate Memories from Those Who Knew Him Best.* Electronic ed. Chicago: Chicago Review Press, 2016.

Your Campaign. Rebel without a Cause exhibitors' marketing guide. Burbank, CA: Warner Bros., 1955.

VIDEO

Note: All digitized kinescopes of James Dean's surviving television appearances were reviewed for this book, but only those described in detail are cited.

Atherton, Ray, prod. *Hollywood Scandals and Tragedies.* MPI Home Video, 1988.

Butler, Robert, dir. *James Dean.* NBC-TV, February 15, 1976.

Connelly, Ray. *James Dean: The First American Teenager.* ZIV International/Disney, 1976.

Corbijn, Anton. *Life.* Cinedigm, 2015.

"The Dark, Dark Hour." *General Electric Theater.* NBC-TV, December 12, 1954.

"Death Is My Neighbor." *Danger.* CBS-TV, August 25, 1953.

George, George W., and Robert Altman, prods. *The James Dean Story.* Warner, 1957.

"James Dean Remembered." *ABC Wide World Special.* ABC-TV, November 13, 1974.

Kazan, Elia, dir. *East of Eden.* Warner Bros., 1955.

Legon, Gary, prod. *James Dean: A Portrait.* Disney Channel, September 30, 1995; ABC (Australia), May 15, 1996.

"A Long Time till Dawn." *Kraft Television Theater.* NBC-TV, November 11, 1953.

Mishory, Matthew, dir. *Joshua Tree, 1951: A Portrait of James Dean.* Iconoclastic Features, 2012.

Ray, Nicholas, dir. *Rebel without a Cause.* Warner Bros., 1955.

Rustam, Mardi, dir. *James Dean: Live Fast, Die Young [James Dean: Race with Destiny].* Mars Productions Corporation, 1997.

Rydell, Mark, dir. *James Dean.* Turner Network Television, August 4, 2001.

"Something for an Empty Briefcase." *Campbell Playhouse.* NBC-TV, July 17, 1953.

Stevens, George, dir. *Giant.* Warner Bros., 1956.

"The Unlighted Road." *Schlitz Playhouse of Stars.* CBS-TV, May 6, 1955.

What Happened? NBC-TV, March 16, 1993.

Index

Babuscio, Jack, 203, 205
Back to Eden (movie), 211
Backus, Jim, 259n56
Baker, Carroll, 168, 262n25
Baldwin, James, 40
"Ballad of James Dean" (song), 183
Barer, Marshall, 95
baseball team, *12*
basketball team, *20*, 26, 31
Bast, William: in Borrego Springs,
    128–29; Brackett home visited by,
    93; as broke and miserable, 171;
    communications lacking with, 71;
    Dean, James, and Sheridan with, 94;
    Dean, James, attraction with, 57–58;
    Dean, James, biography written by,
    190, *191*; Dean, James, death news
    to, 175, 265n1; Dean, James, image
    protected by, 206–7; Dean, James,
    introduced to, 57; Dean, James, left
    by, 71–72, 236n21; Dean, James,
    living with, 63, 95, 235n1; Dean,
    James, love valued by, 70; Dean,
    James, prostituting himself from,
    236n20, 239n14; Dean, James,
    sharing stories with, 63–64; Dean,
    James, to live with, 171–72, 174,
    264n39; Dean, James, true friend of,
    17, 61; Dean, James, unconventional
    behavior confusing, 64–65; Dean,
    James, visited by, 93–94; Dean,
    James, with separate rooms from,
    104–5, 246n30; Draesemer story
    from, 234n21; draft board strategy
    from, 81–83; fans visiting and calling,
    192–93; on gay underground, 210;
    James Dean by, 7; "James Dean
    Remembered" by, 206; lawsuit by,
    207; mourning what could not be,
    144; as no heroic equal, 98, 244n10;
    off to Los Angeles, 105; Sheridan
    and Dean, James, roommates with,
    99–100; theatrical seduction scene

for, 96–98; Whitmore introduced
    by, 69; Wills engagement broken by,
    94; Wills to marry, 88; Wilson on
    comments from, 269n67
Batman and Robin, 117
Battle Cry (movie), 110, 121–22, 164
Beat the Clock (television), 87
Beecham, Thomas, 180
beefcake photo, of Dean, James, *111*
behaviors: dangerous, 13, 20–21, 265n7;
    as difficult and unpleasant, 120; of
    excitement and intensity, 103–4;
    poor manners, 77; sulking and surly,
    113–14; unconventional, 64–65;
    unpleasant and unlikeable, 122–23
Behrman, S. N., 256n18
Bellah, James, 57, 59, 64, 80, 234n21
Bergler, Edmund, 9, 201, 272n13
Best Actor nominations, 186
biblical stories, 13
Bigelow Theatre drama, 72
Billy the Kid, 13, 24, 161
bisexuality, 9
bisexual psychopath, 201, 273n16
bizarre meals, 68, 89, 242n41
black humor, 143
Blum, Daniel, 145
Boetticher, Budd, 78, 238n5
Bolton, Whitney, 201, 272n12
Bomba the Jungle Boy (movie), 118
Borrego Springs, 128–29, 264n39
Boulevard of Broken Dreams
    (Alexander), 207
Bowers, Scotty, 60, 77
Bracker, Lew, 166, 176, 208, 261n19
Brackett, Rogers, 236n22; Ayers getting
    pressure from, 101–2; Bast at home
    of, 93; Bellah visiting, 80; Broadway
    musical revue plans of, 85, 240n23;
    CBS headshot of, *73*; Dean, James,
    accepting work from, 98; Dean,
    James, given books from, 78; Dean,
    James, incestuous feelings of, 77–78;

destiny, making your own, 94
van Deuseun, Anna M., 180
DeWeerd, James: Dean, James, close
    friendship with, 29, 231n40; Dean,
    James, drawn to, 27–28; Dean, James,
    in Chicago with, 86; Dean, James,
    relationship with, 39, 230n39; funeral
    presided over by, 178–79; half-baked
    proverbs from, 64; Hyams rumor
    about, 230n39; Indianapolis 500
    trip with, 34; as "King of the Wood,"
    104; moral teachings of, 28; personal
    immortality from, 28–29, 33; teenage
    boys fondness of, 27
Diamond, David, 108–9
Dickens, Charles, 35
Dietrich, Marlene, 164
dirty cartoons, 65
Dos Passos, John, 4, 194–95, 208
Douglas, Alfred, 43
Draesemer, Isabelle, 74–75, 234n21,
    237n28, 239n15
draft board, 81–83, *82*, 162, 240n18
dramatic oratory, 35, 37
Dr. Seuss. *See* Geisel, Theodor
duality, of Dean, James, life, 43, 55, 112,
    179
dual legacy, 5
DuBois, Roland, 33, 36
Dufy, Lisette, 267n35

earthy language, of McCarthy, 244n15
East of Eden (movie), 122, 142, 250n16;
    Kazan's preparing for, 128; negative
    reviews for, 156–57; premiere of, 144,
    146; Stock's photos promoting, 149
Ebert, Roger, 210
effeminate sissies, 40
Eisenhower, Dwight D., 4
Ellis, Royston, 201, 236n20, 263n36,
    273n16
Ellroy, James, 211, 275n42
Elordi, Jacob, 215

Elson, Edward L. R., 138
emotional connection, 96, *113*
emotional intimacy, 29
emotions, masculinity betrayed by, 215
The End of Men (documentary), 216–17
Les Enfants Terribles (Cocteau), 90
Esquire (magazine), 6, 184
estate, of Dean, James, 202
Eubanks, Robert, 213
Europe, 180
Everybody's Girl (movie), 68
evil influence, of homosexuality, 18
exhibitionist fairies, 104
existential pencil, 131

Fabrikant, Louis, 98, 244n11
Fairmount, Indiana, *15*, 15–16; Dean,
    James, funeral in, *178*; Dean, James,
    leaving, 38–39; Dean, James, racing
    motorcycle through, 19; Dean, James,
    visiting home in, 46–47, 101–2
Fairmount High School: baseball team
    of, *12*; Dean, James, enrolled in,
    11–12; Dean, James, in plays at, 31;
    Dean, James, on basketball team
    of, *20*; grades at, 19; senior year in,
    33; two-day expulsion from, 36;
    Washington, D. C., field trip in, 38
Fairmount Museum Days, 218, 276n7
Falkenburg, Jinx, 2–3, 122
Fall Fantasy (musical revue), 1, *2*
The Fall of Valor (Jackson), 23, 40
families, two unsatisfactory, 44
family farm, *15*
fan clubs, 186, 268n41
fans, of Dean, James, 192–93
farming town, 15–16, 21
fate: marked for success by, 123; out of
    his hands, 134–35; submission to,
    101; we attract our own, 94
Father Knows Best (television), 154
Father Peyton's Television Theater, 69
Faulkner, William, 9

perverted masochists, 201
photos, 112, 149–50
The Pickwick Papers (Dickens), 35
Pierangeli, Anna Maria. *See* Angeli, Pier
Pierangeli, Enrichetta, 130, 253n33
Pittman, Tom, 195
A Place in the Sun (movie), 86
Plan 9 from Outer Space (movie), 194
Plato (fictional character), 153–54, 157–60, *159*, 258n43
Platonic ideal, 89
plays. *See specific plays*
pole vaulting record, 31
police, vigilantes and, 38
pool parties, 60
popularity, of Dean, James, 177
Porsche 550 Spyder, 170, *173*, 270n1
Porter, Cole, 41
Porter, Darwin, 209, 254n3
Post, Emily, 11
Powell Library, at UCLA, *50*
powers, 33–34, *143*, 156
Preble, Bob, 163
Presley, Elvis, 193–94, 202, 257n38
Preston, Johnny, 272n9
Prince, Danforth, 209
Private Lives (tabloid), 176
Production Code (1934), 41, 68
professional success, 70
proverbs, half-baked, 64
psychoanalysis, 171, 263n36; Dean, James, seeing several, 136, 253n44; homosexuals cured through, 17–18; promise to start seeing, 130
public safety announcement, 170

"Queen of the Black Shore" (Howard), 247n21
queer history, 6–7
queer people, 8, 16
Quetzalcoatl (god), 101
Quinn, Joseph, 213

racism, 16
radio interview, 102
Rave (magazine), 191
Ray, Johnnie, 118, 164, *165*
Ray, Nicholas, 140; Dean, James, befriended by, 142; Dean, James, ceded power by, *143*, 156; Dean, James, desperate vulnerability from, 142, 255n8; Shulman removed by, 148
Ray, Tony, 142
The Razor's Edge (movie), 40
reading, 11–12, 232n24, 245n19; as armor against cruel world, 22; Brackett giving books for, 78; of *The Little Prince*, 78, 238n8; of old books and magazines, 21–22
Reagan, Ronald, 137
Real (magazine), 8
reality, myth entwined with, 205–6
Rebel (Ellis), 201
rebels, 23–24
Rebel without a Cause (Lindner), 139
Rebel without a Cause (movie): Brando turned down role in, 26; as CinemaScope color picture, 157; costars dining together, 175; critics on, 186–88; Dean, James, to star in, 140–41; Dean, James, with Mineo in, 5, 157–60, *158–59*; final script for, 153; half-finished script of, 118; intimacy and attraction in, *155*; Jim kisses Plato idea for, 153–54; Plato and Jim in, 157–60; Presley entranced by, 193; Ray, N., removing Shulman as script writer for, 148; release of, 185–90; Russo related to, 188–89; Shulman's script for, 146–48; social issues in, 24; Stern molding script for, 148–49; Wald to produce, 22–23; Warner Bros. securing rights to, 23; Wood to star in, 5

.